THE WHO'S WHO OF
DERBY COUNTY

THE WHO'S WHO OF
DERBY COUNTY

GERALD MORTIMER

BREEDON
BOOKS
SPORT

First published in Great Britain by
The Breedon Books Publishing Company Limited
44 Friar Gate, Derby DE1 1DA
1992.

ISBN 1 873626 31 2

Printed and bound by The Bath Press Limited, Bath and London.
Jacket printed by BDC Printing Services Ltd of Derby.

Contents

Foreword

by Roy McFarland

IT is 25 years since I first came to Derby and, in that time, I have spent only 18 months away. Even then, when I was with Bradford City, we kept our house so, although there are still family ties with Liverpool, I have come to count Derby as my home. I know how important Derby County is to the community and I remember Sam Longson saying that the County part was as significant, that the support is from all around Derbyshire. I think that still applies.

Brian Clough and Peter Taylor always maintained that Derby was a football hotbed and, looking through the proofs of this book, I am reminded that there have been a long line of great players at the Baseball Ground. I am particularly struck by the quality of the photographs: they bring back memories more quickly than anything. With this book, you can pick it up and start anywhere. It is great to dip into and, on every occasion, you will learn something about Derby County and the players.

In terms of atmosphere, the Baseball Ground has always been very important to the club and the players. It is a marvellous place to play and last season's play-off against Blackburn Rovers reminded me of the League Cup ties against Chelsea and Everton and the big European nights. People of Derby have always responded to class and there is plenty of it in these pages.

I have always been fascinated by listening to old players. In my early days, Sammy Crooks was the only man allowed to put his head around the dressing-room door before matches and Jack Bowers was the physio. I have spent a lot of time with Tim Ward, who loves to tell us what great players Raich Carter and Peter Doherty were. Jack Stamps always came to the matches, even when he was blind, and always gave us a gruff greeting. At the first Former Players' Association dinner, Jim Bullions said that he had lived off Jack's back, with his FA Cup winners' medal. "It was a team," said Jack and that was a great remark in the context. It was that kind of thing which made the formation of the Former Players' Association such a success.

I wish Gerald Mortimer success with this publication. I have known him for more than 20 years and although, from opposite sides of the fence we have not always seen eye to eye, I would class him as a good friend. He has studied the history of the club and loves talking to players past and present. There is a great deal of his knowledge in this book and everybody interested in Derby County will find it fascinating.

Introduction

IN 1984, the year that Derby County celebrated their centenary, Breedon Books published *Derby County: A Complete Record*. The book was the result of several people's work, most notably that of Gerald Mortimer and Mike Wilson, both of whom had been collating statistics on the club and its players for a number of years. In 1988, a second, updated, edition of that title was published, this time containing not just biographies of 100 star players to have appeared for the Rams down the years but a biography for every player to have played for the club in a recognised competitive first-team game since Derby were founder members of the Football League in 1888.

This latest book, *A Who's Who of Derby County*, takes that work even further, for in the intervening years Gerald has continued to update and amend the original players' details, adding, of course, the men to have arrived at, and in some cases already departed, the Baseball Ground. The addition of many photographs, not published for many years until now, will add still further to readers' enjoyment and for these and the more modern pictures we are indebted to the *Derby Evening Telegraph*, the Hulton Picture Library, the EMPICS agency of Nottingham and W.W.Winter of Derby for use of the Rams FA Cup Final group.

The details are current to the last day of August 1992 and inevitably some material will be out of date before the book reaches the shops. For instance, Derby made the signing of Lincoln City's Shane Nicholson well before we went to print, but he had yet to make a first-team appearance and so did not qualify for inclusion. Two players who have now made the 'cut' are Billy Redfern and Jim Wilson. They were omitted from previous lists because they played only in the abandoned 1939-40 season, but it has now been felt proper to include them as the games were valid when they made their appearances for the Rams, although they are not included in the statistical section.

Anyone with new information about the players in this book, particularly dates of births and deaths and transfers, is invited to write to the author c/o Breedon Books.

The Who's Who of Derby County

ABBOTT
Shirley Wray *Wing-half*

Born: Alfreton, 19 February 1889. Died: Portsmouth, 26 September 1947.
Career: Alfreton Town. Derby County June 1911. Portsmouth June 1913. Queen's Park Rangers May 1923. Chesterfield September 1924. Trainer, Chesterfield May 1928 to May 1939.
Division Two champions 1911-12.

Shirley Abbott.

Abbott made only one appearance for Derby, in an away game against Huddersfield Town in the 1911-12 Second Division championship season but he spanned World War One with Portsmouth. He helped them to win the Southern League title in 1919-20 and was a member of their first team in the Football League the following season.

ABBOTT
William Lee *Winger*

Career: Riddings. Derby County February 1894. Poolsbrook United May 1895. Riddings July 1896. Chesterfield August 1897. Riddings January 1898. Clowne Rovers October 1893. Walgrave October 1900. Market Harborough September 1901.

William Abbott's Football League career was limited to four consecutive games at outside-left for Derby County in March 1894. He continued to play as a professional locally.

ABDALLAH
Tewfik *Inside-forward*

Born: Egypt, 23 June.
Career: International Sporting Club, Cairo. Derby County September 1920. Cowdenbeath July 1922. Hartlepools United March 1924. Coaching in United States 1924.

Abdallah, nicknamed 'Toothpick', was the second Egyptian to play in the League. He followed Hassan Hegazi, a Cambridge Blue who was with Dulwich Hamlet and had one match for Fulham in 1911. Tommy Barbour served in Egypt during World War One and it may have been this connection which brought Abdallah to Derby in 1920. He was described as a born footballer with excellent close control but was slow. He was also trying to make his way in a struggling Derby team.

ABLETT
Gary Ian *Midfield/defender*

Born: Liverpool, 19 November 1965.
Career: Apprentice, Liverpool: professional November 1983. Derby County, loan, January 1985. Hull City, loan, September 1986. Everton January 1992.

Ablett spent two months on loan at Derby when Arthur Cox was trying to rebuild the club in his first season as

Gary Ablett, on loan to the Rams he later gained honours on Merseyside.

manager. Although a player of some style, he did not establish a regular place. Another loan spell followed at Hull before he made his debut for Liverpool in December 1986. With Liverpool prepared to spend huge fees, Ablett found it hard to break out of the Central League team at Anfield Road until 1987-8, when he won a Championship medal and played in the FA Cup Final. He was in Liverpool's 1989 FA Cup-winning team before joining Everton for £750,000 in 1992.

ACKERMAN
Alfred Albert Eric   *Centre-forward*

Born: Daspoort, Pretoria, 5 January 1929. Died: Dunnottar, Transvaal, 10 July 1988.
Career: Pretoria Municipal. Clyde 1947. Hull City July 1950. Norwich City August 1951. Hull City October 1953. Derby County March 1955. Carlisle United November 1956. Millwall January 1959. Player-manager,
Dartford, July 1961 to June 1966. Manager, Gravesend and Northfleet November 1968 to February 1974.
Division Three North champions 1956-7.

In a last, unsuccessful attempt to prevent Derby County being relegated from Division Two for the first time, Jack Barker bought Ackerman and Ken Harrison from Hull City in a joint £6,600 deal. Ackerman's goals earned him a good living and he hit four for the Rams against Accrington Stanley at home in April 1956. He scored 15 League goals in 1955-6 but Harry Storer sold him to Carlisle for £2,250 in November 1956, when it had become clear that Ray Straw was to be the main striking weapon in the Third Division North championship team.

ADLINGTON
Terence   *Goalkeeper*

Born: Blackwell, 21 November 1935. Career: Stonebroom YC. Blackwell CW. Amateur, Derby County, December 1955: professional, October
1956. Torquay United May 1962. Baltimore Bays 1967. Dallas Tornado 1968. Boston United January 1969. Player-manager, Dover Town March 1969: manager to May 1975. Manager Maidstone United May 1975 to February 1977.
Division Three North champions 1956-7

Strongly-built goalkeeper who emerged through local trials and played one match in the Third Division North championship season. Mostly a reserve to Terry Webster or Ken Oxford,

Terry Adlington.

Adlington's best season at Derby was 1960-61. He had more League opportunities after joining Torquay United for £1,000. In November 1963, he scored for Torquay in an FA Cup tie against Barnet, having come out of goal because of an injured wrist. A finger injury forced him to retire from Torquay in December 1965 before he became one of the early players in the North American Soccer League. He returned to join Boston United but was unable to play because international clearance was not received and was released to take the player-manager's job at Dover.

AINSWORTH
Charles   *Outside-left*

Born: Ashbourne, 1885. Died: 1955. Career: Derby County August 1908. Grimsby Town August 1909.

Ainsworth spent one season at the Baseball Ground before a brief stay with Grimsby Town.

Alf Ackerman, scored four times against Accrington in April 1956.

AINSWORTH
Fred   *Inside-forward*
Born: Loughborough, 29 June 1894.
Died: Redcar, 5 January 1981.
Career Loughborough. Derby County
August 1919. Ashington.

One of many players who appeared
briefly in the early seasons after World
War One. His solitary League appearance was against Blackburn Rovers in
December 1919.

ALDERMAN
Albert Edward   *Winger/inside-*
forward

Born: Alvaston, Derby, 30 October
1907. Died: Frimley, 6 June 1990.
Career: Alvaston House. Derby County
March 1927. Burnley August 1934.
Division One runners-up 1929-30.

A speedy player, who spent most of his
Derby County career in the Reserves
before Burnley bought him for £200.
Alderman provided cover for two
positions but won more lasting fame
as a cricketer. He played for Derbyshire
from 1928 to 1948, including 12 centuries in his 12,376 runs. An opening
batsman, outstanding all-round fielder
and occasional wicketkeeper, Alderman helped Derbyshire to win their
only Championship in 1936. Coached
in New Zealand and, after his retirement, at Repton School and RMA
Sandhurst. He was on the first-class
umpires' list from 1966 to 1968.

ALLAN
John   *Winger/inside-forward*
Career: Glasgow Thistle. Derby
County August 1893. Notts County
December 1894. Heanor Town.

Allan was an ever-present in his only
full season with Derby, spending most
of it as a right-winger. Derby finished
third, their best up to that point, but
Allan moved to Notts County the
following December.

ALLEN
Henry   *Outside-left*
Born: Spondon. Died: Bulawayo,
September 1939.
Career: Alvaston. Derby County
October 1898. Leicester Fosse December
1899. Alvaston and Boulton 1900.
Derby County March 1901.
FA Cup Finalists 1898-9.

Of all those who were involved in
Derby County's four FA Cup Final
teams, Harry Allen made fewest senior
appearances, only 20. He emigrated to
Rhodesia to work on the railways and
reached the rank of captain in the 1st
Rhodesian Regiment in World War
One, during which he fought against
the Germans in South-West Africa.
Became assistant general manager of
Rhodesian railways, vice-president of
the Bulawayo FA and president of the

Rhodesian amateur boxing association.

ALTON
Thomas William   *Right-back*
Born: Chesterfield, 1917.
Career: New Tupton Ivanhoe. Derby
County November 1936.

Alton played in three First Division
matches in 1937 when David Bell was
unfit.

George Antonio, joined the Rams when he was 32.

ANTONIO
George Rowlands *Inside-forward*
Born: Whitchurch, 20 October 1914.
Career: Oswestry Town. Stoke City
February 1936. Derby County March
1947. Doncaster Rovers October 1948.
Mansfield Town October 1949. Player-
manager, Oswestry Town, July 1951.
Player-coach, Wellington Town, July
1954; player-manager January 1955 to
May 1957. Player-manager, Stafford

Rangers, September 1957. Player-coach, Oswestry Town, July 1958; player-manager June 1959 to June 1962.

Antonio, who had been adopted by an Italian family, was 32 when Derby County signed him for £4,000. He filled in after the sale of Peter Doherty but without great success. In 1937-8, when he was with Stoke, Antonio was picked by Wales but did not play when it was discovered he had been born on the wrong side of the border, not a detail which would cause much concern now.

ARKESDEN
Thomas A. *Inside-forward/winger*
Born: Warwick. Died: Hulme, June 1921.
Career: Burton Wanderers April 1897. Derby County January 1898. Burton United July 1901. Manchester United February 1903. Gainsborough Trinity July 1907.
FA Cup Finalists 1898-9.

Arkesden appeared in only one FA Cup tie for Derby, the 1899 Final against Sheffield United. He could play either at inside-forward or on the right-wing but never completely established himself with Derby. With another ex-Derby player, Richard Wombwell, Arkesden played a part in Manchester United's 1905-06 promotion from Division Two.

ARMSTRONG
Arthur *Outside-right*
Born: c1887. Died: Wolverhampton, 13 August 1962.
Career: Ripley Athletic. Bakewell. Derby County October 1906. Brighton & Hove Albion June 1909. Pontypridd. Loughborough Corinthians. Heanor Town.

Trained as an acrobat with Sanger's Circus, touring with them for three seasons before his brief spell with Derby County. A telegraphist with the Great Northern Railway.

ASTLEY
David John *Forward*
Born: Dowlais, 11 November 1909. Died: Birchington, Kent, 7 November 1989.
Career: Dowlais Welfare. Merthyr Town, amateur, July 1927, professional, August 1927. Charlton Athletic January 1928. Aston Villa June 1931. Derby County November 1936. Blackpool January 1939. Retired during the war. Coach, Internazionale Milan. Coach, Sampdoria. Coach, Djurgårdens.

Few footballers until Johnny Morris can have enjoyed such a start to a career with a new club as did Welsh international (16 goals in 14 League appearances and four in three FA Cup ties) Dai Astley with the Rams. Astley came to the Baseball Ground in November 1936 and in his first 30 matches for the Rams he scored 29 goals, including

Dai Astley, scored 20 goals in his first 17 games for Derby.

three hat-tricks. He was a centre-forward who had both punch and craft, yet another of the Rams' forward line of the late 1930s who could both make and score goals. Charlton wanted to re-sign him when he was ready to leave Villa, but Astley had a philosophy of 'never going back' and the Rams side attracted him because it contained so many fine internationals. He was at home at both centre-forward and inside-left and did not want to leave this club when George Jobey told him that he was on offer.

ATKIN
John Thomas *Full-back*
Born: Newhall, 1883. Died: Midway, 15 December 1961.
Career: Newhall Swifts. Derby County May 1907.
Division Two champions 1911-12, 1914-15 (captain).

When Jimmy Methven went to sign him from Newhall Swifts in 1907, Jack Atkin would not agree unless Derby took his brother, Harry, as well.

Jack Atkin, signed for Derby only after they agreed to take his brother too.

Methven agreed and the brothers shared the 15s per week wages. In Atkin's final season with the Swifts they reached the last qualifying round of the FA Cup before losing 2-1 to Second Division Glossop, a team which included the former Rams star Johnny McMillan. Atkin often trained at Newhall with another native of the village, Ben Warren, who was a Rams international. Atkin gave the Rams many years of loyal service, including being ever-present in 1919-20 when, at the age of 34 and after wartime army service, he helped Derby stave off relegation with his first goal in 13 years — a header against Everton which started a remarkable run in which the Rams won enough points to stay in Division One. The following season Atkin scored four goals in successive matches — two penalties followed by two own-goals. In 1921-2, the Rams skipper played his last game, a 'far from convincing performance' in the 6-1 FA Cup defeat at Villa Park. Atkin was unlucky not to win an England cap but the great Bob Crompton of Blackburn monopolised the international right-back position. His only representative honour was to play for an FA team against Cambridge University in 1920

in the same side as Puddefoot of West Ham United and the great Spurs left wing of Bliss and Dimmock.

ATTLEY
Brian Robert　　　　　*Full-back*
Born: Cardiff, 27 August 1955.
Career: Apprentice, Cardiff City: professional August 1973. Swansea City February 1979. Derby County February 1982. Oxford United, loan, March 1983. Gresley Rovers July 1984. Stapenhill March 1986.

John Newman, temporary manager at the time, moved quickly to sign Brian Attley for £25,000 after Steve Emery suffered a fractured leg at Rotherham. Attley had been involved in three promotions, from Division Three with Cardiff (1975-6) and Swansea (1978-9) and out of Division Two with Swansea (1980-81). He helped Derby to retain their Second Division status in his first season but had little success in Peter Taylor's regime.

BACON
Arthur　　　　　　　　*Forward*
Born: Birdholme, 1905. Died: Derby, January 1941.

Career: New Tupton BB. New Tupton Ivanhoe. Chesterfield September 1923. Derby County October 1923. Manchester City December 1928. Reading June 1929. Chesterfield June 1932. Coventry City June 1933. Retired with an eye injury but returned with Burton Town, March 1937.
Division Two promotion 1925-6.

Arthur Bacon.

Bacon was a reserve with Derby County and, after his £1,500 transfer, with Manchester City but proved a prolific scorer elsewhere. In April, 1931, he scored six for Reading against Stoke City (Division Two). In 1933-4, when he was playing for Coventry City (Division Three South), he hit five goals in an away game against Gillingham and followed this with four against Crystal Palace the following week. He was killed while serving as a special constable during Derby's worst air-raid of the war.

BAGSHAW
John James　　　　　*Wing-half*
Born: Derby, 25 December 1885. Died: Nottingham, 25 August 1966.
Career: Fletcher's Athletic. Graham Street Prims. Derby County October 1906. Notts County February 1920. Watford May 1921. Ilkeston United August 1922. Grantham July 1924.
Division Two champions 1911-12, 1914-15.

Jimmy Bagshaw was born in Russell Street, Derby, close by the Baseball Ground, on Christmas Day 1885, when the Rams still played at the County Ground. His first club was Graham Street Prims and he also had a few games for his works side, Fletcher's Athletic, before becoming a full-time professional with the Rams, making his debut in their 2-0 win at Sunderland. After being reserve for England

Brian Attley was involved in three promotions before joining Derby.

Jimmy Bagshaw.

Tony Bailey.

against Scotland in 1918, he played in the Victory international against Wales and was later capped against Ireland. By then, Bagshaw was the Rams' longest-serving player and in 1920 he moved to Notts County for whom he had guested during the war. He returned to the East Midlands after a spell with Watford, later working for Raleigh Industries in Nottingham and scouting for both Forest and County.

BAILEY
Anthony David *Defender*
Born: Burton-on-Trent, 23 September 1946.
Career: Burton Albion June 1966. Derby County February 1970. Oldham Athletic, loan, January 1974. Oldham Athletic March 1974. Bury December 1974. Mossley November 1980.
Division One champions 1971-2.

Signed from Burton Albion on the same day that Derby paid their first £100,000 fee, for Terry Hennessey, Tony Bailey made one League appearance in the 1971-2 championship season, in a 3-0 defeat at Leeds. Moved to Oldham for £6,000 and had his best days with Bury.

BAILEY
Horace Peter   *Goalkeeper*

Born: Derby, 3 July 1881. Died: Biggleswade, 1 August 1960.
Career: Derby County Reserves September 1899. Crich 1901. Ripley Athletic December 1902. Leicester Imperial 1905. Leicester Fosse January 1907. Derby County April 1910. Birmingham February 1911. Retired 1913.

Spent most of his career as an amateur and won a gold medal for Great Britain in the 1908 Olympic Games football in London. An England amateur international, he also won five full caps in 1907-08 while with Leicester Fosse. He worked at the LMS railway and played tennis for Derbyshire.

BAILEY
Leslie Albert   *Centre-half*

Born: Worksop, 2 October 1916. Died: Worksop, 27 June 1980.
Career: Gainsborough Trinity. Bradford May 1936. Derby County March 1937.

Leslie Bailey was signed soon after Derby had won an FA Cup third round tie at Park Avenue and, in the last full season before World War Two, took over from Jack Barker for long spells. He left professional football in 1939 to join the Nottingham City Police.

BAKER
John   *Full-back*

Career: Derby County November 1890.

A full-back who made ten League and Cup appearances in Derby's third League season.

BAKER
William Edward   *Left-winger*

Born: Woolwich, 11 May 1892. Died: Plymouth, 8 March 1980.
Career: Dartford. Derby County May 1914. Plymouth Argyle July 1921. Retired 1927.
Division Two champions 1914-15.

Baker was first choice outside-left when Derby won the Second Division by three points before competitive football ceased because of World War One. He was still there after the war but Alf Quantrill superceded him. Baker was a regular with Plymouth Argyle for three seasons, the start of a record run in which they were Third Division South runners-up six times consecutively.

BAKEWELL
George   *Right-winger*

Career: Derby Midland. Derby County 1884. Notts County July 1891.

Bakewell was the second player to be signed, after Haydn Morley, when Derby County were formed in 1884.

George Bakewell.

The fact that they took one of Derby Midland's best players, a process that was to continue, caused resentment around local clubs. Bakewell scored twice in Derby's opening League game at Bolton and after a spell with Notts County, served on the Derby County committee.

BALKWILL
Alexander   *Centre-forward*

Career: Alvaston. Derby County July 1900. Ripley Town August 1901.

Came out of local football but managed only one goal in his 11 League games in 1901-02.

BANOVIC
Vjekoslav   *Goalkeeper*

Born: Bihac, Yugoslavia, 12 November 1956.
Career: Adelaide Croatia 1972. Toronto Metros 1977. Melbourne Croatia. Heidelburg United. Derby County August 1980. Melbourne Croatia 1984.

Yakka Banovic emigrated with his family from Yugoslavia and was an Australian international when Colin Addison signed him for £40,000 from the Melbourne club Heidelberg. Banovic was a colourful goalkeeper, spectacular on his line, and was unfortunate that he did not join a more settled club. He returned to Australia when Derby freed him.

BARBOUR
Thomas   *Wing-half/full-back*

Born: Largs, 1887. Died: Marlpool, 29 August 1967.
Career: Kilbirnie. Derby County July 1908. Darlington July 1921.
Division Two champions 1911-12, 1914-15.

Manager Jimmy Methven had to move fast when he secured Tommy Barbour from the Ayrshire junior club Kilbirnie in 1908. George Morrell, manager of Woolwich Arsenal, had reached agreement with the club but Methven completed negotiations through Tommy's brother. Either at wing-half, the position for which he was signed, or full-back, Barbour gave Derby excellent value for 13 years, broken by World War One. He served with the Derbyshire Yeomanry at Gallipoli, in Egypt and on the Italian front. He and Jack Atkin, both well over 30, helped to keep Derby in Division One when peacetime football resumed. Barbour was in the first Football League team ever fielded by Darlington but left them in 1922 because he was not allowed to train in Derby, where he was a publican. Later licensee of the Jolly Colliers in Heanor.

BARCLAY
Robert   *Inside-forward*

Born: Scotswood, 27 October 1906. Died: Huddersfield, 13 July 1969.
Career: Scotswood United Church. Bell's Close Juniors, Allendale. Scotswood. Derby County February 1927. Sheffield United June 1931. Huddersfield Town March 1937. Hurst FC May 1946.
Division One runners-up 1929-30.

Bobby Barclay was one of the high-class players George Jobey discovered in non-League football. An inside-forward of quality, Barclay could also score goals, 26 in 64 senior games for the Rams including a hat-trick against Sheffield Wednesday in April 1930. Sheffield United paid £3,500 for him and Barclay played three times for England while he was at Bramall Lane,

Yakka Banovic, Australian international.

Tommy Barbour, joined Derby rather than Arsenal.

Bobby Barclay, discovered by George Jobey.

two of them against Scotland. He was on the losing side in two FA Cup Finals, for Sheffield United in 1936 and Huddersfield Town in 1938.

BARKER
Frederick Charles

Inside-forward
Died: Derby, 25 November 1904.

Career: Derby County March 1903.

Barker scored twice in his four appearances for Derby but died at a tragically young age while still on their books.

BARKER
John William
Centre-half
Born: Denaby, 27 February 1907. Died: Derby, 20 January 1982.

Career: Denaby Rovers. Denaby United 1926. Derby County April 1928. Manager, Bradford City, May 1946. Manager, Dundalk, January 1947. Coach, Oldham Athletic, November 1948 to January 1949. Manager, Derby County, November 1953 to April 1955.

Division One runners-up 1929-30, 1935-6 (captain).

Rams skipper Jack Barker takes the field at Highbury in 1936. Barker also captained England in his final international.

Jack Barker and Cliff Bastin tussle at Highbury in February 1938. The Champions-elect won 3-0.

Jack Barker was one of the giants in the fine team George Jobey created in the 1930s, a centre-half who was commanding, hard and physically imposing. He was also a throw-back to another era. Despite the 1925 change in the offside law that gave birth to the stopper centre-half, Barker always had an eye on attack. He could do it by accurate long passing, but also joined in when the Rams were going forward. Full-backs Tommy Cooper and George Collin believed he attacked too much and Sammy Crooks felt that was true of the whole team. "That was why we came close, rather than winning the League or the Cup," he said in later days. All acknowledged that Barker was a magnificent footballer and he played 11 times for England, captaining them in his final appearance, against Wales at Ninian Park in 1936. There might have been more caps but some selectors considered he was too rough. It was not an accusation that worried him, a tough ex-miner who had survived a pit disaster. When he was on the way to play Scotland at Hampden Park for the first time, Barker was asked by Ivan Sharpe, journalist and former Derby player, if he was worried about the Hampden Roar. "I told him I had heard far worse than that, the roar of a pit falling in," Barker said. His footballer philosophy

was simple: "I followed the ball and played as I knew how." Sadly, his brief period as Derby's manager was a failure and he resented taking orders from directors.

BARKER
Richard   *Forward*

Born: Derby, 23 November 1939.
Career: Morris Sports. Burton Albion October 1960. Loughborough United May 1962. Matlock Town July 1963. Burton Albion November 1963. Primo Hamilton (Canada), loan, April 1965. Derby County October 1967. Notts County December 1968. Peterborough United September 1971. Coach, Shrewsbury Town February 1974: manager, February 1978. Assistant-manager, Wolverhampton Wanderers, November 1978. Manager, Stoke City, June 1981 to December 1983. Manager, Notts County, November 1984 to April 1985. Manager, Ethnikos 1985. Manager Zamalek, Egypt, 1986. Chief coach Luton Town, August 1988. Assistant manager Sheffield Wednesday, February 1989.

Division Two champions 1968-9.

A draughtsman and an experienced non-League player who worked under Peter Taylor for Burton Albion before he entered League football when almost 28. Richie Barker scored valuable goals

Richie Barker, a late starter.

Horace Barnes, immediately impressed manager Jimmy Methven.

for Derby but was allowed to move when the Second Division championship team took shape. Helped Notts County to win the Fourth Division in 1970-71 but a broken leg while with Peterborough hastened his move into management, initially as Alan Durban's assistant at Shrewsbury.

BARNES
Horace   *Forward*
Born: Wadsley Bridge, 3 January 1890.
Died: 12 September 1961.
Career: Wadsley Bridge. Derby County October 1908. Manchester City May 1914. Preston North End November 1924. Oldham Athletic November 1925. Ashton National 1927 to cs 1931.
Division Two champions 1911-12.

Horace Barnes burst on the Derby County scene after being signed from Wadsley Bridge. An outing in the Reserves was so impressive that he was instantly drafted into the first team and scored on his debut at Blackpool. He was inside-left for the rest of the 1908-09 season and, inevitably, the combination with Alf Bentley and Fred Bevan, joined by Jimmy Beauchop the

following season as Bevan moved on, came to be known as the Busy Bees. Barnes had a fierce shot in his left foot, which helped to bring him 78 goals in 167 appearances for the Rams. He developed steadily and was leading scorer in 1913-14 with 24 League goals in 37 games, but the Rams were relegated. Barnes stayed in the First Division, signing for Manchester City after a transfer which also involved Arsenal, Newcastle, Liverpool and Sheffield Wednesday. He was engaged to a Manchester girl and the fee of £2,500 equalled the record. It brought the usual debate about inflationary fees and Leslie Knighton, an Arsenal manager, wrote in his book *Behind the Scenes in Big Football*: "Men argued with each other in pubs up and down England, not about the menace of the Kaiser's steel-helmeted hordes, but about the price paid for Horace Barnes." The closeness of World War One made the transfer a risk but Barnes, who formed a fine partnership with Tommy Browell, repaid City with 125 goals in 235 senior games, including their first at Maine Road. He played in a Victory international against Wales and represented the Football

League twice, against the Irish League and the Scottish League.

BARNES
James   *Outside-left*
Born: New Delaval, 21 July.
Career: Harkford. Derby County August 1921. Rochdale 1921.

One of many players who flickered in and out of the club in the seasons following World War One.

BARROWCLIFFE
Geoffrey   *Full-back*
Born: Ilkeston, 18 October 1931.
Career: Heanor Athletic 1949. Ilkeston Town August 1950. Derby County October 1950. Boston United July 1966. Heanor Town July 1969. Moorgreen Colliery January 1970. Long Eaton United September 1973: manager August 1974. Manager, Kimberley Town, November 1977 to 1981. Coach, Radford, August 1987: manager, January 1988. Assistant manager, Rolls-Royce, cs 1990.
Division Three North champions 1956-7.

The displays of a young full-back playing for Ilkeston Town in the Central Alliance quickly brought scouts to the Manor Ground in 1950. Wolves were among the clubs interested in signing the teenaged miner called Geoff Barrowcliffe but Derby County, closer to home, won the race and so began one of the greatest careers in the Rams' history. Barrowcliffe started as a part-time professional, training in the evenings after a day down the pit. In September 1951 he was rewarded with a first-team debut against Stoke. Barrowcliffe played at left-back in those early days but after the departure of Bert Mozley and a brief tenure by Roy Patrick, right-back became his position. Unlucky to play in a Rams team heading in the wrong direction, Barrowcliffe was one of the best footballing full-backs in England and Reg Ryan, his skipper in Derby's Third Division North days, is convinced that England caps would have come had he been with a more fashionable and successful club. Barrowcliffe was not the hardest tackler, but his ball control and distribution were immaculate. He played a few games at centre-forward and, in the 1955 Christmas holiday, turned out on the left wing. The crowd jeered when it was announced as a team change, but after only a few minutes he laid on a goal for Jesse Pye. Barrowcliffe was a high-scoring full-back, many of his 39 goals coming from powerfully-struck penalties.

BAUCHOP
James Rae   *Inside-forward*
Born: Sauchie, 24 May 1886. Died: Bradford, June 1948.
Career: Alloa Athletic 1905. Glasgow

Geoff Barrowcliffe, a stylish full-back who might have won an England cap with a more successful club. He made 503 League and Cup appearances for the Rams.

Celtic January 1906. Norwich City May 1907. Crystal Palace March 1908. Derby County May 1909. Tottenham Hotspur May 1913. Bradford December 1913. Doncaster Rovers June 1922. Lincoln City May 1923.

Division Two champions 1911-12.

Jimmy Methven first tried to sign Jimmy Bauchop from Celtic, where he was understudy to Scottish international Jimmy Quinn, in 1907. The Derby manager was outbid by Norwich City, but did not return empty-handed, taking Ted Garry from the Glasgow giants. Methven had to wait a couple of years before tracking down his man, but he was well-rewarded when Bauchop scored goals consistently. One of the most important was at Oakwell, when the Rams clinched the Division Two title in 1912 and found 20,000 delighted fans waiting for them when their train pulled into Derby. Although he played centre-forward on occasions,

Jimmy Bauchop.

Bauchop was happiest at inside-left where he had three major wing partners — Jack Davis, Davie Donald and Ivan Sharpe. He was always a potential scorer, whatever the state of the game, one of the reasons why he was called the 'catch of the season' when he arrived from Crystal Palace. He hit 72 goals in 135 games for the Rams, helped Bradford into Division One in 1914 and only World War One interrupted 20 seasons in the game.

BARTLETT
Paul   *Outside-left*

Born: Grimsby, 17 January 1960.
Career: Apprentice, Derby County:
professional December 1977. Boston
United December 1980. Kettering
Town cs 1983.

Paul Bartlett.

Showed some promise in the Youth
and Reserve teams without being able
to bridge the gap into League football.

BARTON
John Stanley   *Full-back*

Born: Birmingham, 24 October 1953.
Career: Boldmere St Michael's. Paget
Rangers. Sutton Coldfield Town 1974.
Stourbridge. Worcester City June 1976.
Everton December 1978. Derby County
March 1982. Player/assistant-manager,
Kidderminster Harriers, August 1984.
Tamworth December 1990. Assistant
manager, Nuneaton Borough, 1991.

After considerable experience in non-
League football, John Barton's career
took a sudden upswing when he was
signed by Everton. He suffered cruelly
from injuries while at Goodison Park
and John Newman signed him on a
free transfer. Barton helped Derby to
avoid relegation in 1982-3 but,
although one of the few consistent
players, he was released a year later.
Barton helped Kidderminster Harriers
to reach the Welsh Cup Final in 1986
and win the FA Trophy a year later.

BAYLISS
Hervey Hugo Robert *Forward*

Born: Burton upon Trent 1895.
Career: Overseal Swifts. Burton All
Saints. Gresley Rovers 1919. Derby
County February 1921. Gresley Rovers
1921.

A favourite with Gresley and stipulated, when he joined Derby, that he
could return if League football did not
suit him. Played only once for Derby,
against Sheffield United in February
1921.

BEDFORD
Harry   *Centre-forward*

Born: Calow, 15 October 1899. Died:
Derby, 24 June 1976.
Career: Grassmoor Ivanhoe. Not-

John Barton, played in the UEFA Cup for Everton.

tingham Forest August 1919. Black-
pool March 1921. Derby County Sep-
tember 1925. Newcastle United
December 1930. Sunderland January
1932. Bradford May 1932. Chesterfield
June 1933. Player-coach, Heanor
Town, August 1934. Trainer, Newcas-
tle United, October 1937. Manager,
Belper Town, January 1954. Manager,
Heanor Town, March 1955 to May
1956.
Division Two promotion 1925-6. Div-
ision One runners-up 1929-30.

George Jobey, manager of Derby
County from 1925 to 1941, signed a
succession of great centre-forwards.
Harry Bedford, who had scored 112
League goals for Blackpool, was the
first, the one against whom others
would be judged. Bedford set a high
standard, 142 League goals for the

Harry Bedford, the first of several great centre-forwards signed by George Jobey. He scored 152 goals in 218 senior games

Rams in 203 games, another ten in 15 FA Cup ties. He was leading scorer in each of his five full seasons and in 1929-30 equalled Alf Bentley's club record of 30 League goals. Three times, he scored four in a game: three on ten occasions. Jobey appreciated courage and Bedford had plenty of that to go with his dash and energy. As Jack Bowers began to emerge, Bedford played at inside-right before a swift and surprising transfer to Newcastle. Sammy Crooks said he was one of the best partners he ever had. Bedford played twice for England while he was at Blackpool and twice scored four goals for the Football League against the Irish League. By the time his League career ended with Chesterfield, Bedford had scored 308 goals in 486 games and it is tempting to speculate on his value in today's transfer market. He settled in Derby and was Derbyshire County Cricket Club's masseur for a time. From 1941 to 1964, he served with the Rolls-Royce Fire Service. Bedford cost Derby £3,500, helped them to promotion in his first season and was instrumental in establishing them as a First Division force before he moved to Newcastle for £4,000

BELL
Colin
Half-back

Born: Horsley, 24 March 1926.
Career: Holbrook MW. Derby County, amateur, May 1945: professional, September 1946. Gresley Rovers June 1955. Long Eaton United July 1957.

Spent much of his career as a Derby reserve and was regarded as a utility player, appearing at full-back and in the forward line as well as at wing-half. When he did break through, Bell found himself in a team declining sharply in the early 1950s.

BELL
David
Right-back/wing-half

Born: Gorebridge, Lothian, 24 December 1909.
Career: Musselburgh Bruntonians. Wallyford Bluebell. Newcastle United May 1930. Derby County June 1934. Ipswich Town October 1938. Retired 1950.

Bell was unlucky with injuries at St James' Park and Derby signed him for £700. He took advantage of injuries to Ted Udall at Derby and established himself at right-back before Jack

Nicholas began a second career in that position. Bell joined Ipswich Town in their first Football League season.

BELLHOUSE
E.W.
Centre-half

Played two matches in the inaugural Football League season.

BENFIELD
Thomas Charles. *Inside-forward*

Born: Leicester, 1889. Died: France, 10 November 1918.
Career: Amateur, Leicester Fosse, February 1907: professional July 1910. Derby County June 1914.
Division Two champions 1914-15.

Benfield proved to be a good signing and was ever-present, scoring 15 goals, when Derby bounced back to win Division Two at the first attempt in 1914-15. He played for both the Rams and Leicester Fosse in wartime football. He represented the Army against the Royal Navy in 1909 before leaving the Leicestershire Regiment to turn professional with Leicester Fosse. He rejoined the army in World War One and was killed by a sniper.

Colin Bell, spent much of his Derby career in reserve.

David Bell, lost his place to Jack Nicholas.

BENTLEY
Alfred
Centre-forward

Born: Alfreton, September 1887. Died: Derby, 15 April 1940.
Career: Alfreton Town. Derby County December 1906. Bolton Wanderers May 1911. West Bromwich Albion June 1913. Alfreton Town.

Alf Bentley.

One of Jimmy Methven's first signings as manager, after his distinguished playing career, was a 5ft 5½ins centre-forward from Alfreton Town, Alf Bentley. Snobby, as he was known, was a bustler but he had quick feet when the ball came to him near goal. Methven paid £50 and was prepared to go higher because Alfreton secretary Ernie Davis tipped off Methven's pedecessor Harry Newbould, then with Manchester City. The Rams were relegated at the end of Bentley's first season, so most of his goals were scored in the Second Division, including successive club records of 27 in the League in 1907-08 and 30 in 1909-10. Bentley moved to Bolton before the Rams recovered their First Division status but his greatest success was to win a League Championship medal with West Bromwich Albion in 1919-20. He finished his playing career with Alfreton and was in the team beaten 8-2 by Port Vale in an FA Cup qualifying match in December 1924.

BESTWICK
T.Harold
Goalkeeper

Career: Long Eaton Rangers. Derby County.

Played in the Cup before the formation of the League and managed one appearance, against Everton, in the first League season.

BETTS
Arthur Charles
Left-back

Born: Scunthorpe, 2 January 1886. Died: 1967.
Career: North Lindsey. Gainsborough Trinity May 1905. Watford May 1907. Gainsborough Trinity May 1910. Newcastle United July 1911. Derby County October 1911. Hull City May 1914. Scunthorpe United June 1920. Player-coach, Normanby Park Steelworks, May 1923. Coach, Lysaghts Sports.
Division Two champions 1911-12.

Charlie Betts was signed after a brief spell with Newcastle United and immediately won a place at left-back in the team which won Division Two in 1911-12. It was an up-and-down period for the Rams and after relegation two years later, Betts joined Hull City.

BEVAN
Frederick William
Centre-forward

Born: Hackney, 1880.
Career: Millwall Athletic, May 1899. Manchester City April 1900. Reading April 1903. Queen's Park Rangers cs 1904. Bury May 1906. Fulham August 1907. Derby County October 1907. Clapton Orient November 1909. Chatham 1913. Coach, Clapton Orient, 1920 to 1923.

Bevan spent almost two season of his varied career with Derby. A strong centre-forward, Bevan gave good support to Alf Bentley in 1907-08 but found goals more elusive the following season.

BIGGINS
Stephen James
Forward

Born: Lichfield, 20 June 1954.
Career: Hednesford Town. Shrewsbury Town December 1977. Oxford United July 1982. Derby County October 1984. Wolverhampton Wanderers, loan, March 1985, Port Vale, loan, March 1986. Telleborg FF (Sweden) July 1986. Exeter City October 1986. Telford United March 1987. Ludlow. Willenhall Town, loan, April 1991.

Steve Biggins, a qualified teacher, was a late entrant into League football. He helped Shrewsbury Town to win Division Three in 1978-9 and did the same with Oxford United in 1983-4. His 24 goals in all competitions that season set an Oxford record, overtaken by John Aldridge a year later. Arthur Cox paid £17,000 for Biggins when Kevin Wilson broke an arm but, despite all his hard work, the Biggins style was not a hit at the Baseball Ground.

Steve Biggins, another late entrant to League football.

Alan Biley, whose career at Derby declined after a fine start.

BILEY
Alan Paul　　　　Centre-forward
Born: Leighton Buzzard, 26 February 1957.
Career: Apprentice, Luton Town. Professional, Cambridge United July 1975. Derby County January 1980. Everton July 1981. Stoke City, loan, March 1982. Portsmouth August 1982. Brighton & Hove Albion March 1985. New York Express July 1986 (transfer never completed). Cambridge United, loan, November 1986. Brest (France), trial, June 1987. Panionios (Greece) July 1987. Swindon Town, trial, August 1989. Welton Rovers November 1989.

Alan Biley's goals in the rise of Cambridge United from Division Four to Division Two persuaded Colin Addison to invest £350,000 on him. Biley began in fine style, even though Derby lost their First Division place, but his second season was less happy. An injury prevented him joining West Bromwich Albion in a deal which would have brought David Mills to Derby and, after a year with Everton, Biley was Portsmouth's leading scorer when they won Division Three in 1982-3. At his best, Biley was a sharp and inventive striker, with his Rod Stewart hairstyle, but there were some downs in a career which foundered at Brighton.

BIRD
Donald William Carlton
　　　　　　　　　　　　Outside-left
Born: Llandrindod Wells, 5 January 1908.
Career: Llandrindod Wells. Cardiff City May 1930. Bury May 1931. Torquay United June 1932. Derby County June 1934. Sheffield United December 1935. Southend United October 1936.
Division One runners-up 1935-6.

As cover for Dally Duncan, Bird's opportunities were limited after he had been signed for £250.

BIRDSALL
George　　　Outside-left/left-back
Born: Saxton, 30 September 1891.
Career: Brompton (Northallerton League). War service. Harpenden Town 1919. Derby County March 1921.

After two League games on the wing, Birdsall's other six were at left-back in his brief stay with the Rams.

BLACKETT
Joseph　　　　　　Left-back
Born: Newcastle upon Tyne, 1875.
Career: Newcastle United. Gateshead. Loughborough Town June 1896. Wolverhampton Wanderers May 1897. Derby County July 1900. Sunderland April 1901. Middlesbrough October 1901. Luton Town May 1905. Leicester

Fosse June 1906. Player-manager, Rochdale, cs 1909. Barrow, August 1912. Trainer, Reading, 1913.

Joe Blackett began 1900-01 as first-choice left-back but his form was apparently affected by poor health. Welsh international Charlie Morris took over and was a fixture in the Derby team for the next decade. Whilst with Wolves, Blackett represented the English XI against the Scottish XI in March 1900, a Players' Union international.

BLADES
Paul Andrew   *Central defender/ right-back*

Born: Peterborough, 5 January 1965. Career: Apprentice, Derby County: professional December 1982. Norwich City July 1990. Wolverhampton Wanderers, loan, August 1992.
Division Three promotion 1985-6. Division Two champions 1986-7.

Paul Blades, whose brother Steve was also on Derby's staff, made his League debut at the age of 17 and won England Youth caps as a centre-half. That is his preferred position but, despite an early start, he made only occasional appearances until Arthur Cox took over as manager. At one stage, Peter Taylor told him to find another club but sanity prevailed. Under Cox, Blades was as liable to appear at right-back as in the centre of defence. In successive promotions, he replaced Charlie Palmer and took over from the injured Mel Sage. Even in his Central League days, Blades always had composure. His speed matched his ability in the air and he showed he could play in two positions at First Division level. When his contract expired in 1990, Blades decided to leave the Baseball Ground. He joined Norwich City for £700,000, a fee fixed by a tribunal

BLESSINGTON
James   *Outside/inside-right*

Born: Linlithgow, 28 February 1874. Died: Newton Abbot, 18 April 1939. Career: Leith Hibernians 1890. Hibernian as an amateur. Leith Athletic 1891. Glasgow Celtic cs 1892. Preston North End February 1898. Derby County June 1899. Bristol City November 1899. Luton Town August 1900. Leicester Fosse May 1903. Team manager, Leicester Fosse, January 1907 to April 1909. Coach, Belfast Celtic, 1913.

Blessington played only twice for Derby but he had enjoyed a distinguished career in Scotland, where he was regarded as one of the leading forwards of the 1890s. He played for Scotland four times, helped Celtic win the Scottish championship in 1892-3, 1893-4 and 1895-6 and played for them in the 1893 and 1894 Scottish Cup Finals.

Paul Blades, shared in two promotions with the Rams.

Steve Bloomer, scored 332 goals for the Rams in 525 senior games and was the club's leading scorer for 13 consecutive seasons.

BLOCKLEY
Jeffrey Paul *Centre-half*

Born: Leicester, 12 September 1949.
Career: Apprentice, Coventry City: professional June 1967. Arsenal October 1972. Leicester City January 1975. Derby County, loan, February 1978. Notts County June 1978. Player-coach, Enderby Town, August 1980. Gloucester City cs 1981. Manager, Leicester United, July 1983. Manager, Shepshed Charterhouse, May 1984 to May 1985. Manager, Hinckley Athletic, April to May 1989.

Jeff Blockley.

Tommy Docherty took Jeff Blockley on loan but played him in only one match, an FA Cup fifth round tie against West Bromwich Albion. Blockley played six times for England Under-23s before his £200,000 move from Coventry to Arsenal. At Highbury, he added four Under-23 appearances and a full cap against Yugoslavia in 1972-3.

BLOOMER
Philip *Left-back*

Born: Cradley Heath.
Career: Derby County May 1895.
Division One runners-up 1895-6.

Steve Bloomer's brother. Made one League appearance in September 1895, a season in which the Rams finished Division One runners-up.

BLOOMER
Stephen *Inside-right*

Born: Cradley, 20 January 1874. Died: Derby, 16 April 1938.
Career: Derby Swifts. Tutbury Hawthorn. Derby County April 1892. Middlesbrough March 1906. Derby County September 1910. Coaching in Berlin 1914. Coach, Derby County, 1919.

Division One runners-up 1895-6. FA Cup Finalists 1897-8, 1898-9. Division Two champions 1911-12 (captain).

Steve Bloomer moved to Derby as a child, learned his football at St James's School and played with Derby Swifts in the Derbyshire Minor League, scoring 14 goals for them in one match. That form brought him to the Rams' attention and in his first game in a Derby shirt, against Darley Dale, he scored four times. Bloomer made his League debut at Stoke in September 1892 and soon established himself as a favourite with the crowd. Pale-faced, almost ill-looking, Bloomer's appearance belied his worth to the side. He scored goals from all angles, plundering them from close range and launching rockets from 25 yards. He was Derby's leading scorer in all matches for 14 seasons and won the first of 23 England caps in 1895, scoring twice in a 9-0 win over the Irish at Derby. Bloomer took his fair share of digging elbows and clogging feet, but nothing could stop this peerless footballer whose rapier shot was matched by exquisite, defence-splitting passes. Some critics said that he played too much for himself and colleagues dreaded a Bloomer stare when the ball was not put to his feet. Yet Bloomer was a legend. One writer said of him: 'He is as crafty as an Oriental and as slippery as an eel and is much given to dealing out electric shocks to goalkeepers at the end of a sinuous run'. In 1906 he went to Middlesbrough, rejoining Derby to a hero's welcome in 1910 and skippering the Rams to promotion. In 1914 he went to coach in Germany where he was interned during World War One. After the war he played with, and coached, the Rams Reserves, then coached in Spain and Holland before returning to the Baseball Ground as a general assistant. In failing health, Bloomer was sent on a cruise, but in April 1938, three weeks after returning home, Derby County's greatest player was dead.

BLORE
Vincent F. *Goalkeeper*

Born: Uttoxeter.
Career: Uttoxeter Amateurs. Burton Town. Aston Villa August 1932. Derby County August 1933. West Ham United July 1935. Crystal Palace October 1936. Exeter City October 1938.

Blore spent two seasons at the Baseball Ground as goalkeeping cover for Jack Kirby.

BOAG
John M. *Centre-forward*

Born: Glasgow.
Career. Cowlairs. Ashfield. East Stirlingshire. Derby County May 1896. Brentford May 1904.

John Boag.

FA Cup Finalists 1897-98, 1898-99, 1902-03.

Cup specialist John Boag played for the Ashfield club which provided the Rams with Stevenson and Maconnachie of the same era. Boag moved to East Stirlingshire and his performances there brought him to the notice of a Rams scout in 1896. A trial was arranged, Boag impressed and he was soon a regular reserve teamer. The well-built forward, though not especially skilful, worked hard and scored goals. In 1897-8, after the Rams drew 1-1 at home to Liverpool in the third round of the FA Cup, the Merseysiders objected to the inclusion of Maconnachie. Boag was called upon to play centre-forward and responded with a hat-trick. Later in the season he played in the Rams' first FA Cup Final. Boag appeared in all three of Derby's early Finals, one of only three players to do so. After the Rams' crushing defeat by Bury in the 1903 Final, Boag stayed at the Baseball Ground for one more season.

BOSWORTH
Samuel *Outside-right*

Career: Long Eaton Rangers. Loughborough Town September 1898. Derby County December 1898. Sheffield Wednesday March 1899. Whitwick White Cross October 1901. Ilkeston United.

Played only twice for Derby and, despite a goal in his second game, gave way to Harry Oakden.

Colin Boulton, whose 344 senior appearances are a record for a Rams goalkeeper.

BOULTON
Colin Donald   *Goalkeeper*

Born: Cheltenham, 12 September 1945. Career: Charlton Kings. Gloucester Police. Derby County August 1964. Southampton, loan, September 1976. Tulsa Roughnecks March 1978. Los Angeles Aztecs July 1979. Lincoln City July 1980.
Division One champions 1971-2, 1974-5.

Only one man played in all 84 games of Derby County's two League Championship seasons, goalkeeper Colin Boulton. He made more appearances than any other goalkeeper in the club's history, beating the record set by Reg Matthews. Boulton was a police cadet in his native Cheltenham when Tim Ward signed him in 1964. He was understudy to Matthews and it came as a setback when Brian Clough signed Les Green from Rochdale in 1968. Not until Green lost form at the end of 1970 was Boulton recalled, but this time he

made the most of it. His handling was high-class, greater experience taught him to deal with crosses and, above all, he was consistent, giving away remarkably few soft goals. In 1971-2, he kept a clean sheet in 23 League games as well as six Cup ties of various kinds. For a time Dave Mackay preferred Graham Moseley, but recalled Boulton shortly before he was sacked as manager. Tommy Docherty ended Boulton's career but, to the day he left, Boulton was, by some way, the best

Frank Boulton, joined the Rams from Arsenal.

Jeff Bourne, forced to wait for his chance.

goalkeeper on the books. Following an unhappy time with Los Angeles Aztecs, Boulton played under Colin Murphy for Lincoln City but, after four games, a severe injury at Crewe put him out of the game.

BOULTON
Frank Preece   *Goalkeeper*

Born: Chipping Sodbury, 12 August 1917. Died: Swindon, June 1987.
Career: Bristol City November 1934. Bath City July 1936. Arsenal October 1936. Derby County August 1938. Swindon Town July 1946. Crystal Palace October 1950. Bedford Town March 1951.

Frank Boulton was one of the unlucky players ruled out of Derby County's 1946 FA Cup team through injury. He was Derby's number one goalkeeper in the last season before World War Two and kept in the first six Cup ties in 1945-6 after serving with the RAF in West Africa. He was badly injured in a clash with Swansea Town's Welsh international Trevor Ford in a League South game and Derby signed Vic Woodley before the semi-finals.

BOURNE
Jeffrey   *Forward*

Born: Linton, 19 June 1948.
Career: Linton United. Derby County January 1969. Dallas Tornado, loan, April 1976. Crystal Palace March 1977. Dallas Tornado March 1978. Atlanta Chiefs 1979. Sheffield United Sep-
tember 1979. Atlanta Chiefs March 1980. Seattle Sounders July 1980. Wichita Wings 1982. Coach, Gresley Rovers, 1986 to June 1987.
Division One champions 1974-5.

Jeff Bourne's goals were important when Derby won the Central League in 1971-2 but he was not given much chance of League football until January 1974, when Dave Mackay brought him out of the shadows. Given the chance, he proved he could be a force at League level and was an important squad player in the 1974-5 Championship. A neat player, with good control, Bourne moved to Crystal Palace for £30,000 and spent five seasons in the North American Soccer League, although he returned for six months with Sheffield United. In 138 League and play-off games in the NASL, Bourne scored 68 goals.

BOWDEN
Oswald   *Inside-forward*

Born: Byker, 7 September 1912.
Career: Newcastle United Swifts. Derby County May 1930. Nottingham Forest June 1935. Brighton & Hove Albion June 1937. Southampton July 1938.

Another of George Jobey's signings from the North-East, Bowden provided useful cover before joining Nottingham Forest.

BOWERS
John Anslow   *Forward*

Born: Leicester, 14 November 1939.
Career: Derby Corinthians. Derby County February 1957. Notts County May 1966.

John Bowers.

Jack Bowers, scored 183 senior goals in 220 games for Derby.

The son of Jack Bowers. A lively forward, with good pace, John Bowers was beginning to establish himself in Derby's Second Division side under Tim Ward, after turning down a move to Lincoln City in 1963, when he sustained a nasty ankle injury in a game against Coventry City in September 1964. Although he returned to the team, he was never again quite as effective and moved to Notts County.

BOWERS
John William Anslow *Centre-forward*

Born: Santon, near Scunthorpe, 22 February 1908. Died: Lichfield, 4 July 1970.
Career: Appleby Works. Scunthorpe United December 1927. Derby County May 1928. Leicester City November 1936. Coach, Notts County Colts, August 1943. Assistant-trainer, Derby County, September 1945: physiotherapist.

Division One runners-up 1929-30, 1935-6.

There has never been a braver centre-forward on Derby County's books than Jack Bowers, who scored on his debut in the 2-1 win over Bolton at the Baseball Ground on 2 February 1929. A week later, as the Rams crushed Portsmouth 5-1 at Fratton Park, the young centre-forward hurled himself at a Crooks centre and scored a goal 'worthy of Steve Bloomer at his best'. Bowers went on to score the first of his 16 hat-tricks that afternoon and

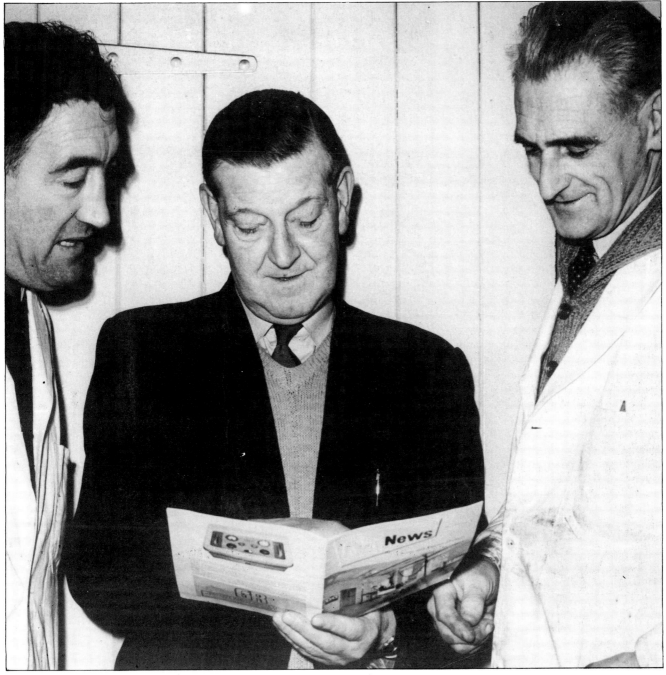

Jack Bowers (right), then assistant trainer at the Baseball Ground, pictured with two other former Rams players Johnny McIntyre (centre), who was then chief scout, and head trainer Ralph Hann.

thereafter became as well-known a Rams star as the great Steve. His courage at diving head first through a forest of legs became legendary and, in 1930-31, he smashed the Rams' scoring record with 37 League goals in only 33 matches. Bowers was the First Division's leading scorer for three consecutive seasons and in 1933 played for the Football League. Three England caps soon followed. In September 1934 he badly injured a knee against Spurs and his recovery was slow, although in 1935-6 his 30 goals for the Reserves helped Derby to the Central League championship. George Jobey brought the great Hughie Gallacher as a short-term replacement. In September

1936, Derby were losing 4-1 at home to Manchester United. Then Bowers struck with four goals in an amazing 15-minute spell to give his side a spectacular victory. Two months later he was sold to Leicester City and scored 33 goals in 27 games to shoot them to the Division Two title.

BOWLER
George Henry
Wing-half

Born: 23 January 1890. Died: 1948.
Career: Gresley Rovers. Derby County May 1911. Tottenham Hotspur June 1913. Luton Town July 1919.

Played only once for Derby, standing in for Tommy Barbour.

BOXLEY
Harry
Wing-half

Born: Stourbridge, c.1894.
Career: Stourbridge. Shrewsbury Town. Wellington Town May 1914. Derby County May 1919. Bristol Rovers August 1920.

One of several players Derby signed from outside the League when peacetime football resumed in 1919. He had appeared once in the Midland Victory League the previous April and played in Bristol Rovers' first League match, having been taken to Eastville by former Derby defender Ben Hall.

BOYD
James Murray   *Outside-right*

Born: Glasgow, 29 April 1907. Died: Bournemouth, March 1991.
Career: Petershill. Edinburgh St Bernard's. Newcastle United May 1925. Derby County May 1935. Bury January 1937. Dundee September 1937. Grimsby Town June 1938.

Division One runners-up 1935-6.

Jimmy Boyd's best days were at Newcastle. Although he played only twice in the 1926-7 Championship team, he was in the side which beat Arsenal in the 1932 FA Cup Final and was capped by Scotland against Ireland in 1933.

BRADBURY
John Jackson Longstaff

Outside-right

Born: South Bank, 1878.
Career: Stockport County. Lincoln City January 1896. Ashton North End September 1896. Blackburn Rovers August 1897. Ashton North End November 1897. Derby County May 1899. Barnsley June 1900. Bristol City June 1901. New Brompton May 1902. Millwall May 1904. Carlisle United cs 1906.

Bradbury spent a season at Derby, providing competition for Richard Wombwell in the outside-right position.

BRAND
Robert.   *Inside-left*

Career: Queen of the South Wanderers. Accrington September 1888. Derby County November 1890.

Played for Accrington in the first two League seasons but appeared only three times for Derby.

BRINTON
John Victor   *Outside-left*

Born: Avonmouth, 11 July 1916.
Career: Avonmouth. Bristol City August 1935. Newport County July 1937. Derby County January 1938. Stockport County July 1946. Leyton Orient August 1948. Chippenham Town 1949.

Brinton cost Derby £1,000 when he was signed as cover for Dally Duncan and was on the books until after World War Two. His brother Ernie was Bristol City's regular left-half for seven seasons in the 1930s, also playing for Newport County and Aldershot.

BRISCOE
Robert Dean   *Midfield.*

Born: Derby, 4 September 1969.
Career: Trainee, Derby County: professional September 1987. Gresley Rovers August 1992.

Robbie Briscoe developed through the Youth team and Reserves, playing as much at left-back as on the left of

Robbie Briscoe.

midfield. He made his debut in the 1989-90 Littlewoods Cup three-match saga against West Ham United and, later that season, scored spectacularly against Arsenal.

BROLLY
Michael Joseph   *Midfield*

Born: Kilmarnock, 6 October 1954.
Career: Juniors, Chelsea: professional October 1971. Bristol City June 1974. Grimsby Town September 1976. Derby County August 1982. Scunthorpe United August 1983. Scarborough July 1986. Goole Town, loan, January 1987. Goole Town March 1987. Boston United February 1988. Holbeach United February 1989.

A Scottish schoolboy international who became a greatly respected wide midfield player in Grimsby Town's rise from Fourth Division to Second. Former Grimsby manager John Newman signed him for Derby on a free transfer and he played in every game of his one season, once as substitute, before Peter Taylor sold him to Scunthorpe for £10,000.

Mick Brolly.

BROMAGE
Enos   *Goalkeeper*

Born: Derby.
Career: Derby Junction. Derby County 1889. Derby Junction.

The first of a Derby footballing family to represent the Rams. Succeeded Joe Marshall at the end of the first League season and was in goal when the Rams lost 11-2 to Everton in the FA Cup, their record defeat.

BROMAGE
Enos   *Outside-left*

Born: Mickleover, 22 October 1898. Died: Derby, 7 April 1978.
Career: Stapleford Town. Sheffield United 1922. Derby County November 1923. Gillingham May 1927. West

Enos Bromage.

Bromwich Albion March 1928. Nottingham Forest October 1929. Chester. Wellington Town.

Division Two promotion 1925-6.

Managed only six senior games in his four years at the Baseball Ground, usually when standing-in for Lionel Murphy.

BROMAGE
Harry   *Goalkeeper*
Born: Derby.
Career: Derby Constitutional. Derby County October 1898. Burton United 1901. Leeds City August 1905. Doncaster Rovers 1911. Bentley Colliery.

Jack Fryer's deputy at Derby and played only rarely. Bromage became a star with Leeds City, playing in their first League game in 1905 and making more than 150 senior appearances.

BROOKS
George   *Wing-half*
Born: Radcliffe. Died in action, 11 November 1918.
Career: Longfield. Manchester City January 1911. Bury April 1912. South Shields. Derby County June 1914.
Division Two champions 1914-15.

Quickly established himself as a reliable performer in the Derby team which won Division Two before World War One halted League football. Brooks was believed to be the only professional footballer killed on Armistice Day.

BROOKS
Joseph T.   *Outside-right*
Career: Melbourne Town. Derby

Frank Broome, 45 goals in 119 senior games for Derby.

County March 1894. Heanor Town September 1895. Melbourne Town February 1896.

Appeared briefly in 1894-5, when Derby avoided relegation only by winning a Test Match.

BROOME
Frank Henry   *Forward*
Born: Berkhamstead, 11 June 1915.
Career: Boxmoor United. Berkhamstead Town. Aston Villa November

1934. Derby County September 1946. Notts County October 1949. Brentford July 1953. Crewe Alexandra October 1953. Shelbourne February 1955. Assistant trainer, Notts County, August 1955: acting manager, January to May 1957: assistant manager to December 1957. Manager, Exeter City, January 1958. Manager, Southend United, May to December 1960. Manager-coach, Bankstown (NSW), July 1961. Manager-coach, Corinthians (Sydney), 1962. Manager, Exeter City, May 1967 to February 1969.

When Frank Broome joined the Rams in September 1946 he was already an established star. He was Aston Villa's leading scorer in the last three seasons before World War Two and, although 31 when he signed for Derby, he soon showed that he had lost none of his speed and exceptional ball control. A thrustful winger, Broome enjoyed a fine striking rate at the Baseball Ground and was adept at switching with his centre-forward. Broome won seven England caps before the war, including one in the infamous Berlin match when the England stars were forced by the Foreign Office to give the Nazi salute. Broome played in four forward positions for his country. In 1947 Broome defied the Chelsea forward line, Tommy Lawton and all, as an emergency goalkeeper for all but five minutes of a fourth-round FA Cup match which ran into extra-time at the Baseball Ground. He was in Villa's Second Division championship team in 1937-8 and helped Notts County to the Third Division South title in 1949-50. After a spell as acting-manager of Notts County in 1957, Broome was disappointed to be passed over in favour of Tommy Lawton. In May 1964, he was appointed coach at Derby County but returned to Australia without taking up the position.

BROWN
Gordon   *Inside-forward*

Born: Ellesmere Port, 30 June 1933.
Career: Juniors, Wolverhampton Wanderers: professional September 1951. Ellesmere Port Town December 1951. Scunthorpe United December 1952. Derby County January 1957. Southampton March 1960. Barrow July 1961. Southport January 1964.
Division Three North champions 1956-7.

With Jack Parry not fully recovered from the previous season's injury, Harry Storer needed a goalscorer to clinch promotion from Division Three North. The Supporters' Association came up with the £5,150 fee for Gordon Brown, who responded with nine goals in 17 games. Brown, an England Youth international in 1951 and 1952, found it harder to score in Division Two but his tally of 20 in 54 senior games helped to attract Southampton's interest.

BROWN
Harold Thomas   *Goalkeeper*

Born: Kingsbury, 9 April 1924. Died: Abingdon, June 1982.
Career: Queen's Park Rangers June 1940. Notts County April 1946. Derby County October 1949. Queen's Park Rangers August 1951. Plymouth Argyle August 1956. Exeter City September 1958.

Spectacular goalkeeper who joined Derby County as part of the deal which took Frank Broome to Notts County. One of several goalkeepers to replace Billy Townsend but be outlasted by him.

BUCHANAN
John   *Forward*

Born: Underwood, near Stirling, 9 June 1928.
Career: Kilsyth Rangers. Clyde 1946. Derby County February 1955. Bradford November 1957. Retired May 1963 and worked as Bradford pools promoter. Team manager, Bradford, May 1964 to March 1967.
Division Three North champions 1956-7.

Jock Buchanan helped Clyde to win the Scottish Second Division in 1951-2 and was one of the players signed by Jack Barker in a vain attempt to avoid relegation to the Third North. Scored five goals in six games in Derby's Third North championship season before leaving in the November.

Jock Buchanan.

BUCKLEY
Franklin Charles   *Centre-half*

Born: Urmston, 9 November 1882. Died: Walsall, 22 December 1964.
Career: Aston Villa April 1903. Brighton & Hove Albion May 1905. Manchester United June 1906. Manchester City September 1907. Birmingham July 1909. Derby County May 1911. Bradford City May 1914. Retired during World War One but made one appearance for Norwich City September 1919. Secretary-manager, Norwich City, March 1919 to July 1920. Manager, Blackpool, July 1923 to May 1927. Manager, Wolverhampton Wanderers, July 1927. Manager, Notts County, March 1944 to January 1946. Manager, Hull City, May 1946 to April 1948. Manager, Leeds United, May 1948. Manager, Walsall, April 1953 to June 1955.
Division Two champions 1911-12.

Frank Buckley was a tough centre-half who reached the peak of his career at the Baseball Ground. Steve Bloomer once said that Buckley, rather than himself, should have skippered the side in 1911-12. Buckley fought in the Boer War and his undoubted leadership qualities were further highlighted in World War One when he joined the 17th Middlesex Regiment — the famous Footballers' Battalion — and was promoted to major, a rank he proudly used for the rest of his life. One of six sons — brother Chris played

Frank Buckley.

Brinsley-born Steve Buckley came the long way round to Derby County but went on to make 366 first-team appearances for the Rams.

for Arsenal and Aston Villa and was later Villa chairman — Frank Buckley managed seven clubs. His managerial success, even though it never brought a trophy, came at Wolves where his methods were innovative — witness the monkey-gland treatment of players — and tough. There is a story of how he made players practise by kicking a ball between two bricks and woe betide any player who was not dead on target. Perhaps the low spot of Buckley's playing career came, curiously enough, in his only England appearance. He was in the side which sensationally lost 3-0 to Ireland in 1914.

BUCKLEY
Steven   *Left-back*
Born: Brinsley, 16 October 1953. Career: Ilkeston Town June 1970. Redfern Athletic (Sunday football) February 1972. Burton Albion May 1973. Luton Town April 1974. Derby County January 1978. Lincoln City August 1986. Boston United November 1988. Eastwood Town, loan, October 1990. Manager, Shepshed Charterhouse, February to May 1991. Assistant manager, Boston United, July 1991. Division Three promotion 1985-6.

Had Derby County been sufficiently alert, they could have snapped up Steve Buckley from Ilkeston Town or Burton Albion long before they paid Luton Town £163,000 for him. Of all Tommy Docherty's signings, Buckley was the only long-term success and was undisputed first choice at left-back for more than eight years. He became the only player in the club's history to complete two separate centuries of consecutive League appearances. Burton signed Buckley as a forward and then manager Ken Gutteridge converted him to left-back, although his attacking instincts produced some spectacular goals for the Rams. He was a favourite at the Baseball Ground, one of the more consistent players in a period of decline and an ever-present in four of his eight complete League seasons. He broke a leg in his 200th League appearance for Derby, against Charlton in 1983, and was obscurely transfer-listed by Peter Taylor the following season, when he was still recovering. Arthur Cox took him off the list and, in helping to re-establish the club, Buckley's Derby career ended on a high note with promotion from the Third Division.

BULLIONS
James Law   *Wing-half*
Born: Dennyloanhead, 12 March 1924. Career: Chesterfield, amateur, December 1942. Clowne cs 1944. Derby County October 1944. Leeds United November 1947. Shrewsbury Town September 1950. Worksop Town August 1955. Gresley Rovers August 1956. Sutton Town December 1956.

Matlock Town October 1958. Alfreton Town, August 1960: Player-manager September 1960: manager to September 1968.

FA Cup winners 1945-6.

The baby of Derby's team, at the age of 22, in the Veterans' Cup Final, Bullions played only 17 peacetime League games for the Rams before giving way to Tim Ward. An industrious wing-half, Bullions was a miner and played part-time. He helped Sammy Crooks to establish Shrewsbury Town as a League club and was a popular manager of Alfreton Town.

BUNYAN
Charles   *Goalkeeper*

Died: Brussels, 1923.
Career: Old Horns (Chesterfield). Hyde. Derby County 1889. Chesterfield Town August 1892. Sheffield United February 1894. Derby County March 1894. Ilkeston Town July 1895. Walsall November 1896. New Brompton cs 1898. Newcastle United January 1901. Ripley Athletic March 1903.

Played only a handful of games for Derby but managed to carve out a good career after being Hyde's goalkeeper when they lost 26-0 to Preston North End in the FA Cup, the highest score in an English competitive senior game. Was on a coaching assignment when he died in Brussels.

BURNS
Kenneth   *Central defender*

Born: Glasgow, 23 September 1953.
Career: Glasgow Rangers. Apprentice Birmingham City: professional July 1971. Nottingham Forest July 1977. Leeds United October 1981. Derby County, loan, March 1983. Derby County, loan, February 1984. Derby

Kenny Burns, helped Derby delay relegation and then stayed on to assist in starting the club's revival under Arthur Cox.

John Burridge, won Second Division championship medals with Palace and Wolves and a Scottish League Cup medal with Hibs.

Noah Burton, Derby's leading scorer in 1919-20.

County March 1984. Notts County, loan, February 1985. Barnsley August 1985. Sutton Town August 1986: joint-manager, March 1987. Stafford Rangers July 1988. Grantham Town 1988. Ilkeston Town July 1989.

Kenny Burns showed himself to be a talented centre-forward at Birmingham but it was in his more normal defensive position that he reached the heights with Nottingham Forest. In 1977-8, when Forest won the League championship and the League Cup, Burns was Footballer of the Year. He also won two European Cup medals in Forest's great period under Brian Clough and Peter Taylor. Burns, capped 20 times by Scotland, helped Taylor to stave off one relegation at Derby and, although unable to prevent it the following year, stayed to assist Arthur Cox in starting the revival.

BURRIDGE
John   *Goalkeeper*
Born: Workington, 3 December 1951. Career: Apprentice, Workington: professional January 1970. Blackpool, loan, April 1971. Blackpool May 1971. Aston Villa September 1975. Southend United, loan, January 1978. Crystal Palace March 1978. Queen's Park Rangers December 1980. Wolverhampton Wanderers, loan, August 1982. Wolverhampton Wanderers September 1982. Derby County, loan, September 1984. Sheffield United October 1984. Southampton August 1987. Newcastle United October 1989. Hibernian August 1991.

John Burridge modelled himself on Peter Shilton and, during 1988-9, passed 600 League appearances. Joined Derby on loan when Eric Steele was injured but preferred to move to Sheffield United rather than stay permanently.

BURTON
John Henry   *Inside-forward*
Born: Derby, 13 August 1875. Died: Derby, 13 May 1949.
Career: Derby St Andrew's. Derby County October 1896. Chatham June 1899. Tottenham Hotspur March 1901.

Never established himself as first choice.

BURTON
Noah   *Forward*
Born: Basford, 18 December 1896. Died: Nottingham, 16 July 1956.
Career: Bulwell St Albans. Ilkeston United August 1915. Derby County December 1915. Nottingham Forest June 1921. Retired 1932.

After helping Nottingham Forest to win the Victory Shield in 1919, Burton was Derby's leading scorer in the first season after World War One. He moved permanently to Forest after two peace-

Barry Butlin, once the Rams record outgoing transfer.

Ian Buxton, the Rams' last footballer-cricketer.

time seasons at the Baseball Ground and helped them to win the Second Division title in 1922. Burton was one of Forest's most popular players in the 1920s and played in 320 League and Cup games, scoring 62 goals.

BUTLIN
Barry Desmond   *Centre-forward*

Born: Rosliston, 9 November 1949.
Career: Juniors, Derby County: professional January 1967. Notts County, loan, January 1969. Luton Town November 1972. Nottingham Forest October 1974. Brighton & Hove Albion, loan, September 1975. Reading, loan, January 1977. Peterborough United August 1977. Sheffield United August 1979.

Barry Butlin's opportunities at Derby were limited by the consistency of John O'Hare and Kevin Hector and much of his early experience came in an extended loan to Notts County, from January to October 1969. The £50,000 paid by Luton was then the highest fee Derby had received. He was a success at Kenilworth Road, leading scorer when they won promotion to the First Division in 1974, and cost £122,000 when he joined Nottingham Forest.

BUTTERWORTH
Charles E.   *Outside-right*

Career: Derby Midland. Derby County June 1891. Loughborough Town 1892. Heanor Town by 1896.

Joined the Rams when Derby Midland folded but played only once, in February 1892.

BUXTON
Ian Ray   *Centre-forward*

Born: Cromford, 17 April 1938.
Career: Matlock Town January 1958. Derby County March 1959. Luton Town September 1967. Notts County July 1969. Port Vale December 1969.

The last player to divide his time between Derby County in the winter and Derbyshire cricket in the summer. His skill as a centre-forward was in holding the ball, although he scored his share of goals, including two on his debut against Ipswich Town in November 1959. Won a Fourth Division championship medal with Luton Town in 1968 and another Fourth Division promotion with Port Vale in 1970. A valuable all-rounder for Derby-

Nigel Callaghan, helped Derby into Division One in 1987 and was happy to return on loan in 1990.

shire from 1959 to 1973. He scored 11,803 runs in first-class cricket, took 483 wickets and held 199 catches. Captain from 1970 to 1972, during which time he shared a Derbyshire fifth-wicket record stand of 203 with Chris Wilkins, against Lancashire at Old Trafford in 1971.

CALLAGHAN
Nigel Ian   *Outside-left/right*
Born: Singapore, 12 September 1962.

Career: Apprentice, Watford: professional July 1980. Derby County February 1987. Aston Villa February 1989. Derby County, loan, September 1990. Watford, loan, March 1991. Huddersfield Town, loan, January 1992. Stafford Rangers March 1992.

Division Two champions 1986-87.

Nigel Callaghan was 17 when he made his debut for Watford and, two seasons later, he was joined by John Barnes to give Graham Taylor's team the most promising wing pair in the League. Callaghan was involved when Watford won promotion from the Second Division in 1982, finished runners-up in the First Division a year later and reached the 1984 FA Cup Final. He played nine times for England Under-21, helping them win the UEFA championship in 1984, and appeared for England 'B'. Derby paid £140,000 for him to give a final push towards the Second Division title. Arthur Cox had used Jeff Chandler, then Graham

The Rams celebrate promotion in 1987. Rob Hindmarch leads the applause, Williams, Callaghan and Steele head the parade.

Harbey on the left flank but saw an extra touch of class in Callaghan. He did an excellent job in the last 18 games of 1986-7, scoring a precious winner at Millwall and a brilliant goal at Ipswich. As the player most likely to create a goal, Callaghan played a significant part in Derby's survival in 1987-8. After two years with the Rams he rejoined Taylor at Villa Park, for £500,000, then a Derby record for an incoming fee. It was not a successful

move for him and he was happy to return to Derby on loan at a time when Cox was unable to buy players. He did well at the Baseball Ground but, when he returned to Villa, his career declined sharply.

CALLAN
William   *Inside-forward*

Born: Glasgow, 10 June 1900.
Career: Shawland Thistle. Pollock.
Derby County May 1921.

Only one senior appearance, in March 1922.

CALLENDER
Reginald H.   *Outside-left*

Killed in World War One.
Career: Stockton School. St John's College, Cambridge. One match for Glossop, 1912-13. Derby County, amateur, March 1914.

A Cambridge Blue and England ama-

Bobby Campbell, a failure at Derby.

Dave Cargill, had a good first season but then faded.

teur international, Callender played five League games when Derby were trying to avoid relegation in 1913-14.

CAMPBELL
Robert McFaul   *Centre-forward*

Born: Belfast, 13 September 1956.
Career: Apprentice, Aston Villa: professional January 1974. Halifax Town, loan, February 1975. Huddersfield Town May 1975. Sheffield United, loan, July 1977. Sheffield United August 1977. Vancouver Whitecaps May 1978. Huddersfield Town September 1978. Halifax Town October 1978. Brisbane City May 1979. Bradford City December 1979. Derby County August 1983. Bradford City, after loan, November 1983. Wigan Athletic October 1986. Guiseley.

Bobby Campbell was a favourite with

Bradford City. When Roy McFarland was manager at Valley Parade, Campbell's 24 goals were crucial to promotion from the Fourth Division in 1981-2, the season in which he was capped twice by Northern Ireland. Derby paid £75,000 for Campbell and lost £45,000 of it when he returned to Bradford City three months later, having completely failed to fit in at the Baseball Ground. But he was again leading scorer when Bradford City won the Third Division in 1984-5 and set a club record of 121 League goals in his two spells. After being freed by Wigan Athletic in 1988 he became part-owner of a night club Huddersfield.

CARGILL
David Anderson   *Outside-left*

Born: Arbroath, 21 July 1936.

Career: Juniors, Burnley: professional July 1953. Sheffield Wednesday September 1956. Derby County April 1958. Lincoln City December 1960. Arbroath February 1962.

Dave Cargill cost £4,250 when Harry Storer bought him to replace Dennis Woodhead. After a reasonable first season, Cargill began to fade and was sold to Lincoln City for £3,265.

CARLIN
William   *Midfield*

Born: Liverpool, 6 October 1940.
Career: Juniors, Liverpool: professional May 1958. Halifax Town August 1962. Carlisle United October 1964. Sheffield United September 1967. Derby County August 1968. Leicester City October 1970. Notts County

Willie Carlin, whose £60,000 move from Sheffield United heralded a 13-match unbeaten run.

September 1971. Cardiff City November 1973.
Division Two champions 1968-9.
Before Willie Carlin joined Derby in August 1968, the Rams had played four League games and failed to win one. After Carlin's £60,000 move — then a Rams record payment — Derby went 13 matches undefeated and by the end of the season had romped away with the Second Division title. Carlin's authority, competitiveness and skill in midfield were big factors in the Rams' promotion. After playing one League game for Liverpool, the 5ft 4ins Carlin went to Halifax and he says that the experience almost cost him his career. He was in Carlisle United's Third Division promotion team of 1964-5 and it was from Brunton Park that Brian Clough and Peter Taylor first tried to sign him. Carlin, still playing well, was shattered when the Rams sold him but he had two more promotions up his sleeve, as Second Division champions with Leicester City in 1970-71 and from the Third Division with Notts County two years later. After retiring, Carlin went into business as a newsagent and later lived in Majorca.

Billy Carr, spent a decade at Derby as a reliable full-back.

East by Cecil Potter but made his debut under George Jobey, playing one match in the Second Division promotion season. For a decade, he was a reliable cover for both full-back positions, clocking up more than 100 senior appearances before moving to Queen's Park Rangers for £350.

CARRUTHERS
Eric   *Forward*

Born: Edinburgh, 22 February 1953.
Career: Heart of Midlothian. Derby County March 1975. Contract cancelled October 1977.

Eric Carruthers.

A £15,000 signing from Hearts who made no impact at Derby. One substitute appearance, against Manchester United in September 1976.

CARTER
Horatio Stratton *Inside-forward*

Born: Sunderland, 21 December 1913.
Career: Amateur, Sunderland November 1930: professional, November 1931. Derby County December 1945. Hull City, player/assistant-manager, March 1948: player-manager May 1948. Resigned as manager September 1951. Retired as player April 1952. Cork Athletic January to May 1953. Manager, Leeds United, May 1953 to June 1958. Manager, Mansfield Town, February 1960. Manager, Middlesbrough, January 1963 to February 1966.
FA Cup winners 1945-6.

By the time he was 24, Raich Carter had won every honour then open to an English footballer — First Division championship medal, FA Cup winners' medal and full England cap. Carter was a brilliant schoolboy international. He signed for Sunderland and

CARR
William Paterson   *Full-back*

Born: Cambois, 6 November 1901.
Career: Seaton Delaval. Derby County February 1924. Queen's Park Rangers August 1935.

Division Two promotion 1925-6. Division One runners-up 1929-30.

Billy Carr was brought from the North-

Raich Carter, then a wartime guest player with Derby, in an unofficial international against Scotland at Wembley in February 1944.

Carter moved to Hull and helped them to the Third Division North title as player-manager. He made a short comeback with Cork Athletic, with whom he gained an FA of Ireland Cup winners' medal. Carter took Leeds United back to the First Division in 1956 and was heading for further promotion, from the Fourth Division, when he left Mansfield Town to join Middlesbrough. The feeling persists that he found it hard to work with players less talented than he had been.

CARTER
Stephen Charles *Outside-right*

Born: Great Yarmouth, 23 April 1953. Career: Apprentice, Manchester City: professional August 1970. Notts County February 1972. Derby County August 1978. Notts County September 1981. AFC Bournemouth March 1982. Torquay United June 1984.

Carter has hit foot on the scales as Reg Harrison is weighed. Jack Howe feigns surprise.

Steve Carter.

made his debut in 1932; by 1937 he had achieved the pinnacle of his career. Carter joined the fire service on the outbreak of war and then transferred to the RAF. He gained permission to guest for Derby because his wife was living in the town with her parents. At the time Carter was posted at Innsworth Lane, Gloucester, but on visits.to Derby he met the CO of RAF Loughborough and gained a posting there to help rehabilitate injured airmen. At Loughborough, Carter teamed up with Peter Doherty and week after week Rams fans enjoyed the spectacle of two of soccer's greatest inside-forwards running opposing defences ragged. Like Doherty with Manchester City, Carter was unsettled with Sunderland's attitude and in December 1945, a midnight taxi dash resulted in him being transferred officially in time for that season's FA Cup competition. It cost Derby £6,000 to sign him — "Sunderland were silly to let me go for that," Carter said later — and it was money amazingly well spent. Carter and Doherty helped Derby to Wembley and both scored freely. Unlike Doherty, Carter stayed at Derby until 1948 when the Rams were beaten by Manchester United in the FA Cup semi-final. Over 35,000 fans turned up to see his last game in a Rams shirt, against Blackpool at the Baseball Ground and, inevitably, he scored.

Involved in Notts County's 1972-3 promotion from the Third Division but joined Derby on a free transfer, arriving as Don Masson went in the opposite direction. This completed a transfer trail which began with Leighton James signing for £300,000, via a James-Masson exchange to frees, with Derby heavily out of pocket. Steve Carter helped to give Bournemouth a final push out of Division Four, under David Webb, in 1982.

Billy Caskey, played six times for Northern Ireland.

Martyn Chalk, scored in his first full match.

CASKEY
William Thomas   *Centre-*
forward

Born: Belfast, 12 October 1953.
Career: Glentoran,. Tulsa Rough-
necks, loan, March 1978. Derby County
September 1978. Tulsa Roughnecks
December 1979. Dallas Sidekicks.
Glentoran 1987.

Billy Caskey, signed by Tommy Docherty at the same time as Vic Moreland, was a determined centre-forward, although he found goals hard to score in English football. In some ways, Caskey was more effective when the opposition had the ball, because he harried and tackled so enthusiastically. Caskey played for Northern Ireland six times while he was with the Rams and made one more appearance when, like Moreland, he had moved into the North American Soccer League. Caskey collected a lengthy

suspension when he was playing indoor soccer in Dallas but returned to Glentoran and represented the Irish League.

CHALK
Martyn Peter Glyn   *Winger*

Born: Swindon, 30 April 1969.
Career: Grimsby Amateurs. Louth
United. Derby County January 1990.

Chalk's £10,000 signing from the Central Midlands League was overshadowed by the capture of Mick Harford on the same day. After making only slow progress and suffering several injuries, Chalk scored in his first full match, at Middlesbrough on New Year's Day 1992, and added a first-minute goal in an FA Cup tie at Burnley the same week.

CHALMERS
Bruce   *Half-back*

Career: Derby County 1890. Sheffield
Wednesday December 1892.

A regular half-back for one season, then Jack Cox took his place. Chalmers spent two seasons with the Wednesday.

CHANDLER
Albert   *Right-back*

Born: Carlisle, 15 January 1897. Died:
Carlisle, January 1963.
Career: Carlisle schools. Army football.
Derby County August 1919. Newcastle
United June 1925. Sheffield United
October 1926. Mansfield Town cs 1929.
Northfleet November 1929. Manchester
Central February 1930. Holme Head
(Carlisle district). Queen of the South.

After joining the Border Regiment in 1915, Chandler was commissioned in the Machine Gun Corps and survived

Jeff Chandler, played an important role in promotion to Division Two.

William Chatterton, played in Derby's first FA Cup tie.

a gas attack in 1918. He signed for Derby after World War One and developed into a reliable right-back. Once he had taken over from Jack Atkin, he was a regular for four seasons, ever-present in 1921-2, until Newcastle United signed him for £3,250. He was not a success with them or with Sheffield United after a £2,625 move but he had served the Rams well.

CHANDLER
Jeffrey George   *Outside-left*

Born: Hammersmith, 19 June 1959.
Career: Apprentice, Blackpool: professional August 1976. Leeds United September 1979. Bolton Wanderers October 1981. Derby County July 1985. Mansfield Town, loan, November 1986. Bolton Wanderers July 1987. Cardiff City November 1989.
Division Three promotion 1985-6.
Division Two champions 1986-7.

Jeff Chandler made a brilliant start with Derby after a transfer tribunal fixed his fee at £38,000. In the early weeks of the Third Division promotion season, he was devastating with his trickery, accurate centres and goals, including the first hat-trick of his career in an FA Cup victory over Telford. He lost his place when Mickey Thomas arrived on loan but was back for the four vital games at the end. Chandler was important to the Third Division success but lost his place to Graham Harbey in the Second Division and returned to Bolton the following summer. With Wanderers, he suffered damaged knee ligaments but recovered to share in the 1988-9 Sherpa Van Trophy success. A spell with Cardiff ended in December 1990 because of a knee injury. In a career which promised much, Chandler played twice for the Republic of Ireland while with Leeds United.

CHATTERTON
William   *Inside-forward*

Born: Birch Vale, 27 December 1861.
Died: Hyde, 19 March 1913.

One of four Test cricketers to play for Derby County, the others being William Storer, Frank Sugg and Arnold Warren. Chatterton appeared in Derby's first FA Cup tie and had five games in the first League season. Chatterton played for Derbyshire from 1882 to 1902, captaining them between 1887 and 1889, and scored seven centuries for the county. In all first-class, he made 10,888 runs and scored 48 in his one Test innings, against South Africa in Cape Town in 1892.

CHERRY
Steven Reginald   *Goalkeeper*

Born: Nottingham, 5 August 1960.
Career: Apprentice, Derby County:

Steve Cherry, still developing as a goalkeeper while with Derby.

for conceding Plymouth Argyle's winner direct from a corner in the 1984 FA Cup sixth round replay. He deserves better. But for his performance at Home Park, there would not even have been a replay and supporters had voted him Derby's Player of the Year in 1982-3. Cherry was still developing as a goalkeeper when he decided to leave Derby. Ironically, after two years with Walsall, he was signed for £19,000 by Plymouth. He was voted Player of the Year at both Fellows Park and Home Park before reaching his peak with Notts County.

CHESTERS
Colin Wayne   Centre-forward

Born: Crewe, 21 November 1959.
Career: Apprentice, Derby County: professional November 1977. Waterford, loan, January 1979. Crewe Alexandra September 1979. Northwich Victoria August 1982. Altrincham August 1984. Weymouth March 1986.

Colin Chesters.

professional March 1978. Port Vale, loan, November 1980. Walsall August 1984. Plymouth Argyle, loan, October 1986. Plymouth Argyle November

1986. Chesterfield, loan, December 1988: January 1989. Notts County February 1989.
Steve Cherry tends to be remembered

His one senior goal for Derby was in the last match of the 1977-8 season. He cost Crewe Alexandra £10,000 and later played in two FA Trophy Finals for Northwich Victoria, on the losing side in 1983 and a winner in 1984, when he scored in both the Final and the replay.

CHIEDOZIE
John Okey *Winger/Centre-forward.*

Born: Owerri, Nigeria, 18 April 1960.
Career: Apprentice Orient: professional March 1977. Notts County August 1981. Tottenham Hotspur August 1984. Derby County August 1988. Notts County January 1990. Chesterfield March 1990. Barking 1990. Bashley 1991.

Chiedozie's career at Tottenham was halted by back trouble and he was given a free transfer after recovering from an operation to fuse vertebrae. Derby gambled on his being able to recover some of his spark but, although he started the first two games in 1988-9, he soon ran into knee problems. He returned to Notts on a non-contract basis but had cost £600,000 when he first moved to Meadow Lane. That was a club record for the remainder of the 1980s, as was the £350,000 they received from Spurs for the Nigerian international.

CHOLERTON
William *Left-back*

Born: Derby, 1 January 1949.
Career: Derby Boys. Apprentice, Derby County: professional December 1966. Mansfield Town August 1968. Rugby Town September 1968. Belper Town October 1969.

Stood in for Peter Daniel in one match, against Cardiff City at Ninian Park in October, 1966.

CHRISTIE
Trevor *Forward*

Born: Cresswell, Northumberland, 28 February 1959.
Career: Apprentice, Leicester City: professional December 1976. Notts County June 1979. Nottingham Forest July 1984. Derby County February 1985. Manchester City August 1986. Walsall October 1986. Mansfield Town March 1989. Kettering Town August 1991. VS Rugby March 1992.
Division Three promotion 1985-6.

Trevor Christie helped Notts County to win a First Division place in 1981 and, although his move across the Trent was not a success, he was vital to Derby's Third Division promotion drive. Arthur Cox bought him for £100,000, knowing that his honesty, ability in the air and goals would make him the ideal partner for Bobby Davison. Christie missed only one League game in 1985-6 and scored the penalty which clinched promotion against Rotherham United. His 15 League goals that season emphasised his importance but, the following August, he moved to Manchester City in part-exchange for Mark Lillis, a deal which did not turn out well for either player.

John Chiedozie, whose career was dogged by injury.

Trevor Christie, another vital member of the Third Division promotion side.

Ted Clamp, one game for the Rams before moving to Oldham.

Jonathan Clark, struggled to make an impact.

CLAMP
Edward   Goalkeeper

Born: Burton, 13 November 1922. Died: Swadlincote, 2 June 1990.
Career: John Knowles. Moira United. Gresley Rovers. Derby County November 1947. Oldham Athletic July 1949. Buxton August 1950.

Replaced Billy Townsend for one League game, on New Year's Day, 1949.

CLARK
Benjamin   Wing-half

Born: North Shields, 14 April 1933.
Career: North Shields. Sunderland August 1950. Yeovil Town, loan, October 1952. Derby County May 1954. Barrow February 1959.

Division Three North champions 1956-7.

Ben Clark gained experience with Yeovil Town while doing his National Service at RAF Netheravon, Sunderland allowing him to go on loan. As reserve to Albert Mays at right-half at Derby, Clark's opportunities were limited. He made one appearance in the Division Three North championship team but managed only 17 senior games in almost five years before moving to Barrow for £1,000. He made 202 League appearances for Barrow.

CLARK
Jonathan   Midfield

Born: Swansea, 12 November 1958.

Career: Apprentice, Manchester United: professional November 1975. Derby County September 1978. Preston North End July 1981. Caretaker manager, Preston North End, March to June 1986. Bury December 1986. Carlisle United August 1987. Morecambe February 1989. Rhyl August 1989.

Tommy Docherty signed Jonathan Clark for £50,000 but, in Derby's struggling team, he found it hard to make any impact. He had the misfortune to be sent off when he played his first League game in his native Swansea, in October 1980. Clark could use the ball well but Docherty's advance praise — "the best thing to come out of Wales since coal" — did him no favours.

CLAYTON
John
Forward

Born: Elgin, 20 August 1961.
Career: Apprentice, Derby County: professional December 1978. Bulova, Hong Kong, August 1982. Chesterfield July 1983. Tranmere Rovers July 1984. Plymouth Argyle August 1985. Fortuna Sittard (Holland) July 1988. FC Volendam (Holland).

John Clayton.

Clayton always looked as if he could score goals but his career did not flourish until he joined Tranmere. In all competitions, he scored 36 goals for Tranmere in 1984-5, forming a potent partnership with Colin Clarke. Plymouth paid £24,000 for Clayton and his goals helped them to promotion from Division Three in the same season as Derby, 1985-6.

CLEAVER
Fred L.
Centre-forward

Born: Ashbourne, c1885.
Career: Ashbourne Town. Derby County February 1906. Preston North End, trial. Watford August 1908.

Cleaver won a place in Derby's team as soon as he had been signed from Ashbourne but did not score goals regularly enough to sustain it.

Nigel Cleevely, scored on his League debut, against Charlton in September 1964.

CLEEVELY
Nigel Robert
Outside-left

Born: Cheltenham, 23 December 1945.
Career: Juniors, Derby County: professional July 1964. Burton Albion February 1968. Ilkeston Town June 1970. Redfern Athletic August 1971.

Tim Ward brought Cleevely from Cheltenham, a birthplace they shared. Cleevely showed some promise without being able to earn a regular place. In his only FA Cup tie, he played at full-back against Norwich City and was one of those moved on when Brian Clough and Peter Taylor arrived.

CLIFTON
G.
Half-back

Career: Long Eaton Rangers. Derby County 1886. Long Eaton Rangers January 1889.

Played in two of Derby's early Cup ties and once in the first season of the Football League.

COLEMAN
Simon
Centre-half

Born: Worksop, 13 March 1968.
Career: Apprentice Mansfield Town: professional July 1985. Middlesbrough

Simon Coleman, enjoyed an excellent first season with the Rams.

September 1989. Derby County August 1991.

After Robert Maxwell had been bought out, Arthur Cox's first concern was to strengthen the defence. Simon Coleman, on Middlesbrough's transfer list, arrived a week after Andy Comyn, the first indications that the Rams were on the move again. Coleman had joined Middlesbrough to replace Gary Pallister, who had moved to Manchester United. His task at the Baseball Ground was to take over from Mark Wright but he did not allow himself to be intimidated by this. Coleman was sent off in Derby's 3-2 victory over Wolverhampton Wanderers at Molineux and their 3-0 triumph over Barnsley at Oakwell but this did not detract from an excellent first season. He was strong in the air, solid in the challenge and determined to improve his game.

COLLIN
George   *Left-back*
Born: Oxhill, 13 September 1905. Died: 1 February 1989.

George Collin.

Career: Juniors, West Ham United. West Stanley. Arsenal February 1924. Bournemouth & Boscombe Athletic August 1925. West Stanley August

George Collin heads clear from a West Ham player at the Baseball Ground in October 1931.

1927. *Derby County November 1927.*
Sunderland June 1936. Port Vale June
1938. Burton Town August 1939.
Division One runners-up 1929-30,
1935-6.

George Collin was one of those safe,
yet unspectacular players who served
his club well for a number of years but
who never caught the eyes of the
international selectors. He played
alongside the brilliant Tommy Cooper,
who inevitably stole the limelight. A
native of the North-East, Collin first
played for Arsenal before failing to
agree terms with the Highbury club.
He followed his manager, Leslie
Knighton, to Bournemouth where he
broke a leg and returned to play with
West Stanley in the North-Eastern
League. When Jobey signed him in
November 1927, he had to deal with
two clubs. On his Rams debut, one
critic wrote. 'Derby have found a class
back. He is cool and discriminate.'
From then until his final season, Collin
was rarely out of the side. After signing
Jack Howe, George Jobey felt safe in
allowing Collin to join Sunderland. It
was at Roker Park in December 1933
that Collin had been sent off, one of
only three Derby players punished in
this way in League games between the
wars. Paterson and Fairclough were the
others.

COMYN
Andrew John   *Central defender.*
Born: Wakefield, 2 August 1968.
Career: Birmingham University. Alve-
church. Aston Villa August 1989. Derby
County August 1991.

Andy Comyn became the first signing
of the post-Maxwell era and the
£200,000 fee was soon revealed to be
an excellent investment. Comyn has a
physics degree from Birmingham
University and combined his course
with part-time football for Alvechurch
in the Southern (Beazer Homes)
League. Within days of joining Villa,
Comyn found himself marking John
Barnes and he also played in the home
leg of the 1990-91 UEFA Cup tie against
Inter-Milan. For the most part Comyn
was a reserve at Villa Park but Arthur
Cox saw enough of him to make an
instant move when he had some
financial leeway. Given responsibilty
and a regular first-team place, Comyn
seized the chance eagerly.

CONWELL
Anthony   *Full-back*
Born: Bradford, 17 January 1932.
Career: Bradford junior football. Shef-
field Wednesday January 1949. Hud-
dersfield Town July 1955. Derby
County June 1959. Doncaster Rovers
July 1962.

An extremely hard-tackling full-back,
very much according to the Harry

Andy Comyn, seized his chance at Derby after being mostly in reserve at Villa Park.

Tony Conwell.

Storer conception of a defender. Tony
Conwell cost Derby £6,000 and was
ever-present in 1960-61. His fearless
style led to several nasty injuries and
he was freed in 1962. He broke a leg
in an FA Cup tie the following
November and, although he battled
back, retired in 1964.

COOKE
John Alfred   *Outside-left*
Career: Mansfield. Derby County
March 1899.

Had his best run early in 1899-1900,
when Hugh McQueen was out of the
side.

COOP
Michael Anthony   *Right-back*
Born: Leamington, 10 July 1948.
Career: Apprentice, Coventry City:

Mick Coop, run ragged by Jeff Chandler and did not play again.

Lewis Cooper, scored twice in Derby's first League game.

professional January 1966. York City, loan, November 1974. Detriot Express, loan, May 1979. Derby County July 1981. Contract cancelled January 1982. AP Leamington. Coventry City coaching staff cs 1987 to cs 1990.

Mick Coop played more than 400 League games for Coventry and Colin Addison hoped his experience would help to revive a promotion challenge for Derby County. Coop had a bad time with the Rams and did not play again after Jeff Chandler had run him ragged in an FA Cup third round defeat by Bolton Wanderers at Burnden Park.

His contract was cancelled the same month. Coop played a few games for AP Leamington and ran an antique shop in his native town before returning as a coach with Coventry City.

COOPER
Lewis   *Forward*

Died: Derby, 12 February 1937.
Career. Darley Dale. Derby County. Grimsby Town. Derby County June 1888.

A versatile forward, usually to be found at outside-left but capable of playing inside-forward. He was one of Derby's early stars and, after a spell with Grimsby, returned to play in the first League game against Bolton Wanderers in September 1888. He scored twice in the 6-3 win at Pike's Lane.

COOPER
Thomas   *Right-back*

Born: Fenton, 9 April 1904. Died: Aldeburgh, 25 June 1940.
Career: Longton. Trentham. Port Vale August 1924. Derby County March 1926. Liverpool December 1934.

Tommy Cooper, skippered the Rams and England as a polished full-back.

Divison Two promotion 1925-6. Division One runners-up 1929-30.

It was a fine performance for Port Vale against the Rams which induced George Jobey to pay £2,500 for snowy-haired full-back Tommy Cooper in March 1926. Cooper went on to become one of the best English full-backs of all time and his polished football made his stand out among his contemporaries. His tackling and distribution soon brought him to the attention of the England selectors and he won 15 caps, all of them with Derby. Cooper would have won many more, but for the injuries which saw him lose cartilages from both knees. Cooper took over the Rams captaincy from Johnny McIntyre in November 1931 and he skippered the side until he moved to Liverpool for £8,000. Cooper also captained Liverpool and England. He scored only one goal for the Rams — against Middlesbrough at the Baseball Ground in February 1932 — but as a defender he had few peers, although goalkeeper Harry Wilkes felt he had a weakness in not being very strong in the air. Tommy Cooper met a tragic end. In December 1940, he was killed in a motor-cycle accident in Suffolk while serving with the Military Police.

CORISH
Robert   *Left-back*
Born: Liverpool, 13 September 1958.
Career: Apprentice, Derby County: professional August 1976. Fort Lauderdale Strikers November 1978.

Bobby Corish showed some promise in the Central League but managed only one substitute appearance at senior level, against Birmingham City in March 1978.

COWELL
William   *Goalkeeper*
Born: Acomb, near Hexham, 7 December 1902.
Career: Newburn. Mickley. Newburn. Huddersfield Town, amateur, 1920: professional December 1920. Hartlepools United September 1924. Derby County May 1926. Grimsby Town February 1927. Millwall June 1928. Carlisle United September 1929.

An England schoolboy international, against Scotland in 1916, Cowell made one League appearance for Derby, as Ben Olney's deputy in a 5-4 defeat by Blackburn Rovers in November, 1926.

COX
John Davies   *Right-half*
Born: Spondon, 1870. Died: Toronto, June 1957.
Career: Spondon. Long Eaton Rangers. Derby County cs 1891.

Division One runners-up 1895-6. FA Cup Finalists 1897-8, 1898-9.

Jack Cox, played in two FA Cup Finals.

Andy Crawford, whose career prospered at Blackburn.

Jack Cox was one of those footballers whose prowess at the game was noted at a very early age. Cox signed for his local club before he had left school and it was his form at half-back which brought him to the notice of Long Eaton Rangers, then one of the leading Midlands clubs and a team which appeared in the FA Cup competition proper. The Rams soon heard about Cox and he made his first-team debut in the last match of 1890-91, signing during the summer. Cox was a wing-half who played accurate passes through to his forwards and, in addition, could tackle hard and was good in the air. All these qualities led to him playing for England against Ireland in Belfast in March 1892. Cox was known to the other Rams players as the 'squire of Spondon'. After leaving the Rams in 1899, Cox emigrated to Canada,

where he went into business as a painter and decorator, although he returned to England to fight in World War One.

CRAWFORD
Andrew   *Forward*

Born: Filey, 30 January 1959.
Career: Filey Town. Apprentice, Derby County: professional January 1978. Manawatu (New Zealand), loan, 1979. Blackburn Rovers October 1979. AFC Bournemouth November 1981. Cardiff City August 1983. Middlesbrough October 1983. Stockport County December 1984. Torquay United March 1985. Poole Town 1988.

A sharp little striker, who might have done well had Derby County persevered with him. Colin Addison accepted a £50,000 bid from Blackburn and Crawford was leading scorer when Rovers

won promotion from the Third Division in 1979-80. He was in another promotion team when Bournemouth, under David Webb, left the Fourth Division in 1981-2.

CRAWFORD
James   *Outside-right*

Born: Leith.
Career: Reading. Sunderland May 1898. Derby County May 1900. Middlesbrough November 1901.

In his 18 months at the Baseball Ground, Crawford established himself as Derby County's regular outside-right until he moved back to the North-East.

CRESSWELL
Peter Frank   *Outside-right*

Born: Linby, 9 November 1935.

Rams full-back Tom Crilly hammers the ball clear at Stamford Bridge in November 1924.

Career: Heanor Town. Derby County, amateur, October 1953: professional April 1954. Peterborough United August 1957. Heanor Town September 1959. Sutton Town January 1962. Matlock Town July 1962. Long Eaton United July 1963. Crewton cs 1965. Division Three North champions 1956-7.

Derby spotted Peter Cresswell while he was with Heanor Town and he provided useful cover on the right wing, playing once in the Division Three North championship team, in a 3-0 win over Carlisle United. He made 14 senior appearances before joining Peterborough, then in the Midland League.

CRILLY
Thomas *Left-back*

Born: Stockton, 20 July 1895. Died: Derby, 18 January 1960.
Career: Stockton. Hartlepools United January 1920. Derby County August 1922. Crystal Palace May 1928. Northampton Town July 1933. Player-manager, Scunthorpe & Lindsey United, May 1935 to April 1937.
Divison Two promotion 1925-6.

When Cecil Potter succeeded Jimmy Methven as manager of Derby County in 1922, he soon went back to his former club, Hartlepools United, for defenders Tom Crilly and Harry Thoms. Both gave Derby excellent service before they again moved together, to Crystal Palace in 1928. Crilly was in Hartlepools' opening game when they entered the Football League in 1921 and immediately established himself at the Baseball Ground. For three years, his full-back partnership with Albert Chandler was interrupted only by injuries and Crilly missed only 24 League and Cup matches in his first five seasons at Derby, such was his steady reliability. In October 1927, Crilly asked to be rested following a 4-2 defeat at Burnley and, having opened the door for first Billy Carr and then George Collin, did not make another senior appearance. He had done a good job for Derby and was an important member of the team which won promotion to the First Division. After ending his career as player-manager of Scunthorpe, he returned to Derby as licensee of the Hilton Arms in Osmaston Road and looked after the Rams Reserves and Colts during World War Two.

CROOKS
Samuel Dickinson *Outside-right*

Born: Bearpark, 16 January 1908. Died: Belper, 3 February 1981.
Career: Bearpark Colliery. Brandon Juniors. Tow Law Town. Durham

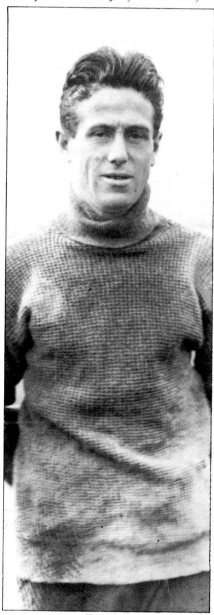

Tom Crilly.

Sammy Crooks comes off second best in a heading duel at Highbury.

Sammy Crooks in a more familar role, speeding down the right wing.

City May 1926. Derby County April 1927. Retired 1947. Chief scout, Derby County, February 1946 to August 1949. Manager, Retford Town, December 1949. Secretary-manager, Shrewsbury Town, May 1950 to July 1954. Gresley Rovers, player, December 1954: player-manager, January 1955 to May 1957. Manager, Burton Albion, May to November 1957. Manager Gresley Rovers June 1958. Manager-coach, Heanor Town, April 1959. Chief scout, Derby County, June 1960 to May 1967. Division One runners-up 1929-30, 1935-6.

A place in Derby's 1946 FA Cup winning team would have crowned

Sammy Crooks' brilliant career but he was not regarded as fit enough to play. He felt that he might have got through the game but it was entirely typical of the man that his comments after the Cup had come to Derby for the first time were in praise of his young deputy, Harrison. "Reg didn't let me down," was Sammy's theme. George Jobey signed Crooks from Durham City, then in Division Three North, for £300. "I stepped off a coal lorry one Thursday and Jobey met me," Crooks recalled. "He told me not to say anything because he knew five other clubs planned to watch me on the Saturday and he wanted me to put one over on

them." It was clear that Derby had another star because Crooks, despite his frail appearance, had pace, a bundle of tricks and a sharp football brain. He was England's outside-right on 26 occasions and played four times for the Football League in an era when there was competition from the likes of Joe Hulme (Arsenal), Albert Geldard (Everton) and, of course, the Stoke City wizard Stanley Matthews. Only Arsenal full-back Eddie Hapgood played more times for England between the wars. Crooks scored more than 100 goals for Derby and his name is still linked with that of left-winger Dally Duncan. "We didn't hit passes from wing to wing," said Crooks. "I would find Dally from midfield and go up to inside-right for the return. We had a great side but the accent was too much on attack for us to win trophies." Even Arsenal could not prise Crooks, Players' Union chairman for 14 years, away from Derby and after the war he served them as chief scout. He was secretary-manager of Shrewsbury Town when they entered the League in 1950. "I was the worst secretary in the world," he once said but they loved him at Gay Meadow. Crooks was a vintage winger whose affection for Derby lasted until he died, without a enemy in the world.

CROPPER
William   *Centre-forward*

Born: Brimington, 27 December 1862. Died: Grimsby, 13 January 1889. Career: Chesterfield Spital. Derby County. Staveley.

A promising all-round sportsman, who played cricket for Derbyshire from 1882 to 1888. Died after a football injury at the age of 26.

CROSS
Steven Charles   *Midfield*

Born: Wolverhampton, 22 December 1959.

Steve Cross.

Career: Apprentice, Shrewsbury Town: professional December 1977. Derby County July 1986. Bristol Rovers September 1991: player-coach May 1992.

Division Two champions 1986-7.

Steve Cross did not have much luck after joining Derby from Shrewsbury Town for £60,000. Arthur Cox saw his versatility as one of the factors to establish Derby in the Second Division, as Cross had done with Shrewsbury after their Third Division championship in 1978-79. But Cross began badly, lost his place to Geraint Williams, suffered a nasty eye injury against Leeds United Reserves and played only six times, three of them as substitute, in Derby's Second Division championship team. He was in his best spell with Derby in the First Division when he was ruled out by a stress fracture in a foot and he joined Bristol Rovers in search of regular first-team football.

CROWSHAW
Allan Alfred   *Outside-left*

Born: Willenhall, 12 December 1932. Career: Bloxwich Wesley. West Bromwich Albion May 1950. Derby County May 1956. Millwall May 1958. Sittingbourne July 1960.

Division Three North champions 1956-7.

Allan Crowshaw.

After Derby County had finished runners-up in the Third Division North in 1955-6, Harry Storer increased his attacking options by the £1,000 signing of Allan Crowshaw. The winger scored six goals in 17 games

during the championship season but Tommy Powell and Dennis Woodhead were ultimately the key men on the flanks.

CRUMP
Frederick   *Centre-Forward*

Career: Stourbridge. Derby County June 1899. Glossop May 1900. Northampton Town 1902. Stockport County August 1905. Brighton & Hove Albion 1908.

Fred Crump spent one season at Derby but did not succeed in taking John Boag's place on a permanent basis.

Former Scottish international Mick Cullen.

CULLEN
Michael Joseph   *Inside-forward*

Born: Glasgow, 3 July 1931. Career: Douglasdale Juniors. Luton Town August 1949. Grimsby Town June 1958. Derby County November 1962. Wellington Town February 1965. Burton Albion February 1966.

Mick Cullen played for Scotland, against Austria in 1955-6, while with Luton Town and Tim Ward, who had been his manager at Grimsby, paid £5,000 to bring him to the Baseball Ground. Cullen was a clever ball-player but did not make much impact with Derby.

Terry Curran, Derby made £15,000 on his transfer.

Dick Cushlow, started late in League soccer because of the war.

CURRAN
Edward   *Outside-right*

Born: Kinsley, 20 March 1955.
Career: Kinsley. Doncaster Rovers July 1973. Nottingham Forest August 1975. Bury, loan, October 1977. Derby County November 1977. Southampton August 1978. Sheffield Wednesday March 1979. Sheffield United August 1982. Everton, loan, December 1982. Everton September 1983. Huddersfield Town July 1985. Panionios (Greece) July 1986. Hull City October 1986. Sunderland November 1986. Grantham September 1987. Grimsby Town November 1987. Chesterfield March 1988. Goole Town August 1988: Coach, March 1989: manager, November 1989.

Terry Curran helped Nottingham Forest out of the Second Division with his exciting play on the right wing but was happy to leave the City Ground in a £50,000 deal. Like most of Tommy Docherty's signings, Curran was not a consistent success at Derby. It was hard for anybody to achieve that as Docherty bought and sold without any detectable

pattern. Derby made a £15,000 profit when Curran was transferred to Southampton and some of his best football was played in Sheffield Wednesday's Third Division promotion team. Curran was one of the cover players when Everton won the League Championship in 1984-5. At his best, he was very good but he was never entirely predictable.

CURRY
William Morton   *Centre-forward*

Born: Newcastle, 12 October 1935.
Died: Mansfield, 20 August 1990.
Career: Juniors, Newcastle United: professional October 1953. Brighton & Hove Albion July 1959. Derby County September 1960. Mansfield Town February 1965. Chesterfield January 1968. Boston FC, loan, October 1968. Trainer, Worksop Town, cs 1969. Manager, Boston FC, February 1971 to May 1976. Manager, Sutton Town, May 1977 to May 1980.

When Harry Storer brought Bill Curry to the Baseball Ground in 1960, the fee of £12,000 was not only the biggest that

the Rams had paid for some time. Curry was also one of the most colourful players to appear in a Derby shirt for many years. He had a swagger to his play and his style, coupled with the fact that he was leading scorer in each of his first three seasons, made him a favourite with the fans. Curry won an England Under-23 cap while with Newcastle United and gave good value to his clubs, with 178 League goals in 394 games.

CUSHLOW
Richard   *Centre-half*

Born: Shotton, 15 June 1920.
Career: Murton Colliery. Chesterfield May 1946. Sheffield United December 1947. Derby County March 1948. Crystal Palace February 1951.

A late starter because of World War Two, Dick Cushlow filled in for Leon Leuty in two games but was never regarded as more than a Central League player at Derby. When Leuty left for Bradford, Ken Oliver took over the centre-half berth.

Bill Curry, in 1960 Derby's biggest signing for some years, scored 76 goals in 164 League and Cup games for the Rams.

Gerry Daly, an attractive player at his best.

Ian Dalziel, unlucky to come into a struggling team.

DAFT

T. *Forward*

Career: Derby Midland. Derby County 1890.

Played three League games in 1890-91.

DALY

Gerard Anthony *Midfield*

Born: Dublin, 30 April 1954.
Career: Bohemians. Manchester United April 1973. Derby County March 1977. New England Tea Men, loan, May 1978 and May 1979. Coventry City August 1980. Leicester City, loan, January 1983. Birmingham City August 1984. Shrewsbury Town October 1985. Stoke City March 1987. Doncaster Rovers July 1988. Player-coach, Telford Uni-

ted, December 1989: manager August 1990.

Gerry Daly was one of the brightest stars in Tommy Docherty's young Manchester United team which reached the FA Cup Final in 1976, beating Derby in the semi-final at Hillsborough. Colin Murphy signed him for £175,000 and Daly made an immediate impact, helping to lift the Rams from the bottom of Division One to a position of safety. At his best, he was a delightful player, quick-footed and inventive with a gift for finding scoring positions. Daly had fallen out with Docherty at Old Trafford and was unhappy when Docherty succeeded Murphy at the Baseball Ground. A transfer request followed and, although this was subsequently withdrawn, the

peace was uneasy. Daly spent two summers in the North American Soccer League before Colin Addison sold him to Coventry City for £300,000. Having helped Manchester United to the Second Division championship in 1974-5, Daly won another promotion with Birmingham City ten years later. He made 14 of his 46 Republic of Ireland appearances while with Derby.

DALZIEL

Ian *Defender/midfield*

Born: South Shields, 24 October 1962.
Career: Apprentice, Derby County: professional October 1979. Hereford United May 1983. Carlisle United July 1988.

A determined player at Central League

level for Derby. He had the difficult
task of trying to learn his trade in a
struggling team and was unlucky to
be sent off against Newcastle United
at St James' Park in December 1983,
catching the backwash of trouble in
other parts of the field. When Dalziel
was freed in 1983, John Newman
snapped him up for Hereford United.
A broken leg interrupted his career with
Carlisle United.

DANIEL
Peter Aylmer   *Defender*

Born: Ripley, 22 December 1946.
Career: Apprentice, Derby County:
professional December 1964. Van-
couver Whitecaps, loan, April 1978.
Vancouver Whitecaps February 1979.
Burton Albion February 1980. Belper
Town October 1980.

Division Two champions 1968-9.
Division One champions 1974-5.

Peter Daniel was a safe but unspectacular player whose consistent efforts
were mostly overshadowed by colleagues of international status. But, for
Daniel, there came a glorious season
of triumph when he helped Derby
County to their Second League championship in 1974-5. Daniel was signed
by Tim Ward in August 1963, as an
apprentice, one of a number of youngsters whose careers began under Ward
and who went on to greater deeds.
Daniel made safe and steady progress
and survived Clough's purge to become
a valued member of the Reserves
especially in the 1971-2 Central League
title team, filling in at full-back
whenever one of the established stars
was injured or on international duty.
Daniel always gave a solid performance
but never threatened to establish a
regular place. He was always the
bridesmaid until an injury to Roy
McFarland in an international match
in May 1974. Daniel did not play a
single game when Derby first won the
title in 1971-2. Now he stepped into
Dave Mackay's side, took the vacant
number-five shirt, played brilliantly as
the Rams marched towards their second
Championship in four seasons and was
voted Player of the Year by supporters.

DARWIN
George Hedworth *Inside-forward*

Born: Chester-le-Street, 16 May 1932.
Career: Wimblesworth Juniors.
Huddersfield Town May 1950. Mans-
field Town November 1953. Derby
County May 1957. Rotherham United
October 1960. Barrow July 1961.

George Darwin had a brilliant first
season after costing Derby £4,000 plus
full-back Keith Savin. With his tight
control, Darwin was an entertainment
in his own right as he scuttled over
the Baseball Ground mud and past
defenders. It seemed that Harry Storer
had made an inspired buy but Darwin

Peter Daniel, played brilliantly in the 1975 Championship team.

George Darwin joins Rotherham, watched by Harry Storer and Tommy Johnston.

never touched the same heights again
and his wife found it hard to settle in
the area. Rotherham paid £5,000 to sign
him but his contribution at Millmoor
was severely limited by a cartilage
injury.

DAVIDSON
Jonathan Stewart   *Defender.*
Born: Werrington, 1 March 1970.
*Career: Trainee, Derby County: profes-
sional July 1988. Preston North End
July 1992.*

Jonathan Davidson.

Jonathan Davidson was another of the
young players pushed into senior
action as a team severely depleted by
injuries and suspensions battled out
three matches with West Ham United
in the quarter-finals of the 1989-90
Littlewoods Cup. Davidson was captain of the Youth team and the Reserves
in his time at Derby, but, although
quick and determined, was short of the
physical stature for a central defender
in the First or Second Divisions.

DAVIES
Frank   *Goalkeeper*
Born: Birkenhead.
Career: Birkenhead. Derby County May

Glyn Davies, a rugged defender who drove Derby to the edge of a promotion race.

*1902. Glossop June 1904. Manchester
City June 1906.*

Third choice behind Jack Fryer and,
once he had arrived from Ripley
Athletic, Harry Maskrey. Davies played
only once for the Rams, in the final
League game of 1902-03.

DAVIES
Glyn   *Defender*
Born: Swansea, 31 May 1932.
Career: Juniors, Derby County, ama-
*teur, May 1949: professional July 1949.
Swansea Town July 1962. Player-
manager, Yeovil Town, January 1964.
Manager, Swansea Town, June 1965 to
October 1966.*

*Division Three North champions
1956-7.*

Glyn Davies was a Welsh schoolboy
international who signed professional
for Derby in 1949 and had to wait well
over four years for his League debut
which came at Rotherham in December

Roger Davies, scored 44 goals in 166 senior games for Derby.

1953. Davies was the possessor of a ferocious tackle and he more than made up for his limited skill with a super-abundance of effort and tireless leadership. In 1958-9 it was his captaincy which inspired the revival which took the Rams to the edge of the promotion race after a poor start to the season. Davies's hard style of play had its critics and during that 1958-9 season he was sent off at Hillsborough after a bad foul on Sheffield Wednesday's Alan Finney. But it was Davies's unquestionable commitment to the game, whether at wing-half or left-back, which left its mark on many a Rams match during the 1950s.

DAVIES
Roger *Centre-forward*

Born: Wolverhampton, 25 October 1950.
Career: Bridgnorth Town. Worcester City August 1971. Derby County September 1971. Preston North End, loan, August 1972. Bruges July 1976. Leicester City December 1977. Tulsa Roughnecks March 1979. Derby County September 1979. Seattle Sounders March 1980. Fort Landerdale Strikers April 1983. Burnley October 1983. Gresley Rovers November 1983. Darlington November 1983. Gresley Rovers February 1984. Player-manager, Gresley Rovers, cs 1984. Player-manager, Stapenhill, November 1985. Manager, Rolls-Royce, 1990
Division One champions 1974-5.

Roger Davies joined Derby from Southern League Worcester City in September 1971 for £12,000, although he made his League debut when on loan with Preston. After returning, Davies, who had been in the Central League-winning team in 1971-2, began to force his way in. He scored a spectacular hat-trick in the great FA Cup replay recovery at Tottenham and was sent-off in the European Cup semi-final against Juventus after reacting to provocation. Davies was a regular member of the 1974-5 Championship-winning side and, that season, scored all five goals against Luton at Derby. In August 1976, Davies signed for Bruges for £135,000, helping them to a Belgian League and Cup double, and then joined Leicester. Between two spells in the North American Soccer League, Davies returned to the Baseball Ground but could do nothing to stave off relegation from Division One.

DAVIS
George Henry *Outside-left*

Born: Alfreton, 5 June 1881. Died: Wimbledon, 28 April 1969.
Career: Alfreton Town 1896. Derby County December 1899. Alfreton Town May 1908.
FA Cup Finalists 1902-03.

George Davis achieved what must be

Bobby Davison, returned on loan and took his goals tally for the Rams past the 100 mark.

a unique double in football. After playing in the Rams side which lost 6-0 to Bury in the 1903 FA Cup Final, thus taking a losers' medal, Davis emigrated to Canada and 19 years later won a Canadian Cup-winners' medal with Calgary Hillhurst. Davis was another Rams find from the Alfreton area. Early this century, Davis formed a fine left-wing partnership with the Castle Donington player George Richards. Like Richards, Davis was capped for England and the friendship between the two resulted in their team mates dubbing them the 'Siamese Twins'. Davis never really recovered from an accident at Villa Park in the

George Davis.

1903 FA Cup semi-final when he stumbled on the matting laid down for the linesman's comfort and struck his head on the asphalt cycle track. Davis was carried off with concussion, although he returned later looking 'fearful bad'. In 1904-05, with the Rams experimenting with their forward line, only George Davis and Steve Bloomer were assured of a place. Davis left the Rams in 1908 at the comparatively early age of 26 and went back to helping Alfreton Town. In 1912, he and his wife sailed for Canada to begin a new life. First Davis coached a Manitoba team, but later he went into the hotel business and made his fortune.

DAVIS
John William   *Wing-forward*

Born: Ironville, 10 April 1882. Died: Ripley, 29 October 1963.
Career: Somercotes. Derby County April 1905. Ilkeston United September 1910. Eastwood Rangers July 1912. Sutton Junction December 1912. Ilkeston United August 1919.

Jack Davis.

Jack 'Pimmy' Davis played in the last match of 1904-05 after being signed from Somercotes and, with his ability to play on either wing, was an important member of the team for the next five years. He played in the lull between Steve Bloomer's departure and triumphant return and was unable to help Derby out of Division Two after their first relegation in 1907. A very good Border League cricketer with Loscoe, Davis played once for Derbyshire in 1920, against Essex at Southend. He worked as a boilermaker at the Butterley Company in Ripley and was then a miner for 35 years.

DAVISON
Robert   *Centre-forward*

Born: South Shields, 17 July 1959.
Career: Seaham Red Star. Huddersfield Town July 1980. Halifax Town August 1981. Derby County November 1982. Leeds United November 1987. Derby County, loan, September 1991. Sheffield United, loan, March 1992. Leicester City August 1992.

Division Three promotion 1985-6. Division Two champions 1986-7.

When Peter Taylor returned to the Baseball Ground as manager in November 1982, his first and best cash signing was Bobby Davison, for £80,000. For the next five years, Davison was Derby's most reliable scorer and his 98 goals in all games took him to tenth in the club's all-time list. After starting with three appearances as substitute, Davison soon became a popular hero with the crowd because of his speed, enthusiasm and, above all, his goals. He gave the Rams a taste of his skill in 1982-3 by scoring three times for Halifax Town in the two legs

of a Milk Cup tie and Roy McFarland had wanted to sign him for Bradford City when he was still manager there. Davison flourished under Arthur Cox. He scored 26 goals in 1982-3, Derby's best since Ray Straw hit 37 in 1956-7, and was the spearhead as the Rams won two promotions in successive seasons. Oxford United, for a totally unrealistic fee, and Watford tried to take Davison into Division One during the Second Division championship season but he saw Derby back to the top flight before joining Leeds United in a £350,000 deal. He gave Derby brilliant service and fully deserved his high standing with supporters. He confirmed that when he returned on loan to transform Derby's 1991-2 Second Division season with eight goals in ten games, including his 100th for the club.

DAVISON
Thomas Reay   *Centre-forward*

Born: West Stanley, 3 October 1901.
Died: Derby, 1 January 1971.
Career: Tanfield Lea Juniors. Durham City August 1920 Wolverhampton Wanderers June 1923. Derby County July 1925. Sheffield Wednesday February 1931. Coventry City July 1932. Player-coach Rhyl Athletic, July 1935. Bath City August 1936.

Division Two promotion 1925-6. Division One runners-up 1929-30.

Tommy Davison and manager George Jobey were involved in Wolverhampton Wanderers' Third Division North championship and both arrived at the Baseball Ground in the summer of 1925. Davison played only once when the Rams were promoted from Division Two, Harry Thoms still being the regular centre-half, but had a good run before the emergence of Jack Barker. In February 1931, Davison and George Stephenson joined Sheffield Wednesday in a swiftly negotiated deal.

DAYKIN
Reginald Brian   *wing-half*

Born: Long Eaton, 4 August 1937.
Career: Ericsson Telephones. Long Eaton Town 1954. Derby County November 1955. Notts County July 1962. Corinthians, Sydney, May 1963. Player-coach, Adamstown Rosebuds (Newcastle, New South Wales), January 1964. Belper Town January 1966. Lockheed Leamington May 1966. Player-manager, Long Eaton Albion 1969. Manager, Long Eaton United, December 1972. Assistant-manager Brighton & Hove Albion, August 1974.

Hard-tackling wing-half who spent most of his Derby days in the Central League. Transferred to Notts County for £1,000 but left for Australia after one season at Meadow Lane. Daykin worked with Peter Taylor at Brighton.

Eamonn Deacy, turned down a permanent move to the Rams.   **Steve Devine, enjoyed a good career at Hereford United.**

DEACY
Eamonn Stephen   *Full-back*

Born: Galway, 1 October 1958.
Career: Limerick 1976. Galway Rovers 1977. Aston Villa March 1979. Derby County, loan, October 1983. Galway United 1984.

Deacy won four Republic of Ireland caps and was an occasional player in Aston Villa's 1980-81 League Championship team before impressing in a month's loan with Derby. Rejected the chance of a permanent transfer.

DEVINE
Stephen Bernard   *Midfield*

Born: Strabane, 11 December 1964.
Career: Apprentice, Wolverhampton Wanderers: professional December 1982. Derby County, March 1983. Stockport County August 1985. Hereford United October 1985.

One of the young players Roy McFarland called up when, as acting-manager following the departure of

Peter Taylor, he was trying to keep Derby in Division Two. He became one of Hereford's most reliable players.

DEVONSHIRE
William J.   *Outside-left*

Career: Derby County, amateur, October 1914: professional December 1914.
Division Two champions 1914-15.

Played seven games in place of Billy Grimes when Derby won the Second Division title in the last season before World War One.

DILLY
Thomas   *Wing-forward*

Born: Arbroath, November 1882. Died: 1960.
Career: Forfar County. Arbroath. Heart of Midlothian. Everton July 1902. West Bromwich Albion March 1906. Derby County October 1907. Bradford June 1908. Walsall. Shrewsbury Town. Worcester City. Kidderminster Harriers. Cadbury Works 1938. Retired 1939.

Derby was a short stop on Dilly's long

career. He was still playing in the Birmingham area when well past 50. Most of his games with the Rams were as replacement for George Davis.

DIX
Ronald William   *Inside-forward*

Born: Bristol, 5 September 1912.
Career: Juniors, Bristol Rovers: professional September 1929. Blackburn Rovers May 1932. Aston Villa May 1933. Derby County February 1937. Tottenham Hotspur June 1939. Reading November 1947. Retired cs 1949.

Ronnie Dix had an early baptism in League football. At the age of 15 years and 173 days he made his debut for Bristol Rovers and showed such brilliant form that he was soon the target of First Division clubs. The Football League was asked to rule on just whose player he was and said he belonged to the Eastville club for whom he signed professional. The former schoolboy international was with Aston Villa when they were relegated for the first time but it did not affect his standing.

Ronnie Dix, played in an all-international forward line at Derby.

He came to the Baseball Ground with a fine reputation as a schemer and showed his best form at inside-left after Napier went to Sheffield Wednesday in March 1938. A few months later Dix won his one England cap and completed an all-international Rams forward line with Crooks, Astley. McCulloch and Duncan. Dix cost Spurs £5,000 in the close season, but after three matches war was declared.

DOBBS
Arthur
Centre-forward

Career: St Roth, Glasgow. Derby County November 1933.

Cost Derby £135 and played three games as stand-in for Jack Bowers.

DOCHERTY
James
Wing-half

Born: Pollokshaw.
Career: Pollokshaw. Clyde. Hibernian. Derby County cs 1893. Luton Town May 1895. Cowes May 1898.

Brought from Scotland to take over from Walter Roulstone and was first choice at left-half for two seasons before Luton tempted him into the Southern League. He was captain of Cowes when they were promoted but they could not sustain the pace in the Southern League First Division and folded.

DOCKERY
George
Goalkeeper

Career: Third Lanark. Derby County August 1893.

Reserve goalkeeper who stood in for Jack Robinson five times in his season with Derby County.

DOHERTY
Peter Dermont
Inside-forward

Born: Magherafelt, 5 June 1913. Died: Fleetwood, 6 April 1990.
Career: Station United (Coleraine). Coleraine, amateur. Glentoran June 1930. Blackpool November 1933. Manchester City February 1936. Derby County December 1945. Huddersfield Town December 1946. Player-manager, Doncaster Rovers, June 1949; retired as player 1953: manager, to January 1958. Manager, Bristol City, January 1958 to March 1960. Manager, Northern Ireland, October 1951 to February 1962. Notts County, joint advisor with Andy Beattie December 1965. Chief scout,

Peter Doherty with the Midland Cup, which Derby won in 1945 when he scored five goals against Villa.

Peter Doherty.

Aston Villa July 1968. Assistant manager, Preston North End, October 1970 to January 1973. Assistant manager, Sunderland.

FA Cup winners 1945-6.

They used to say that Peter Doherty, the flame-haired Irishman who danced his brilliant way through English football with Blackpool and Manchester City in the 1930s, was a discontented footballer. Doherty was not pompous or petulent, sulky or ill-mannered. Indeed, it would be impossible to meet a more gentle and courteous man. Doherty's discontent was with the system — he was a football trade unionist ahead of his time — and it manifested itself in the need to be more exciting and innovative than any other player. The former Coleraine junior bus conductor who became an Irish national hero was already a famous star when he joined Derby in World War Two as a guest player. Doherty was a member of the Manchester City team which won the League championship

in 1937. His style of play was never to stand still. One minute he would be back helping out in his own penalty area, the next he would be dancing through the oppositon's 18-yard box. Doherty helped the Rams win the Midland Cup in 1945, scoring five times when they beat Aston Villa in the second leg of the Final at Derby. Less than a year later Manchester City had let him go for £6,000 and he was scoring at Wembley as the Rams won the FA Cup. Doherty played a handful of games when the Football League started up again in 1946. He wanted to take over the Arboretum Hotel near the Baseball Ground, but the Derby directors refused permission and told him that they thought it might affect his game. Said Doherty. "If they thought that, then they didn't know me. I had no option but to leave, though it almost broke my heart because I loved Derby." Doherty was listed in the Huddersfield programme as their new player on Boxing Day 1946, but the deal had not quite gone through and he played one more game for the Rams, bowing out in style with two goals in the 5-1 win over Everton. After Huddersfield he led Doncaster Rovers to the Third Division North title in 1949-50 and managed Northern Ireland when they reached the World Cup quarter-finals in Sweden in 1958.

DONAGHY
Edward   *Left-half*

Born: Grangetown, 8 January 1900.
Career: Grangetown. Middlesbrough February 1922. Bradford City May 1923. Derby County May 1926. Gillingham July 1927.

As Sid Plackett began to fade, George Jobey's search for a left-half brought in Ted Donaghy, whose brother Peter also played for Bradford City, for six games in 1926-7. He gave way to Bernard McLaverty but the longer-term answer proved to be dropping Harry Storer back from inside-forward.

DONALD
David Morgan   *Outside-left*

Born: Coatbridge. Died: Derby, 19 January 1932.
Career: Albion Rovers. Bradford July 1908. Derby County March 1910. Chesterfield June 1912. Watford June 1913. Queen's Park Rangers cs 1914. Hamilton Academical July 1922.
Division Two champions 1911-12.

Davie Donald went straight into the Derby team, succeeding Jack Davis, when he was signed from Park Avenue. Donald was first choice for a season but gave way to Ivan Sharpe in the Second Division championship team. He had played in Bradford's first Football League match in 1908.

DRAPER
Derek   *Midfield*

Born: Swansea, 11 May 1943.
Career: Juniors, Swansea Town: professional May 1962. Derby County April 1966. Bradford September 1967. Chester January 1969.

Draper, a Welsh Under-23 international, was seen as a possible threat to Alan Durban but never presented a serious challenge and managed only nine senior games for Derby County. He played more than 300 League games for Chester, becoming a popular player at Sealand Road, and was in their 1974-5 Fourth Division promotion team. Draper joined Chester's commercial department in 1977-8 before buying a milk round in the city.

DUNCAN
Douglas   *Outside-left*

Born: Aberdeen, 14 October 1909. Died: Brighton, 2 January 1990.

Dally Duncan.

Career: Aberdeen Richmond. Hull City August 1928. Derby County March 1932. Player-coach, Luton Town, October 1946: player-manager June 1947: retired as player cs 1948. Manager, Blackburn Rovers, October 1958 to July 1960.

Division One runners-up 1935-6. FA Cup winners 1945-6.

Derby County knew that they were getting a goalscoring winger when they signed Douglas 'Dally' Duncan from Hull City in 1932. The Aberdonian had

David Donald.

John Duncan.

Jimmy Dunn.

averaged more than a goal every three games for the Tigers. It cost the Rams £2,000 to bring him to Derby, but he repaid the fee many times over. Duncan took over from Georgie Mee on the Rams left wing and was soon seen by the Scottish selectors as the natural successor to the legendary Alan Morton. His friendly rivalry with Sammy Crooks over who would be Derby's top-scoring winger was good for Derby County and in the late 1930s it was the Rams' goalscoring from the wings which helped them to become one of the best teams in the land. Duncan worked at the Derby Carriage and Wagon Works during World War Two and, aged 36, helped the Rams to win the FA Cup in 1946. He joined Luton Town and, as manager, steered them into Division One for the first-time in 1955. Duncan also managed Blackburn and took them to the 1960 FA Cup Final.

DUNCAN
John Pearson   *Forward*

Born: Lochee, 22 February 1949.
Career: Dundee April 1966. Tottenham Hotspur October 1974. Derby County September 1978. Player-manager, Scunthorpe United, June 1981: manager to February 1983. Manager, Har-

tlepool United, April 1983. Manager, Chesterfield, June 1983. Manager, Ipswich Town, June 1987 to May 1990.

John Duncan, in Dundee's 1974 League Cup winning team, repaid Tottenham Hotspur's £125,000 fee by being leading scorer in their 1977-8 Second Division promotion. He was always a regular scorer but also suffered from frequent injuries, although Tommy Docherty paid £150,000 for him. Duncan went into management and was poorly treated by Scunthorpe United, who sacked him when promotion from the Fourth Division was in sight. In 1985, he steered Chesterfield to the Fourth Division championship, a feat which earned him the Ipswich Town post. After three years at Portman Road he went into teaching and in August 1992 was appointed one of England manager Graham Taylor's observers.

DUNN
George   *Inside-forward*

Appeared once for Derby, in the final match of the 1890-91 season.

DUNN
James   *Inside-forward*

Born: Edinburgh, 25 November 1923.

Career: St Teresa's, Liverpool. Wolverhampton Wanderers, amateur, 1941: professional, November 1942. Derby County November 1952. Worcester City July 1955. Runcorn June 1957 to May 1959. Trainer, West Bromwich Albion.

Son of a member of Scotland's 1928 Wembley Wizards team, so named following their 5-1 win, Jimmy Dunn junior earned an FA Cup winners' medal with Wolves in their 1949 victory over Leicester City. Jesse Pye was in the same team. Stuart McMillan signed Dunn in the hope that he would help to preserve Derby's First Division status. Only six weeks after joining the Rams, Dunn was forced out by knee trouble which necessitated a cartilage operation.

DURBAN
William Alan

Inside-forward/midfield

Born: Cardiff, 7 July 1941.
Career: Juniors, Cardiff City: professional September 1958. Derby County July 1963. Player-assistant manager, Shrewsbury Town, September 1973: acting manager December 1973: player-manager, February 1974. Manager, Stoke City, February 1978. Manager, Sunderland, June 1981 to March 1984.

Alan Durban, 403 senior games for Derby, First and Second Division championship medals and 27 Welsh caps.

pace, nor was he a particularly good tackler but he had a wonderful feel for the flow of the game and a delicate touch. Perhaps his greatest attribute was an ability to find space in crowded penalty areas, arriving late to score a large percentage of his goals from close range. He earned 27 Welsh caps before joining Shrewsbury Town, where he became player-manager and steered them out of the Fourth Division in 1974-5. Durban played more than 550 League games (on all 92 grounds) before he retired. He became manager of Stoke City in February 1978, and was involved in another promotion success in 1978-9, third place in Division Two. After an unhappy spell with Cardiff he became manager of the Telford Tennis Centre.

EADIE
William Phillips   *Centre-half*
Born: Greenock.
Career: Morton. Manchester City, August 1906. Derby County June 1914. Retired during World War One.
Division Two champions 1914-15.

When Derby County were relegated from the First Division in 1914 and Frank Buckley joined Bradford City, Jimmy Methven needed an experienced centre-half. He signed Bill Eadie, who had played in 205 League and Cup games for Manchester City and been in their 1909-10 Second Division championship team. Eadie's one season at Derby brought another Second Division medal but his career ended with the onset of World War One.

EDWARDS
John W.   *Inside-forward*
Career: Carr Vale, Bolsover. Derby County January 1909.

Edwards made two League appearances soon after arriving from north Derbyshire, scoring to earn a point off Blackpool in the second of them.

EGGLESTON
Thomas   *Wing-half*
Born: Mitcham, 21 February 1920.
Career: Derby County, amateur, December 1936: professional, February 1937. Leicester City July 1946. Watford February 1948. Trainer, Brentford, September 1954. Coach, Watford, May 1957. Coach, Sheffield Wednesday, October 1958. Coach, Everton, June 1961. Manager, Mansfield Town, August 1967. Manager, Ethnikos (Greece), July 1970. Manager, Panahaiki (Greece), 1971. Youth coach, Everton, February 1972: assistant manager May 1972 to June 1973. Physiotherapist, Plymouth Argyle. Physiotherapist, Ipswich Town, December 1978 to retirement.

Tommy Eggleston's career was ham-

Manager, Cardiff City, September 1984 to May 1986.
Division Two champions 1968-9.
Division One champions 1971-2.

Alan Durban was 22 when Tim Ward signed him from Cardiff City for £10,000 in July 1963. It was money well spent, for Durban was one of the few to survive and play a significant part in the Clough era. He had two distinct phases at Derby, the first as a goalscoring inside-forward and the second as an intelligent midfield player. In his first role, he formed a productive partnership with Eddie Thomas which brought them 24 goals each in 1964-5 after Thomas had arrived from Swansea Town. Durban went on to score more than 100 goals for Derby, including four hat-tricks, but his best days were in midfield. He had no great

Tommy Eggleston, a good career in coaching and management.　　**Steve Emery, whose Derby career was ended by a broken leg.**

pered by World War Two, during which he served as a Petty Officer in the Royal Navy. He played only one peacetime game for Derby, in the FA Cup third round, second leg against Luton Town in 1946. His best playing days were with Watford, after which he became a respected coach, manager and, finally, physiotherapist.

EKINS
Frederick George　　*Forward*

Born: New Brompton, 27 September 1871.
Career: New Brompton Rovers. Chatham. Derby County October 1891. Burton Swifts August 1893. Luton Town May 1895.

Ekins was given a good run at inside-left when he joined Derby but, in his second season, played only intermittently on the right-wing. He had the distinction of scoring Luton Town's first goal after they joined the Football League in 1897.

EMERY
Stephen Roger　　*Midfield/full-back*

Born: Ledbury, 7 February 1956.
Career: Apprentice, Hereford United: professional April 1974. Derby County September 1979. Newport County

March 1983. Hereford United June 1983. Wrexham August 1985. Gloucester City February 1987. Westfields April 1987: manager.

Steve Emery was Hereford's first apprentice and Colin Addison, who had known him at Edgar Street, paid £100,000 to sign him for Derby. He was unlucky with injuries, fracturing a cheekbone against Chelsea in 1980 and having a leg broken by a wild tackle from Gerry Gow at Rotherham in February 1982. Gow was ordered off and Emery did not play another senior game for Derby. He showed great courage by reviving his career in the lower divisions after such an unpleasant injury.

EMSON
Paul David　　*Outside-left*

Born: Lincoln, 22 October 1958.
Career: Athletico FC, Grimsby Sunday League. Brigg Town cs 1978. Derby County September 1978. Grimsby Town August 1983. Wrexham August 1986. Darlington August 1988. Kettering Town March 1991. Gateshead October 1991.

Frank Blunstone, Tommy Docherty's assistant, watched Paul Emson play for Brigg and Derby promptly paid £5,000 for him. Emson had terrific pace and,

Paul Emson.

if his final pass and shooting were erratic, he might have flourished in a better or more settled team. He had three good years for Grimsby before tasting European football with Wrexham.

EVANS
George   *Centre-forward*
Born: Sutton-in-Ashfield, 1865. Died: c1930.
Career: Derby Midland/St Luke's. Derby County 1884. West Bromwich Albion May 1889. Brierley Hill Alliance 1890. Oldbury Town. Oldbury St John's. Retired 1901.

Scored six FA Cup goals in five games before the start of the Football League.

EVANS
William   *Outside-left*
Career: Clay Cross. Derby County October 1907.

Played one League game soon after arriving from Clay Cross.

EXHAM
Percy George   *Left-half*
Born: Cork, 16 June 1859. Died: Repton, 7 October 1922.

A master at Repton School, Exham played in Derby's first FA Cup tie, a 7-0 defeat by Walsall Town. He also played cricket for Derbyshire, once, and Ireland.

FABIAN
Aubrey Howard   *Inside-forward*
Born: Barnet, 20 March 1909. Died: Cranbrook, 6 September 1984.

Howard Fabian.

Career: Casuals and Corinthian Casuals 1928 to 1946. Cambridge University 1929 to 1931. Derby County December 1931 to May 1933. Sutton United. Fulham December 1934 to February 1935.

Educated at Highgate, where he was later a master, Howard Fabian was a good enough amateur to be accepted into Derby County's richly-talented team of the early 1930s. That could have happened only to a player of considerable gifts. Fabian played in the 1933 FA Cup semi-final against Manchester City and was in the Casuals' team when they won the Amateur Cup in 1936. A Cambridge cricket and football Blue, he later combined his teaching duties with football journalism.

FAGAN
Fionan   *Wing-forward*
Born: Dublin, 7 June 1930.
Career: Transport. Hull City March 1951. Manchester City December 1953. Derby County March 1960. Player-manager, Altrincham, June 1961; manager to April 1962; player to May 1963. Ashton United September 1963. Northwich Victoria.

Paddy Fagan was in Manchester City's beaten FA Cup Final team in 1955 and won two of his eight Republic of Ireland caps while at Maine Road. Another six came after his £7,500 transfer to Derby and, in 1960-61, he was the Republic of Ireland's Player of the Year while spending most of his time in Derby's Central League team. From a club point of view, the signing was not a great success.

FAIRCLOUGH
Albert   *Centre-forward*
Born: St Helens, 4 October 1891. Died: Stockport, 5 November 1958.
Career: Windle Villa. Eccles Borough. Manchester City April 1913. Southend United May 1920. Bristol City March

Albert Fairclough.

1921. Derby County July 1924. Gillingham February 1927.
Division Two promotion 1925-6.

Albert Fairclough had a brilliant scoring record with Derby, 26 goals in 37 League games. He was leading scorer in 1924-5, after arriving from Bristol City, with 22, including four against Fulham and a hat-trick against Portsmouth. He played only twice in the 1925-6 promotion team because George Jobey felt he had signed a better centre-forward in Harry Bedford.

FAZACKERLEY
Stanley Nicholas   *Forward*
Born: Preston, 3 October 1891. Died: Sheffield, 20 June 1946.
Career: Lane Ends United. Preston North End August 1909. Charlestown, Boston League, USA, 1910. Accrington Stanley. Hull City April 1912. Sheffield United March 1913. Everton November 1920. Wolverhampton Wanderers November 1922. Kidderminster Harriers, while on Wolves' transfer list, March 1925. Derby County August 1925. Retired April 1926.
Division Two promotion 1925-6.

Stan Fazackerley.

One of three centre-forwards tried by George Jobey in the first six games of 1925-6 before Harry Bedford was signed. Fazackerley had a varied and, at times, distinguished career. He gained a Boston League championship medal and scored one of the goals in Sheffield United's 3-0 FA Cup Final victory over Chelsea in 1915. Everton paid a British record £4,000 for him in 1920 and he was a member of Jobey's Wolverhampton Wanderers team which won the Third Division North in 1924-5. He retired on medical advice.

FELLOWS
Percy J.   *Outside-left*
Career: Dudley. Derby County January 1914.

Fellows played two matches in 1913-14, a relegation season for the Rams.

FEREDAY
David T.   *Outside-right*
Born: Walsall Wood.
Career: Walsall Wood. Walsall August 1927. Derby County February 1928. West Ham United May 1931. Yeovil.
Division One runners-up 1929-30.

A useful winger, whose chance of more regular senior appearances was limited by the emerging brilliance of Sammy Crooks.

FERGUSON
Archibald   *Full-back*
Career: Heart of Midlothian. Derby County cs 1888. Preston North End. Ardwick April 1894. Baltimore October 1894.

One of those who launched Derby County on their League career in 1888, Ferguson was the regular left-back for the first two seasons and most of the third. He made a couple of appearances for Ardwick before leaving for the United States, with Tommy Little among others.

FERGUSON
Robert Burnitt   *Left-back*
Born: Dudley, near Newcastle, 8 January 1938.
Career: Dudley. Newcastle United May 1955. Derby County October 1962. Cardiff City December 1965. Player-manager, Barry Town, December 1968. Player-manager, Newport County, July 1969. Dismissed as manager November 1970: player to cs 1971. Youth coach, Ipswich Town, July 1971: reserve-team coach 1973: coach August 1979: manager July 1982 to May 1987. Manager Al-Arabi (Kuwait), June 1987. Assistant manager, Birmingham City, June 1989 to January 1991. Coach, Sunderland, June 1992.

Bobby Ferguson cost £4,000 when he was signed from Newcastle United, enabling Tim Ward to have a specialist left-back instead of playing Ray Young out of position. Hard and determined, Ferguson gave Derby good service, missing only two games out of 131 before Peter Daniel emerged to take his place.

FIFE   *Goalkeeper*
Played two League games in February 1890.

FINDLAY
John Williamson   *Goalkeeper*
Born: Blairgowrie, 13 July 1954.
Career: Apprentice, Aston Villa: professional June 1972. Luton Town November 1978. Barnsley, loan, September 1983. Derby County, loan, January 1984. Swindon Town July 1985. Peterborough United January 1986. Portsmouth January 1986. Coventry City August 1986.

Jake Findlay, Luton Town's goalkeeper when they won the Second Division in 1981-2, was signed on loan by Peter Taylor. Findlay played only once, in a home defeat by Charlton Athletic, and was promptly dropped.

FINDLAY
Thomas   *Full-back*
Born: Port Glasgow.
Career: Port Glasgow Athletic. Derby County March 1922. Merthyr Town May 1925.

Played four games as deputy for either Albert Chandler or Tom Crilly before joining Merthyr Town, then in the Third Division South.

FISHER
William   *Inside-forward*
Career: Kilmarnock. Derby County May 1896. Burton Swifts October 1897. Bristol Eastville Rovers May 1898.

Had a good run in his only season with Derby when his fellow-Scot Jimmy Stevenson was out of action. His scoring rate was excellent, eight in 15 senior games, and his goals helped Derby towards the 1897 FA Cup semifinal. Fisher was in the Bristol Rovers team which entered the Southern League in 1899, along with George Kinsey, John Leonard and John Paul.

FLANDERS
Frederick   *Left-back*
Born: Derby, 1 January 1894. Died: Birmingham, 1967.
Career: Derby Boys. Shelton United. Derby County May 1910. Newport County August 1913. Hartlepools United June 1922.

From Gerard Street School, Fred Flanders was captain of the Derby Boys team which won the English Schools Shield in 1908. Derby Boys were still looking for a repeat more than 80 years later. Flanders also led England in a junior international against Wales at Aberdare in 1907 and made his League debut for Derby at the age of 16 years and 287 days, in all probability the youngest until Steve Powell.

FLETCHER
Frederick   *Outside-left*
Career: Derby County August 1892. Notts County November 1894.

Played in three League games early in 1894-5 before his move to Notts County.

Archie Ferguson (above) and Fred Flanders (below).

FLETCHER
Thomas   *Forward*
Born: Heanor, 15 June 1881. Died: Derby, 29 September 1954.
Career: Hill's Ivanhoe. Derby Nomads. Leicester Fosse April 1902. Derby Nomads. Derby County November 1904.

A versatile forward, who played all across the front line in his days with Derby. Tom Fletcher remained an amateur and was also an extremely useful cricketer, representing Derbyshire against the West Indians in 1906.

FORD
David   *Goalkeeper*
Career: Derby County July 1898.
Chesterfield October 1899.

Reserve goalkeeper who made six
appearances in place of Jack Fryer early
in 1898-9.

FORDHAM
Norman M.   *Centre-forward*
Born: Maidstone.
Career: Ashford. Derby County
February 1914.
Division Two champions 1914-15.

Fordham, who came out of Kent
League football, helped to set the 1914-
15 Second Division campaign off on
the right foot with an opening-day hat-
trick in Derby's 7-0 home win against
Barnsley. He played in the first six
matches before Harry Leonard returned
and later made one appearance at
centre-half. A brother-in-law of the
great Kent and England cricketer Frank
Woolley.

FORMAN
Frank   *Half-back*
Born: Aston-upon-Trent, 23 May 1875.
Died: West Bridgford, 4 December 1961.
Career: Aston-upon-Trent. Beeston
Town. Derby County March 1894.
Nottingham Forest December 1894.
Retired 1905.

Frank Forman played only a handful
of matches for Derby before joining his
brother Fred at Nottingham Forest. It
was Derby's loss. Frank Forman,
described as a born leader, appeared for
England nine times while with Forest
and was in the team which beat Derby
in the 1898 Cup Final. In 1899, Frank
and Fred became the eighth pair of
brothers to play in the same England
team — and the last until Bobby and
Jack Charlton in 1965. Frank Forman
was a member of the Forest committee
from 1903 to 1961 and a building
contractor in partnership with Harry
Linacre, his brother-in-law.

FORMAN
Frederick Ralph   *Outside-left*
Born: Aston-upon-Trent, 8 November
1873. Died: 14 June 1910.
Career: Beeston Town. Derby County
January 1892. Nottingham Forest 1893.
Retired 1903.

He played for England at outside-left
but his four games for Derby County
were on the right-wing or at inside-
right. Only briefly with Derby, like his
brother. A railway draughtsman by
profession.

FORSYTH
Michael Eric   *Left-back*
Born: Liverpool, 20 March 1966.
Career: Apprentice, West Bromwich

Michael Forsyth, one of the Rams' most consistent players in good times and bad.

Albion: professional November 1983.
Northampton Town, loan, March
1986. Derby County March 1986.
Division Two champions 1986-7.

For six seasons, Michael Forsyth was one
of Derby's consistent players, in the bad
times as well as the good. He stepped
into the left-back vacancy created when
Steve Buckley left after the 1986 Third
Division promotion and went on to play
for England Under-21 and England 'B'.
Forsyth was a Youth international with
West Bromwich Albion and cost the
Rams £26,000 when they beat the 1986
transfer deadline. He had just gone on
loan to Northampton Town but was
recalled to The Hawthorns without
playing for them when Derby's bid came
in. For the remainder of that season,
Forsyth played as a central defender, his
recognised position, in the Central

League championship team. He was
given first chance to replace Buckley
and, as he said: "Started on a trial and
error basis." He adapted to the position
well enough to be voted Player of the
Year in 1987-8 and only suspensions,
plus an occasional injury, kept him
out. When Blades partnered Forsyth,
the Rams had outstanding heading
ability at full-back. With his strength
in the tackle and absolute determination, Forsyth became an established
First Division defender, although the
Rams always hoped for more from him
in the other half of the field. After a
memorable equaliser against Liverpool
and another goal in an important
victory at Coventry in March 1988,
Forsyth did not score again until
October 1991, in a League Cup tie at
Oldham. He succeeded Geraint Williams as captain in 1992.

George Foster.

FOSTER
George Walter *Centre-half*
Born: Plymouth, 26 September 1956.
Career: Apprentice, Plymouth Argyle:
professional September 1974. Torquay
United, loan, October 1976. Exeter
City, loan, December 1981. Derby
County June 1982. Mansfield Town
August 1983: player-manager February
1989.

Foster played for all three clubs in the South-West before John Newman brought him to Derby for £40,000. When Peter Taylor took over as manager, Foster's place was less certain but he helped in a successful fight against relegation from the Second Division. Captained Mansfield Town to promotion from the Fourth Division in 1986 and the Freight/Rover Trophy in 1987. As player-manager he took his total of League appearances past 600.

FOX
Walter *Goalkeeper*
Born: Derby.
Career: Matlock Town. Alfreton Town.
Derby County, amateur, August 1925:
professional, September 1925.
Division Two promotion 1925-6.

Ben Olney missed only one match in the 1925-6 promotion season and Fox stood in successfully in a 2-0 home win against South Shields.

FRAIL
Joseph *Goalkeeper*
Born: Burslem, 1873.
Career: Burslem Port Vale June 1892.
Glossop North End April 1895. Derby
County June 1896. Chatham June
1898. Middlesbrough May 1900. Luton
Town May 1902. Brentford May 1903.
Middlesbrough May 1904. Stockport
County November 1905. Glossop May
1906.

Frail was in the first team Burslem Port Vale ever fielded in League football, in 1892, and joined Derby as reserve to Jack Robinson. When Robinson shook the football world by joining New Brighton Tower, Frail began 1897-8 as first choice but gave way to Jack Fryer in October.

FRANCIS
Kevin Michael Derek
Centre-forward
Born: Birmingham, 6 December 1967.
Career: Redditch April 1988. Mile Oak
Rovers July 1988. Derby County
February 1989. Stockport County
February 1991.

Kevin Francis.

Derby paid a nominal fee for Kevin Francis in a gamble on his physical qualities. He is 6ft 7ins tall and, when in full stride, has startling pace. His football improved at the Baseball Ground and, in the Reserves, he was always likely to make something happen. He scored only one senior goal, in an FA Cup replay defeat by Port Vale, but found more regular League football with Stockport County, helping them to promotion

from the Fourth Division in 1990-91, and to the Third Division play-offs a year later, after moving for £60,000. He was following the trail of Brett Angell, who never played first-team football at Derby but joined Southend United from Stockport County for £100,000.

FRANCIS
Percy Ollivant *Outside/inside-right*
Died: Derby, 21 June 1947.
Career: Amateur. Registered with
Derby County 1893.
Division One runners-up 1895-6.

An amateur who played occasionally over three seasons, including once in the team which finished runners-up in Division One for the first time. A solicitor in Derby and for many years a director of the club as well as serving on the Derbyshire CCC committee.

FRITH
Robert William *Defender*
Born: Hassop.
Career: Sheffield United April 1909.
Derby County December 1910. Luton
Town July 1913. South Shields July
1919. Rotherham County March 1920.

Played only once for Derby, in the final match of the 1910-11 season.

FRYER
John Spencer *Goalkeeper*
Born: Cromford 1877. Died: West-
minster, 22 December 1933.
Career: Abbey Rovers, Cromford. Clay
Cross Town August 1895. Derby
County September 1897. Fulham May
1903. Retired 1910.

Jack Fryer.

FA Cup Finalists 1897-8, 1898-9, 1902-03.

The 6ft 2ins Jack 'String' Fryer played in a variety of positions for his local side in the Derbyshire Minor League until one day the regular goalkeeper failed to arrive and the tallest man on the pitch was asked to deputise. When Fryer was signed by the Rams, he expected to play mostly in the Reserves. But when Frail, Robinson's replacement, failed to distinguish himself, Fryer was quickly promoted to the League side and by the end of the season found himself in an FA Cup Final. In the second round match at Wolverhampton, with Bloomer unfit, Fryer withstood a 90-minute bombardment to help Derby win 1-0. The goalkeeper was carried shoulder-high from the field and any lingering doubt that he would not be capable of filling Robinson's place were dispelled. A fine cricketer who kept wicket for the Ind Coope brewery team at Burton where he worked, Fryer won the hearts of the Rams fans until his feeble performance in the 1903 FA Cup Final, when he played with an injured thigh. It was his last match for the Rams and he moved to Fulham where he kept goal in the 1905-06 and 1906-07 Southern League championship teams. Fryer later kept a pub near the Chelsea ground.

FULTON
William   *Inside-forward*

Born: Alva.
Career: Alva Albion Rangers. Trial for Preston North End. Sunderland May 1898. Bristol City June 1900. Derby County May 1901. Alloa Athletic June 1902.

Scored on his Derby debut against Grimsby at Blundell Park in September 1901, but held the inside-left position for only a month before Ben Warren took over. Injury hampered him at Derby and he took over a pub at Alloa. In 1904 he was reinstated as an amateur.

FUTCHER
Paul   *Central defender*

Born: Chester, 25 September 1956.
Career: Apprentice, Chester: professional January 1974. Luton Town June 1974. Manchester City June 1978. Oldham Athletic August 1980. Derby County January 1983. Barnsley March 1984. Halifax Town July 1990. Grimsby Town, loan, January 1991. Grimsby Town February 1991.

Still a teenager when Luton paid £100,000, the first of four expensive moves for Paul Futcher. Manchester City paid £350,000, Oldham £150,000 and Derby £115,000 when Peter Taylor tempted him to help in the fight against relegation. With 11 England Under-21 caps, Futcher's considerable skill was never in doubt but he and Taylor were

Paul Futcher.

increasingly on a different wavelength. Derby's financial crisis helped to force Futcher's sale to Barnsley for £30,000, with Calvin Plummer involved in the same deal, and the player was happy to get away. His twin brother Ron played for several of the same clubs, but not Derby. Barnsley had six good years from Paul.

GABBIADINI
Marco   *Centre-forward*

Born: Nottingham, 20 January 1968.
Career: Apprentice, York City: professional September 1985. Sunderland September 1987. Crystal Palace September 1991. Derby County January 1992.

Arthur Cox, backed by Lionel Pickering's massive investment, began to form a new strike force when he signed Marco Gabbiadini for £1 million. Paul Simpson, Paul Kitson and Tommy Johnson followed within weeks. Gabbiadini emerged as a teenager at York and followed manager Denis Smith to Sunderland for £80,000. He was a big hit at Roker Park, averaging 20 goals a season as well as winning England Under-21 and 'B' caps. Crystal Palace signed him for £1.8 million but his four months at Selhurst Park were extremely unhappy. Although he scored the winner at

Marco Gabbiadini.

Portsmouth on his debut for the Rams, Gabbiadini needed a few weeks to rid himself of the Palace experience.

GALLACHER
Hugh Kilpatrick   *Centre-forward*

Born: Bellshill, 2 February 1903. Died: Low Fell, Gateshead, 11 June 1957.
Career: Bellshill Athletic March 1920. Queen of the South December 1920. Airdrieonians May 1921. Newcastle United December 1925. Chelsea May 1930. Derby County November 1934.

Hughie Gallacher hammers in a shot for Derby County.

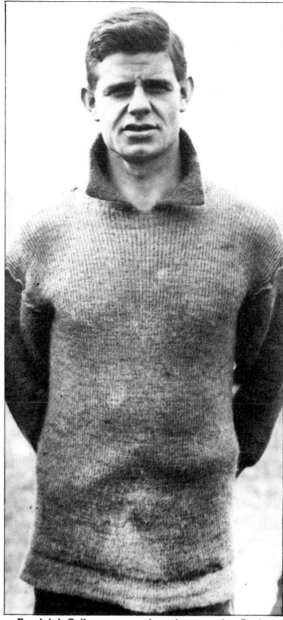

Randolph Galloway, a good scoring record at Derby.

Notts County September 1936. Grimsby Town January 1938. Gateshead June 1938. Retired September 1939.

Division One runners-up 1935-6.

In 1934, Derby manager George Jobey, confronted with a serious injury to centre-forward Jack Bowers, paid £2,750 for Chelsea's Scottish international striker Hughie Gallacher. Jobey knew that he was buying more than one of the greatest centre-forwards who ever lived and that Gallacher had a reputation off the field. Married at 17, and divorced at 23, his debts were so high that Derby had to pay them off as part of the transfer deal. His Derby debut, against Birmingham in November 1934, was watched by nearly 20,000 fans, who turned up at the Baseball Ground despite driving rain. He scored within six minutes and, in December 1934, hit all five against Blackburn Rovers at Ewood Park. A member of the famous Wembley

Wizards team which beat England 5-1 in 1928. Gallacher won a Scottish Cup medal at Airdrie and captained Newcastle United to the 1926-7 League Championship. When he returned after a £10,000 move to Chelsea, there were 68,386 in St James' Park to smash Newcastle's attendance record. He died in June 1957, throwing himself in front of the Edinburgh-York express train while facing a charge of cruelty to his son.

GALLOWAY
Septimus Randolph

Centre-forward

Born: Sunderland, 22 December 1896. Died, 10 April 1964.
Career: Army, boy musician. Yorkshire Regiment in World War One. Sunderland Tramways. Derby County October 1922. Nottingham Forest November 1924. Luton Town June

1927. Coventry City January 1928. Tottenham Hotspur September 1928.

Although a late entrant into League football, Randolph Galloway had a good scoring record at Derby, 30 goals in 76 senior games. A good enough schoolboy full-back to represent the North, Galloway became a centre-forward while serving with the Yorkshire Regiment. He was in the Derby team a month after arriving from Sunderland Tramways and stayed until he was deposed by Albert Fairclough. That was the signal for Cecil Potter to accept a £2,500 offer from Nottingham Forest.

GAMBLE
Francis

Forward

Born: Liverpool, 21 August 1961.
Career: Burscough. Derby County, loan, March 1981. Derby County May 1981. Barrow November 1982. Rochdale December 1984. Morecambe

Frank Gamble, upset by the turmoil at Derby.

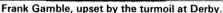

Andy Garner, hat-trick as a teenager.

March 1986. *Northwich Victoria, loan, October 1987. Southport November 1987. Rhyl October 1989.*

Frank Gamble showed touches of skill in his few appearances but walked out of Derby County in October 1982 because he felt lost in the turmoil of the club, then facing financial problems and changes of chairman and manager. He returned to the League two years later with Rochdale.

GARDEN
Henry Whitworth   *Centre-half*
Career: Derby Midland. Derby County June 1891. Long Eaton Rangers 1893.

Played only once, in the opening game of the 1892-3 season.

GARDNER
William   *Centre-forward*
Born: Langley Moor, 7 June 1893.
Career: Bishop Auckland. Derby County August 1920. Spennymoor United November 1921. Queen's Park Rangers March 1923. Ashington July 1923. Grimsby Town October 1925. Darlington September 1927. Torquay United June 1928. York City July 1929. Crewe Alexandra July 1931. Rochdale September 1932.

Gardner, short but powerful, made his name with Bishop Auckland, playing in the 1915 FA Amateur Cup Final, which they lost to Clapton. In 1919-20, he scored 64 goals, 56 for his club, five for England amateurs, including four against Wales at Merthyr, and three for County Durham. Derby brought him into the paid ranks but he played only five League games before embarking on his travels.

GARNER
Andrew   *Forward*
Born: Stonebroom, 8 March 1966.
Career: Apprentice, Derby County: professional January 1985. Blackpool August 1988.
Division Three promotion 1985-6.
Division Two champions 1986-7.

Andy Garner first played in Derby County's Central League side as a powerfully built 15-year-old and made his senior debut in an FA Cup fifth round tie against Norwich City in February 1984. He scored a Second Division hat-trick against Crystal Palace just over a month after his 18th birthday but, under Arthur Cox, was regarded as a squad player. He scored valuable goals in the Third Division promotion season, none more welcome than the winner at Blackpool, but appeared only twice as substitute when Derby won the Second Division.

Garner always scored goals but lack of pace hampered him at the top level.

GARRY
Edward   *Inside-forward/wing-half*
Born: Dumbarton, c.1885. Died: Derby, 28 May 1955.
Career: Dumbarton Hearts. Glasgow Celtic. Ayr United September 1905. Glasgow Celtic March 1906. Derby County May 1907. Bradford May 1913. Dumbarton during World War One. Coached in Spain.
Division Two champions 1911-12.

Ted Garry's career is linked with that of Jimmy Bauchop. In 1907, Jimmy Methven wanted to sign Bauchop from Celtic but was outbid by Norwich City. Garry made a good second prize and started spectacularly, with three goals against Lincoln City at the Baseball Ground on his debut. Garry had moved to wing-half when Derby won the Second Division in 1911-12, with Bauchop also in the side. They shared another promotion at Park Avenue, when Bradford were Second Division runners-up in 1913-14.

GEE
Phillip John   *Striker*
Born: Pelsall, 19 December 1964.
Career: Riley Sports. Gresley Rovers July 1985. Derby County September 1985. Leicester City March 1992.

Phil Gee, whose goals helped Derby into Division One.

Division Three promotion 1985-6. Division Two champions 1986-7.

Phil Gee, a painter and decorator in Walsall, had played only a few games for Gresley Rovers when the club's chairman, David Nish, mentioned his potential to Derby County. Events moved swiftly and Gee was soon rattling in Central League goals, 31 in 28 games as the Rams surged to the title in 1985-6. As substitute, he scored in the vital Third Division promotion game against Rotherham United and went on to worry Second Division defences with his pace and fierce shooting. When he had completed 25 senior appearances, the fee had become £5,000, this for a man who scored 15 goals in the Second Division triumph. After two years of unbroken success, he found it infinitely harder to score goals in the First Division but his unflagging efforts reflected strength of character in difficult times. The arrival of Paul Goddard, Dean Saunders and Mick Harford ended Gee's time as a regular and he moved to Leicester as part of the Paul Kitson deal.

Archie Gemmill, an inspiration when Derby won the title again.

GEMMILL
Archibald   *Midfield*

Born: Paisley, 24 March 1947.
Career: Drumchapel Amateurs. St Mirren 1964. Preston North End May 1967. Derby County September 1970. Nottingham Forest September 1977. Birmingham City August 1979. Jacksonville Tea Men March 1982. Wigan Athletic September 1982. Derby County November 1982. Released May 1984. Coach, Nottingham Forest, August 1985: registered as player January 1986.
Division One champions 1971-2, 1974-5 (captain).

Archie Gemmill cost Derby County £66,000 when he was signed from Preston to take over from Willie Carlin in midfield. So keen was Brian Clough to complete the deal that he stayed overnight in the Gemmills' house. Pace was the first important ingredient Gemmill added but he soon developed into one of the finest midfield players in Britain. He began running every August and did not stop until the following May, urging the rest of the team, competing in every area of the field and using his speed as the ace. After a stunning UEFA Cup performance against Atletico Madrid in Spain, Argentine manager, Juan Carlos Lorenzo, embraced an embarrassed Gemmill shouting "Magnifico". Gemmill made 40 appearances for the 1971-2 champions, and, in the absence of Roy McFarland, was an inspirational captain when the title returned to Derby three years later.

The Rams with the League Championship trophy in 1975. Back row (from left to right): Dave Mackay, Roger Davies, Henry Newton, Colin Boulton, Roy McFarland, Alan Hinton, Francis Lee, David Nish, Peter Daniel (partly hidden), Colin Todd and Steve Powell. Front row: Rod Thomas, Bruce Rioch, Archie Gemmill and Kevin Hector.

He won a third championship medal in 1977-8, after joining Nottingham Forest in what was for Derby a disastrous exchange deal which brought in goalkeeper John Middleton and £25,000. He played 43 games for Scotland, 22 of them while with Derby, and gained a League Cup winners' medal with Forest but was disappointed to be left out of Forest's 1979 European Cup Final team. He was the first signing after Peter Taylor's appointment as manager and did more than most in a successful fight against relegation. In 1983-4, Taylor fell out with Gemmill and although McFarland restored him to the team, his career ended sadly with relegation to Division Three.

GEORGE
Charles Frederick   *Forward/*
midfield

Born: Islington, 10 October 1950.
Career: Apprentice, Arsenal: professional March 1968. Derby County July 1975. St George Budapest, NSW, loan, May 1977. Minnesota Kicks, loan, May 1978. Southampton December 1978. Nottingham Forest, loan, January 1980. Bulova, Hong Kong September 1981. AFC Bournemouth March 1982. Derby County March 1982.

Dave Mackay interrupted a holiday in Scotland and flew to London when, in July 1975, he heard that Charlie George might be available. Mackay wanted to

add even more skill to his League champions and was exceptionally pleased with himself when he captured George, a member of Arsenal's 1970-71 double side, for £100,000. George made his competitive debut at Wembley in the Charity Shield and had a brilliant first season. His shooting was deadly, his passing both exquisite and startling in its vision. Until he dislocated a shoulder against Stoke at the Baseball Ground in March 1976, Derby had a realistic chance of the double. George was the first Midlands Player of the Year but was upset when Mackay was sacked in November 1976. He never again reached the same heights, although one England appearance was poor reward for his skill. He had knee problems when Tommy Docherty sold him to Southampton for £400,000 in December 1978. John Newman brought him back to Derby in March 1982, a short-term move which helped Derby to stay up for another season, but they could not meet his terms for a longer stay.

GIBSON
Aidan Michael   *Outside-left*
Born: Clayton, 17 May 1963.
Career: Apprentice, Derby County: professional May 1981. Exeter City July 1982. Stourbridge August 1983. Willenhall Town.

Gibson's only appearances were as substitute but he was a bright left-sided player in the Central League.

GILCHRIST
Leonard   *Inside-forward*
Career: Burton United February 1903. Derby County May 1904.

Signed from Burton United, then a Second Division club, Gilchrist provided useful cover for George Richards in 1904-05.

GILL
James   *Inside-forward*
Born: Sheffield, 9 November 1894.
Career: Sheffield Wednesday June 1913. Cardiff City July 1920. Blackpool October 1925. Derby County February 1926. Crystal Palace May 1928.

Jimmy Gill.

Charlie George, injured as Derby chased the double.

Paul Goddard, in 1989 the Rams' record sale.

Division Two promotion 1925-6.

George Jobey leaned heavily on forwards from Blackpool when Derby regained their First Division status in 1926. Harry Bedford arrived from Bloomfield Road in September of the promotion season and in February, Jobey bought Jimmy Gill and George Mee at a joint cost of £3,500. They gave an impetus at the right time. Gill, a former England schoolboy international, had been involved in Cardiff City's Second Division promotion in 1920-21 and played for them in the 1925 FA Cup Final defeat by Sheffield United. He was renowned for his pace and, if this was fading by the time he reached the Baseball Ground, he was still sharp enough to be joint leading League scorer with Bedford in 1926-7, when Derby settled back in the First

Division. The following year, his experience aided the development of Sammy Crooks.

GILLETT
Leonard Francis   *Goalkeeper*

Born: Borrowash, 21 January 1861.
Died: Harbertsford, 23 November 1915.

He helped the Old Carthusians to win the FA Cup in 1881, 3-0 against Old Etonians, but was beaten seven times when he played in Derby's first-ever tie, against Walsall Town. After leaving Oxford University, where he gained a football Blue in 1882, Gillett worked as a civil and mining engineer.

GODDARD
Paul   *Centre-forward*

Born: Harlington, 12 October 1959.

Career: Apprentice, Queen's Park Rangers: professional July 1977. West Ham United August 1980. Newcastle United November 1986. Derby County August 1988. Millwall December 1989. Ipswich Town January 1991.

Paul Goddard cost £425,000 and made a big impact in his 16 months at the Baseball Ground. With his ability to hold the ball, he was at his most effective after Dean Saunders was signed from Oxford United. Goddard also scored his share of goals and it came as a shock when he joined Millwall for £800,000, then the highest fee Derby had received. He had continued to live in Gerrards Cross and Arthur Cox promised to keep him informed if a London club came in with an acceptable offer. The move

Archie Goodall, probably the most colourful character in the Rams' early history. He made 423 senior appearances for the Rams

cussedness when he tried to back out of the move to them. Primarily a centre-half in the days when that posiition was not merely that of a stopper, Archie scored over 50 goals for Derby. He was one of the greatest characters ever to play for the club, causing alarm before the 1898 Cup Final because he was outside trying to unload tickets on which he had speculated, and once refusing to play extra-time in a United Counties League Cup Final because he said that his contracted ended after 90 minutes. He toured Europe and America with a strongman act, 'walking' around a giant metal hoop, and was a great follower of country sports. He was an Ireland regular and his records of consecutive appearances for Derby, 167 in all matches and 151 in the League, survived into the 1990s.

GOODALL
John   *Forward*

Born: Westminster, 19 June 1863. Died: Watford, 20 May 1942.
Career: Kilmarnock Athletic. Great Lever 1883. Preston North End August 1885. Derby County May 1889. New Brighton Tower October 1889. Glossop February 1901. Watford, player-manager, May 1903. Manager to May 1910. Ended playing career with Mardy in 1913.

Division One runners-up 1895-96 (captain). FA Cup Finalists 1897-8 (captain).

Derby County had good reason to remember John Goodall. He scored five goals for Great Lever in the Rams' first match in 1884. Derby never forgot him and after he played in the 1888-9 Preston double-winning side, the Rams signed Goodall in time for the League's second season. It was a sensational signing, considering his status in the Preston team, and Goodall, one of the great footballers of his time, did not disappoint Derby supporters. Although the two were dissimilar players, Goodall taught Steve Bloomer much about the game. He knew just when to pass or shoot and his great strength was to bring out the best in those around him. Though born in England — he played 14 times for his country — Goodall was raised in the Scottish school of soccer and was a pioneer of scientific football and the passing game. Such was his exemplary character, he was known as Johnny All-Good. He also played cricket for Derbyshire and Hertfordshire.

GOODCHILD
George   *Outside-right*

Career: Ryhope Colliery. Sunderland June 1894. Derby County June 1896. Nottingham Forest March 1897. Burton Swifts October 1897. Jarrow July 1899. South Shields Athletic July 1901.

Appeared twice for Derby in 1896-7.

turned out to be a disaster, because it had never been likely that Goddard and Millwall would be compatible. He left The Den on a free transfer and rejoined John Lyall, his former West Ham United manager, at Ipswich. Although hampered by ankle trouble, he helped them to the Second Division title in 1991-2. The Hammers had paid £800,000 to take him across London in 1980 and, with them, he was capped by England, as substitute against Iceland in 1982. He also played once for England 'B' and eight times at Under-21 level.

GOLBY
Joseph Allen   *Centre-half*

Born: Burton upon Trent 1897.
Career: Burton All Saints. Derby County August 1922. Halifax Town July 1926.

Played only once for Derby, in the final League match of the 1922-3 season.

GOODALL
Archibald Lee   *Centre-half*

Born: Belfast, 19 June 1864. Died:London N10, 29 November 1929. Career: Liverpool Stanley. Preston North End. Aston Villa October 1888. Derby County May 1889. Plymouth Argyle May 1903. Glossop January 1904. Wolverhampton Wanderers October 1905.

Division One runners-up 1895-6. FA Cup Finalists 1897-8, 1902-03.

Born in Ireland and raised in Scotland, Archie Goodall was as rumbustuous as his brother John was gentle. He played for several clubs, including the Rams, before 1888 and when the Football League was formed he played for Preston and Aston Villa. His move to Preston from Villa was the first transfer to be approved by the League. *Athletic News* reported: 'Goodall's arrival at Perry Barr led to a good deal of bickering. Derby had a first taste of his

John Goodall, as gentle as his brother Archie was rumbustuous. He appeared in 238 League and Cup games, scoring 85 goals.

GRANT
Alexander Frank   *Goalkeeper*

Born: Camerton, 11 August 1916.
Career: Doncaster Rovers (midweek-League). Sheffield United, amateur. Bury August 1937. Aldershot May 1938. Leicester City December 1941. Derby County November 1946. Newport County November 1948. Leeds United

August 1949. York City March 1950.

Grant took over from veteran Vic Woodley for part of the first League season after World War Two. When he left Derby, Grant's wages were 3d (1.25p) a week. The nominal sum was paid so that he could be retained as a professional and remain eligible for the full government family allowance while training as a teacher. As a wartime guest, Grant played in both

legs of the 1944-5 Midland Cup Final success against Aston Villa.

GREEN
Joseph James   *Goalkeeper*
Career: Derby Bedford Rangers. Derby County January 1894. Belper Town.

Green stood in for England goalkeeper Jack Robinson seven times in 1894-5.

Les Green, won a Second Division medal with the Rams.

GREEN
Leslie   *Goalkeeper*
Born: Atherstone, 17 October 1941.
Career: Atherstone Town. Hull City August 1960. Nuneaton Borough July 1962. Burton Albion June 1965. Hartlepools United November 1965. Rochdale April 1967. Derby County May 1968. Durban City August 1971. Manager, Durban City. Commercial manager, Nuneaton Borough, 1989: manager September 1989 to January 1991. Manager, Hinckley Town, April 1991. Nuneaton Borough.
Division Two champions 1968-9.

Brian Clough and Peter Taylor were only too happy to allow Les Green to leave Hartlepools United after troubles off the field but they remembered his good handling and organisational ability when they paid Rochdale £7,000 to sign him for Derby. He was a big hit in the team which sailed away with the Second Division title, when he 19 clean sheets, and made 129 consecutive appearances, 107 in the League, before his form betrayed him. After knocking around in non-League football for so long, Green grabbed his chance with Derby but, once dropped after a 4-4 draw against Manchester United, never played League football again. His career was ended by a broken leg in South Africa.

GREEN
Robert Edward   *Inside-forward*
Born: Tewkesbury. Died: Cheltenham.

Career: Bournemouth & Boscombe Athletic, amateur, February 1929: professional, March 1929. Derby County May 1931. Manchester United June 1933. Stockport County July 1934.

His only appearance for Derby County came in the opening game of the 1931-2 season.

GREENWOOD
Roy Thornton   *Forward*
Born: Leeds, 26 September 1952.
Career: Apprentice, Hull City: professional October 1970. Sunderland January 1976. Derby County January 1979. Swindon Town February 1980. Huddersfield Town August 1982. Tranmere Rovers, loan, November 1983. Scarborough June 1984.

Sunderland paid £140,000 for Roy Greenwood to give them a final push for the Second Division title in 1975-6. Greenwood was a useful winger but Tommy Docherty played him as a central striker. Despite his willing efforts, he was not suited to the position.

GREGORY
John Charles   *Midfield*
Born: Scunthorpe, 11 May 1954.
Career: Apprentice, Northampton Town: professional January 1973. Aston Villa June 1977. Brighton & Hove Albion July 1979. Queen's Park Rangers June 1981. Derby County November 1985. Coach, Portsmouth,

August 1988: manager January 1989 to January 1990. Playing registration, Derby County to Portsmouth, August 1989. Plymouth Argyle January 1990: temporary manager February 1990. Bolton Wanderers March 1990. Coach, Leicester City, June 1991.
Division Three promotion 1985-6.
Division Two champions 1986-7.

Arthur Cox began to build a promotion team in his first season at the Baseball Ground but needed an extra dimension in midfield in 1985-6, especially when Steve McClaren was ruled out by injury. He spent £100,000 on John Gregory, who had won the last of his six England caps only 18 months earlier. Gregory had been involved in two expensive moves, £250,000 from Aston Villa to Brighton & Hove Albion and another £300,000 when he joined Queen's Park Rangers. He played for Rangers in the 1982 FA Cup Final and was an ever-present when they won the Second Division 12 months later. Gregory's experience was invaluable in two promotions with the Rams. Injury hampered him in the Third Division but he was an ever-present in the Second Dvision championship, contributing vital goals from midfield. "John improved the standard of our passing," said Cox. Gregory helped Derby stay in the First Division and was a good partner for the industrious Geraint Williams. He had a spell in attack which, although it did not bring him a goal, helped to turn the results after eight successive League defeats and showed his willingness to help the team effort.

GRIMES
William John   *Outside-right*
Born: Hitchin, 27 March 1886. Died: near Biggleswade, 6 January 1936.
Career: Hitchin Town. Watford May 1906. Glossop May 1907. Bradford City December 1908. Derby County March 1910. Tottenham Hotspur during World War One. Watford April 1917. Luton Town July 1919.
Division Two champions 1911-12, 1914-15.

Billy Grimes took over from George Thompson when he arrived from Bradford City and for the five seasons up to World War One was Derby County's most regular ouside-right. His goals were rare but he was an integral part of both Second Division championship teams in a yo-yo period for the Rams. His Derby career continued during World War One. After retiring in 1920 he resumed his previous trade as a bricklayer.

GROVES
Arthur   *Inside-forward*
Born: Killamarsh, 27 September 1907. Died: Derby, 27 September 1979.
Career: Langwith Colliery. Halifax

Roy Greenwood.

John Gregory's midfield skills helped the Rams to consecutive promotions.

Arthur Groves.

Billy Grimes tries a high kick, watched by Chelsea's Danish international Nils Middelboe.

Town May 1927. Blackburn Rovers January 1929. Derby County July 1933. Portsmouth January 1936. Stockport County June 1939. Atherstone Town July 1945. Player-coach, Heanor Athletic, November 1946.

Division One runners-up 1935-6.

A creative inside-forward who helped to provide the openings for Jack Bowers after being signed from Blackburn Rovers for £550. The contemporary feeling was that Groves and Peter Ramage were too similar, although both were players of considerable skill. Groves played his last senior game for Derby against Portsmouth on Christmas Day, 1935. The following month, he was back at Fratton Park as a £1,500 signing. His son John played for Luton Town in the 1959 FA Cup Final.

GWYNNE
Revd Llewellyn Henry
Centre-forward

Born: Kilvey, near Swansea. Died: Epping, 3 December 1957.
Career: Derby County 1888.

The only bishop ever to play for Derby County. Llewellyn Gwynne was a typical muscular Christian of the Victorian era and was curate of St Chad's when he represented the Rams in an FA Cup game at Crewe. After parish work in Nottingham, Gwynne went to Khartoum as a missionary and became Archdeacon of the Sudan in 1904. From 1920 to 1946, he was Bishop in Egypt and the Sudan and frequent use of air travel around his see earned him the title of the Flying Bishop. When the cathedral and his house were looted in the Cairo riots of 1946, King Farouk sent an envoy to express his horror. Bishop Gwynne was in his nineties when he died in Epping.

HADDOW
David
Goalkeeper

Born: Dalserf, Lanarkshire, 12 June 1869.
Career: Coatbridge junior football. Albion Rovers c.1888. Derby County August 1890. Albion Rovers January 1891. Glasgow Rangers cs 1891. Motherwell 1895. Burnley December 1895. New Brighton Tower August 1898. Retired 1899. Returned with Tottenham Hotspur November 1899.

Haddow did not have a distinguished stay with Derby, conceding 69 goals in his 16 League games. The defence in front of him must shoulder much of the blame and Haddow's career flourished later. In 1893-4, he earned a Scottish Cup winners' medal with Rangers in their 3-1 win over Celtic and played for Scotland against England, his one cap. He was Burnley's goalkeeper when they won the Second Division title in 1897-8 and gained a Southern League championship medal with Tottenham Hotspur in 1899-1900.

HAGAN
James
Inside-forward

Born: Unsworth, 21 January 1918.
Career: Liverpool, amateur, January 1932. Derby County, amateur, May 1933: professional, January 1935. Sheffield United November 1938. Retired 1958. Manager, Peterborough United, August 1958 to October 1962. Manager, West Bromwich Albion, April 1963 to May 1967. Manager, Benfica, March 1970 to September 1973. Coached in Kuwait. Manager, Oporto.

Division One runners-up 1935-6.

Jimmy Hagan was one of the greatest talents to escape from the Baseball Ground. He cost Sheffield United £2,500 but played almost 20 years for them. He took part in two Second Division promotions with them, as runners-up in 1938-9 and champions in 1952-3. Hagan was a schoolboy international and added a full England cap, against Denmark in September 1948, but one appearance was regarded as a poor return for an inside-forward of Hagan's quality. Although he was with the Rams for only a short time, Hagan was one of the major League footballers in the decade after World War Two. He was managing Benfica when they met Derby in the 1972-3 European Cup.

HAIG
James
Wing-half

Career: Derby County May 1898. Kilbarchan 1899. Chesterfield November 1900. Retired 1908.

Haig played only three times for Derby, standing in for Jack Cox, but had a long career with Chesterfield before emigrating to Canada in 1908.

HALES
Derek David
Centre-forward

Born: Lower Halston, 15 December 1951.
Career: Dartford. Luton Town March 1972. Charlton Athletic, loan, July 1973. Charlton Athletic October 1973. Derby County December 1976. West Ham United September 1977. Charlton

Derek Hales, a regular scorer who found life difficult in Division One.

Athletic July 1978. Gillingham March 1985.

Derek Hales was the major signing of Colin Murphy's spell as manager, costing £330,000. Hales had been a big success with Charlton Athletic, leading scorer when they were promoted from the Third Division in 1974-5, but found it hard to adapt to the First Division in a struggling side. He was soon moved on by Tommy Docherty, although the £110,000 West Ham paid represented a huge loss. Within a year, he was back at The Valley and leading scorer in another Third Division promotion, in 1980-81. During his two spells with Charlton, Hales scored 148 League goals in 320 games.

HALEY
William Thomas

Inside/Centre-forward

Born: Bexleyheath, 1904. Died: Rochester, 20 January 1960.
Career: Bostall Heath. Charlton Athletic May 1924. Derby County February 1925. Fulham June 1928. Queen's Park Rangers May 1931. Dartford cs 1932. Sheppey United August 1935.
Division Two promotion 1925-6.

In contrast to his four hat-tricks for Fulham in 1929-30, Haley had a lean time at the Baseball Ground. He scored only one goal, in a 2-0 win over Middlesbrough in the Second Division promotion campaign, and was never regarded as more than a useful reserve.

HALFORD
David
Outside-left

Born: Crossley Green, 19 October 1915.
Career: Rowntrees FC. Scarborough amateur August 1932: professional October 1932. Derby County December 1932. Bolton Wanderers June 1936. Oldham Athletic June 1938.
Division One runners-up 1935-6.

An England schoolboy international, David 'Spider' Halford had only limited opportunities at Derby as understudy to Dally Duncan.

HALL
Benjamin
Centre-half

Born: Ecclesfield, 6 March 1879. Died: 1963.
Career: Grimsby Town January 1900. Derby County August 1903. Leicester Fosse August 1911. Hyde 1912. South Shields 1913. Coach, Grimsby Town. Coach, Heywood United. Trainer, Hednesford Town, 1919. Manager, Bristol Rovers, July 1920 to May 1921. Manager, Loughborough Corinthians.

When Archie Goodall left the Rams for Plymouth in 1903 the club knew that they needed to sign a first-class centre-half to fill the gap left by the Irish international. They turned to Grimsby

Ben Hall.

Town's Ben Hall and brought to the Baseball Ground one of the most skilful half-backs in the Football League. In the days when a centre-half was the key man, linking defence with attack, Hall's immaculate ball control and delightful passing were vital. Grimsby had dropped into Division Two and Hall wanted to continue in the top flight, which made Derby's task of signing him easier. He stayed at Derby when they, too, were relegated. He relied on skill rather than brawn and was considered a gentlemanly player. A good cricketer, Hall was popular with both players and spectators. He returned to play some wartime games for Derby in 1915-16, along with his brother Ellis. Hall was manager of Bristol Rovers when they entered the League in 1920 and later scouted for Southend United.

HALL
Ian William
Midfield

Born: Sutton Scarsdale, 27 December 1939.
Career: Amateur, Wolverhampton Wanderers. Amateur, Derby County, August 1958: professional, September 1959. Mansfield Town September 1962. Tamworth August 1968. Burton Albion March 1972. Derbyshire Amateurs. Tamworth 1974.

An England Schools and Youth international, Ian Hall signed professional for Derby County in the same year as he made his first-class cricket debut for Derbyshire. A creative midfield player, who was in Mansfield Town's 1962-3 Fourth Division promotion team after Raich Carter signed him for the Stags. An opening batsman and good close catcher, Hall scored 11,666 runs for Derbyshire (average 25.86) and his nine centuries included two in the match against Kent at Folkestone in 1965.

Ian Hall.

HALLIGAN
William
Forward

Born: Athlone, c.1890.
Career: Belfast Distillery. Leeds City May 1909. Derby County February 1910. Wolverhampton Wanderers June 1911. Hull City May 1913. Preston North End July 1919. Oldham Athletic January 1920. Nelson August 1921.

Billy Halligan spent 16 months with Derby, winning one of his two caps for Ireland in that time. His second was with Wolverhampton Wanderers after his £450 move.

HAMILTON
John
Forward

Born: Ayr, 1872.
Career: Ayr United. Wolverhampton Wanderers. Derby County November 1894. Ilkeston Town May 1895.

Hamilton played a dozen games in the forward line in 1894-5.

HAMPTON
John William
Goalkeeper

Born: Wolverhampton.
Career: Wellington Town. Oakengates Town. Wolverhampton Wanderers May 1920. Derby County June 1927. Preston North End May 1930. Dundalk June 1931.
Division One runners-up 1929-30.

Hampton had played under George Jobey for Wolves. At Derby, he provided goalkeeping cover for Harry Wilkes who, like Hampton, had played for Wellington Town.

HANDLEY
George *Outside-right*

Career: Loughborough. Notts County December 1895. Coalville Town. Derby County November 1897. Newark Town.

Handley offered a useful variation in attack during 1897-8 but did not play in any of the FA Cup ties as Derby reached successive Finals in 1898 and 1899.

Ralph Hann.

HANN
Ralph *Wing-half*

Born: Whitburn, 4 July 1911. Died: Derby, 17 July 1990.
Career: Marsden Colliery. Amateur, Sunderland, April 1929: professional January 1930. Newcastle United August 1930. Derby County March 1932. Trainer, Crystal Palace, September 1946: registered as player, April 1947. Trainer-masseur, Luton Town, July 1947. Head trainer, Derby County, November 1953 to May 1967.
Division One runners-up 1935-6.

Ralph Hann was in a Newcastle cinema when a message was flashed on the screen telling him to report to St James' Park. George Jobey was there, waiting to sign him and Duncan Hutchison in a joint £3,100 deal. His chances were limited by the consistency of Jack Nicholas and Eric Keen but Hann established himself in 1938-9, when he was ever-present. He played one League game for Crystal Palace after the war, then was called in as trainer by old friends in Dally Duncan at Luton and Jack Barker at the Baseball Ground. He lost his job in 1967 because Brian Clough wanted a complete clear-out.

HANNAY
John *Outside-right*

Career: Newcastle district. Derby County October 1920.

Played only one League game, in May 1921, on trial after relegation had been settled.

HANNIGAN
John Leckie *Forward*

Born: Glasgow, 17 February 1933. Career: Morton. Sunderland July 1955. Derby County May 1958. Bradford June 1961. Weymouth July 1964.

Johnny Hannigan.

Johnny Hannigan was a versatile forward, who could play on either wing or in the middle. Derby signed him for £6,000 from Sunderland, where he had been one of the players who had received illegal bonus payments offered by the club — a practice familiar at the Baseball Ground between the wars. Bradford bought Hannigan for £2,400.

HARBEY
Graham Keith

Left-back/midfield

Born: Chesterfield, 29 August 1964. Career: Apprentice, Derby County: professional August 1982. Ipswich Town July 1987. West Bromwich Albion, loan, November 1989. West Bromwich Albion December 1989. Stoke City July 1992
Division Three promotion 1985-6. Division Two champions 1986-7.

Graham Harbey was on non-contract terms when he made a brilliant debut against Charlton Athletic at The Valley in September 1983. Peter Taylor

Graham Harbey.

promptly offered him a full contract. His opportunities at left-back were few while Steve Buckley remained and he played only as substitute in the Third Division promotion. He had an important spell in midfield when Derby were on the way to the Second Division championship. When his contract was up, he joined Ipswich Town for £65,000 in search of more regular senior football.

HARBOARD *Wing-half*

When Derby went to Anfield Road, then the home of Everton, with only ten men in October 1888, they had to borrow a player from the opposition to make up the numbers. Nothing is known of Harboard and even the spelling is in some doubt.

HARDCASTLE
Douglas S. *Inside-forward*

Born: Worksop.
Career: Worksop Town. Derby County May 1905. Worksop Town August 1907.

In two seasons at the Baseball Ground,

Hardcastle appeared in six senior games, usually filling in for George Richards or allowing him to move to wing-half.

HARDMAN
John A. *Half-back*
Born: Miles Platting, 1889. Died: France, February 1917.
Career: Longfield. Oldham Athletic, amateur, December 1910; professional, March 1911. Pontypridd August 1912. Derby County August 1913. Bristol Rovers October 1914.

Division Two champions 1914-15.

Hardman joined Derby after going out of the Football League. Most of his games were in the 1913-14 First Division relegation season although he played once, in place of Bill Eadie, when Derby bounced back a year later. One of the professionals to fall in World War One.

HARDY
Arthur *Inside-forward*
Career: Derby Midland. Derby County June 1891. Heanor Town cs 1893.

One of the players to join Derby County when Derby Midland folded.

HARDY
John James *Centre-half*
Born: Sunderland, 10 February 1899. Died: Sunderland, January 1932.
Career: Sunderland Celtic. South Shields April 1921. Derby County August 1924. Grimsby Town July 1925. Oldham Athletic January 1927. South Shields October 1927. Scarborough Town August 1930. West Stanley December 1930. Clapton Orient September 1931.

Hardy stood in for Harry Thoms three times in 1924-5, when Derby missed promotion from the Second Division by two points. He found more success in Grimsby Town's Third Division North championship team the following season. Hardy was only 32 when he died after falling ill with pneumonia.

HARFORD
Michael Gordon *Centre-forward*
Born: Sunderland, 12 February 1959.
Career: Lambton Star BC. Lincoln City July 1977. Newcastle United December 1980. Bristol City August 1981. Newcastle United March 1982. Birmingham City March 1982. Luton Town December 1984. Derby County January 1990. Luton Town September 1991. Chelsea August 1992.

One of the most feared and respected target men in the League, Mick Harford was over 30 when he joined Derby County for £480,000 as the replacement for Paul Goddard. Harford played twice for England, against Israel and Denmark, in his first spell with Luton,

John Hardy.

Mick Harford.

towards the end of which he suffered a series of injuries. The artificial pitch at Kenilworth Road may have been a factor but Harford helped Luton to win the Littlewoods Cup in 1988 and reach the Final again a year later. He was unfortunate to be at Derby when Robert Maxwell's chairmanship prevented any development and money was still tight when he returned to Luton. Uniquely, Harford was on the books of three League clubs in one day in March 1982. Bristol City, in severe financial trouble, could not maintain payments on the £160,000 fee they owed Newcastle, so he returned, technically, to St James' Park, so that Birmingham City could pay Newcastle £100,000.

HARRISON
Kenneth *Outside-right*
Born: Stockton, 20 January 1926.
Career: Billingham Synthonia and army football. Hull City April 1947. Derby County March 1955. Goole Town July 1956.

Arrived with Alf Ackerman as Jack Barker vainly tried to stave off relegation to the Third Division North. Raich Carter's right-wing partner in Hull City's 1948-9 Third North championship team but suffered a bad injury in 1954, when he fractured a knee in three places.

HARRISON
Reginald Frederick *Outside-right*
Born: Derby, 22 May 1923.

Reg Harrison.

Career: Derby Corinthians. Derby County March 1944. Boston United July 1955. Player-coach, Long Eaton United May 1957: player-manager, January 1958. Coach, Wilmorton and Alvaston, May 1962. Player-coach, Alfreton Town, July 1962. Manager, Crewton, July 1966. Coach, Belper Town, June 1970.

FA Cup winners 1945-6.

Little Reg Harrison could hardly have expected to win an FA Cup winners' medal so early in his career. A hard-running outside-right who scored his fair share of goals, Harrison returned to the Rams team for the semi-final matches against Birmingham when Sammy Crooks was injured. Crooks was not risked at Wembley, although he had managed a League South game earlier, and manager McMillan had no worries in handing over the number seven shirt to Harrison. The player has always paid tribute to the help he received from Crooks and from Raich Carter, who took the baby-faced winger into his charge. After war service with the Royal Artillery, Harrison proved himself a highly skilled as well as enthusiastic player. He was of First Division quality but stayed while the club declined. Harrison was in the Boston United team which won 6-1 at the Baseball Ground to provide an FA Cup humiliation and later did an immense amount for junior football in Derby.

HARRISON
Thomas William   *Goalkeeper*

Career: South Normanton Town August 1899. Stanton Hill Town September 1899. South Normanton Town March 1901. Ripley Athletic November 1901. Derby County December 1901. Pinxton September 1902.

Played once in April 1902 and would have appeared a second time had he not missed his train from South Normanton, forcing Arthur Latham, the trainer and former full-back, into an unwelcome comeback as goalkeeper.

HART
John Leslie   *Centre-forward*

Career: Mansfield Town. Derby County January 1926.

Division Two promotion 1925-6.

Hart was signed as cover for Harry Bedford and scored in his first two games in the Second Division promotion season under George Jobey.

HARVEY
John Arthur H.   *Half-back*

Career: Partick Thistle. Derby County July 1894. Ilkeston Town March 1895. Abercorn January 1896.

Covered for all three half-back posi-

tions in a poor season for Derby, when they needed victory in a Test Match to stay in the First Division.

HASLAM,
Harry B.   *Outside-left*

Career: Gresley Rovers. Belper Town January 1897. Derby County March 1901. Belper Town August 1902.

Arrived as a winger but also played a few games at half-back in his eight senior appearances.

HAVENHAND
Keith   *Inside-forward*

Born: Dronfield, 11 September 1937. Career: Juniors, Chesterfield: professional September 1954. Derby County October 1961. Oxford United December 1963.

An England Youth international in 1957, Havenhand cost £10,000 when he arrived from Chesterfield. He had a good first season, scoring 14 goals in 29 games, but a cartilage operation halted his progress and he moved to Oxford for £4,000. Injury curtailed his career.

Keith Havenhand.

HAWDEN
Kenneth   *Centre-forward*

Born: Huddersfield, 16 September 1931. Career: Ashenhurst SC, Huddersfield. Derby County April 1953. Belper Town. Sutton Town February 1955. Gresley Rovers August 1958.

One of 31 players used in 1953-4 as Derby were in the process of sliding from the First Division to the Third North in two seasons.

HAYWARD
Steve Lee   *Midfield*

Born: Pelsall, 8 September 1971. Career: Trainee, Derby County: professional September 1988.

After only a handful of Reserve appearances, Steve Hayward made his debut as substitute in March 1990. He became a regular England Youth player but had yet to earn a regular senior place with Derby by the end of 1991-2.

HAYWOOD
Frederick   *Centre-forward*

Career: Mexborough Town. Derby County April 1907.

Haywood's only appearance was in the final game of 1906-07.

HAZLEDINE
Donald   *Inside-forward*

Born: Derby, 10 July 1929. Career: Notts Regent. Derby County August 1951. Northampton Town June 1954. Boston United July 1955. Skegness Town July 1961. Holbeach United July 1962. Bourne Town August 1965. Coach, Boston United Reserves, July 1966: joint-coach with brother Geoff, August 1966.

Played most of his games in Derby County's disastrous 1952-3 season when they were bottom of the First Division and on the slide. Along with his brother Geoff, he was among six ex-Derby players in the Boston United team which won 6-1 at the Baseball Ground in December 1955, an FA Cup humiliation marking the lowest point in the Rams' history.

HAZLEDINE
Geoffrey   *Forward*

Born: Derby, 27 December 1932. Career: Ransome & Marles. Derby County July 1952. Boston United September 1954. Southport July 1957. Skegness Town July 1958. Loughborough United July 1960: player-manager designate June 1962: player-manager May 1963 to May 1965. Bourne Town September 1965. Joint coach, Boston United Reserves, August 1966.

Geoff Hazledine appeared once, in a 0-0 draw at Oldham in February 1954. In 1961-2, Hazledine caused the aban-donment of Loughborough's Midland

Steve Hayward.

Don Hazledine.

Geoff Hazledine.

Trevor Hebberd.

League match at Belper by refusing to leave the field when sent off. The game was replayed and he was again ordered off. As player-manager designate, he led Loughborough to the Midland League title in 1962-3

HEBBERD
Trevor Neal   *Midfield*

Born: Winchester, 19 June 1958.
Career: Apprentice, Southampton: professional July 1976. Washington Diplomats, loan, March 1981. Bolton Wanderers, loan, September 1981. Leicester City, loan, November 1981. Oxford United March 1982. Derby County August 1988. Portsmouth October 1991. Chesterfield November 1991.

Not until he joined Oxford United, in a deal which took Mark Wright and Keith Cassells to Southampton, did Trevor Hebberd have a regular League

place. He made the most of his opportunity at the Manor Ground. He was an ever-present when Oxford won the Third and Second Divisions in successive seasons, a star when they beat Queen's Park Rangers in the 1986 Milk Cup Final. Primarily a midfield player, Hebberd could also play in attack, as a sweeper or at full-back. Derby signed him in 1988, Mickey Lewis going to Oxford in part-exchange. Hebberd was a key ingredient of the Derby team which finished fifth in Division One in 1988-9 but, because of the overall financial situation, stayed too long at the Baseball Ground and was released on a free transfer. At his best, he was an inventive midfield man with a good touch and the ability to score goals.

HECTOR
Kevin James   *Forward*

Born: Leeds, 2 November 1944.

Career: Juniors, Bradford: professional July 1962. Derby County September 1966. Vancouver Whitecaps January 1978. Boston United, loan, September 1978. Burton Albion, loan, November 1979. Burton Albion September 1980. Derby County October 1980. Gresley Rovers September 1982. Shepshed

Kevin Hector and David Nish parade the League Championship trophy around the Baseball Ground at the end of the 1974-5 season.

Kevin Hector, whose 589 senior appearances are a Rams record.

Charterhouse October 1982. Burton Albion December 1982. Gresley Rovers September 1983. Belper Town July 1984. Eastwood Town August 1987. Heanor Town July 1988.

Division Two champions 1968-9. Division One champions 1971-2, 1974-5.

Kevin Hector had scored 113 League goals in 176 games for Bradford when Tim Ward astonished supporters by signing him for £40,000. Derby, pottering along unambitiously in the Second Division, were not expected to pay fees of that size but Hector was an instant success. He was christened the King by supporters and retained the nickname, even when he became one fine player among many in the great days of the early 1970s. He did more than survive the advent of Brian Clough and Peter Taylor; he was an integral part of the teams which won the Second Division and two League Championships. He was gifted with pace and a marvellous balance, so the goals flowed regularly. Between 1970 and 1972, he played in 105 consecutive League games. Sir Alf Ramsey should have given him an earlier England run and his debut, against Poland in October 1973, was farcical, a couple of minutes as substitute to try and get England through to the World Cup Finals. He nearly did it too, being denied only by a Polish kneecap on the goal-line. His only other cap was also as substitute. Tommy Docherty sold Hector to Vancouver Whitecaps and he spent the English seasons playing for Boston United and Burton Albion before Colin Addison brought him back in October 1980. By the time he bowed out, with a goal against Watford in a match Derby had to win to ensure their Second Division place, Hector had made more appearances than any other player in Derby's history and

Terry Hennessey, whose fine career was ended by injuries.

scored 201 goals, a total surpassed only by Steve Bloomer. He gave supporters immense pleasure through his style, his goals and his manner on and off the field. He was still a winner in Belper Town's Northern Counties (East) League championship team of 1984-5.

HENNESSEY
William Terrence
Central defender/midfield

Born: Llay, 1 September 1942.
Career: Juniors, Birmingham City: professional September 1959. Nottingham Forest November 1965. Derby County February 1970. Manager, Tamworth, April 1974. Advisory coach, Kimberley Town, September 1976: temporary manager, November 1977. Asssistant-manager, Tulsa Roughnecks, 1978: Shepshed Charterhouse August 1978 to October 1980. Assistant coach, Tulsa Roughnecks, November 1980: chief coach 1981 to 1983. Assistant coach, Vancouver Whitecaps. Man-

ager, Heidelberg, 1987 to 1988.
Division One champions 1971-2.

Terry Hennessey was the first £100,000 signing made by Derby County when he joined the Rams from Nottingham Forest as a replacement for Dave Mackay, who made it clear that he would have to work for the position. He won eight of his 39 Welsh caps while at the Baseball Ground. Hennessey was a dominant figure at the City Ground and it was a surprise when Forest let him go to their near-neighbours and most deadly rivals. A powerful wing-half, Hennessey's career at Derby was interrupted, then ended, by injuries to his knees and an Achilles tendon. His signing for a six-figure fee showed supporters that Derby County were well and truly among the big spenders of football, after years of modest signings, and it was a great pity that Hennessey was unable to share in more triumphs at the Baseball Ground. He did, however, manage at least one

golden memory, playing in the team which beat Benfica at Derby in the 1972-3 European Cup and defending magnificently in the second leg.

HICKINBOTTOM
Ernest   *Half-back*

Born: Darley Abbey, Derby, c1865.
Died: Derby, 2 September 1939.
Career: Darley Abbey. Derby Midland. Derby County.

One of the most reliable players in Derby County's early years and, like many at that time, moved around the local clubs. Hickinbottom died at the Baseball Ground while watching the Rams play Aston Villa in the final League game before World War Two.

HICKLING
William   *Full-back*

Career: Somercotes United April 1902. Derby County April 1903. Middlesbrough September 1906. Tottenham Hotspur 1907. Mansfield Mechanics. Ilkeston United cs 1909.

A reserve defender who stood in for both Jimmy Methven and Charlie Morris during 1903-04.

HIGGINS
Alexander F.   *Centre-forward*

Born: Kilmarnock, c1865. Died: 17 April 1920.
Career: Kilmarnock. Derby County August 1888. Nottingham Forest July 1890. Retired April 1894.

Sandy Higgins must be one of the unluckiest players ever to stop at a

Sandy Higgins.

Gordon Hill, knocked Derby out of the FA Cup.

Rob Hindmarch, led Derby brilliantly to two promotions.

single international appearance, as he scored four goals in Scotland's 8-2 victory over Ireland in March 1885. He played in Derby's first League game and was their leading scorer for two seasons before joining Nottingham Forest and appearing in their first League team. His son Alex played for Kilmarnock, Newcastle United and Nottingham Forest, winning four Scotland caps.

HILL
Andrew Robert   Centre-forward
Born: Ilkeston, 10 November 1960.
Career: Kimberley Town. Derby County June 1981. Carlisle United September 1983. Boston United January 1987. Shepshed Charterhouse July 1987. Hinckley Athletic November 1987.

Andy Hill did not score many goals for Derby but one which is remembered is the second, and clincher, in the 1983 FA Cup victory over Nottingham Forest. An accountant by profession.

HILL
Gordon Alec   Outside-left
Born: Sunbury, 1 April 1954.
Career: Staines Town. Slough Town. Southall. Millwall January 1973. Chicago Sting, loan, April 1975. Manchester United November 1975. Derby County April 1978. Queen's Park Rangers November 1979. Montreal Manic January 1981. Chicago Sting May 1982. HJK Helsinki. Twente Enschede. Northwich Victoria September 1986: caretaker-manager, December 1986. Stafford Rangers August 1987. Northwich Victoria January 1988: player-manager May 1988: player-coach to October 1988. Radcliffe Borough March 1990.

Tommy Docherty signed Gordon Hill three times, most significantly for Manchester United at a fee of £70,000. While he was at Old Trafford, Hill played six times for England and appeared in two FA Cup Finals, as a loser in 1976, after his two goals had beaten Derby in the semi-final, and a

winner in 1977. In both Finals, he was replaced by substitute David McCreery. He cost Derby £275,000 and went on the 1978 England 'B' tour, but he was not the right man for a struggling side. Docherty paid £150,000 to take him to Queen's Park Rangers.

HINCHLIFFE
Thomas   Inside-forward
Born: Denaby, 6 December 1913. Died: Rushcliffe, 1978.
Career: Denaby United. Grimsby Town October 1933. Huddersfield Town February 1938. Derby County November 1938. Nottingham Forest May 1946.

Tom Hinchliffe was an inside-forward who was given a brief run after Dai Astley had been sold to Blackpool. World War Two took out his best years.

HIND
F.   Full-back
Career: Derby Junction. Derby County.
Hind stood in once for Arthur Latham,

in March 1890. He was a member of the famous Derby Junction team, FA Cup semi-finalists in 1888.

HINDMARCH
Robert   *Centre-half*

Career: Apprentice, Sunderland: professional April 1978. Portsmouth, loan, December 1983. Derby County July 1984. Wolverhampton Wanderers June 1990.

Division Three promotion 1985-6 (captain). Division Two champions 1986-7 (captain).

Rob Hindmarch had been captain of Sunderland as a teenager but was allowed to leave Roker Park on a free transfer. Arthur Cox moved in quickly, saying: "I would have signed Rob had I still been manager of Newcastle United in the First Division." Hindmarch was a magnificent capture. He was appointed captain in 1985 and led Derby brilliantly in their two promotions. Although not blessed with pace, he is tremendous in the air, solid on the ground and has moral as well as physical strength. When Mark Wright was signed, Hindmarch was left out after one game as his partner and was not recalled for almost six months. With Hindmarch back in, the Rams began to move towards safetly and Wright clearly appreciated his presence. At the end of the season, Cox spoke of Hindmarch as the backbone of the club: "A man's man." The mystery was that no other club had come in with an offer the Rams could not refuse while Hindmarch was playing in the Central League. When his contract was up, Hindmarch joined Wolverhampton Wanderers for £300,000 but he was right out of the picture in his second season at Molineux and did not make a senior appearance.

HINTON
Alan Thomas   *Outside-left*

Born: Wednesbury, 6 October 1942.
Career: Juniors, Wolverhampton Wanderers: professional October 1959. Nottingham Forest January 1964. Derby County September 1967. Borrowash Victoria August 1976. Dallas Tornado March 1977. Player/assistant coach, Vancouver Whitecaps, October 1977. Head coach, Tulsa Roughnecks, October 1978 to August 1979. Head coach, Seattle Sounders, November 1979 to January 1983. Head coach, Vancouver Whitecaps, April 1984. Head coach, Tacoma Stars, 1986 to 1990.
Division Two champions 1968-9. Division One champions 1971-2, 1974-5.

Alan Hinton had won three England caps, one with Wolverhamapton Wanderers and two with Nottingham Forest, before Brian Clough and Peter

Alan Hinton, Derby's leading scorer when they won the Championship in 1971-2.

Taylor signed him from the City Ground for £30,000 in September 1967. Some Forest committee men were heard to suggest that Derby would be asking for their money back but they were absolutely wrong. Hinton's ability to cross the ball from any position and with either foot amounted almost to genius. His explosive goals were a bonus. He was Derby's creator-in-chief as they won the Second and First Division titles in the space of four years as well as their acknowledged artist from free-kicks and corners. He had a short run in the 1974-5 Championship success, giving Derby a different shape at a time when they were beginning to lose their way, but played little in the next season after the tragic death of his son Matthew. He went into the North American Soccer League and set a new record for 'assists' in 1978, laying on 30 goals to beat the mark set by Pelé and George Best. He was a successful coach, going indoors after the collapse of the NASL. As Peter Taylor predicted, he was fully appreciated at Derby only after he had left.

HODGKINSON
William H.   *Centre-forward*

Career: Hinckley Town. Derby County March 1901. Hinckley Town July 1902. Derby County May 1903. Plymouth Argyle May 1904.

William Hodgkinson was as near to a regular centre-forward as Derby had in 1903-04, scoring nine times in 16 games, including a hat-trick against Sunderland. Despite his record, he was allowed to leave. His brother Albert, also on Derby's books without playing a senior game, was later capped for Wales while with Southampton.

HODGSON
William   *Outside-left*

Born: Govan, 9 July 1935.
Career: St Johnstone. Guildford City, loan, September 1956. Sheffield United May 1957. Leicester City September 1963. Derby County June 1965. Rotherham United, player-coach, September 1967. York City, player-coach, December 1967: temporary manager August 1968. Coach, Sheffield United, July 1970.

Billy Hodgson.

Billy Hodgson was almost 30 when Tim Ward signed him but he did a good job for Derby in his two years at the Baseball Ground, his 20 goals including a hat-trick against Middlesbrough.

HOFFMAN
Ernest Henry   *Goalkeeper*

Born: South Shields, 16 July 1892.
Career: Tottenham Hotspur during World War One. Hebburn Argyle. South Shields cs 1919. Derby County April 1923. Ashington August 1923. Darlington August 1924. Manager, Jarrow.

Played only once for Derby, in place of Ben Olney in the final match of 1922-3.

HOLMES
Samuel   *Inside-forward*

Career: Crich. Derby County November 1889.

Sam Holmes.

An inside-forward with an eye for goals in the early years of the Football League.

HOLYOAKE
James Ernest   *Full-back*

Career: Derby County January 1900. Ripley Town September 1902.

Deputised for Charlie Morris on one occasion in 1901-02.

HOOKS
Paul   *Midfield*

Born: Wallsend, 30 May 1959.
Career: Apprentice, Notts County: professional July 1977. Derby County March 1983. Mansfield Town, non-contract, August 1985. Boston United August 1985. Cotgrave Miners' Welfare 1987.

A player of considerable but, as far as Derby County were concerned, largely unfulfilled potential. He was in the Notts County team which gained

Paul Hooks.

promotion to the First Division in 1980-81 and, at his best, could glide past opponents. Hooks was, however, liable to disappear from games for long periods and the Rams did not get value for their £60,000 fee, especially when he left on a free transfer.

HOPE
John   *Inside-forward*

Born: Bishop Auckland, 10 June 1905.
Career: Crook Town. Derby County January 1927. Bury February 1930. Falkirk October 1932.

Division One runners-up 1929-30

Arrived from Crook Town with Ted Nelson at a joint fee of £100. Hope was given a few chances to replace Jimmy Gill but never established himself before moving to Bury for £1,250.

HOPEWELL
W.   *Centre-half*

Career: Grimsby Town. Derby County

September 1888. *Grimsby Town December 1888.*

Hopewell played in five matches during Derby County's first League season. All were lost, part of a club record run of eight consecutive League defeats. This was equalled in 1987-8 but was still intact after more than 100 years.

HOPKINS
William   *Full-back*

Career: Derby Junction. Derby County 1890. Ardwick cs 1891.

Hopkins began the 1890-91 season as full-back partner to Arthur Latham but was unable to consolidate his place.

HOPKINSON
Michael Edward *Midfield/full-back*

Born: Ambergate, 24 February 1942. Career: West End Boys Club. Juniors, Derby County: professional, June 1959. Mansfield Town July 1968. Port Vale July 1970. Boston United June 1971. Coach, Belper Town, November 1973: manager, January to September 1974. Coach, Burton Albion: assistant manager, November 1978.

Mick Hopkinson.

Mick Hopkinson established himself as a versatile player under Tim Ward. He played in more than 100 League games and a spectacular goal against Liverpool in October 1961 lived in the memory. He played in Brian Clough's first season before joining Mansfield Town for £5,500. A great trier, popular with the crowd but not quite up to the standards Clough was seeking.

HOUNSFIELD
Reginald Edward *Outside-right*

Career: Sheffield FC. Sheffield Wednesday March 1902. Derby County October 1903.

Reputed to be one of the fastest players

Jack Howe leads out the Rams, followed by Reg Harrison.

ever to appear for Derby County. He made good progress in 1903-04 but gave way to Jack Davis the following season.

HOWARD
E.   *Centre-half*

Career: Northampton Town. Derby County April 1899.

He deputised for Archie Goodall once, in December 1899.

HOWARD
Frederick Julian *Inside-forward*

Born: Long Eaton. Career: Stapleford Brookhill. Long

Eaton. Derby County May 1919. Gillingham July 1920.

One of several players brought in when League Football resumed after World War One, Howard joined Gillingham for their opening Third Division season.

HOWE
John Robert   *Left-back*

Born: West Hartlepool, 7 October 1915. Died: Hartlepool, 5 April 1987. Career: Hartlepools United June 1934. Derby County March 1936. Huddersfield Town October 1949. Player-

Jack Howe (extreme left) and Errington Keen watch as Rams goalkeeper Ken Scattergood dives towards the ball at The Den in February 1937, when a ground record crowd of 48,672 saw Millwall score a shock FA Cup win over Derby.

manager, King's Lynn, July 1951: manager to May 1953: player to May 1955. (Appointed player-manager Long Sutton United in August 1955 but did not take it up). Wisbech Town August 1955.

Division One runners-up 1935-6. FA Cup winners 1945-6.

Jack Howe was one of the best two-footed full-backs in Britain. Standing six-feet tall. Howe could kick a ball equally hard and accurately with either foot. Another George Jobey capture from the North-East, Howe made his debut as Derby were finishing eight points behind champions Sunderland and was a regular until the war when he joined the Cameron Highlanders and guested for Hearts, Falkirk, Aberdeen and St Mirren. He played for the Scottish League against the British Army and, after service in India, he was demobbed in time to earn an FA Cup winners' medal playing centre-half in the semi-final replay and left-back at Wembley. Howe never shirked a tackle, was totally dominant and took over the captaincy when Carter went to Hull in 1948. When he won the first of his three England caps it was considered long overdue. Howe, among Derby's greatest defenders, was one of the first professional sportsmen to wear contact lenses. He was over 40 before he ended his career with Wisbech Town.

HUGHES
Alan   *Outside-right*

Born: South Shields.
Career: Wigan Athletic. Chesterfield

May 1933. Derby County September 1934. Everton June 1935.

Hughes was one of a succession of understudies to Sammy Crooks and was in a similar position behind another England winger, Albert Geldard, when he joined Everton.

HUGHES
Gordon   *Outside-right*

Born: Washington, 19 June 1936.
Career: Tow Law Town. Newcastle United August 1956. Derby County August 1963. Lincoln City March 1968. Boston United March 1971.

Gordon Hughes was a small, stocky winger whose most obvious asset was his speed. He had played 143 senior games for Newcastle United before Tim Ward paid £10,000 for him, hoping he would increase the supply of chances for Bill Curry and Barry Hutchinson. Unfortunately, they were beginning to fade but Hughes gave Derby five enthusiastic seasons before Brian Clough sold him to Lincoln City for £5,000. In the season of transition when Clough and Peter Taylor arrived, Hughes helped Derby to their best League Cup run, reaching the semi-finals in which they lost to Leeds United. After succeeding Don Roby, Hughes was first choice in Ward's time and played with spirit and bustle in a team never good enough to be serious promotion candidates.

HUGHES
William   *Forward*

Born: Coatbridge, 30 December 1948.

Career: Coatbridge Juniors. Juniors Sunderland: professional February 1966. Derby County, loan, August 1977. Derby County September 1977. Leicester City December 1977. Carlisle United, loan, September 1979. San José Earthquakes April 1980.

Like his brother John, Billy Hughes was a Scottish international. His one appearance was as substitute against Sweden in April 1975. Hughes had a fine career with Sunderland. He was in their 1973 FA Cup Final team, epic winners over Leeds United, and in the side which won the Second Division in 1975-6. Colin Murphy brought him to Derby as an experienced forward and he was leading scorer when Tommy Docherty inexplicably sold him. Hughes was bitterly disappointed and his career never picked up again.

HUNT
Archibald   *Centre-forward*

Career: Bulwell United. Whitwick White Cross. Derby County August 1904. Walsall.

Archie Hunt had a good run in 1904-05 but managed only one goal.

HUNT
David   *Defender/midfield*

Born: Leicester, 17 April 1959.
Career: Apprentice, Derby County: professional May 1977. Notts County March 1978. Aston Villa July 1987. Mansfield Town June 1989. Burton Albion August 1991. Leicester United September 1991.

Billy Hughes, an FA Cup hero with Sunderland.

Gordon Hughes, 24 goals in 201 senior games for Derby.

David Hunt, sold for £40,000 when still a teenager.

David Hunt was still a teenager, with five League games behind him, when Notts County paid £40,000 for him. It was an excellent capture by Jimmy Sirrel as Hunt played in more than 300 League games for Notts and was ever-present when they were runners-up in the Second Division in 1980-81. Graham Taylor signed him for Aston Villa on a free transfer and he was a useful squad player in their 1987-8 promotion from Division Two.

HUNT
John
Wing-half

Career: Alvaston and Boulton September 1899. Derby Hill's Ivanhoe August 1900. Derby County March

1902. Ripley Athletic August 1902. Three games for Glossop in 1903-04. Derby County August 1905.

John Hunt, who played as an amateur, had two spells with Derby County but appeared in only five senior games.

HUNT
Ralph Arthur Robert *Centre-forward*

Born: Portsmouth, 14 August 1933. Died: Grantham, 17 December 1964. Career: Juniors. Portsmouth: professional August 1950. Bournemouth & Boscombe Athletic February 1954. Norwich City July 1955. Derby County August 1958. Grimsby Town July 1959. Swindon Town July 1961. Port Vale December 1961. Newport County July 1962. Chesterfield July 1964.

Ralph Hunt.

A strapping centre-forward, signed from Norwich City by Harry Storer for £4,200. Ralph Hunt's season at the Baseball Ground was one of his less

successful periods, for he scored 186 League goals for his nine clubs. He was with Chesterfield when, on the way back from watching a match at Peterborough, he was seriously injured in a car crash and died in the Grantham and Kesteven Hospital. His brother Dennis played for Gillingham and Brentford.

HUNTER
George Irwin *Goalkeeper*

Born: Troon, 29 August 1930. Died: Nottingham, 10 May 1990. Career: Glasgow Celtic. Derby County June 1954. Exeter City August 1955. Yiewsley July 1960. Darlington June 1961. Weymouth July 1962. Burton Albion July 1963. Lincoln City September 1965. Matlock Town August to September 1966.

George Hunter kept goal for Celtic when they beat Motherwell in the 1951 Scottish Cup Final but stayed with Derby County for only one season. After 14 games, he lost his place to Terry Webster and did not appear again until the last five games of the season in which the Rams dropped into the Third Division North for the first time.

HURST
William *Forward*

Career: Walker Celtic. Derby County September 1922. Queen's Park Rangers August 1923.

Cecil Potter made one of this periodic raids on the North-East to sign Hurst but he played only three senior games before moving on.

HUTCHINSON
James Barry *Inside-forward*

Born: Sheffield, 27 January 1936. Career: Amateur, Bolton Wanderers. Professional, Chesterfield, April 1953. Derby County July 1960. Weymouth July 1964. Lincoln City July 1965. Darlington February 1966. Halifax Town November 1966. Rochdale July 1967. Bangor City August 1968. Hyde United September 1968.

Barry Hutchinson joined Derby in a three-way deal. Chesterfield took Albert Mays and Roy Martin, plus £2,025. Hutchinson had an excellent scoring record with the Rams, averaging almost a goal every two games (57 in 116). He was at his best in partnership with Bill Curry and might have made a bigger name for himself in the game.

HUTCHISON
Duncan *Inside-forward*

Born: Kelty, Fife, 3 March 1903. Died: 1972. Career: Rosewell (Edinburgh). Dunfermline Athletic. Dundee United 1925. Newcastle United August 1929. Derby County March 1932. Hull City July 1934. Dundee United June 1935.

Newcastle United brought Hutchison from Scotland after he had shared in Dundee United's Second Division championship success in 1928-9. He joined Derby at the same time as Ralph Hann, in a joint deal, but was only one of several players scrapping for a regular inside-forward place. Later a director of Dundee United and there when the Rams played them in the Texaco Cup.

IMLACH
James John Stewart *Outside-left*

Born: Lossiemouth, 6 January 1932. Career: Lossiemouth United. Lossiemouth. Bury May 1952. Derby County May 1954. Nottingham Forest July 1955. Luton Town June 1960. Coventry City October 1960. Crystal Palace June 1962. Dover January 1965. Chelmsford City February 1965. Player-coach, Crystal Palace, February 1966. Youth coach, Notts County, March 1967. Assistant coach, Everton, 1969: first-team trainer, July 1972 to January 1976. Coach, Blackpool, June 1976 to August 1977. Coach, Bury, June 1978 to October 1979.

Stewart Imlach arrived at Derby in a three-way deal, with Cecil Law and Norman Nielson joining Bury. His year at the Baseball Ground was unsuccessful, the Rams sinking into the Third Division North, but he fared better with Nottingham Forest. He was in Forest's 1959 FA Cup Final victory over Luton Town and played four times for Scotland in 1957-8. His last two international appearances, against Yugoslavia and France, were in the 1958 World Cup Finals in Sweden.

JACKSON
James Herbert *Centre-forward*

Born: Bollington, 27 December 1897. Career: Bollington Cross. Macclesfield Town. Derby County amateur, December 1920: professional, December 1921. Bollington Cross 1922. Norwich City June 1923.

Jackson scored on his debut, against West Ham United on Christmas Eve 1921, as Derby County tried to rebuild following relegation to the Second Division. He did well for Norwich City but a broken leg in February 1927, shortened his career.

JAMES
Leighton *Outside-left*

Born: Llwchwyr, 16 February 1953. Career: Apprentice, Burnley: professional February 1970. Derby County November 1975. Queen's Park Rangers October 1977. Burnley September 1978 Swansea City May 1980. Sunderland January 1983. Bury August 1984. Newport County August 1985. Burnley July 1986: youth coach, June 1986. Youth coach, Bradford City, February

Duncan Hutchison.

Stewart Imlach, fared better with Forest.

Leighton James, a regular for Wales.

1990: acting-manager November to December 1991.

Leighton James became Derby's first £300,000 player when Dave Mackay signed him from Burnley. A regular in the Wales team, James played 13 times while with the Rams and reached 54 international appearances. He had tremendous ability, pace, two good feet, a teasing centre and an eye for goals. James was an early casualty of Tommy Doherty's management and, in October 1977, went to Queen's Park Rangers in an ill-fated exchange deal which brought Don Masson to Derby. The players were valued at £180,000 each but Masson, at 33, was nine years older than James. Within a year, Masson had joined Notts County for a second spell on a free transfer, so Derby had written off £300,000. James played only 33 games for Queen's Park Rangers before moving back to Burnley and then helped Swansea City to reach Division One for the first time. With a third spell at Burnley he appeared in 656 League games.

JARDINE
R.J. *Inside-left*

Career: Notts County 1888. Heanor Town. Derby County October 1889.

Heanor Town. Nottingham Forest 1889.

Jardine scored in his only game for Derby County, a 2-1 victory over champions Preston North End in October 1889. It was one of only four games Preston lost in the first two seasons of the Football League.

JEFFRIES
Alfred *Outside-right*

Born: Bishop Auckland, 21 September 1914.
Career: Norwich City August 1934. Bradford City May 1935. Derby County February 1937. Sheffield United June 1939.

Alf Jeffries was a talented winger, one of many through the 1930s whose opportunities were limited by the brilliance of Sammy Crooks. World War Two broke out when he was starting with Sheffield United.

JESSOP
Frederick Samuel *Half-back*

Born: Barrow Hill, 7 February.
Career: Barrow Hill. Staveley Works. Amateur, Derby County, January 1926: professional, March 1926. Sheffield

United December 1937. Atherstone Town 1945.
Division One runners-up 1935-6.

Freddie Jessop was essentially a wing-half but his versatility made him invaluable to Derby County in the 1930s as he played all across the half-back line, at inside-forward and at left-back. He was the kind of utility player regularly summoned to fill a gap and might have established himself more fully had he not suffered a broken leg in an FA Cup fifth round tie against Manchester City in 1932. A fierce tackler, he was with Sheffield United when they won the Second Division in 1938-9.

JOHNSON
Thomas *Forward*

Born: Newcastle upon Tyne, 15 January 1971.
Career: Trainee Notts County: professional January 1989. Derby County, loan, March 1992. Derby County March 1992.

Derby County's transfer record, £1.3 million for Paul Kitson, was only ten days old when Tommy Johnson's signing beat it. He made his debut on loan and the deal was completed the

Alf Jeffries, a talented winger who found Sammy Crooks barring his way.

Freddie Jessop.

Tommy Johnson, a record signing for Derby.

Roger Jones.

following week for £1,375,000. Johnson was developed by Notts County and made his debut as a 17-year-old before helping them to successive promotions from Third Division to First, both times through the play-offs. He scored in the two Wembley Finals. An England Under-21 international with both clubs.

JOHNSTON
John M.   *Centre-forward*

Career: Seaton Delaval. Derby County December 1923. Rotherham County May 1924.

Another Cecil Potter capture from the North-East, Johnston deputised once for Randolph Galloway in January 1924.

JONES
Norman Edward   *Inside-right*

Born: Liverpool.
Career: Walker Celtic 1919. Derby County May 1922. Gillingham June 1923.

Although born in Liverpool, Norman Jones was signed from non-League football in the North-East like many others in the early seasons after World War One. Released after one season.

JONES
Roger   *Goalkeeper*

Born: Upton-upon-Severn, 8 November 1946.
Career: Apprentice, Portsmouth: professional November 1964. Bourne-

mouth & Boscombe Athletic May 1965. Blackburn Rovers January 1970. Newcastle United March 1976. Stoke City February 1977. Derby County July 1980. Birmingham City, loan, February 1982. York City July 1982. Coach, Sunderland.

After Derby County had been relegated from the First Division in 1980, Colin Addison made a sound investment by signing Roger Jones from Stoke City for £20,000. Jones won an England Under-23 cap, against Hungary in 1968, while playing for Bournemouth and was Blackburn's goalkeeper when they won the Third Division in 1974-5. Shoulder and knee injuries hampered him at Newcastle but he earned another promotion, with Stoke from Division Two in 1978-9, before an outstanding first season with the Rams culminated in the Player of the Year award. Further promotion followed as captain of York City, runaway Fourth Division champions in 1983-4.

Jason Kavanagh, made a mark at right-back.

Errington Keen, 237 senior games and four England caps.

Denis Smith took Jones to Sunderland as coach and he was Malcolm Crosby's assistant when they reached the 1992 FA Cup Final.

JONES
Verdun A. *Inside-forward*

Career: Aston Villa September 1936. Derby County November 1937. Southend United May 1948.

A £550 signing from Aston Villa who played twice in 1937-8.

KAVANAGH
Jason Colin *Defender*

Born: Birmingham, 23 November 1971. Career: Schoolboy, Birmingham City. FA School of Excellence. Derby County trainee June 1988; professional December 1988.

Derby County had to pay compensation to Birmingham City, £50,000 by the time he had completed a handful of senior appearances, when they signed Jason Kavanagh from the School of Excellence. He and Steve Hayward were England Youth team regulars and Kavanagh made a mark in 1991-2 at right-back. Injuries to Mel Sage and Mark Patterson gave Kava-

nagh a chance which he accepted eagerly.

KEAY
Walter *Inside-forward/wing-forward*

Born: Whiteinch, August 1871. Died: Winchester, January 1943.
Career: Partick Thistle. Darlington. Derby County July 1893. Southampton St Mary's May 1895.

Watty Keay had two seasons with Derby County, playing on both wings as well as his more favoured inside-left position. He was enticed away by Southampton, who were unrestricted by the Football League's maximum wage rules and helped them to win three successive Southern League titles, in 1896-7, 1897-8 and 1898-9. He was later employed as a shipwright and coached Southampton Reserves in 1923.

KEEN
Errington Ridley Liddell
Left-half

Born: Walker-on-Tyne, 4 September 1910. Died: Fulham, July 1984.
Career: Nun's Moor. Newcastle United September 1927. Derby County December 1930. Chelmsford City May

1938. Player-manager, Hereford United, July 1939. Leeds United December 1945. Bacup Borough July 1946. Hull City, trial, 1946. Coached in Hong Kong.
Division One runners-up 1935-6.

Blond-haired wing-half 'Ike' Keen played just one game for his first club, Newcastle United. It was against the Rams and, two months later, he signed for Derby, George Jobey having seen enough to convince him that Keen, a powerful half-back, would do a useful job at the Baseball Ground. He quickly established himself as a fine player and in December 1932 won the first of his four England caps. Keen was one of four Rams stars — Crooks, Barker and Cooper were the others — to play for England against The Rest in a trial match in March 1933. In March 1936 Keen took a £650 benefit cheque for the Rams, but the business in which he invested it foundered and he found fhimself in Derby Bankruptcy Court. Keen was a fine attacking wing-half, but his defensive qualities were often questioned and against Leicester, in January 1938, he gave away a goal when trying to dribble his way out of trouble only a dozen yards from his goal-line. Shortly afterwards Tim Ward took his place and Keen went into the Southern League.

KEETLEY
Frank
Forward

Born: Derby, 23 March 1901. Died: Worcester, 13 January 1968.
Career: Victoria Ironworks. Derby County February 1921. Doncaster Rovers June 1926. Bradford City November 1929. Lincoln City May 1931. Margate July 1933. Player-manager, Worcester City.

Division Two promotion 1925-6.

Frank Keetley.

Frank Keetley was a member of an astonishing Derby family, one of nine brothers all signed at some stage by professional clubs — Albert, Arthur, Bill, Charlie, Harold, Jack, Joe and Tom being the others. Frank was the only one who played for Derby and one of four, along with Harold, Joe and Tom, who were with Doncaster Rovers. Frank was in and out of the Derby County team and moved to Doncaster after promotion to the First Division had been gained. In January, 1932, Frank completed a unique family double when he scored six goals in 21 minutes for Lincoln City against Halifax Town. In February 1929, Tom had scored six for Doncaster against Ashington, also in the Third Division North.

KELHAM
Harold J.
Wing-half

Career: Derby County April 1907.

Kelham stood in for George Richards for his solitary appearance, against Birmingham in April 1909.

KELLY
Daniel
Outside-right

Born: Blantyre.
Career: Hamilton Academical. Derby County February 1927. Torquay United

June 1928. York City July 1930. Doncaster Rovers June 1932. Dundalk cs 1935.

A £300 buy from Hamilton Academical, Kelly was understudy to two England wingers, George Thornewell and Sammy Crooks, during his 16 months at the Baseball Ground. He cost Torquay £150 when he moved.

KIDD
James
Goalkeeper

Career: Blackpool July 1910. Bolton Wanderers March 1915. Derby County September 1919. Fleetwood.

Jimmy Kidd spent three seasons at the Baseball Ground and was regarded as reserve to George Lawrence until Ben Olney was signed.

KIFFORD
John
Full-back

Born: Paisley, 1878.
Career: Paisley FC. Abercorn. Derby County June 1898. Bristol Rovers July 1900. West Bromwich Albion June 1901. Millwall May 1905. Player-manager, Carlisle United, cs 1906. Coventry City cs 1907.

Jack Kifford was a reserve full-back at Derby but was a regular in West Bromwich Albion's 1901-02 Second Division championship team. He retired in 1909 to join Fred Karno's Troupe.

KING
Francis Oliver
Goalkeeper

Born: Alnwick, 13 March 1917.
Career: Blyth Spartans. Everton October 1933. Derby County May 1937. Assistant trainer, Leicester City, 1954. Trainer, Luton Town, 1958.

Frank King played in the last three games of 1937-8, the fourth goalkeeper used by Derby County in that season. He cost £200 and his contract was cancelled in October 1938.

KING
Jeffrey
Midfield

Born: Fauldhouse, 9 November 1953.
Career: Fauldhouse United. Albion Rovers December 1972. Derby County April 1974. Notts County, loan, January 1976. Portsmouth, loan, March 1976. Walsall November 1977. Sheffield Wednesday August 1979. Sheffield United January 1982. Chesterfield October 1983. Stafford Rangers November 1983. Altrincham February 1984. Burton Albion August 1984. Kettering Town 1984. Torquay United August 1985.

Dave Mackay signed Jeff King from Albion Rovers for £7,000 and also took him to Walsall when he became manager at Fellows Park. A fiery midfield player, King produced some of his best football in Sheffield where he was involved in two promotions, from the Third Div-

Jeff King.

ision with Wednesday in 1979-80 and as Fourth Division champions with United in 1981-2.

KING
W. George
Outside-right

Career: Derby County January 1906.

Played in one match, against Woolwich Arsenal, in March 1906.

KINSEY
George
Left-half

Born: Burton upon Trent, June 1866. Died: January 1911.
Career: Burton Crusaders 1883. Burton Swifts 1885. Mitchell St George's 1888. Wolverhampton Wanderers August 1891. Aston Villa June 1894. Derby County May 1895. Notts County March 1897. Eastville Rovers cs 1897. Burton Swifts 1900. Burton Early Closing September 1902. Reinstated as amateur August 1904.

Division One runners-up 1895-6.

George Kinsey made his name with Wolverhampton Wanderers. He won

George Kinsey.

two England caps and was left-half in their 1893 FA Cup winning team but his transfer to Aston Villa worked out badly. Derby had faith in his ability and he was ever-present in his first season, when the Rams were runners-up in Division One and reached the FA Cup

semi-finals for the first time. He played twice more for England while with Derby, against Ireland and Wales in 1896. Kinsey was the first professional to be signed by Eastville Rovers, then in the Birmingham & District League.

KIRBY
John   *Goalkeeper*

Born: Overseal, 30 September 1910. Died: Derby, 15 June 1960.
Career: Newhall United. Derby County April 1929. Player-manager, Folkestone Town, August 1938.
Division One runners-up 1929-30, 1935-6.

Jack Kirby joined Derby in 1929, but he had to wait until 1932 before he could establish a regular first-team place, succeeding Harry Wilkes. Kirby had been in the habit of making the occasional glaring error when called upon to deputise and Rams fans began to think of him more for his faults than for his attributes. Yet when Wilkes suffered a knee injury and Kirby took over, he seized the opportunity with both hands and it was a save during the epic FA Cup quarter-final replay at Roker Park in March 1933 which finally won Kirby the fans' seal of approval. Seventy-five thousand fans were already roaring 'goal' when Sunderland's Davis fired for the

top corner of Kirby's net in the dying seconds of injury time. But Kirby was more than equal to it. He got to the ball and, instead of diverting it, he amazed the crowd by catching it cleanly. It was the save which put Derby into the semi-final and set the seal on Kirby's place. For the next few years he was rarely out of the side and might have won an England cap but for the brilliance of goalkeepers like Harry Hibbs and Ted Sagar. The nearest he came was an international trial match in March 1936.

KITSON
Paul   *Forward*

Born: Merton, 9 January 1971.
Career: Trainee Leicester City: professional December 1988. Derby County March 1992.

Brian Little gave Paul Kitson a regular place in the Leicester City team and he won England Under-21 caps as well as appearing for the Second Division representative side in Italy. Derby had watched Kitson since his Youth team days and moved in when Lionel Pickering's arrival on the board gave Arthur Cox spending power. Phil Gee and Ian Ormondroyd went to Leicester as part of a £1.3 million deal, with the Rams paying £800,000. The move worked well for both clubs and Kitson was quick to show his quality.

Jack Kirby, 191 League and Cup games for Derby.

Paul Kitson, valued at £1.3 million.

KNOWLES
Frederick Edmund *Centre-half*

Born: Derby, 21 June 1901.
Career: YMCA Derby. Derby County November 1921.

Knowles was plucked out of local football and given three Second Division games in 1921-2.

LAMB
Samuel *Outside-left*

Born: Alfreton.
Career: Alfreton Town. Derby County October 1905. Alfreton Town cs 1907. Sutton Town December 1907. Plymouth Argyle May 1909. Swindon Town May 1910. Millwall April 1913. Rotherham County August 1919. Caerphilly July 1920.

Sam Lamb was a talented winger from Alfreton Town, who became first choice as soon as he joined Derby County. In his second season, he was superceded by an even better outside-left from Alfreton, George Davis. Lamb returned to his native town but later had considerable success in the Southern League. He helped Swindon Town to win the title in 1910-11 and played for the Southern League against the Football League in 1912.

LAMPH
Thomas *Wing-half*

Born: Gateshead, 1893. Died: 24 February 1926.
Career: Pelaw United. Spennymoor. Leeds City May 1914. Manchester City October 1919. Derby County March 1920. Leeds United February 1921. Retired cs 1922.

Tom Lamph helped manager Jimmy Methven to stave off relegation in 1919-20 but was unable to hold his place the following season, when the Rams went down. He was one of the players, along with George Stephenson, sold by auction when Leeds City were expelled from the League in 1919.

LANE
Moses Alexander E. *Centre-forward*

Born: Willenhall, 17 February 1895. Died: Cannock, 1949.
Career: Willenhall Pickwick. Willenhall 1921. Birmingham April 1922. Derby County June 1924. Wellington Town May 1925. Worcester City October 1926. Walsall June 1927. Brierley Hill Alliance.

Mo Lane served in France and Italy during World War One and was decorated with the Military Medal. In his season at the Baseball Ground, Lane did not play in a League match. His only appearance was in an FA Cup defeat by Bradford City but he became a favourite at Walsall.

Tommy Lamph.

Moses Lane.

David Langan.

LANE
Sean Brendon *Outside-left*

Born: Bristol, 16 January 1964.
Career: Apprentice, Hereford United: professional March 1981. Derby County May 1983. Australia cs 1984.

Sean Lane had one senior appearance in November 1983 but made little impact in his year with Derby.

LANGAN
David Francis *Right-back*

Born: Dublin, 15 February 1957.
Career: Apprentice, Derby County: professional June 1976. Birmingham City July 1980. Oxford United August

1984. *Leicester City, loan, October 1987. AFC Bournemouth, loan, November 1987. AFC Bournemouth December 1987. Peterborough United August 1988.*

In February 1977, a new star arrived at the Baseball Ground although, a pleasant change in that era, he did not cost a massive fee. David Langan had been an industrious but unexceptional midfield player in the Central League when Colin Murphy gave him his debut at right-back against Leeds United. Langan, who had joined the Rams from school, was an immediate success and maintained his standards in a struggling team. He had pace, tackled well and went forward eagerly but became unsettled when, under Colin Addison, relegation from the First Division was increasingly likely. He refused to travel with the team for an FA Cup tie against Bristol City in 1980 then, when he did turn up, was sent home and fined. In an attempt to ease Derby's financial problems, Langan was sold to Birmingham for £350,000. By then Langan had won four of his 24 Republic of Ireland caps but, after two reasonably successful years, his career collapsed at Birmingham. A knee injury began his troubles and he was on crutches after a fourth operation when he cracked a vertebra. He missed all the 1983-4 season and Ron Saunders gave him a free transfer. Jim Smith, the man who had signed him for Birmingham, came to the rescue and offered him a trial with Oxford United, Langan not only proved his fitness but helped Oxford into the First Division and won back his international place in the most romantic story of 1984-5. He capped that with a fine Wembley display in Oxford's 1986 Milk Cup Final victory.

LANGLAND
A. *Inside-forward*

Played twice in 1889-90.

LATHAM
Arthur *Right-back*

Career: St Luke's. Derby Midland. Derby County 1886. Trainer, Derby County, 1891. Trainer, Norwich City, 1919.

Arthur Latham was one of the men who formed the basis of the Derby team when the Football League was inaugurated and was an automatic choice for the first two seasons. He became trainer after he had finished playing. Having made his last League appearance at full-back in November 1890, the non-arrival of goalkeeper Tom Harrison forced Latham to keep against Blackburn Rovers in April 1902. Latham was England trainer on several occasions and joined Frank Buckley at Norwich in that capacity in 1919.

LAW
Cecil Richard *Outside-left*

Born: Salisbury, Rhodesia, 10 March 1930.
Career: Alexandra FC, Salisbury. Derby County August 1951. Bury May 1954.

A bustling winger of considerable pace, Cecil Law was in a struggling Derby County team after being signed from Rhodesia. His control was not up to League standards and he moved to Bury as part of the deal that took Stewart Imlach to the Baseball Ground.

LAWRENCE
George Harold *Goalkeeper*

Born: Basford, 10 March 1889. Died: Derby, 1 March 1959.
Career: Manners Rangers. Ilkeston United 1909. Derby County May 1910. Bristol City September 1924. Lincoln City August 1925. Ilkeston United November 1926.
Division Two champions 1914-15.

After Jack Robinson's controversial move to New Brighton Tower in 1897, Derby County were well served by locally-produced goalkeepers for the next 25 years. Jack Fryer was succeeded by the England pair, Harry Maskrey and Ernald Scattergood, both from Ripley Athletic. Then came George Lawrence, a reluctant reserve to Scattergood to judge by the number of tansfer requests he put in. When Scattergood went to Bradford, Lawrence won a Second Division championship medal and stayed until after World War One, moving to Bristol City for £100 in 1924.

LEACH
Samuel *Left-back*

Career: Derby County May 1897. Heanor Town.

Leach stood in for Joe Leiper once, in March 1898.

LECKIE
Charles T. *Half-back*

Born: Alva.
Career: Dundee. Derby County December 1898.

For seven years, Leckie was close to being a fixture in the Derby County team without quite being first-choice. He provided such valuable cover, not only across the half-back line but in both full-back positions, that he was seldom idle for long. He was the type of player who provides constant competition and gives strength in depth.

Francis Lee and Roy McFarland parade the League Championship trophy in 1975.

Cecil Law.

Francis Lee, signed off with two goals against Ipswich.

George Lawrence.

LEE
Francis Henry   *Forward*

Born: Westhoughton, 29 April 1944.
Career: Juniors, Bolton Wanderers:
professional May 1961. Manchester City
October 1967. Derby County August
1974. Retired April 1976.

Division One champions 1974-5.

An inspired signing by Dave Mackay, Francis Lee created a lasting impact at the Baseball Ground. When he retired to look after his waste paper conversion business in Bolton, he left a host of friends as well as the feeling that he could have had at least one more season. After joining Manchester City, Lee won League, FA Cup, League Cup and European Cup-winners' Cup medals as well as 27 England caps. Mackay paid City £100,000 in August 1974, rightly thinking that Lee could score goals and, as important, give a good side extra aggression. Lee, full of bustle in oppos- ing penalty areas, promptly added another League Championship medal to his collection. His second season was marred by a brawl with Norman Hunter in the League match against Leeds United at Derby. Lee, sent off for allowing his lip to be cut by Hunter's fist, attacked the Leeds man on the way to the tunnel and was later suspended for four weeks. He went out with a typical flourish, scoring twice against Ipswich Town at Portman Road in the last two minutes of his 500th and final League game. He later became a race-horse trainer.

LEE
Jack   *Centre-forward*

Born: Sileby, 4 November 1920.
Career: Quorn Methodists. Leicester City, amateur, December 1940: professional, February 1941. Derby County June 1950. Coventry City November 1954.

When Stuart McMillan signed Leicester City's bustling centre-forward Jack Lee for £18,500, he promised the player that he would win a full England cap. Just four months later Lee scored in England's 4-1 win in Belfast, the last Derby player to be capped by England until Roy McFarland 20 years later. Despite his goal, it proved to be Lee's only international. McMillan and First Division football tempted Lee to the Baseball Ground after he had been

Jack Lee.

Leicester's leading League scorer in the first four seasons after World War Two and played for them in the 1949 FA Cup Final defeat by Wolverhampton Wanderers. On the way to Wembley, he scored four goals in a 5-5 draw with Luton Town. He was an instant hit at Derby and his 29 goals in 1950-51 included four in the 6-5 win over Sunderland and two hat-tricks. In the First Division, only Blackpool's England international Stan Mortensen scored more but a knee injury in the final home match meant a cartilage operation for Lee. Another followed and he was never again as effective, retiring after one season with Coventry. Lee was an accomplished cricketer, playing once for Leicestershire and dismissing Glamorgan opener Arnold Dyson with the first ball he sent down.

LEES
John   *Inside-forward*

Career: Sawley Rangers. Derby County August 1887.

Lees played intermittently in the first two seasons of the Football League.

LEIGH
Alfred Sidney   *Centre-forward*

Born: Derby.
Career: Osmaston. Derby County June 1914. Bristol Rovers July 1920.

Sid Leigh played only twice for Derby County but he was Bristol Rovers' leading scorer in their first two seasons in the Football League before injury ended his League career.

LEIPER
Joseph   *Left-back*

Born: Partick.
Career: Minerva. Partick Thistle. Derby County August 1892. Grimsby Town July 1900. Chesterfield July 1902. Partick Thistle May 1903. Motherwell. Hull City August 1904. Aberdare October 1904.
Division One runners-up 1895-6. FA Cup Finalists 1897-8.

Joe Leiper, known to the Derby players as 'Fossil', was one of the club's early giants after being signed from Scotland. He made his debut at right-back. in the only game Jimmy Methven missed in 1892-3, but from then he was Methven's regular partner for more than five years. In that period, the Rams were runners-up for the first time and Leiper played in three FA Cup semi-finals as well as the 1898 Final against Nottingham Forest. Described as 'dashing and fear-less', Leiper succeeded Jonathon Staley, who remained faithful, either as stand-in left-back or at left-half. And when Leiper was injured against Bury in September 1898, it was Staley who took over again. In his first season after leaving Derby, Leiper helped Grimsby Town to win the 1900-01 Second Division championship.

LEONARD
Henry Droxford   *Centre-forward*

Born: Sunderland, 1886. Died: 3 November 1951.
Career: Sunderland West End. Newcastle United November 1907. Grimsby Town May 1908. Middlesbrough March 1911. Derby County October 1911. Manchester United September 1920. Heanor Town June 1921.
Division Two champions 1911-12, 1914-15.

Harry Leonard was a high-scoring centre-forward who led the Rams' line with gusto before World War One. He was signed in 1911 to replace Alf Bentley and, coupled with Steve Bloomer's second spell at the Baseball Ground, made Derby a potent attacking force. He scored 17 League goals in the Second Division championship side, including four against Fulham, in his first winter. Two years later he missed three months of the season through injury when the Rams were relegated, but 12 months on he was celebrating promotion once more. Leonard ended 1914-15 second-highest scorer and continued to find the net regularly in wartime games. He was still at the Baseball Ground when League soccer resumed in 1919, but was by then a veteran and landlord of the Albert Vaults, Brook Street, Leonard went to Manchester United in 1920, having given Derby the best years of his football career.

LEONARD
John   *Outside-right*

Career: St Mirren. Derby County May 1897. Notts County March 1898.

Leonard scored in his only League game, against Sheffield Wednesday in February 1898, and also helped Derby County towards their first FA Cup Final with the only goal in the second round away win over Wolverhampton Wanderers.

LEUTY
Leon Harry   *Centre-half*

Born: Meole Brace, 23 October 1920. Died: Nottingham, 19 December 1955.
Career: Derby County, amateur, 1936. Notts County wartime guest. Derby Corinthians. Rolls-Royce. Derby County, amateur, August 1943: professional, May 1944. Bradford March 1950. Notts County September 1950.
FA Cup winners 1945-6.

No less a centre-forward than Tommy Lawton once nominated Leon Leuty as the most difficult centre-half to have faced him. In the late 1940s Leuty established his reputation as a calm, confident pivot who possessed more footballing skill than most First Division stoppers, although he never won a full England cap. He was unlucky to play at the same time as Stoke's Neil Franklin, one of England's greats until he went to Bogota to break free of the maximum

Joe Leiper.

Leon Leuty, 158 games for Derby and an FA Cup winners' medal.

Harry Leonard.

wage. Leuty, an impressive member of the 1946 FA Cup-winning team, captained England 'B' while at Derby and appeared in the unofficial Bolton Disaster Fund international. Like other senior players, he became unsettled by the arrival of Billy Steel and moved to Bradford for £20,000, then to Notts County for £25,000 six months later. He was still a young man when he died but he was unchallenged as Derby's best postwar centre-half until the emergence of Roy McFarland.

LEWIS
Alan Trevor *Left-back*

Born: Oxford, 19 August 1954.
Career: Apprentice, Derby County: professional May 1972. Peterborough United, loan, March 1974. Brighton & Hove Albion, loan, January 1975. Brighton & Hove Albion March 1975.

Sheffield Wednesday, loan, May 1977. Reading July 1977. Witney Town 1982.

Alan Lewis was a member of the England team which won the European Youth tournament in 1972 and 1973. Along with Steve Powell, another Youth international, Lewis made his debut in a Texaco Cup match against Stoke City in 1971. His career did not flourish in the same way as Powell's and his best days were in midfield with Reading, where he was in the 1978-9 Fourth Division championship team.

LEWIS
Michael *Midfield*

Born: Birmingham, 15 February 1965.
Career: Apprentice, West Bromwich Albion: professional February 1982. Derby County November 1984. Oxford United August 1988.
Division Three promotion 1985-6.

Mickey Lewis, helped to end a run of eight League defeats.

Mark Lillis, his goal took Derby nearer promotion.

Mickey Lewis won England Youth caps in 1982 and 1983 while with West Bromwich Albion. Arthur Cox signed him for £30,000 and he soon showed himself to be an enthusiastic and keen tackler. Lewis lost his place to Geraint Williams early in Derby County's Third Division promotion season and he did not play another League game until they were back in the First. In a struggling team early in 1988, Lewis made a useful contribution with his defensive qualities and helped to end a run of eight consecutive League defeats. He moved to Oxford United in part-exchange for Trevor Hebberd and was voted their Player of the Year for 1988-9.

LEWIS
Wilfred Leslie   *Inside-right*

Born: Swansea, 1 July 1905. Died: Swansea, 1976
Career: Baldwins Welfare. Swansea Amateurs. Swansea Town March 1924. Huddersfield Town November 1928. Derby County April 1931. Yeovil and Petters United July 1932. Bath City December 1933. Cardiff City August 1934. Haverfordwest August 1936.

Wilf Lewis was one of nine players to appear at inside-right for Derby County in 1931-2. He did not solve George Jobey's obvious problem, although he scored three times in his eight games. Lewis hit goals for Swansea Town and earned five Welsh caps while he was at Vetch Field. Another cap followed when

he joined Huddersfield Town but he made little impact in the First Division.

LIEVESLEY
Wilfred   *Inside-forward*

Born: Staveley, 6 October 1902.
Career: Staveley Old Boys. Derby County May 1920. Manchester United October 1922. Exeter City August 1923. Wigan Borough May 1928. Cardiff City May 1929.

Wilf Lievesley's solitary appearance came in September 1920, one of 32 players used in the relegation season. He built a solid career in the lower divisions with Exeter City and Wigan Borough. He was part of a football family. Joseph Lievesley had three sons, Denis, Leslie and Horace: Wilfred and Ernest were cousins to them.

LILLIS
Mark Anthony *Forward/midfield*

Born: Manchester, 17 January 1960.
Career: Manchester Boys. Manchester City, schoolboy. Huddersfield Town July 1978. Manchester City June 1985. Derby County August 1986. Aston Villa September 1987. Scunthorpe United September 1989. Stockport County September 1991. Witton Albion August 1992.
Division Two champions 1986-7.

Mark Lillis was one of the stars of Huddersfield Town's Third Division promotion team in 1982-3 but had an unlucky year at the Baseball Ground.

He was ruled out with injured knee ligaments after three League games and by the time he was fit, Bobby Davison and Phil Gee had formed an effective partnership in attack. His only goal was vital, an Easter Monday winner against Bradford City which took Derby close to promotion. He was involved in another promotion when Aston Villa returned to Division One in 1987-8.

LINACRE
Henry James   *Goalkeeper*

Born: Aston upon Trent, 26 March 1881. Died: Nottingham, 11 May 1957. Career: Loughborough GS. Aston upon Trent. Draycott Mills. Derby County December 1898. Nottingham Forest August 1899.

Linacre played only twice for Derby County but like the Forman brothers, who also came from Aston upon Trent, made his name with Nottingham Forest and rose to international level. He played for England against Wales and Scotland in 1905 and won a Second Division championship medal with Forest in 1906-7. He was later a building contractor, in partnership with his brother-in-law Frank Forman.

LITTLE
Thomas   *Inside/outside-left*

Born: Dumfries, April 1872

Career: Derby County December 1892. Manchester City June 1894. Baltimore October 1894. Manchester City November 1894. Ashton North End November 1895. Wellingborough cs 1896. Luton Town August 1897. Swindon Town May 1898. Barnsley August 1899. Dumfries March 1900.

Tommy Little was John McMillan's regular partner on the left wing in the second half of 1892-3 but did not go on to establish himself.

LLOYD
Albert
Centre-half

Career: Ripley Athletic. Derby County December 1902.

Albert Lloyd's only senior appearance for Derby was in February 1904, when Ben Hall was rested between two FA Cup replays against Wolverhampton Wanderers.

LLOYD
George Henry
Half-back

Born: Derby.
Career: Derby County December 1900. New Brompton July 1903.

Lloyd provided cover across the half-back line and played in the FA Cup semi-final first replay against Sheffield United in 1902. He was later a director of Gillingham.

LONG
James
Forward

Career: Clyde. Grimsby Town February 1902. Reading May 1904. Derby County May 1906.

Jimmy Long joined a Derby County team struggling after the departure of Steve Bloomer. He was capable of playing in most forward positions and in 1906-7, when Derby lost their First Division place, was joint leading League scorer with George Davis.

LOVATT
John
Right-back

Born: Newcastle upon Tyne, 21 January 1962.
Career: Apprentice, Derby County: professional January 1980. Whitby Town August 1983. Guisborough Town.

Lovatt was a sound performer at Central League level. He played four times, twice as substitute, in the successful 1981-2 battle to stay in the Second Division.

LOWELL
Eric James
Inside-forward

Born: Cheadle, 8 March 1935.
Career: Juniors, Derby County: professional March 1952. Stoke City May 1955. Stafford Rangers September 1956.

Ted Lowell scored in his only game for Derby County, the last one in 1953-4.

LYLE
Robert C.
Centre-half

Career: Partick Thistle. Derby County May 1910.

With Ben Hall's Derby County career nearing an end, Lyle was given an opportunity in 1910-11 but did not suggest he would be a permanent replacement. The Rams signed Frank Buckley for 1911-12.

LYONS
James
Inside-right

Born: Hednesford, 27 September 1897.
Career: Hednesford Town. Derby County January 1920. Wrexham July 1925.

For three seasons, Jimmy Lyons was one of Derby County's most reliable scorers and hit all four goals in a

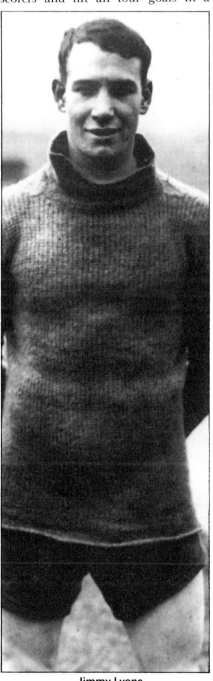

Jimmy Lyons.

Second Division match against Rotherham County in April 1922. The advent of Jackie Whitehouse and Harry Storer pushed him into the background but 33 goals in 86 senior games was a good return. Derby also suspended him permanently for what was described as insubordination.

McALLE
John Edward
Central defender

Born: Liverpool, 31 January 1950.
Career: Apprentice, Wolverhampton Wanderers: professional February 1967. Sheffield United August 1981. Derby County, loan, February 1982. Derby County April 1982. Harrisons August 1984.

John McAlle had a tremendous career with Wolverhampton Wanderers, making his debut as a teenager in 1967-8 and going on to play 407 League

John McAlle.

games. He helped them to win the Texaco Cup in 1971, the League Cup in 1974, the Second Division in 1976-7 and reach the UEFA Cup Final in 1971-2. When John Newman replaced Colin Addison as manager, he made four important signings, McAlle among them, aimed to keep Derby County in the Second Division. McAlle was also one of several players with whom Peter Taylor fell out during his spell as manager.

McALLISTER
Alexander
Centre-half

Born: Kilmarnock.
Career: Kilmarnock. Sunderland December 1896. Derby County June 1904.

Sandy McAllister was an ever-present

in Sunderland's 1901-2 League Championship season. He was essentially a defensive centre-half and supporters presented him with a piano and a gold watch when he scored his first goal. After eight years with Sunderland, McAllister spent one season at the Baseball Ground.

McANDREW
Robert   Left-back

Born: Derby, 6 April 1943.
Career: Derby Boys. Derby County, amateur, June 1958: professional, April 1960. Lockheed Leamington June 1965. Ilkeston Town September 1965. Loughborough United May 1970.

Bob McAndrew made only one senior appearance, standing in for Bobby Ferguson in April 1964, but he was a force at Midland League level.

McCAFFERY
Aiden   Central defender

Born: Newcastle upon Tyne, 30 August 1957.

Career: Apprentice, Newcastle United: professional January 1975. Derby County August 1978. Bristol Rovers August 1980. Bristol City February 1982. Bristol Rovers March 1982. Torquay United, loan, March 1985. Exeter City July 1985. Hartlepool United February 1987. Whitley Bay cs 1987. Player-coach, Carlisle United, January 1988: youth coach May 1990: acting manager March 1991: manager April 1991.

An England Youth international, McCaffery was signed by Tommy Docherty but given more opportunities by Colin Addison before joining Bristol Rovers for £70,000. He gave excellent value at Eastville and at one stage crossed to Bristol City, who had just reached agreement with eight players to cancel their contracts in order to reduce the wage bill and alleviate a grave financial crisis. They signed three new players, including McCaffery, but were ordered to return them to their former clubs in March 1982.

McCANN
John   Outside-left

Born: Govan, 23 July 1934.
Career: Bridgeton Waverley. Barnsley December 1955. Bristol City May 1959. Huddersfield Town October 1960. Derby County September 1962. Darlington August 1964. Chesterfield October 1964. Skegness Town August 1966. Lockheed Leamington June 1967.

When Tim Ward was manager of Barnsley, he bought John McCann from Scottish junior football for £500 and developed him into a Scotland 'B' player, against England in 1956-7. McCann cost £6,000 when Ward signed him a second time and he was Derby County's first choice at outside-left for two seasons before he was released.

McCLAREN
Stephen   Midfield

Born: Fulford, 3 May 1961.
Career: Apprentice, Hull City: profes-

Aiden McCaffery.

Johnny McCann, signed for a second time by Tim Ward.

sional April 1979. Derby County August 1985. Lincoln City, loan, February 1987. Bristol City February 1988. Oxford United August 1989.

Division Three promotion 1985-6.

Steve McClaren was in Hull City's Third Division promotion team in 1984-5 and Derby County hoped for a repeat when they paid £70,000, a fee set by tribunal, for him. McClaren began promisingly but was injured against Rotherham United. Arthur Cox bought John Gregory and McClaren was unable to re-establish himself before joining Bristol City for £50,000. When he moved to Oxford, McClaren also coached the Reserves.

McCORD
Brian John *Midfield*

Born: Derby, 24 August 1969.
Career: Apprentice, Derby County: professional June 1987. Barnsley, loan, November 1989. Barnsley March 1990. Mansfield Town, loan, August 1992.

McCord rose through Derby Boys and first joined Derby as an associate school-boy. McCord made his senior debut as substitute in a Simod Cup match against Birmingham City in November 1987 and scored one of the goals which put Derby through. His first three senior games were in different competitions, Simod Cup, League and FA Cup, but there was a gap

of almost two years before he appeared again. Three months after completing a loan with Barnsley, he joined them for £80,000.

McCORMICK
Harry *Outside-left*

Born: Coleraine, 10 January 1924.
Career: Coleraine. Derby County November 1946. Everton July 1948. Coleraine September 1949.

A tiny outside-left with a few tricks. He returned to Northern Ireland after brief spells with Derby County and Everton.

McCULLOCH
David *Centre-forward*

Born: Hamilton, 5 October 1911. Died: Hamilton, May 1979.
Career: Hamilton Amateurs. Shotts United. Third Lanark 1932. Heart of Midlothian June 1934. Brentford December 1935. Derby County October 1938. Leicester City July 1946. Bath City December 1946. Player-coach, Waterford, August 1949. Player-manager, Alloa Athletic July 1951 to August 1952.

Dave McCulloch was a strong centre-forward, particularly powerful in the air. He made his name with Hearts, where he won the first of his seven Scottish caps, and Brentford paid

Dave McCulloch.

Steve McClaren.

Brian McCord.

Harry McCormick.

£6,000 for him. His goals helped to keep Brentford in the First Division and he scored four against Derby County in May 1936. George Jobey paid a club record £9,500 for McCulloch and he played his last two games for Scotland, against Wales and Hungary, while at the Baseball Ground. He was part of an all-international forward line at Derby, with Crooks, Astley, Dix and Duncan but World War Two stifled McCulloch's career, although he scored five against Mansfield Town, in a wartime League match in January 1943.

MacDONALD
William James   *Inside-left*

Born: Inverness.
Career: Dundee. Derby County December 1898. Dundee June 1900.
FA Cup Finalists 1898-9.

The transfer of Jimmy Stevenson to Newcastle United left Derby County with an inside-left problem in 1898-9. They played Tom Arkesden there for two months but put Mac-Donald in as soon as he was signed from Dundee. MacDonald played in the FA Cup Final defeat by Sheffield United but was less prominent the following season and returned to Scotland.

McDONNELL
Martin   *Centre-half*

Born: Newton-le-Willows, 27 April 1924. Died: Coventry, 13 April 1988.
Career: Everton August 1942. Southport August 1946. Birmingham City May 1947. Coventry City October 1949. Derby County July 1955. Crewe Alexandra July 1958.
Division Three North champions 1956-7.

Harry Storer had great faith in Martin McDonnell, signing him for Bir-

Martin McDonnell.

mingham, Coventry and Derby. Storer took over at the Baseball Ground when Derby were in the Third Division North for the first time and started the rebuilding process with two experienced players he knew well, McDonnell and Paddy Ryan. His trust was not misplaced for whether at centre-half or

right-back, McDonnell set a tremendous example of fitness and enthusiasm, giving Storer great service for three years.

MacDOUGALL
Alexander Lindsay   *Right-half*

Born: Motherwell.
Career: Wishaw Juniors. Wolverhampton Wanderers February 1925. Derby County August 1928.

MacDougall played twice in 1928-9 when Johnny McIntyre was out of action.

McFARLAND
Roy Leslie   *Centre-half*

Born: Liverpool, 5 April 1948.
Career: Edge Hill Boys Club. Tranmere Rovers July 1966. Derby County August 1967. Player-manager, Bradford City, May 1981. Assistant manager, Derby County, November 1982: registered as player August 1983; caretaker manager, April 1984; assistant manager, June 1984.
Division Two champions 1968-9. Division One Champions 1971-2 (captain), 1974-5.

Brian Clough and Peter Taylor had seen Roy McFarland playing for Tranmere Rovers when they were in charge of Hartlepool and made him their second signing at Derby. He was then 19 and had been snatched from under the noses of Liverpool, the team he supported. For less than £25,000, Clough and Taylor bought a player who, they felt sure, would develop into the best centre-half in England. With Dave Mackay alongside him to speed up his maturing process in 1968-9, McFarland was a key-figure in the team which romped away with the Second Division title. He made his England debut in Malta in February 1971, and led Derby to the 1971-2 League Championship. McFarland had the football

Rams' squad with the League Championship trophy, won in 1974-5 for the second time in the club's history. Back row (left to right): Des Anderson (assistant manager), Webster, Daniel, Todd, Boulton, Moseley, Bourne, Powell, Thomas, Newton, Hector, Gordon Guthrie (physiotherapist). Front row: Lee, George, Rioch, McFarland, Dave Mackay (manager), Gemmill, Nish, Davies, Hinton.

Roy McFarland, one of the all-time greats, made 530 senior appearances for the Rams.

Shilton. Sadly for McFarland, the best part of his playing career came first and, in a declining side, he was increasingly susceptible to injuries. He became player-manager of Bradford City, and promptly led them to promotion from Division Four in 1981-2 before returning to Derby in controversial circumstances. He played a few matches when he was team manager under Taylor in the first part of the sad 1983-4 season. At his peak, he was one of Derby's all-time greats, skilful, consistent and ruthless; a superb professional and one of England's best post-war defenders.

McGILL
James   *Inside-forward*
Born: Kilsyth, 10 March 1926.
Career: Bury December 1945. Derby County March 1947. Kilmarnock October 1949. Berwick Rangers January 1951.

Jimmy McGill.

After eight games at inside-forward or on the left-wing, Jimmy McGill joined Kilmarnock in part-exchange for Hughie McLaren.

McGOVERN
John Prescott   *Midfield*
Born: Montrose, 28 October 1949.
Career: Apprentice, Hartlepools United: professional May 1967. Derby County September 1968. Leeds United August 1974. Nottingham Forest February 1975. Player-manager, Bolton Wanderers, June 1982 to January 1985. Horwich RMI February 1985. Assistant manager, Chorley, December 1989:

world at his feet, although he suffered a black week in 1973 when Clough and Taylor resigned and England were knocked out of the World Cup in the qualifying stages because they were unable to beat Poland at Wembley. It was also at Wembley, in May 1974, that McFarland sustained the severe Achilles tendon injury which was to keep him out of all but the last four games in the 1974-5 Championship triumph. He was able to regain his England place briefly and his 28 appearances set a record for a Rams player, passing Alan Durban's 27 for Wales but later overtaken by Peter

manager March 1990. Assistant manager Plymouth Argyle March 1992.
Division Two champions 1968-9. Division One champions 1971-2.

John McGovern's headmaster was reluctant to allow him to join Hartlepools United from a rugby-playing grammar school. Even then, however, McGovern was his own man, showing the strength of character which he needed to sustain him through a career in which success was never matched by whole-hearted appreciation from the stands and terraces. His total dedication to the team effort tended to mask skill and a lovely touch on the ball but, above all others, Brian Clough and Peter Taylor appreciated his value. He followed Clough from Hartlepools to Derby for £7,500, then to Leeds and Nottingham Forest, whom he captained to two European Cup successes as he reached his peak. McGovern looked frail, but he was as tough physically as he was mentally. He oiled

the midfield wheels in Derby's first League Championship and, after sharing Clough's unhappy experiences at Leeds, led Forest to their first Championship in 1977-8. He was self-effacing, closing down the opposition's key man and keeping his own side ticking by pushing around simple passes. He was an intelligent player, accepting his own limitations and devoting himself to the needs of the his team, an approach he continued as manager of Bolton Wanderers before he fell victim to internal politics. He played briefly for Horwich RMI while waiting for another job in the League but it was seven years, including a period in the Canaries, before Peter Shilton took him to Plymouth.

McINTYRE
John McMutrie   *Right-half*
Born: Glasgow, 19 October 1898. Died: Derby, 7 June 1974.
Career: Perthshire (Glasgow Junior

League). Stenhousemuir 1918. Derby County June 1921. Chesterfield December 1931. Retired 1933. Derby County 'A' team coach/scout, 1944: assistant manager, November 1953; scout to May 1960.
Division Two promotion 1925-6. Division One runners-up 1929-30 (captain).

Johnny McIntyre cost the Rams no more than a £10 signing-on fee when he came from Stenhousemuir as an inside-forward. Seldom has a football club spent a tenner more wisely and McIntyre settled down to become a key member of the Rams side for more than a decade. He made his debut against Blackpool on 27 August 1921 and scored in the Rams' 4-2 defeat at Bloomfield Road. He was also tried at outside-left, but eventually found his true position at right-half. It was there that he became a regular, although injury dogged his career and but for that ill-luck he would have played many more games. McIntyre was a

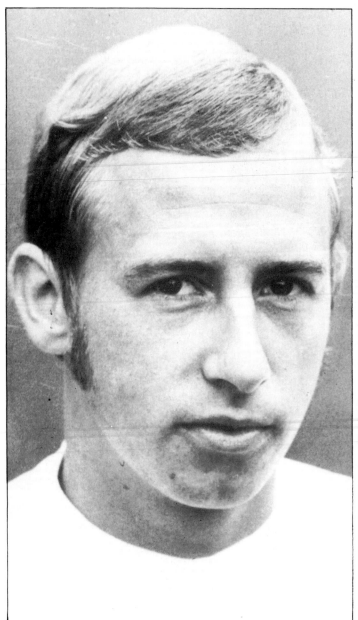

John McGovern, 237 games for Derby but never fully appreciated.   **Johnny McIntyre, 369 League and Cup appearances.**

player of polish, precision and determination, unchallenged in his position until Jack Nicholas took over.

MACKAY
David Craig *Wing-half*

Born: Edinburgh, 14 November 1934. Career: Slateford Athletic. Newtongrange Star. Heart of Midlothian April 1952. Tottenham Hotspur March 1959. Derby County July 1968. Swindon Town May 1971: player-manager, November 1971. Manager, Nottingham Forest, November 1972. Manager, Derby County, October 1973 to November 1976. Manager, Walsall, March 1977. Manager, Al-Arabi, Kuwait, August 1978. Manager, Alba Shabab, Dubai, 1986. Manager, Doncaster Rovers, December 1987 to March 1989. General manager Birmingham City, April 1989 to January 1991. Coach, Zamalek, September 1991.

Division Two champions 1968-9 (captain).

For three unforgettable seasons. Dave Mackay conducted a master class at the Baseball Ground. He was already a legend in two countries before he joined Derby County. In five seasons with Heart of Midlothian, Mackay won Scottish League, Cup and League Cup winners' medals before Bill Nicholson signed him for Tottenham Hotspur. With them, he was in the first team this century to win the League and FA Cup double in 1960-61, helped to retain the FA Cup the next year and led Spurs to a third FA Cup victory in 1967 after twice breaking his left leg. When Brian Clough announced that he had signed Mackay for £5,000, many Derby people could not grasp it fully until they had seen him in a Rams shirt. Clough later called that: "The best day's work of my life." Mackay, the inspiration of Tottenham's midfield, was to patrol at the back, tell the young players where to go and what to do, tidy up the loose ends, and, most important, lead. At the time he was the highest paid player in the League and was worth every penny because he was a natural captain. He was supremely skilful, a lovely kicker of the ball however it came to him, and he inspired Derby. They raced away with the Second Division championship in 1968-9 and Mackay was joint Footballer of the Year with Manchester City's Tony Book. He then proved that, in his mid-30s, he remained a force in the First Division. He finished at Derby in 1970-71 with a full house of 42 League appearances for the first time in his career. Only one mystery persists about his career — why he played for Scotland on only 22 occasions. He would have been a great player in any era and returned as manager to lead the Rams to their second Championship.

McKELLAR
David *Goalkeeper*

Born: Ardrossan, 22 May 1956. Career: Apprentice, Ipswich Town: professional March 1974. Colchester United, loan, September 1974. Peterborough United, loan, December 1975. Ardrossan Winton Rovers. Derby

Dave Mackay, spent three unforgettable seasons at the Baseball Ground.

David McKellar.

County March 1978. Brentford, loan, September 1980. Brentford October 1980. Hong Kong FC April 1983. Carlisle United August 1983. Hibernian August 1985. Manchester City, loan, December 1985. Newcastle United, loan, February 1986. Hamilton Academical July 1986. Dunfermline Athletic January 1988. Hartlepool United, loan, August 1988. Carlisle United, loan, October 1988. Carlisle United November 1988. Kilmarnock March 1990. Glasgow Rangers August 1991.

Tommy Docherty signed David McKellar for £2,500. McKellar shared the goalkeeping duties with John Middleton for two seasons before joining Brentford for £25,000. He had good days without reaching a consistent level but proved remarkably durable, with a string of clubs.

MACKEN
Anthony   Midfield
Born: Dublin, 30 July 1950.
Career: Waterford. Derby County August 1974. Portsmouth, loan, November 1975 and February 1976. Washington Diplomats, loan April 1976 and May 1977. Dallas Tornado July 1977. Walsall October 1977. Waterford 1982. Player-manager Drogheda United. Home Farm 1987.

Tony Macken joined Derby County for £30,000 and provided sound cover in midfield. He was capped for the Republic of Ireland, one of a Derby County record number of nine players

Tony Macken.

to appear in international matches in 1976-7. Dave Mackay signed him a second time, for Walsall. As a defender, he gave excellent value for the £10,000 fee for five years at Fellows Park before returning to Ireland.

McLACHLAN
James   Inside-forward
Career: Vale of Leven. Derby County cs 1890. Notts County September 1893. Derby County September 1894. Ilkeston Town May 1895.

Jimmy McLachlan was an automatic choice in his first two seasons with Derby County, slotting in after the departure of Sandy Higgins. In his second spell with Derby, he played most of his games on the right-wing.

McLACHLAN
Stephen   Wing-half
Born: Kirkudbright, 19 September 1918. Died: Kircudbright July 1990.
Career: Dalbeatie. Derby County March 1938. Kilmarnock June 1953.

A faithful reserve who spent 15 years at the Baseball Ground without ever making himself an undisputed first-choice. Derby County tended to turn to McLachan only when they were in

Steve McLachlan.

trouble and his experience was valuable. Always one of the toughest men on Derby's books.

McLAREN
Hugh   Outside-left
Born: Hamilton, 24 June 1926. Died: Derby, 8 December 1965.
Career: Kilmarnock. Derby County October 1949. Nottingham Forest January 1954. Walsall July 1955. Burton Albion July 1956. Gresley Rovers June 1957.

Hugh McLaren cost Derby £7,000 and replaced Frank Broome, who left for Notts County the same month. McLaren instantly achieved an ambition by partnering his idol, Billy Steel. He was speedy and had fine close ball control, although some critics felt that he was inclined to be a shade overelaborate. A hard shot in either foot made him especially dangerous and although he played in a Derby side which was largely on the decline, he enjoyed a superb scoring rate for a winger, 56 goals in 131 senior games. Although inclined to be erratic, McLaren was justifiably a favourite at the Baseball Ground but he did not stay long with Nottingham Forest or Walsall, ending his career by playing three seasons for Gresley Rovers.

MacLAREN
Ross   Defender
Born: Edinburgh, 14 April 1962.
Career: Juniors, Glasgow Rangers. Shrewsbury Town August 1980. Derby County July 1985. Swindon Town August 1988.
Division Three promotion 1985-6.
Division Two champions 1986-7.

Chic Bates, then manager of Shrewsbury Town, was furious when an independent tribunal fixed a fee of £67,500 for Ross MacLaren. "We have lost a good player at less than his value," said Bates. "Where can I find a replacement for that kind of money?" MacLaren made an immediate impact at the Baseball Ground as partner to Rob Hindmarch, with his firm tackling and the certainty of his kicking. Supporters elected him Player of the Year after the Third Division promotion and MacLaren, ever-present for his first two League seasons, was as influential when the Rams won the Second Division the following year. He lost his place in the centre of defence in the First Division but was never far from the squad and did good work at right-back for four months. Unable to find a guarantee of first-team football at Derby, MacLaren joined Swindon Town for £150,000, the fee again being set by tribunal and later adjusted upwards, by £25,000 plus interest, after disciplinary action against Swindon, who had not revealed all their payments to him.

McLAVERTY
Bernard   *Half-back*

Born: Chester Moor, 15 March 1898.
Died: Duffield, 24 December 1952.
Career: Chester Moor. Leadgate Park.
Durham City December 1919. Derby
County May 1920. Norwich City Jan-
uary 1928. Heanor Town December
1932.
Division Two promotion 1925-6.

When Derby County were struggling
in the early seasons after World War
One, much of their scouting was
concentrated in the North-East. Bernard McLaverty was one success from
this activity, playing more than 100
games for the Rams. He always faced
stiff competition for the half-back
positions and played only four times
when Derby were promoted in
1925-6. He did, however, have a big part
in re-establishing the Rams as a First
Division club and scored his only goal
against Tottenham Hotspur in October
1926. He was later a licensee in
Duffield.

McMILLAN
John Stuart   *Inside-left*

Born: Port Glasgow, 16 February 1871.
Died: Derby, 4 November 1941.
Career: Port Glasgow Athletic. St
Bernards cs 1890. Derby County
December 1890. Leicester Fosse May
1896. Small Heath January 1901.
Bradford City May 1903. Glossop May
1906: trainer 1908. Trainer, Bir-
mingham, August 1909. Manager,
Gillingham, July 1920 to August 1923.
Division One runners-up 1895-6.

Derby County made an important
signing when they engaged Johnny
McMillan from the Edinburgh club St
Bernards, a source which was to
produce Jimmy Methven the following

Ross MacLaren.   **Bernard McLaverty.**

John McMillan.   **Hugh McLaren, achieved an ambition by playing alongside Billy Steel.**

year. McMillan added class on the left of the attack, whether at inside-forward or on the wing, and scored 50 senior goals for the Rams, including five in a 9-0 victory over Wolverhampton Wanderers in his seventh League game. He was a front-line Derby player until Jimmy Stevenson was signed. He was Bradford City's captain when they entered the League in 1903, elected by the players, and managed Gillingham before becoming a Derby licensee. Father of Stuart McMillan.

McMILLAN
Stuart Thomas   *Outside-right*

Born: Leicester, 17 September 1896. Died: Ashbourne, 27 September 1963. Career: Derby County December 1914. War service with Derbyshire Yeomanry. Chelsea cs 1919. Gillingham March 1921. Wolverhampton Wanderers June 1922. Bradford City May 1924. Nottingham Forest June 1927. Clapton Orient August 1928. Manager, Derby County, January 1946 to November 1953.

Division Two champions 1914-15.

Stuart McMillan played once for Derby County, standing in for Billy Grimes in January 1915, but earned a unique place in the club's history as manager of the 1946 FA Cup winning team. Under George Jobey, one of his predecessors as manager of Derby, McMillan was involved in Wolverhampton Wanderers' Third Division North championship in 1923-4. He played four first-class cricket matches for Derbyshire in the early 1920s.

McMINN
Kevin Clifton   *Midfield*

Born: Castle Douglas, 28 September 1962. Career: Glenafton Athletic. Queen of the South November 1982. Glasgow Rangers October 1984. Seville January 1987. Derby County February 1988.

Arthur Cox chased Ted McMinn for five years before signing him for £300,000 from Seville and was rewarded by seeing him become one of Derby's most popular players. McMinn was close to the Scotland side when, in November 1989, he severely damaged knee ligaments in a victory over Tottenham Hotspur at White Hart Lane. It was 14 months before he played again but, after a tentative return in the 1990-91 relegation season, McMinn was back to his colourful best the following season and was voted Derby's Player of the Year. Tall for a winger, McMinn loves to take on opponents, although his scoring record was poor. Cox first chased McMinn, then with Queen of the South, when he was manager of Newcastle United but Rangers had more appeal. After joining Derby, Cox had two more tries and, on the second occasion, McMinn

Ted McMinn, lit up many a game at the Baseball Ground.

followed his Rangers manager Jock Wallace, son of a former Derby goalkeeper, to Spain. The persistent Cox at last landed his man in February 1988 and ended a depressing period in which Robert Maxwell, squabbling with the League over his proposed purchase of Watford, put a block on transfers.

MACONNACHIE
Alexander   *Forward*

Career: Ashfield. Derby County May 1897. Notts County March 1898. Third Lanark 1901. Ripley Athletic August 1902. Ilkeston United. Alfreton Town.

Maconnachie had a productive season at Derby before joining Notts County. He began at inside-left but, after Jimmy Stevenson had been signed, appeared on the right wing and at centre-forward. He missed out on Derby's first FA Cup Final.

McQUEEN
Hugh   *Outside-left*

Born: Harthill, 1 October 1873. Died: Norwich, 8 April 1944. Career: Leith Athletic 1890. Liverpool October 1892. Derby County July 1895. Queen's Park Rangers May 1901. Gainsborough Trinity July 1902. Player-trainer, Fulham, October 1903. Trainer, Norwich City.

Division One runners-up 1895-6. FA Cup Finalists 1897-8.

Hugh McQueen signed for Liverpool at the same time as his brother Matt, who was later manager. They were among a team of eight Liverpool 'Macs' and while at Anfield, Hugh narrowly escaped drowning when he dived off the springboard at Southport baths where the team was training. He was hauled out only with difficulty and

Hugh McQueen.

admitted later that he could not swim. Derby County signed him after he had been in the Liverpool team which won the Second Division in 1893-4, their opening League season, and the fans at the Rams' new home, the Baseball Ground, soon came to appreciate the Scotsman's speed and pinpoint accuracy. Two of the Rams' goals in the 1898 FA Cup semi-final came from McQueen centres. After that year's Final, McQueen was awarded a gold medal by the magazine *Football Chat* for being the best player on the losing side.

McQUILLAN
Dennis   *Outside-right*

Born: Derby, 16 March 1934.
Career: Derby Boys. Juniors, Derby County: professional March 1951. Aldershot July 1956. Luton Town March 1957. Banbury Spencer July 1957. Long Eaton United June 1958: joint player-manager, with Reg Harrison, April 1960 to August 1961.

McQuillan made his debut as a teenager but, like other young players at the time, had to make his way in a team which was constantly struggling.

MALLOCH
Gavin Cooper   *Left-half*

Born: Glasgow, 18 July 1905. Died: Scotland, 1974.
Career: Benburb. Derby County January 1927. Sheffield Wednesday December 1931. Millwall August 1936. Barrow August 1937.
Division One runners-up 1929-30.

Gavin Malloch cost £140 when George Jobey signed him from the Glasgow junior club Benburb and he was carefully nurtured in the Reserves until Harry Storer joined Burnley in 1929. From then until the arrival of Ike Keen, Malloch was Derby County's first choice at left-half and became a polished First Division player. He also excelled as an eccentric dancer and a contemporary report tells how he astonished the Danes on a Derby tour with 'Weird but graceful gyrations'. He was part of the traffic between the Rams and Sheffield Wednesday, following Jackie Whitehouse, Tommy Davison and George Stephenson to Hillsborough. His father Jock had won a League Championship medal with Wednesday in 1902-03.

MANN
Herbert Henry   *Outside-left*

Born: Nuneaton, 30 December 1907.
Career: Griff Colliery. Derby County February 1926. Grantham August 1929. Manchester United May 1931. Ripley Town November 1933.

Bert Mann played six senior games in 1928-9 before being released. He was later a butcher in Derby and in 1958 was elected president of the Derby and District Master Butchers' Association.

MARSHALL
Joseph   *Goalkeeper*

Born: Mosborough, 25 July 1862. Died: Derby, 15 January 1913.
Career: Staveley. Derby County 1887. Derby Junction 1889.

Derby County's first Football League goalkeeper, the most frequently used of the four called upon in the opening season. He played first-class cricket for Derbyshire in 1887.

MARTIN
Blakey   *Right-half*

Born: Bradford.
Career: Castleford 1913. Glossop July 1914. Derby County August 1919. Southend United August 1920. Llanelli cs 1922.

Blakey Martin had a distinguished record in World War One. He served in France and Gallipoli with the Royal Marines and was awarded the Military Medal and bar. He was signed by Jimmy Methven after the war, then helped Southend in their opening Third Division season.

MARTIN
Robert   *Left-back*

Born: Kilwinning, 16 May 1929.
Career: Kilwinning Rangers. Birmingham City March 1950. Derby County March 1956. Chesterfield July 1960. Burton Albion July 1961. Long Eaton United July 1963.
Division Three North champions 1956-7.

Roy Martin, as he was always known, was an excellent, composed full-back. Harry Storer went back to one of his old clubs, Birmingham City, to sign Martin, who played a vital part in the Third Division North championship before he was ruled out by a broken leg. He was never quite such a force again and moved to Chesterfield with Albert Mays in the deal which involved Barry Hutchinson. He retired in May 1966, after three Midland League seasons with Long Eaton United.

MASKREY
Harry Mart   *Goalkeeper*

Born: Unstone, nr Dronfield, 8 October 1880. Died: Derby, 21 April 1927.
Career: Ripley Athletic. Derby County December 1902. Bradford City October 1909. Ripley Town May 1911. Mansfield Mechanics July 1913. Celanese FC. Derby County September 1920. Burton All Saints August 1921.

Derbyshire has long had a tradition of producing top-class goalkeepers, from the Rams' Robinson and Fryer, and Sheffield United's 'Fatty' Foulke, down the years, to Ernald Scattergood of Derby and Sam Hardy of Liverpool and Villa, and, more recently, West Brom's John Osborne and the great Gordon Banks. Harry Maskrey is most worthy

Harry Maskrey.

of a place in that gallery of great goalkeepers. Soon after he succeeded Jack Fryer he was described as having 'all the collier's contempt for hard knocks'. Maskrey, while not as tall as the man he replaced, was still quite a size. He stood over 6ft tall and measured 77ins from finger-tip to finger-tip of his outstretched arms, a physique which helped him into the Grenadier Guards in World War One. Maskrey spent only a short time in the Reserves before establishing himself as the regular first-team goalkeeper and he was remarkably assured. He played for the Football League against the Irish League and was capped by England against Ireland in Belfast in February 1908. He was playing for Celanese when he returned to Derby County in an emergency in 1920. Maskrey collapsed and died at his pub, the New Inn in Russell Street, Derby.

MASSON
Donald Sandison   *Midfield*

Born: Banchory, 26 August 1946.
Career: Apprentice, Middlesbrough:

professional September 1963. Notts County September 1968. Queen's Park Rangers December 1974. Derby County October 1977. Notts County August 1978. Minnesota Kicks May 1981. Notts County September 1981. Bulova, Hong Kong, April 1982. Player-manager, Kettering Town April to October 1983. Player-manager, Los Angeles Kickers, March 1987.

Don Masson had a justifiably high reputation as a midfield player. He was in the Notts County team which climbed from Fourth Division to Second and, after a £100,000 move, helped Queen's Park Rangers to finish as First Division runners-up in 1975-6. He played for Scotland 14 times while with Queen's Park Rangers and won three more caps, the last against Peru in the 1978 World Cup Finals, after Tommy Docherty had exchanged him for Leighton James. Masson had a bad season with Derby and rejoined Notts on a free transfer, thus making a nil return on the £300,000 originally paid for James. With Notts, he took part in a third promotion, to the First Division in 1980-81.

MATTHEWS
Reginald Derrick   *Goalkeeper*

Born: Coventry, 20 December 1932.
Career: Modern Machine Tools FC. Juniors Coventry City: professional May 1950. Chelsea November 1956. Derby County October 1961. Manager, Rugby Town, August 1968 to May 1969.

Reg Matthews was a natural goalkeeper. His lightning reflexes and immense courage allied themselves to great agility and sound positional sense to make him, for a decade, one of the best in Britain. Harry Storer signed him for his local club, Coventry City, and after a break for National Service, Matthews became one of the outstanding young goalkeepers of the age. It was no surprise when he won five England caps although he was still a Third Division player, and in 1956 Chelsea paid £20,000 for him, at the time a record fee for a 'keeper. Harry Storer signed him for a second time, paying £6,300 to bring him to Derby. His acrobatic saves and courage in hurling himself at forwards' feet were

Don Masson, exchanged for Leighton James in a bad deal for Derby.

Reg Matthews.

loved by the supporters and he set a club record, later beaten by Colin Boulton, with 246 appearances in goal. Matthews totally dominated his own penalty area and fellow defenders had to be as wary as opposing forwards. For one season Matthews kept the Rams in Division Two virtually single-handed.

MATTHEWS
William
Wing-half

Born: Derby.
Career: Ripley Athletic. Aston Villa October 1903. Notts County December 1906. Derby County July 1912. Newport County August 1913.

Matthews made only one senior appearance in his season at the Baseball Ground.

MAY
Hugh
Centre-forward

Born: Hamilton.
Career: Wishaw United. Glasgow Rangers December 1901. Derby County July 1902. Fulham May 1903.

The brother of Johnny May, Hugh had a run of six games in October and November 1902, but could not produce a goal.

MAY
John
Wing-half

Born: Cambusnethan, 5 August 1880.
Career: Paisley. Wishaw Thistle. Abercorn. Derby County May 1898. Glasgow Rangers May 1904. Morton cs 1910.

FA Cup Finalists 1898-9, 1902-03.

"Johnny May was one of the finest half-

Johnny May.

backs who ever kicked a ball," said Steve Bloomer about the Scotsman whose injury was a key factor in the Rams losing the 1899 FA Cup Final to Sheffield United. May fell heavily after colliding with Bennett and despite showing great pluck in continuing for a while, eventually had to retire. The subsequent need to reorganise the team, together with some missed chances by May's great admirer, Bloomer, cost the Rams the game. After joining Derby, May quickly developed into one of the best half-backs in the Football League and, not long after he signed, the *Derby Daily Telegraph* described him as 'a fine tackler and not deficient in making a game for his forwards. He has been a great acquisition to the Derby club and, depending as he does on purely scientific methods, is a very instructive player to watch'. May played in another Final for the Rams, the thrashing of 1903, and then moved to Glasgow Rangers where he won five Scottish caps and captained his country. May ran a chain of billiard halls in Falkirk and Glasgow, one of them managed by John Boag.

MAYS
Albert Edward
Wing-half

Born: Ynyshir, 18 April 1929. Died: Derby, 5 July 1973.
Career: Allenton Juniors. Derby County, amateur, July 1943: professional, May 1946. Chesterfield July 1960. Burton Albion June 1961.

Division Three North champions 1956-7.

Born in the Rhondda, the son of a former Wrexham and Wales footballer,

Albert Mays, 281 games and 21 goals for the Rams.

Albert Mays was in fact a product of local Derby football, his father working on the maintenance staff at Derby Police Station when Albert was a youngster. He made his League debut in 1949-50 and established a place at wing-half. Mays, who was also an accomplished snooker player and cricketer, had a bullet-like shot and scored some of his goals from free-kicks taken outside the penalty area. Mays was not always as effective in the tackle as he might have been, although when he was going forward in attack, he showed some delightful touches. Mays was also something of a character — he once offered his shirt to a Popular Side barracker — and he was the man the crowd either loved or hated. He would have been ideal in later tactical formations as a creative midfield player and, if a bad back-pass in a 1959 FA Cup tie against Preston North End was to haunt him, he was one of the key men in Harry Storer's Third Division North championship team. Mays missed only one match in that season and represented the Third North against the Third South in October 1956. He later managed the Regent Billiard Hall in Derby and was a licensee when he died.

MEE
George Wilfred   *Outside-left*

Born: Bulwell, 12 April 1900. Died: Poulton-le-Fylde, 9 July 1978.
Career: Highbury Vale United. Notts County August 1919. Blackpool July 1920. Derby County February 1926. Burnley September 1932. Mansfield Town July 1933. Great Harwood November 1934. Accrington Stanley October 1935. Rochdale July 1938. Accrington Stanley January to May 1939.
Division Two promotion 1925-6. Division One runners-up 1929-30.

On a Friday evening in Sunderland in the late 1920s, Derby County players

George Mee.

were following their eve-of-the-match tradition by attending a show. A pretty poor show it was turning out until a small dark-haired man jumped on to the stage, grabbed the microphone and proceeded to astonish the audience with his professional patter and fine singing voice. The Rams players were not surprised, however, because the man was their left-winger, 5ft 4ins Georgie Mee, inevitably known as 'Shortie', who had been a vocalist before turning to soccer. Mee was a model of consistency with Blackpool, ever-present in four consecutive seasons, and joined Derby in a joint £3,750 deal with Jimmy Gill to give a late push towards promotion in 1925-6. He fell ill with typhoid fever in September 1928, and was out for five months before recovering fully. His brother Bertie was on Derby County's books and managed Arsenal to the League and FA Cup double in 1970-71. After World War Two, George ran an hotel in Blackpool until his retirement in 1965.

MERCER
John Thompson   *Outside-right*

Born: Belfast, 1879. Died: January 1947.
Career: Belview. Ligoneil. 81st North Lancashire Regiment. Preston North End. 8th Belfast Boys' Brigade. Linfield Swifts. Distillery. Brighton United May 1899. Leicester Fosse February 1900. Linfield cs 1900. Distillery March 1903. Derby County October 1903. Director, Glentoran. Director, Distillery.

An established Irish international when Derby County signed him, Mercer played the last three of his 11 international matches while he was at the Baseball Ground. Leicester Fosse still held his League registration, so Derby had to negotiate with two clubs, but Mercer's contribution was limited by injuries. Mercer became a businessman in Belfast, was a director of Glentoran for 20 years and later chairman of Distillery. He earned Irish Cup winners' medals with Linfield in 1902 and Distillery in 1903. Mercer was chairman of the Irish League in 1941-2.

METCALFE
Ronald   *Outside-left*

Born: South Shields, 8 December 1947.
Career: Marsden Colliery Juniors. Derby County January 1965. Burton Albion November 1967.

Metcalfe played only once, against Plymouth Argyle in the final match of 1966-7 when, after sacking Tim Ward, the directors picked the team.

METHVEN
James   *Right-back*

Born: Perth, 7 December 1868. Died: Derby, 25 March 1953.
Career: Leith. Heart of Midlothian. St

Jimmy Methven.

Bernards. Derby County May 1891. Manager, Derby County, August 1906 to June 1922.
Division One runners-up 1895-6. FA Cup Finalists. 1897-8, 1898-9 (captain), 1902-03 (captain).

Jimmy Methven was unchallenged at right-back for Derby County for 15 years after joining them from Edinburgh St Bernards. Methven, who also played a few games for Leith and Hearts, was reserve for Scotland against England in 1890. He had turned down a contract with Burton Swifts because it included a hotel managership which his wife did not want, and it was a former St Bernards team mate, Johnny McMillan, who persuaded him to join Derby. Methven was ever-present in five seasons and with Boag and Fryer played in all three of Derby's early FA Cup Finals. Towards the end of his career he had slowed considerably but even on his last appearance, after becoming Derby manager in 1906, he still showed his cool, confident style. He was, according to one writer 'one of the wonders of the football world'.

METHVEN
James junior   *Inside-forward*

Career: Everton Reserves. Ilkeston United November 1912. Derby County, amateur, March 1914. Cardiff City August 1914.

The son of Jimmy Methven. He played once in 1913-14, when Derby County were on their way towards relegation from the First Division.

Gary Micklewhite, 277 senior games for the Rams.

white was made available but continued to play his part, often as substitute, in a promotion bid that foundered at the play-off stage. For seven years with the Rams he was an excellent player and a model professional.

MIDDLETON
Francis   *Outside-left*

Born: Whitwick.
Career: Whitwick White Cross. Derby County November 1901. Leicester Fosse August 1906.

Frank Middleton went straight into Derby County's First Division team when he was signed but always faced stiff competition for the outside-left position from George Davis and Sam Lamb. He was one of five players with Derby connections in Leicester Fosse's Second Division promotion team in 1907-08, the others being Horace Bailey, Joe Blackett, James Blessington and Tommy Shanks.

MIDDLETON
John   *Goalkeeper*

Born: Lincoln, 24 December 1956.
Career: Apprentice, Nottingham Forest: professional November 1974. Derby County September 1977.

John Middleton played for the England Youth team in 1975 and made three England Under-21 appearances while he was with Nottingham Forest. After Forest had won the Anglo-Scottish Cup

John Middleton.

MICKLEWHITE
Gary   *Midfield*

Born: Southwark, 21 March 1961.
Career: Apprentice, Manchester United: professional March 1978. Queen's Park Rangers July 1979. Derby County, February 1985.

Division Three promotion 1985-6.
Division Two champions 1986-7.

The sale of Kevin Wilson to Ipswich Town in January 1985 financed two significant purchases by Arthur Cox, Trevor Christie from Nottingham Forest and, for £92,500, Gary Micklewhite from Queen's Park Rangers. Micklewhite was signed for Rangers by

Tommy Docherty and played for them in the 1982 FA Cup Final, as substitute in the first game and as a starter in the replay. He was in their Second Division championship team a year later but Derby's ambition and potential persuaded him to take what he felt was a temporary drop into the Third Division. In a run of 112 consecutive League games, he was an essential part of two promotions, covering the ground tirelessly on the right and scoring his share of goals. Two major operations, on an Achilles tendon in September 1987 and knee ligaments in December 1989, set back his career but he returned both times. After Derby's big transfer splash in 1992, Mickle-

Ray Middleton, helped Boston United to a sensational Cup win over the Rams.

Derby County out of the FA Cup with a 6-1 victory at the Baseball Ground in 1955. He was elected a town councillor in Boston and managed Rumbelows' store for 11 years. His brother Matt was also a League goalkeeper with Southport, Plymouth, Bradford City and York.

MILARVIE
Robert   *Outside-left*
Career: Stoke October 1888. Port Vale 1889. Derby County November 1889. Newton Heath July 1890. Ardwick cs 1891.

Milarvie played for Stoke in the opening season of the Football League. He spent one season at Derby, who had a tussle with Port Vale before clinching his registration.

MILLER
David   *Centre-half*
Born: Middlesbrough, 21 January 1921. Career: Middlesbrough September 1938. Wolverhampton Wanderers August 1945. Derby County April 1947. Doncaster Rovers January 1948. Aldershot March 1954. Boston United July 1954.

A reserve defender whose only senior appearance was at centre-forward against Sunderland at Roker Park in September 1947. He played a dozen games in Doncaster Rovers' Third Division North championship team in 1949-50 and was in the Boston United side which beat the Rams 6-1 in 1955. Miller stayed with Boston United until 1960.

MILLER
John   *Centre-forward*
Born: Dumbarton.
Career: Clyde. Derby County June

John Miller.

and promotion from the Second Division in 1976-7, Brian Clough bought Peter Shilton and transferred Middleton to Derby County for £25,000 plus Archie Gemmill. It meant that Colin Boulton was prematurely discarded and Forest did much better from the deal than Derby. A persistent shoulder injury forced Middleton to retire in 1980.

MIDDLETON
Raymond   *Goalkeeper*
Born: Boldon, 6 September 1919. Died: Boston, 12 April 1977.
Career: Washington Church. North Shields. Chesterfield, amateur, August

1937: professional, October 1937. Derby County June 1951. Player-manager, Boston United, April 1954. Manager, Hartlepools United, May 1957 to October 1959. manager, Boston United, June 1960 to May 1961: director February 1963: secretary 1972.

Ray Middleton, who insured his hands for £2,000 when he was working as a miner, was a miracle of consistency with Chesterfield. He played four times for England 'B' and became a Justice of the Peace in his Saltergate days. Stuart McMillan signed him to replace Harry Brown and he was Derby's first-choice goalkeeper for three seasons. He returned as player-manager of the Boston United team which dumped

1895. Bolton Wanderers November 1897.

Division One runners-up 1895-6.

Derby County's regular centre-forward for two seasons after being signed from Scotland, Miller provided a steady, rather than spectacular, supply of goals.

MILLIN
Alfred   *Outside-left*
Born: Rotherham, 18 December 1933.
Career: Juniors, Derby County: professional August 1951. Brush Sports August 1956. Gresley Rovers June 1957. Heanor Town June 1958. Gresley Rovers August 1959.

Alf Millin appeared in one Third Division North match, against Scunthorpe United in September 1955.

MILLS
Gary Roland   *Midfield*
Born: Northampton, 11 November 1961.
Career: Apprentice, Nottingham Forest: professional November 1978. Seattle Sounders March 1982. Derby County October 1982. Seattle Sounders April 1983. Nottingham Forest December 1983. Notts County August 1987. Leicester City March 1989.

Gary Mills.

An England Youth international, Gary Mills played in Nottingham Forest's 1980 European Cup Final victory over Hamburg while still a teenager. He won two England Under-21 caps while with Forest. Derby signed him from Seattle Sounders on an extended loan and, under complicated agreements in force between the Football League and the North American Soccer League, he was still Forest's player but unable to turn out for them in 1982-3. Instead, he played a considerable part in Derby's successful battle to avoid relegation from the Second Division. He moved on round the East Midlands with Notts County and Leicester City.

MILLS
Samuel   *Outside-right*
Career: Derby Midland. Derby County June 1891. Loughborough Town 1893. Heanor Town November 1896.

One of the players who strengthened Derby County when Derby Midland folded, Mills was first choice at outside-right for most of his two seasons with the Rams.

MINNEY
George   *Centre-forward*
Career: Hertfordshire junior football. Derby County 1920.

One of many players to make fleeting appearances in the difficult years after World War One. Minney played in the last two games of 1920-21.

MITCHELL
Harry   *Outside-right*
Born: Barrow Hill, Staveley.
Career: Derby County May 1905.

A reserve who made one League appearance in February 1906.

MITCHELL
James Donald   *Goalkeeper*
Born: Ilkeston, 1 July 1937.
Career: Horsley Woodhouse MW. Ilkeston Town 1955. Derby County amateur May 1958: professional October 1958. Ilkeston Town June 1961. Matlock Town November 1965.

Recommended to Harry Storer while he was doing his National Service with the Sherwood Foresters. He played six League games before returning to Ilkeston Town for three seasons and concentrating on the family coal business.

MONEY
Richard   *Central defender*
Born: Lowestoft, 13 October 1955.
Career: Lowestoft Town. Scunthorpe United July 1973. Fulham December 1977. Liverpool May 1980. Derby County, loan, December 1981. Luton Town, loan, March 1982. Luton Town

Richard Money.

April 1982. Portsmouth August 1983. Scunthorpe United October 1985: acting manager February 1987: youth development officer. Youth coach, Aston Villa, September 1989.

Richard Money played for England 'B', as substitute, while with Fulham and cost Liverpool £333,333. He did not break through at Anfield Road, although he played in the away leg of their 1980-81 European Cup semi-final against Bayern Munich, and Derby County took him on loan in the troubled 1981-2 season.

MONKS
Isaac   *Centre-half*

Monks played centre-half in Derby County's first three League games in September 1888, but had scored when he played at centre-forward in an FA Cup tie against Staveley the previous season.

MOORE
James   *Inside-forward*
Born: Handsworth, 11 May 1889.
Career: Quebec Albion. Glossop May 1911. Derby County October 1913. Chesterfield March 1926. Mansfield Town November 1927. Worcester City March 1929.

Division Two champions 1914-15. Division Two promotion 1925-6.

'Gentleman' Jim Moore joined Derby County as a centre-forward from

Glossop, but it was as an inside-forward that he made his mark, for it was there he could show his dribbling powers off to their best advantage. It cost Derby £1,500 to bring Moore to the Baseball Ground and although World War One soon intervened, the club had full value. Moore skippered the side which reached the FA Cup semi-final in 1923 and although he was on the losing side that day, he could look back to a fine scoring feat not long before. On Christmas Day 1922, Moore scored the first five as Derby hammered Crystal Palace 6-0 at the Baseball Ground. Modest Moore shrugged it off: "The ball just came to me at the right time." The arrival of Harry Storer cut down his appearances and then, having just regained this place, he had the misfortune to suffer a knee injury which resulted in an operation. Moore, who won one England cap, was the

only survivor of the 1914-15 Second Division championship team to appear in the promotion 11 years later.

MOORE
John   *Forward*
Career: Burton United. Derby County January 1905.

Played on the wing and at inside-forward in his five League appearances for Derby.

MOORE
John Leslie   *Centre-half*
Born: Sheffield, 7 July 1933.
Career: Sheffield FC. Worksop Town August 1957. Derby County October 1957. Boston FC July 1965. Lincoln City October 1965. Lockheed Leamington July 1967. Buxton August 1968: player-manager May to November

Jimmy Moore (above left), played in promotion sides 11 years apart. Les Moore (above) joined the Rams from Midland League soccer for £1,000.

1970. Manager, Worksop Town, June 1972 to July 1973.

Les Moore was a late entrant into League football and remained a part-time professional. Derby were having defensive problems in their first season back in the Second Division after promotion and Harry Storer paid Worksop Town £1,000 for Moore. He soon made the transition from the Midland League and his sturdy defending was important to the Rams for the next seven seasons. He was always contending for the centre-half spot with the more elegant Ray Young but was also a hard man to beat. He steered Worksop to the Midland League title in his only season as manager.

MOORE
Ralph *Inside-forward*

Career: *Crewton United. Derby County June 1919.*

Made one League appearance in October 1919.

MOORE
William C. *Full-back*

Career: *Graham Street Prims. Derby County October 1906. Stockport County August 1909. Ilkeston United March 1911.*

Known as Doggy Moore, he was on the staff for three seasons, one of the reserves for Jack Nicholas senior and Charlie Morris.

MORAN
John *Inside-forward*

Born: *Cleland, 9 March 1933.*
Career: *Coltness United. Derby County November 1954. St Mirren August 1955.*

Moran made two senior appearances in November 1954, when Derby were on their way to a second relegation in three seasons.

MORELAND
Victor *Defender/midfield*

Born: *Belfast, 15 June 1957.*
Career: *Glentoran. Tulsa Roughnecks, loan, March 1978. Derby County September 1978. Tulsa Roughnecks March 1980. Dallas Sidekicks. Wichita Wings.*

Vic Moreland, signed in a joint deal with Billy Caskey, played six times for Northern Ireland while he was with Derby County. His aggressive style was best suited to midfield and his enthusiasm often provided a lift, even if he was not the most tactically disciplined of players. He could profitably have stayed longer at the Baseball Ground but was always keen to return to the North American Soccer League. He was in the Tulsa team which, with Terry Hennessey as coach, won the 1983 Soccer Bowl.

MORLEY
Haydn Arthur *Full-back*

Born: *Derby, 26 November 1860. Died: Hathersage, May 1953.*
Career: *Derby County 1884. Notts County. Derby County 1889. Sheffield Wednesday 1889.*

Haydn Morley, who also played cricket for Derbyshire, was the first player to be signed after the formation of Derby County in 1884. His brother William and their father, William senior, were the moving spirits in starting the football club. He played in Wednesday's 1889-90 FA Cup Final defeat by Blackburn Rovers.

Vic Moreland.

MORRIS
Charles Richard *Left-back*

Born: *Oswestry, 29 August 1880. Died: Chirk Bank, 18 January 1952.*
Career: *Chirk. Derby County April 1900. Huddersfield Town August 1910. Wrexham May 1911.*
FA Cup Finalists 1902-03.

Charlie Morris worked down a Welsh mine for eight years and played football for Chirk, winning three Welsh caps before signing for the Rams to replace Joe Blackett, whose form had been affected by poor health. Morris made his debut against Blackburn Rovers and it was soon obvious that the Rams had made an important capture. He became one of the finest defenders to represent Derby and was a regular choice for Wales during his ten years at the Baseball Ground, winning 21 of his 27 caps. After the 1903 FA Cup Final disaster, Morris went from strength to strength and Derby appointed him skipper in succession to Archie Goodall. Morris was one of the best players in British football in the early 1900s, a brilliant international full-back and a First Division star. It was written of him: 'Morris not only knows the game from A to Z but he is also a model

Charlie Morris.

Johnny Morris.

footballer'. In the close season of 1910 he moved to Huddersfield who had just been elected to Division Two. Morris is the only player to have been asked to replace the goalkeeper in both an FA Cup Final and an international. He took over from Fryer at the Crystal Palace in 1903, and in March 1908 stood in for the injured Roose against England, although Wales were allowed to call upon regular goalkeeper Davies of Bolton in the second half. From 1910 to 1916 he was cricket professional to the Duke of Westminster's XI at Eaton Hall. He was a Methodist lay preacher in Chirk.

MORRIS
John *Inside-right*

Born: *Radcliffe, 27 September 1924.*
Career: *Juniors, Manchester United. Derby County March 1949. Leicester City October 1952. Player-manager,*

Johnny Morris of Derby County (right) and Wilf Mannion of Middlesbrough at a muddy Baseball Ground.

Corby Town, May 1958. Kettering Town June 1961. Manager, Great Harwood, cs 1964. Manager, Oswestry Town, October 1967.

Derby County broke the British transfer record for the second time in less than two years when they paid £24,500 to bring Manchester United inside-forward Johnny Morris to the Baseball Ground. Twenty-one months after the record signing of Billy Steel, the Rams bought Morris to form, with the Scotsman, a new 'Carter-Doherty' duo. Morris made a brilliant start at the Baseball Ground, with 13 goals in 13 games, but it was impossible to emulate Carter and Doherty. Morris, who was in Manchester United's 1948 FA Cup winning team against Blackpool and played for the Football League, was a player Matt Busby confessed he could never understand. Liverpool were the favourites to sign him until Stuart McMillan stepped in with a record cheque. Morris was a fine dribbler who

was difficult to dispossess and he combined artistry with power in front of goal. He won his three England caps at Derby before leaving a declining team to move to Leicester where he played more than 200 games and helped the Filbert Street club to the Second Division championship in 1954. Morris and Steel were highly talented players but, for the supporters, nothing could dim the memory of the 1946 FA Cup Final pairing.

MORRISON
Angus Cameron   *Forward*

Born: Dingwall, 26 April 1924.
Career: Ross County. Derby County October 1944. Preston North End November 1948. Millwall October 1957. Player-manager, Nuneaton Borough, June 1958 to January 1961. Player-manager, Belper Town, April 1961 to April 1964. Coach, Ripley MW, September 1966: manager, August

1967. Manager, Belper Town, January 1970 to December 1973.

Angus Morrison was signed for a box of cigars, the gift Derby County sent in return for the recommendation. Morrison was in the RAF at the time and proved an extremely talented forward, either in the centre or at outside-left, with an excellent scoring record. He was one of those unsettled by the arrival of Billy Steel and, at £8,000, proved a fine buy for Preston North End. He was in the team which finished runners-up in the First Division in 1952-3 and scored in Preston's FA Cup Final defeat by West Bromwich Albion in 1954. When Morrison returned to the Derby area, he spent many years with Belper Town.

MORTON
William Henry   *Wing-half*

Born: Ilkeston, 16 December 1896.
Career: West Hallam. Ilkeston St

Bill Morton.

Graham Moseley.

Angus Morrison in action against Grimsby Town.

John's. War service. Ilkeston United August 1919. Derby County August 1920. Newcastle United September 1921. Lincoln City August 1922. Wigan Borough June 1923.

A sturdy wing-half in a struggling Derby County team. In his first season, the Rams lost their First Division place and he moved to Newcastle United the following September, although he did not play in their first team. He served with the Sherwood Foresters in World War One and was taken prisoner after 18 months at the front.

MOSELEY
Graham   Goalkeeper

Born: Urmston, 16 November 1953.
Career: Apprentice, Blackburn Rovers: professional September 1971. Derby County September 1971. Aston Villa, loan, August 1974. Walsall, loan, October 1977. Brighton & Hove Albion November 1977. Ipswich Town, loan, March 1984. Cardiff City August 1986.

Peter Taylor spotted Moseley's potential when he was a teenager with Blackburn Rovers, who rapidly signed him as a professional to collect a fee, but it took him a long time to dislodge Colin Boulton. Moseley had talent but was prone to errors. He had a good run under Dave Mackay but Boulton battled back and Moseley joined Brighton. He shared the goalkeeping duties with Eric Steele when Brighton were promoted from the Second Division in 1978-9 and played in the 1983 FA Cup Final. An England Youth international in his Derby days, Moseley was injured in a car accident while with Cardiff and was forced to retire.

Bert Mozley, made 321 senior appearances for Derby.

'Spud' Murphy, took over from Quantrill and made 235 sppearances.

MOZLEY
Bert   *Right-back*

Born: Derby, 23 September 1923.
Career: Derby Boys. Shelton United.
Nottingham Forest, amateur, 1944.
Derby County, amateur, May 1945:
professional, October 1945.

Bert Mozley went about his business in such an unflappable manner that he always appeared to have plenty in reserve, yet throughout the late 1940s and into the 1950s he had few equals as a First Division right-back of international class. His League debut came in the first post-war season and in 1949-50 he won three England caps before losing his place through injury. Mozley was unlucky that his replacement was Tottenham's Alf Ramsey, who established himself as an England regular. The Rams' dressing-room jester, Mozley was always organising

practical jokes. He was also a skilled defender who delighted in coming forward to try speculative shots, although they brought him only two goals in over 300 first-team appearances. With Tim Ward he went on the FA Canadian tour in 1950 and four years later emigrated to that country, taking over an hotel. He played for Western Canada All Stars against a touring Russian side in Winnipeg.

MURPHY
Lionel   *Outside-left*

Born: Hovingham Spa, 15 September 1895. Died: Derby, 27 October 1968.
Career: Melton Mowbray. Derby County February 1922. Bolton Wanderers January 1928. Mansfield Town September 1929. Norwich City May 1931. Luton Town October 1934.
Division Two promotion 1925-6.

When Alf Quantrill left for Preston in the close season of 1921, Derby County struggled hard to fill the vacant outside-left spot until Lionel 'Spud' Murphy, a former army footballer, made the position his own soon after signing. A few days after joining the Rams, Murphy made his League debut against Clapton Orient and midway through the following season one local journalist wrote: 'Spud Murphy, the Derby County left winger, is a genius. All his work is done without effort, and yet the results he gets with one touch of the ball often equal the results secured by other players after they have expounded pounds of energy. That marks a true-born player, but we must hope that the Melton lad won't play to the gallery. A hint in time might save him from a terrible complaint which shall be nameless.' Presumably Murphy took the hint. He missed only

The rugged Musson in action against Wolves.

'Chick' Musson.

four matches when the Rams won promotion in 1925-6 and scored 12 goals, starring at inside-left towards the end of the season when Georgie Mee came from Blackpool. Murphy moved to Bolton in part-exchange for another outside-left, Albert Picken.

MURRAY
William   *Inside-forward*

Born: South Church, Bishop Auckland.
Career: Eildon Lane. Bishop Auckland 1919. Derby County August 1920. Middlesbrough July 1921. Heart of Midlothian June 1923. Dunfermline November 1934.

Murray won an England amateur international cap against Belgium while he was with Bishop Auckland but spent only one season with Derby County. He was the regular inside-left in 1919-20, when the Rams were relegated from the First Division. Known as 'Tiddler', he emigrated to Australia in 1963 after retiring from Rolls-Royce foundry.

MUSSON
Walter Urban   *Left-half*

Born: Kilburn, 8 October 1920. Died: Loughborough, 22 April 1955.
Career: Holbrook St Michael's. Derby County, amateur, March 1936: professional, October 1937. Player-manager, Brush Sports, June 1954.

FA Cup winners 1945-6.

'Is Chick playing today?' asked more than a few nervous opposing forwards in the late 1940s. The rugged little wing-half, who was known all his playing days by that misleading nickname, certainly knew how to 'put himself about' and few, if any, opposing forwards relished a visit to the Baseball Ground when he was in the side. Musson was one of the band of local youngsters who helped restart Derby County in 1942 after the closure for war. Musson could play on either flank, but it was as a left-half that he forced his way into the team and he was a key member of the 1946 Cup-winning side. His ferocious tackling was well-known on the First Division circuit, but under Peter Doherty's tuition Musson developed his skills and the primarily defensive wing-half became a useful supporter of the attack, although he never scored a goal for the Rams. Musson played for the Football League against the Irish League in April 1950, and missed only five games in the first five post-war seasons. Sadly, like Leuty, Musson died in his mid-30s.

Les Mynard.

MYNARD
Leslie Daniel   *Wing-forward*

Born: Bewdley, 19 December 1925.
Career: Bewdley. Wolverhampton Wanderers, amateur, 1942-3: professional, May 1945. Derby County July 1949. Scunthorpe United August 1952.

Les Mynard could play on either wing and had a run on the right when Reg Harrison was injured. Derby were not short of talented wingers and Mynard spent most of his time in the Reserves.

NAPIER
Charles Edward   *Inside-forward*

Born: Bainsford, Falkirk, 8 October 1910.
Career: Maryhill Hibernian. Glasgow Celtic June 1929. Derby County June 1935. Sheffield Wednesday March 1938. Falkirk September 1945. Stenhousemuir September 1946. Retired 1948.
Division One runners-up 1935-6.

Charlie Napier seemed to be a permanent fixture at Celtic until the club refused his request for a benefit at the end of 1934-5. The Scottish international went on the transfer list and the Rams bought him for £5,000. Within 12 months Napier had played in every forward position for Derby and Baseball Ground fans loved his electrifying dashes through opposition defences. Napier was the rapier thrust of an international-class forward line and his resumed partnership with fellow Scottish international Dally Duncan won many a game for Derby County. Napier was both stylish and positive and the

Charlie Napier, 26 goals in 88 games for Derby.

former Glaswegian electrician was christened 'Happy Feet' by the Derby fans. Once, both Bowers and Gallacher were injured before a match at mighty Arsenal and it was Napier who led the attack and helped the Rams to a rare Highbury point. Napier earned two of his five Scottish caps while with Derby. His father, Charles Edward senior, was secretary of Falkirk FC and a brother, George, was a defender with Kilmarnock and Cowdenbeath.

NEAL
Richard Marshall *Wing-forward*

Born: Fence, 14 January 1908. Died: Fence, 26 December 1986.
Career: Dinnington Main. Blackpool, amateur, January 1926: professional, February 1926. Derby County May 1931. Southampton February 1932. Bristol City May 1937. Accrington Stanley June 1938.

Neal played mostly on the right-wing for Blackpool, more often on the left for Derby. It was a problem position for the Rams in 1931-2, solved only when Dally Duncan was signed. Neal had five extremely good years with Southampton in the Second Division. His son, also Richard Marshall, played more than 350 League games for Lincoln City, Birmingham City and Middlesbrough, winning four England Under-23 caps.

NEEDHAM
George Wright   *Wing-half*

Born: Staveley.
Career: Staveley. Derby County August 1919. Gillingham June 1920. Northampton Town February 1924.

George Needham played only five times for Derby County. Gillingham signed him for their first Football League season and he had a good career in the lower divisions.

NEEDHAM
Thomas   *Forward*

A versatile forward who played in Derby's first two Football League seasons.

NELSON
Edward   *Wing-half*

Born: Bishop Auckland, 21 April 1907. Died: Durham West, 1972.
Career: Crook Town. Derby County January 1927. Doncaster Rovers June 1928.

Nelson was signed in a joint deal with John Hope — £100 the pair — but played only twice in Derby County's first team, standing in for Johnny McIntyre.

NELSON
James *Outside-left*

Nelson scored twice on his debut in an 8-5 victory over Blackburn Rovers in September 1890 but made only three more appearances.

NEVE
Edwin *Outside-left*

Born: Prescot, 1885. Died: August 1920. Career: St Helens Recreational. Hull City May 1906. Derby County August 1912. Nottingham Forest July 1914. Chesterfield April 1916.

Neve shared the left-wing duties with Ivan Sharpe in 1912-13 and succeeded him as first-choice the following season. Unfortunately for Neve, this coincided with relegation to the Second Division.

NEWBERY
Peter John *Centre-forward*

Born: Derby, 4 March 1938. Career: Derby Boys. Derby County, amateur, May 1953: professional, March 1955. Burton Albion July 1961. Lockheed Leamington July 1962. Derbyshire Amateurs 1964. Long Eaton United August to October 1966.

Peter Newbery was a useful Central League player but was short of pace for League level. He scored twice in his five senior games before going into non-League football. He retired from Long Eaton United in October 1966, on medical advice because of knee trouble.

NEWTON
Henry Albert *Midfield*

Born: Nottingham, 18 February 1944. Career: Juniors, Nottingham Forest: professional June 1961. Everton October 1970. Derby County September 1973. Walsall July 1977.

Division One champions 1974-5.

Henry Newton took a roundabout route to Derby from Nottingham Forest, where he made 315 senior appearances and won four England Under-23 caps. Because of the success of Alan Hinton and the £100,000 move of Terry Hennessey, not to mention Derby's later attempt to sign Ian Moore, Forest became increasingly reluctant to do business with Brian Clough and Peter Taylor. So Newton went to Everton and Clough and Taylor had to wait almost three years before they got their man for £100,000. It was their last major signing, for they left Derby the following month. Along with others players, Newton was upset by the turn of events but his reward came in 1974-5, when he won a League Championship medal. He was a player of great courage and one of the fiercest tacklers in the game. Newton's versatility enabled him to play in midfield,

Henry Newton, whose 156 appearances took in the 1974-5 Championship season.

the centre of defence and at left-back. He had to battle against injuries and his move to Walsall in May 1977 was a prelude to retirement. Arthritis caught up with him and in 1984, when he was running a sub-Post Office in Derby, he underwent a hip operation.

NICHOLAS
John Thomas *Right-half/right back*

Born: Derby, 26 November 1910. Died: Nottingham, 4 February 1977. Career: Juniors, Swansea Town. Derby County December 1927. Acting player-manager 1942 to March 1944. Retired 1947. Chief scout, Derby County.

Division One runners-up 1929-30, 1935-6. FA Cup winners 1945-6 (captain).

Derby County have had many fine servants but there has never been one more loyal than Jack Nicholas. Son of a former Rams defender, Nicholas was born in Derby but soon moved to Wales with his family where he won schoolboy international honours. Swansea Town wanted to sign him but Nicholas chose the Rams. Known as 'Owd Nick' on the Popular Side, Nicholas set out in September 1931 on a run of 328 out of a possible 331 League games to the end of 1938-9, adding another three in the first post-war season. He took over

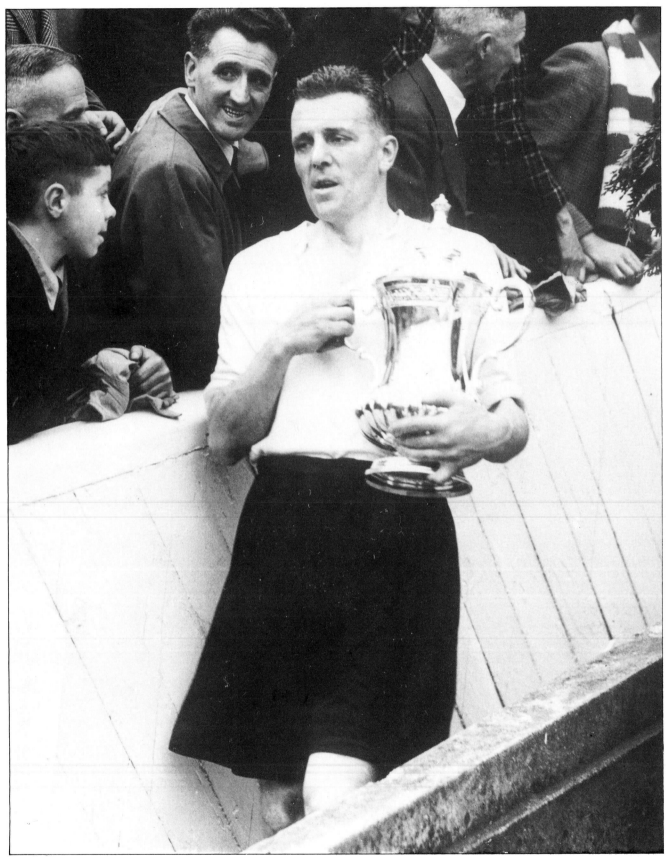

In 1946, Jack Nicholas mades history as the first – and so far only – Rams skipper to receive the FA Cup.

from Johnny McIntyre at right-half, played occasionally at centre-half and full-back and in 1938 became Jack Howe's regular partner at right-back. Nicholas, along with Jack Webb, was largely responsible for starting the Rams up again in 1942 and his reward was to lead the club to Wembley four years later. Nicholas was a fearsome and rugged defender and a hard man — there were stories of him taking cold showers even on freezing days. In Derby's first 108 years, he was unique, the only Rams skipper to have lifted the FA Cup.

NICHOLAS
William Joseph   *Right-back*
Born: Staines.
Career: Staines. Derby County April 1905. Swansea Town August 1912.

Jack Nicholas senior, father of Derby County's FA Cup winning captain,

Teatime at the Nicholas household. Mrs Nicholas serves (from left to right) Jack junior, Dally Duncan and Jack senior.

took over the right-back position on a permanent basis when Jimmy Methven stepped up to become manager in 1906. Nicholas was there until Jack Atkin began to emerge, then left to help Swansea Town in their first year as a professional club. He did great work there and later returned to live in Derby, taking young Jack with him.

NIELSON
Norman Fred   *Centre-half*

Born: Johannesburg, 6 December 1928. Career: Arcadia Pretoria. Charlton Athletic July 1949. Derby County September 1951. Bury May 1954. Hull City April 1957. Corby Town July 1958. Gresley Rovers August 1959. Hinckley Athletic November 1959. Long Eaton United May 1960. Wilmorton 1966. Ripley MW July 1967.

A giant of 6ft 3ins who came from South Africa to Charlton Athletic, a familiar path in the late 1940s. He could kick the ball with extraordinary power and, although centre-half was his best position, it was not unusual to see him at centre-forward. Nielson was a colourful player, unfortunate to arrive when the club was starting a sharp decline.

Jack Nicholas senior.

Norman Nielson.

David Nish, made 237 senior appearances for Derby.

American Soccer League and even at the end of his career, he remained upset that what he thought was an equaliser in the 1976 FA Cup semi-final against Manchester United had been disallowed because other players were offside. "I had worked out exactly how I would beat their offside trap," he said, "and I was annoyed that the referee penalised others who were coming back." Nish worked at Middlesbrough with Bruce Rioch and Colin Todd before returning to Leicester.

OAKDEN
Harry — *Outside-right*
Born: Derby.
Career: Alvaston and Boulton. Derby County November 1898. Distillery 1899. Brighton United cs 1900. Swindon Town September 1901.

Harry Oakden made a rapid transition from local football to the First Division and played in the first three FA Cup ties as Derby County moved towards their second successive FA Cup Final. But John Goodall returned for the semi-final and Tom Arkesden played at Crystal Palace.

O'BRIEN
Michael Terence — *Centre-half*
Born: Kilcock, 10 August 1893. Died: Uxbridge, 21 September 1940.
Career: Walker Celtic. Wallsend. Blyth Spartans. Newcastle East End. Glasgow Celtic. Alloa Athletic. Norwich City August 1919. South Shields December 1919. Queen's Park Rangers May 1920. Leicester City March 1922. Hull City June 1924. Brooklyn Wanderers May 1926. Derby County December 1926. Walsall June 1928. Norwich City May 1929. Watford June 1931. Manager, Queen's Park Rangers,

NISH
David John — *Left-back*
Born: Burton upon Trent, 26 September 1947.
Career: Measham. Amateur, Leicester City: professional July 1966. Derby County August 1972. Tulsa Roughnecks February 1979. Seattle Sounders March 1980. Shepshed Charterhouse April 1982. Player-manager, Gresley Rovers, June 1982: chairman, cs 1985. Youth coach, Middlesbrough, July 1988: reserve-team coach, March 1989: assistant manager April 1990 to March 1991. Youth development officer, Leicester City, July 1991.
Division One champions 1974-5.

Derby County were reigning champions when in August 1972, they broke the British record transfer fee for the third time since the war, signing David Nish for £225,000 from Leicester City to follow Billy Steel and Johnny Morris, their big signings of the 1940s. Nish had led Leicester in the 1969 FA Cup Final by Manchester City at the age of 21 and was one of the most elegant defenders ever seen at Derby. He was geared to attack and had the delicate touch of a skilful inside-forward. Nish relished the arrival of Charlie George and could always find his runs on the Derby left. His brief international career of five games was then over. Illness, requiring immediate surgery, put him out of an England tour to Eastern Europe and he was not picked again. His effectiveness was gradually curtailed by three operations on his right knee, the result of an injury sustained when scoring against Sheffield United at Derby in December 1975. He joined Alan Hinton in the North

Mick O'Brien.

May 1933 to April 1935. Assistant manager Brentford 1935. Manager, Ipswich Town, May 1936 to August 1937.

In 18 months at the Baseball Ground, Mick O'Brien played in only five senior games but appeared for two countries. He won 10 caps for Ireland and four for the Irish Republic, gained with seven different English clubs and one for each country while with Derby. O'Brien joined Derby after an unhappy spell in New York and his registration was held up pending a League inquiry, after which Derby and Hull were fined £100 each. O'Brien fought at the Battle of Jutland during World War One. He was in the first Queen's Park Rangers team to play in the Football League.

O'BRIEN
Raymond Christopher

Left-back

Born: Shelbourne, 21 May 1951.
Career: Shelbourne. Manchester United May 1973. Notts County March 1974. Derby County, loan, September 1983. Boston United July 1984: caretaker-manager, November 1985: manager, January 1986. Manager, Corby Town, November 1987. Manager, Arnold Town, August 1991.

After being signed from Manchester United for £40,000, Ray O'Brien played more than 300 League games for Notts County, helped them to win promotion to the First Division and appeared four times for the Republic of Ireland. He was Notts' leading League scorer in 1979-80 with ten goals, seven from penalties, but he was nearing the end of his League career when Peter Taylor signed him for Derby on a month's loan.

O'HARE
John

Centre-forward

Born: Renton, 24 September 1946.
Career: Drumchapel Amateurs. Juniors, Sunderland: professional October 1963. Derby County August 1967. Leeds United August 1974. Nottingham Forest February 1975. Dallas Tornado, loan, April 1977: May 1978. Belper Town August 1981. Carriage and Wagon 1982. Manager, Ockbrook. Manager, Stanton, March 1988.

Division Two champions 1968-9. Division One champions 1971-2.

When Brian Clough took over as manager he was soon in touch with Sunderland over a centre-forward he had coached in the Youth team. John O'Hare became Clough's first signing, for £20,000 and he was an immediate fixture in the team, missing only four League games in his first five seasons. In that time he made 13 appearances for Scotland. O'Hare was a steady rather than prolific scorer. He had no great pace, nor was he a battering ram,

John O'Hare, 81 goals in 308 first-team games for Derby.

so supporters regarded him with certain reservations. They soon began to realise, however, that he was absolutely essential to Derby's style. He had marvellous ball control, could accept and hold passes under intense pressure from behind, and was totally unselfish. As Alan Durban said: "Anybody in defence or midfield knew that he would be available. You only had to glance up to find him and if Solly was given the ball, it was his. It would not fizz back past you and put the defence under pressure." Solly was his universal

nickname. O'Hare was involved in a Second Division promotion, another League Championship and a League Cup victory with Nottingham Forest, ending his senior career by coming on as substitute in their second European Cup triumph against Hamburg in Madrid.

OLIVER
James Henry Kenneth *Centre-half*

Born: Loughborough, 10 August 1924.

Ken Oliver.

Career: Brush Sports. Sunderland August 1946. Derby County September 1949. Exeter City January 1958.

Division Three North champions 1956-7.

Ken Oliver was signed from Sunderland for £6,750 with a daunting, some would say impossible, task. His brief was to take over from Leon Leuty, England's number two centre-half, whom the Rams were resigned to losing. Oliver, who had begun as a centre-forward at Roker Park, did not have the class of Leuty, but he gave Derby reliable service for more than eight years. He was affectionately known to the crowd as 'Rubberneck' because he had a long neck and his clearing headers had the force of his whole body behind them. There were several challengers to Oliver's position — Norman Nielson, Ray Young and Martin McDonnell — but he stayed loyal to the Rams and played a dozen games in the Third Division North championship side. After two years with Exeter City, Oliver's career was ended by knee trouble. He continued to live in Derby where he was a director of a sports goods business.

OLIVER
Joseph Alan   *Outside-left*

Born Blyth, 8 September 1924.
Career: Crofton CW. Derby County October 1946. Stockport County August 1950. Gateshead July 1954.

Alan Oliver was on the fringe of the

Ben Olney, 240 senior appearances before moving to Villa.

Derby County team for three seasons. He played several good games in the formidable side of the late 1940s without making himself first choice.

OLNEY
Benjamin Albert   *Goalkeeper*

Born: Holborn, 30 March 1899. Died: Derby, 23 September 1943.
Career: Fairleys Athletic. Aston Park Rangers. Stourbridge. Derby County April 1921. Aston Villa December 1927. Bilston United July 1930: player-manager May 1931. Walsall August 1931. Shrewsbury Town August 1932. Moor Green.

Division Two promotion 1925-6.

Rams fans had special reason to celebrate Christmas 1927. For the first time in 37 years their team had done the double over Aston Villa, winning

5-0 at the Baseball Ground on Boxing Day and 1-0 at Villa Park 24 hours later. Villa's reaction to this was immediate. Two days later they went back to Derby and signed the Rams' out-of-favour goalkeper Ben Olney. Within five months, Olney was in the England team which played in France and Belgium. Olney, a Londoner raised in Birmingham, requested a move after losing his place to Harry Wilkes and negotiations had been in progress a fortnight before he joined Villa. He set an appearances record for a Derby goalkeeper, 240 senior games, which survived until Reg Matthews passed it, and missed only 11 games through illness and injury between February 1922 and September 1927. Olney was a pillar of George Jobey's Second Division promotion team, being absent only once. He was working at Rolls-Royce at the time of his death.

Donald O'Riordan.

Ian Ormondroyd.

Keith Osgood.

O'RIORDAN
Donald Joseph *Defender/midfield*

Born: Dublin, 14 May 1957.
Career: Apprentice, Derby County: professional July 1975. Doncaster Rovers, loan, January 1978. Tulsa Roughnecks February 1978. Preston North End October 1978. Tulsa Roughnecks, loan, May 1979. Carlisle United August 1983. Middlesbrough August 1985. Player-coach, Grimsby Town, August 1986: player/assistant-manager, July 1987. Notts County July 1988. Mansfield Town, loan, September 1989.

Showed considerable promise but Tommy Docherty allowed him to join Tulsa on a free transfer, one of the American deals which came under review when the police investigated Derby County's affairs in 1979. O'Riordan returned from America to have a long and successful career. At Notts County he combined playing with coaching but was injured after helping them to win promotion to the First Division in 1990-91.

ORMONDROYD
Ian *Forward*

Born: Bradford, 22 September 1964.
Career: Manningham Mills. Thackley. Bradford City August 1985. Oldham Athletic, loan, March 1987. Aston Villa February 1989. Derby County, loan, September 1991. Derby County December 1991. Leicester City March 1992.

Mick Harford's return to Luton left Derby County's attack thin in autumn 1991, when money was still short. Arthur Cox's counter was to sign Ian Ormondroyd and Bobby Davison on loan on the same day. Davison's homecoming helped the 6ft 4in Ormondroyd to ease his way in and they quickly formed an effective partnership. When Davison returned to Leeds, Ormandroyd accepted the scoring responsibility and, after three months on loan, signed permanently for £300,000. He was settling in with Marco Gabbiadini when, without warning, he joined Leicester City as part of the Paul Kitson deal.

O'ROURKE
John *Centre-forward*

Career: Willington Athletic. Derby County January 1901.

O'Rourke played five games in place of John Boag towards the end of the 1900-01 season.

OSGOOD
Keith *Central defender*

Born: Isleworth, 8 May 1955.

Career: Apprentice, Tottenham Hotspur: professional May 1972. Coventry City January 1978. Derby County October 1979. Orient December 1981. HJK Helsinki May 1984. Cambridge United November 1984. Burton Albion February 1986. Stapenhill March 1986.

Keith Osgood, an England Youth international in 1973, cost Derby County £150,000, part of a total outlay of around £1.3 million in Colin Addison's first season. Osgood, a fine athlete, was also prone to lapses of concentration and the Rams lost heavily when he moved to Orient for £20,000.

OSMAN
Rex Charles Herbert *Wing-half*

Born: Derby, 4 April 1932.
Career: Juniors and Derby County office staff: professional, July 1949. Boston United July 1956. Ilkeston Town August 1957. Gresley Rovers September 1959: player-coach, November 1959.

Osman spent several years in Derby's Central League team but played only two senior games. His son Russell played for Ipswich Town, Leicester

City, Southampton and Bristol City, winning 11 England caps. At one stage, Rex ran Ipswich Town's restaurant at Portman Road.

OXFORD
Kenneth   *Goalkeeper*

Born: Oldham, 14 November 1929.
Career: Ardwick LC. Manchester City November 1947. Derby County December 1948. Chesterfield June 1950. Norwich City July 1951. Derby County December 1957. Doncaster Rovers July

Ken Oxford.

1964. Port Vale March 1965. Boston United November 1965 to June 1967. reserve-team coach, 1968. Boston FC October 1968: caretaker manager April 1969: manager May 1969: general manager, May 1970.

Derby County signed goalkeeper Ken Oxford from Norwich City for £4,000, yet they once had him for nothing. Oxford had played one game for Manchester City — keeping a clean sheet against Arsenal — before they released him and he arrived at Derby in 1948 for a trial. The Rams decided he would not make the grade and he drifted to Chesterfield, where Ray Middleton denied him a League game. When Oxford signed for Norwich, he was again understudy, this time to Ken Nethercott. Eventually, he made his debut on Christmas Day 1953, the first of 136 senior games for the Canaries. Oxford represented the Football Combination against a Dutch X1 and the Third Division South against the North. Harry Storer signed him to replace Terry Webster and he was a

Charlie Palmer.

regular for two-and-a-half seasons, occasionally giving way to Terry Adlington or Jim Mitchell until November 1961, when Storer signed former England goalkeeper Reg Matthews. On the opening day of 1962-3, new manager Tim Ward found that Matthews was ill and Oxford came in, saving a penalty in the 3-3 draw at Huddersfield. He kept his place until the following March before moving to Doncaster. Even in his early 60s, Oxford was still keeping goal enthusiastically for the ex-Rams team.

PALMER
Charles Anthony   *Right-back*

Born: Aylesbury, 10 July 1963.
Career: Apprentice, Watford: professional July 1981. Derby County July 1984. Hull City February 1987. Notts County, loan, February 1989. Notts County March 1989.
Division Three promotion 1985-6.

Charlie Palmer was Arthur Cox's first signing at Derby and one of the most popular. He had only limited senior experience with Watford, although he played in the UEFA Cup. His athleticism made him a pleasure to watch but financial considerations led to his being sold to Hull City. Palmer had his best days with Notts County, helping them to win promotion from the Second Division and doing well in the First, despite relegation.

PALMER
Desmond Frederick   *Forward*

Born: Swansea, 23 September 1931.
Career: Juniors, Swansea Town: professional April 1950. Liverpool March 1959. Johannesburg Ramblers 1960. Derby County June 1961. Wellington Town July 1962. Slavia Melbourne 1963. Yugal, Sydney, 1964. Player-manager, Llanelli, 1965.

Des Palmer played three times for Wales while he was with Swansea Town, scoring a hat-trick in his second international, against East Germany, but his move to Liverpool turned into a disaster when he suffered knee ligaments damage. After Palmer had played in South Africa, Harry Storer took a gamble on him and he scored twice on his debut against Middlesbrough at Ayresome Park. The move was only a short-term success.

PARKIN
Albert Geoffrey   *Centre-forward*

Born: Mansfield, 11 April 1928.
Career: Juniors. Derby County May 1946. Ilkeston Town November 1952.

Geoff Parkin deputised in three forward positions during 1949-50 but did not score in his nine League appearances.

PARKIN
Reginald   *Goalkeeper*

Career: Folkestone Town. Derby County May 1936.

Reg Parkin played in only one League game for Derby, a 3-3 draw against Huddersfield Town in March 1937.

PARNELL
Gresham Frederick   *Outside-right*

Born: Sutton-in-Ashfield, 1886.
Career: Skegby United. Pinxton. Derby County December 1903. Leeds City August 1905. Exeter City May 1908. Preston North End May 1909. Exeter City July 1910. Sutton Junction June 1912.

Fred Parnell was given nine games at outside-right when Derby County were struggling to fill the position, injuries having hampered Mercer's career at the Baseball Ground.

PARR
Jack   *Left-back*

Born: Derby, 21 November 1920. Died: Derby, 28 March 1985.
Career: Little Eaton St Peter's. Derby County, amateur, December 1937:

Jack Parr.

professional March 1938. Shrewsbury Town July 1953. Gresley Rovers August 1956. Burton Albion June 1957. Gresley Rovers November 1957. Belper Town May 1958: player-coach May 1959.

Jack Parr was one of the unlucky trio, along with Frank Boulton and Sammy Crooks, who missed the 1946 FA Cup Final through injury. Parr, a pre-war junior, made his senior debut when the Rams arranged some friendlies in 1941-2 and played through the 1946 Cup campaign, missing only the Final. He broke an arm when Derby were playing Luton Town in the League South 24 days before the Wembley date. Jack Howe took Parr's place at left-back and went on to play for England. Parr's cultured style won considerable praise and he played for an England 'B' team against the Army in 1946-7 but by the time he became a regular in League football, Derby were falling into decline. He joined Crooks at Shrewsbury Town before finishing his career in non-League football.

PARRY
Anthony John   *Midfield*

Born: Burton upon Trent, 8 September 1945.

Two unlucky footballers. Jack Parr (left) and Peter Croker (centre) take their places before the 1946 FA Cup Final.

Tony Parry.

Jack Parry, one of only ten to score 100 goals for Derby.

Career: Burton Albion amateur 1963: professional May 1964. Hartlepools United November 1965. Derby County January 1972. Mansfield Town, loan, January 1974. Gresley Rovers 1976. Local football. Gresley Rovers August 1981.

Tony Parry was a tough tackler in midfield and did well for Brian Clough and Peter Taylor at Hartlepools United. He joined Derby County for £3,000 and made his debut in the first leg of the Texaco Cup Final against Airdrieonians at Broomfield Park. He had two spells with Gresley Rovers, who made him club captain and awarded him a testimonial.

PARRY
Jack　　　　*Inside-forward/wing-half*
Born: Derby, 29 July 1931.
Career: Juniors, Derby County: professional, July 1948. Boston United June 1967.

Division Three North champions 1956-7.

Jack Parry came from a Derby football family. One brother, Ray, played for Bolton and England, while another, Glyn, was on Derby County's staff and Cyril played for Notts County. Jack played for Derby Boys and signed for the Rams when Raich Carter and Billy Steel were still there. He was still at the Baseball Ground 20 years later, having set a club record of 517 appearances which survived until Kevin Hector overtook it. Like Geoff Barrowcliffe and Albert Mays, Parry might have made a bigger name in football had he moved to a more successful club. He was a lively inside-forward and had a brilliant year when the Rams found themselves in the Third Division North in 1955-6. He scored 24 goals in 34 League games but his season was ended by injury in the key clash with Grimsby Town, watched by 33,330 at the Baseball Ground. Ray de Gruchy's chal-

lenge left Parry with a back injury, limiting his contribution to the Third North championship the following season. In the Second Division he established himself at wing-half and was club captain. He lost his place in 1965-6 and was unable to establish himself again, spending a final season with Boston United. Parry's wit made him a popular member of the dressing-room and once Ralph Hann was treating him in a match. Fearing concussion, Hann asked him where he was. "I'm at Wembley," said Parry. "We're beating Brazil 2-0 — and I've scored both."

PATERSON
Robert　　　　*Centre-half*
Born: Glasgow.
Career: Clyde. Derby County October 1897. Coventry City.
FA Cup Finalists 1898-9.

Paterson spent two seasons at the

Baseball Ground, mostly as a reserve to Archie Goodall. He did, however, earn a surprise place in the 1899 FA Cup Final against Sheffield United, when Goodall was suspended by the club for 'inattention to training'.

PATERSON
William *Centre-forward*

Born: Hill o' Beath, 5 March. Died: Cowdenbeath, 1970.
Career: Cowdenbeath 1914. Derby County January 1921. Cowdenbeath June 1924. Armadale, loan. Coventry City August 1925. Springfield 1926. Fall River. Player-manager, Providence. Gold-Bugs. New York Nationals.

Bill Paterson.

A shortage of goals was a main reason for Derby losing their First Division place in 1921. Bill Paterson arrived during the summer but, although he was leading scorer in his first season, did not entirely solve the problem. He faded as Randolph Galloway began to emerge. He played in the United States for several years.

PATON
Thomas H. *Centre-forward*

Born: Larkhall.
Career: Glasgow Rangers. Derby County May 1904. Sheffield United March 1906. St Mirren.

After the departure of John Boag and William Hodgkinson, Derby County signed Paton but he found goals scarce, managing only four in 38 senior games.

PATRICK
Roy *Right-back*

Born: Overseal, 4 December 1935.
Career: Juniors, Derby County: professional December 1952. Nottingham Forest May 1959. Southampton June 1961. Exeter City March 1963. Burton Albion August 1965.

Roy Patrick was an early starter. He made his League debut against Sunderland at Roker Park in September 1952, at the age of 16 years and 277 days. It was his only appearance that season and Derby were relegated twice before he was 20. After playing in 1955-6, when the Rams were runners-up in the Third Division North, Patrick made only rare appearances.

PATTERSON
Mark *Defender*

Born: Leeds, 13 September 1968.
Career: Trainee, Carlisle United: professional August 1987. Derby County November 1987.

Mark Patterson.

After only 22 Fourth Division games for Carlisle United, Mark Patterson was signed for £60,000 as a player for the future. His runs from right-back made him popular at Brunton Park and he quickly settled with Derby Reserves, making occasional senior appearances. His best chance to establish a regular place came when Mel Sage was injured in November 1991. Patterson was doing

well and scored a marvellous goal in an FA Cup third-round replay against Burnley. Sadly for him, the game was abandoned because of fog, so the goal did not count, and he finished the night needing an operation on damaged knee ligaments.

PATTISON
John W. *Outside-left*

Born: Durham, 10 April.
Career: Framwellgate Moor. Durham City January 1920. Langley Moor. Newcastle United April 1920. Durham City November 1920. Derby County July 1921. Bristol Rovers September 1922. Durham City August 1925. South Shields 1926. Torquay United July 1927. Bath City 1930.

Pattison had a run in Derby County's Second Division team between the departure of Alf Quantrill and the arrival of Lionel Murphy.

PAUL
David Dryburgh *Goalkeeper*

Born: Kircaldy, 19 February 1936.
Career: Juniors, Derby County: professional February 1953. Boston United July 1956. Matlock Town July 1961. Belper Town September 1963. Matlock Town September 1964. Crewton May 1967.

A Scottish schoolboy international goalkeeper, on the short side for League football. One of several Derby County players who joined Boston United in the 1950s.

PAUL
John *Wing-forward*

Career: Hibernian. Derby County November 1894. Bristol Rovers May 1898.
Division One runners-up 1895-6.

John Paul.

Paul played on both wings for Derby County, settling on the right as cover for John Goodall.

PAYNE
Frank Ernest.   *Goalkeeper*

Born: Ipswich, 18 March 1926.
Career: Ollerton Colliery. Derby County December 1947. Hull City August 1948. Lincoln City August 1949. Kippax Legionaires September 1950. Swillington Welfare July 1951. Farsley Celtic October 1956.

Frank Payne played only once for Derby County, in an FA Cup fifth round tie against Middlesbrough at Ayresome Park in February 1948. He had only a handful of Central League games behind him but an injury to Billy Townsend forced Payne's inclusion. Payne was on the winning side but the Rams signed veteran Jock Wallace to see them through to the semi-finals.

PEART
John George   *Centre-forward*

Born: South Shields, 3 October 1888.
Died: Paddington, 3 September 1948.
Career: South Shields Adelaide 1905. Sheffield United May 1907. Stoke June 1910. Newcastle United March 1912. Notts County February 1913. Birmingham November 1919. Derby County January 1920. Player-manager, Ebbw Vale, August 1920. Port Vale January 1922. Norwich City July 1922. Player-manager, Rochdale, March 1923. Retired as player May 1924: manager to July 1930. Manager, Bradford City, July 1930 to March 1935. Manager, Fulham May 1935 until his death.

Jack Peart had a long and sometimes distinguished career, as player and manager, but he did not solve Derby County's scoring problem in 1919-20. Peart played for the Football League in 1913-14, the season in which he was involved in Notts County's Second Division championship. Two years earlier, while with Stoke, he played three times for the Southern League, against the Irish League, the Scottish League and the Football League. He managed Fulham for 13 years, building the team which won the Second Division in 1948-9 but not living to see the success.

PEART
Ronald   *Centre-forward*

Born: Brandon, 8 March 1920.
Career: Langley Moor. Hartlepools United September 1938. Derby County May 1939. York City June 1948. Spennymoor United 1949.

Derby County had an unsettled forward line in 1946-7 after Peter Doherty left. Ron Peart, a pre-war George Jobey signing, was given one outing, against Blackpool, in February 1947.

PEMBRIDGE
Mark Anthony   *Midfield*

Born: Merthyr Tydfil, 29 November 1970.
Career: Trainee, Luton Town: professional July 1989. Derby County June 1992.

Mark Pembridge was the first of Arthur Cox's major signings in summer 1992, joining the Rams from Luton Town for £1,250,000. Pembridge's dynamic displays in midfield impressed Michael Harford, who returned from Derby to Kenilworth Road early in September 1991. In that season, Pembridge won his first full caps for Wales, having represented them at Under-21 and 'B' levels.

Jack Peart.

Mark Pembridge with manager Arthur Cox and Rams owner Lionel Pickering.

PENNEY
David Mark
Forward

Born: Wakefield, 17 August 1964.
Career: Pontefract Collieries. Derby County September 1985. Oxford United June 1989. Swansea City, loan, March 1991.

Division Two champions 1986-7.

David Penney was snapped up from the Northern Counties League (East) and immediately played a part in Derby County's 1985-6 Central League championship. He made one substitute appearance in the Second Division championship team, while continuing to show lively pace and an eye for goals in the Reserves. Penney made more appearances in the First Division, becoming a valuable member of the squad before he joined Oxford United for £175,000.

PHILBIN
John
Inside-forward

Career: Washington Colliery. Derby County December 1933. Torquay United May 1936. Brighton & Hove Albion June 1938.

Philbin, who cost Derby £150, played one League game, as replacement for Arthur Groves in April 1935.

PHILLIPS
Justin Lee
Centre-half

Born: Derby, 17 December 1971.

Career: Trainee, Derby County: professional July 1990.

A regular in the England Schools team, Justin Phillips was always destined for the Baseball Ground. Unfortunately, his career suffered a major setback when, still in his teens, he needed two operations to repair knee ligaments. He battled back and played three First Division games at the end of 1990-91, scoring against Southampton. He won an England Youth cap.

PICKERING
Nicholas
Midfield

Born: Newcastle upon Tyne, 4 August 1963.
Career: Apprentice, Sunderland: professional August 1981. Coventry City January 1986. Derby County August 1988. Darlington October 1991.

Nick Pickering played for England at left-back, against Australia in 1983, won 15 Under-21 caps and was in Coventry City's 1987 FA Cup winning team. He left Coventry because he wanted to play in midfield rather than the left-back spot which was planned, and with such a solid First Division career behind him, appeared to be a good signing at £250,000. Nothing went right for him at Derby. He was unable to win a regular place and, on the occasions when he began to show a glimmer of form, was unfortunate with injuries. After being released on a free transfer, Pickering joined Darlington.

PITMAN
Reuben John
Goalkeeper

One of four goalkeepers used by Derby in the first Football League season.

PLACE
Charles Arthur
Outside-left

Born: Ilkeston, 26 November 1937.
Career: Juniors, Derby County: professional November 1954. Ilkeston Town July 1956. Bourne Town November 1958. Stamford June 1959. Long Eaton United July 1960.

Charlie Place played two League games in September 1955, Derby County's first season in the Third Division North.

PLACKETT
Henry
Forward

Career: Long Eaton Midland. Derby County 1888. Nottingham Forest April 1889.

One of Derby County's original League players, Harry Plackett partnered his brother on the left of the attack through much of the opening League season.

David Penney.

Justin Phillips.

Nick Pickering.

Syd Plackett, recovered from war wounds to make 156 appearances for Derby.

Whitwick, near Coalville, May 1950. Career: Sawley United Church. Service in World War One. Sawley Discharged Soldiers' Federation March 1919. Derby County January 1921. Notts County February 1927.

Division Two promotion 1925-6.

Syd Plackett was wounded in fighting on the Somme in 1916 but recovered to build an excellent League career and was ever-present when Derby County won promotion from the Second Division in 1925-6. He arrived at the Baseball Ground as a centre-forward but gradually found his niche as a left-half. He first played there regularly when Harry Storer was injured and was so successful that Storer returned as an inside-left. Plackett completed a formidable half-back line with Johnny McIntyre and Harry Thoms, an utterly reliable trio in Jobey's promotion team. Notts County, one of the clubs most interested when he was playing in Sawley, eventually signed him in 1927.

PLUMMER
Calvin Anthony   *Outside-right*

Born: Nottingham, 14 February 1963. Career: Apprentice, Nottingham Forest: professional February 1981. Chesterfield, loan, December 1982.

Calvin Plummer.

Chesterfield January 1983. Derby County August 1983. Barnsley March 1984. Nottingham Forest, amateur, October 1986: contract, December 1986. Lahden Reipas (Finland) May 1987. Nottingham Forest October 1987. Derry City, loan, March 1988. Plymouth Argyle, loan, September 1988. Plymouth Argyle October 1988. Chesterfield July 1989. Gainsborough 1991.

PLACKETT
Lawrence   *Forward*

Career: Long Eaton Alexandra. Derby County 1886. Nottingham Forest cs 1889.

Lol Plackett was the first Derby County player to complete an ever-present season in the Football League. He scored twice in Derby's opening League game, against Bolton Wanderers at Pike's Lane, and was at outside or inside-left throughout 1888-9. In 1890, after leaving Derby, he played in an England international trial at Nottingham.

PLACKETT
Sydney   *Left-half*

Born: Sawley, 21 September 1898. Died:

Peter Taylor wanted to sign Calvin Plummer before he went to Chesterfield. Plummer joined the Rams for £10,000 but had not completed his first season when he was sold to Barnsley, along with Paul Futcher, to alleviate desperate financial problems. When Barnsley released him two years later, Brian Clough gave him another chance with Nottingham Forest and, after a summer in Finland, he played in a successful First Division team in 1987-8 before moving down the League.

POPPITT
John   *Right-back*
Born: West Sleekburn, 20 January 1923. Career: West Sleekburn. Derby County May 1945. Queen's Park Rangers September 1950. Chelmsford City July 1954. Burton Albion June 1955. Banbury Spencer May 1957. Corby Town June 1958. Long Eaton United January 1960. Player-coach, Matlock Town, June 1965.

John Poppitt.

A neat full-back who made his League debut in February 1947, as an emergency centre-forward. Most of his Derby career was spent in the Central League, as reserve to Bert Mozley, but he made 106 League appearances for Queen's Park Rangers.

POWELL
Barry Ivor   *Midfield*
Born: Kenilworth, 29 January 1954. Career: Apprentice, Wolverhampton Wanderers: professional January 1972. Portland Timbers, loan, April 1975. Coventry City September 1975. Derby County October 1979. Portland

Barry Powell, found life difficult in a struggling team.

Timbers, temporary transfer, April 1981. Bulova, Hong Kong, August 1982. Burnley July 1984. Swansea City February 1985. South China FC, Hong Kong, July 1986. Wolverhampton Wanderers November 1986: youth coach, August 1987 to June 1991.

Barry Powell earned four England Under-23 caps while he was with Wolverhampton Wanderers and came on as substitute when they won the 1974 League Cup Final against Manchester City. Colin Addison paid around £340,000 to sign Powell from Coventry but he struggled at Derby. He was the type of midfield player to keep a good team ticking over, rather than the one to transform an ailing side. He moved

to Hong Kong in 1982, with Derby having lost heavily on their investment.

POWELL
Kenneth   *Outside-left*
*Born: Mansfield, 2 March 1920. Died: 1976.
Career: Mansfield CWS. Derby County May 1939. Southport June 1947.*

Ken Powell served in the Royal Navy during World War Two and returned to make his bid for the outside-left position when Dally Duncan moved to Luton Town. He played 13 League games in the first post-war League season but moved on during the following summer.

Steve Powell, 420 senior appearances for the Rams.

POWELL
Stephen   *Midfield/central-defender*

Born: Derby, 20 September 1955.
Career: Apprentice, Derby County: professional, November 1972. Arcadia Shepherds, loan, May 1977. Tulsa Roughnecks, loan, May 1979. Player-coach, Shepshed Charterhouse, June

1986: player-manager, March 1987. Assistant coach, Albany Capitals, April 1988. Shepshed Charterhouse 1988: caretaker player-manager December 1988. Player-manager Burton Albion, February 1990 to April 1991. Manager, Belper Town, June 1991.
Division One champions 1971-2, 1974-5.

Steve Powell was 16 years and 30 days old when he made a remarkable debut against Stoke City in a Texaco Cup tie at the Baseball Ground in October 1971. His father, Tommy, had been a distinguished Rams player. Steve, educated at Bemrose School like his father, was captain of England Boys and, in 1973, led the England Youth team to victory in the UEFA tournament in Florence. Even more amazingly mature than his debut, was Powell's performance in the final League match of 1971-2 against Liverpool. He played at right-back in the victory which gave Derby their first Championship. He was playing European football in his teens and, during those early seasons, England caps seemed inevitable. He was equally happy in midfield or defence but, as his career developed, he suffered a great deal from injuries. The most serious brought about an operation on damaged knee ligaments in 1981-2. He also had back and pelvic trouble and, in 1982-3, a broken jaw. Some of his problems seemed to have stemmed from a summer with Tulsa Roughnecks in 1979, but Powell battled against injuries as he always competed on the field. He turned from a schoolboy star into a fine League professional who, despite playing in a declining side, was totally dedicated to Derby County. Experience and knowledge of the game enabled him to overcome a lack of pace, but his international honours stopped at an Under-23 appearance against Scotland in 1974-5.

POWELL
Thomas   *Inside-forward/Winger*
Born: Derby, 12 April 1925.
Career: Derby Corinthians. Derby County April 1942. Retired 1962. Northcliffe United. Player-manager, Redfern Athletic, November 1965 to October 1966. Manager, Northcliffe United to August 1984.
Division Three North champions 1956-7.

Tommy Powell first played on the Baseball Ground in the 1930s for the Firs Estate Junior School in a local schools cup final. He went on to Bemrose School and on Christmas Day 1941 played for the Rams as a 16-year-old against an RAF team, Derby's first match since re-forming after the outbreak of war. The *Derby Evening Telegraph* reported: 'Tom, a big lad with a long stride, need not be too downhearted if he felt out of it before the course was run . . .he did get at least one chance to show that he had a fine shot in his gun . . .' Powell was a great success in wartime soccer. He was called up and played in the BAOR side, his National Service preventing him making League debut until 1948. Although not obviously strong, Powell

Tommy Powell, 406 first-team games after his League debut was delayed.

Dick Pratley.

PRATLEY
Richard George   *Centre-half*

Born: Banbury, 12 January 1963.
Career: Banbury United. Derby County July 1983. Scunthorpe United, loan, March 1984. Shrewsbury Town February 1988: youth coach 1991.

Division Three promotion 1985-6. Division Two champions 1986-7.

Dick Pratley was spotted in Southern League football, playing for the club which produced Kevin Wilson. After appearing in a stipulated number of games, Pratley cost £9,000, so Derby made a handsome profit when he joined Shrewsbury Town for £60,000. A valuable squad member in two promotions, Pratley was captain of the Central League championship side in 1985-6 when Derby became the first Third Division club to lift the title. Pratley became Shrewsbury's captain, but knee trouble ended his career.

PUMFORD
George Leslie   *Centre-forward*

Born: Ruabon.
Career: Manchester North. Derby County January 1925. Walsall July 1926.

Pumford stood in twice for Albert Fairclough during 1924-5.

---

had immaculate ball control, and perhaps his two best years came when the Rams were in Division Three North. Seldom had the Third Division seen such skill and when Derby won promotion, Powell had the perfect understanding with Ray Straw, able to drop the ball in from all angles to exploit the centre-forward's strength in the air. Powell's deceptive body swerve and complete mastery of the ball made

him vital to the side. In 1953, Derby and Hull agreed on a fee of £10,000, but Powell did not want to leave his beloved Derby. In his younger days many considered him unlucky not to have won an England cap. He retired in 1961, but made a brief comeback the following season until an injury against Portsmouth in a League Cup replay at the Baseball Ground ended his career for good.

Jesse Pye, 16 goals in Derby's first Division Three North season.

Alf Quantrill.

PYE
Jesse
Centre-forward

Born: Treeton, 22 December 1919. Died: Blackpool, 20 February 1984.
Career: Treeton. Sheffield United December 1938. Notts County September 1945. Wolverhampton Wanderers May 1946. Luton Town July 1952. Derby County October 1954. Wisbech Town July 1957: player-manager March 1960: manager to December 1966.
Division Three North champions 1956-7.

Jesse Pye was in the veteran stage when Jack Barker signed him for Derby County and, despite his considerable skill, he was unable to halt the slide towards the Third Division North. Pye played in a Victory International while he was with Notts County but his best days were with Wolverhampton Wanderers. He scored twice when

Wolves beat Leicester City 3-1 in the 1949 FA Cup Final, played three times for England 'B' and earned his solitary full cap, against the Republic of Ireland in September 1949. Pye was on the fringe of the Rams team when they won the Third North but spent more than nine years as player and manager in the Southern League with Wisbech Town.

PYNEGAR
Algernon
Inside-forward

Born: Heanor, 1883. Died: 23 June 1948.
Career: Marlpool. Derby County August 1904. Grimsby Town August 1905.

Pynegar's solitary League appearance was as stand-in for Steve Bloomer in a 6-0 defeat by Manchester City in December 1904.

QUANTRILL
Alfred Edward
Outside-left

Born: Punjab, 22 January 1897. Died: Trefriw, 19 April 1968.
Career: Boston Swifts. Derby County August 1914. Preston North End July 1921. Chorley August 1924. Bradford September 1924. Nottingham Forest May 1930. Retired May 1932.
Division Two champions 1914-15.

Alf Quantrill was born in India, but it was in a Lincolnshire Cup match for Boston Swifts that the Rams spotted him. Quantrill signed a week after the outbreak of World War One and played three games in the 1914-15 promotion side. After service with the Derbyshire Yeomanry — he contracted malaria in Salonika — Quantrill resumed his career in 1919 and, within six months of his First Division debut, was picked to play for England. His debut came in the surprising 2-1 defeat by Wales at Highbury in February 1920. Quantrill was the only forward to retain his place for the game against Scotland at Hillsborough the following month, scoring in a thrilling 5-4 victory. Quantrill had tremendous speed, but his international career lasted only two more games and he moved to Preston when Derby lost their First Division place. A son-in-law of Steve Bloomer, Quantrill later managed the Manchester headquarters of the Scottish Union Insurance Company.

Alan Ramage, also a Yorkshire cricketer.

Craig Ramage, badly injured before the start of 1992-3.

RAISBECK
William
Wing-half

Born: Wallacetown, 1876.
Career: Clyde. Sunderland, December 1896. Royal Albert. Clyde October 1897. Sunderland August 1898. Derby County May 1901. New Brompton July 1902. Reading June 1904.

One of the brothers of the great Liverpool and Scotland centre-half Alex Raisbeck, William spent a season with Derby, filling in at wing-half on three occasions.

RAMAGE
Alan
Centre-half

Born: Guisborough, 29 November 1957.
Career: Apprentice, Middlesbrough: professional December 1975. Derby County July 1980.

Colin Addison paid £150,000 for Ramage after Derby County had been relegated from the First Division but he never settled and was forced into premature retirement by a knee injury. This also curtailed his cricket career. A fast bowler, he played for Yorkshire from 1979 to 1983.

RAMAGE
Craig Darren
Midfield

Born: Wirksworth, 30 March 1970.
Career: Trainee, Derby County: professional July 1988. Wigan Athletic, loan, February 1989.

After developing as a striker in the Youth team, Craig Ramage found his place in midfield. He made his League debut while on loan to Wigan Athletic and found it hard to make his way in Derby's 1990-91 relegation season. He came back the following season after

a knee-ligaments operation. Ramage earned two England Under-21 caps, a reward for his skill on the ball.

RAMAGE
Peter
Inside-left

Born: Bonnyrigg, 26 March 1908. Died: Ballyclare, 17 December 1982.
Career: Tranant Juniors. Newtongrange Star. Coventry City June 1927. Derby County August 1928. Chesterfield August 1937. Chelmsford City May 1939. Atherstone Town July 1945. Ilkeston Town September 1947 to October 1948.

Division One runners-up 1929-30, 1935-6.

Derby County supporters consistently undervalued Peter Ramage because, they felt, he did not score enough goals. His record will bear examination, 60 goals in 255 appearances, and for five

Peter Ramage scores for Derby at Highbury in November 1935, watched by Sammy Crooks (far left).

seasons he was an automatic choice at inside-forward. Ramage played 28 times for Coventry City before George Jobey signed him in time for the 1928-9 season. He scored on his debut, a 5-1 defeat of FA Cup holders Blackburn Rovers, but did not gain a regular place until George Stephenson moved to Sheffield Wednesday. Ramage's creative skill earned him the respect of other players and Jack Barker said he had helped more others to international status than anybody he knew. Ramage's most famous goal was the FA Cup replay winner against Sunderland in 1933, when 75,118 squeezed into Roker Park to see the sixth-round tie resolved.

RAMSELL
Ernest A.   *Wing-half*
Born: Stanton, near Burton upon Trent.
Career: Stanton. Derby County January 1906.

Ramsell took over on five occasions when Ben Warren was either injured, on England duty or playing centre-forward.

RANCE
Charles Stanley   *Centre-half*
Born: Bow, 28 February 1889. Died: Chichester, 29 December 1966.
Career: Clapton 1904. Tottenham Hotspur July 1910. Derby County March 1921. Queen's Park Rangers September 1922. Coached in Holland. Secretary-manager, Guildford City, April 1925 to June 1927.

Jimmy Methven hoped that the signing

Peter Ramage.

Charlie Rance.

of Harry Storer and Charles Rance would help to keep Derby County in the First Division but they were still relegated in 1921. Harold Wightman regained his place from Rance the following season. Rance scored the winner for Clapton against Stockton in the 1907 FA Amateur Cup Final and was a member of Tottenham Hotspur's Second Division championship team in 1919-20.

RANDALL
James   *Outside-left*
Born: Guide Post, Northumberland, 12 December 1904.
Career: Ashington Colliery Welfare. Sleekburn Albion. Bedlington United. Ashington June 1925. Bradford City October 1928. Derby County May 1930. Bristol City May 1935.

Randall was a member of Bradford City's Third Division North championship team in 1928-9 and Derby County offered him the chance of First Division football. He was one of several contestants for the outside-left position, a problem George Jobey solved only when he signed Dally Duncan.

RANSFORD
James   *Centre-forward*
Born: Blackwell.
Career: Blackwell. Ripley Athletic February 1904. Blackwell. Alfreton Town 1906. Derby County September 1906. Alfreton Town.

Ransford was given a good run in 1906-07 but was unable to produce enough goals to make the centre-forward spot his own.

RATCLIFFE
Emor   *Left-back*
Born: Hyde.
Career: Loughborough Corinthians. Derby County May 1902. Middlesbrough March 1906.

Jack Ratcliffe joined Derby County as reserve to Charlie Morris but covered in several defensive positions before joining Middlesbrough as part of the deal which involved Steve Bloomer moving to Ayresome Park. With a second player involved, Derby could pull in a more realistic fee for Bloomer under the transfer regulations then in force.

RAYBOULD
Samuel   *Outside-right*
Born: Chesterfield, 1875.
Career: Chesterfield Town (trial) February 1894. Derby County 1894. Ilkeston Town January 1895. Poolsbrook United. Ilkeston Town February 1898. Bolsover Colliery. New Brighton Tower October 1899. Liverpool January 1900. Sunderland May 1907. Woolwich Arsenal May

Sam Raybould.

1908. Chesterfield Town September 1909. Sutton Town August 1911.

Sam Raybould scored on his debut for Derby County and played five games on the right-wing before joining Ilkeston Town for £10. The Rams had failed to spot his potential because, as centre-forward, Raybould won two League Championship medals with Liverpool, played three times for the Football League and also earned a Second Division medal. His 31 League goals in 1902-03 was a Liverpool record for 28 years.

READER
Albert Richard   *Outside-right*
Born: Derby, 3 June 1894.
Career: Ripley Athletic. Derby County December 1913. Bristol City June 1914. Luton Town June 1922.

Reader replaced Billy Grimes for four games in 1913-14, when Derby County were relegated from the First Division.

REDFERN
William Joseph   *Inside-forward*
Born: Connah's Quay, 15 October 1910.

Billy Redfern.

Died: Deeside, Flintshire, September 1988.
Career: Hollywell Arcadians 1931. Bangor City 1933. Newry Town. Luton Town July 1937. Derby County August 1939. Wrexham during World War Two.

George Jobey had a new right-wing pair in two of the three matches in 1939-40 before the outbreak of World War Two. Wilfred Walsh replaced Sammy Crooks and Billy Redfern was signed from Luton Town to take over from Ronnie Dix, sold to Tottenham Hotspur. Reg Stockill went to Kenilworth Road as part of the Redfern deal. By the time the war was over and the fixtures replayed in 1946-7, Redfern's League career was over. He played in a wartime international for Wales against Ireland in November 1939.

REID
Anthony James   *Midfield*
Born: Nottingham, 9 May 1963.
Career: Apprentice, Derby County: professional May 1980. Scunthorpe United, loan, February 1983. Newport County March 1983. Chesterfield July 1985. Stafford Rangers December 1987. Burton Albion September 1988. Matlock Town October 1988.

Tony Reid.

Tony Reid was starting to emerge as an exciting midfield prospect with Derby County when his progress was halted by a nasty injury to knee ligaments against Luton Town in November 1981. Reid, a good user of the ball, was only 18 at the time but similar injuries hampered him at Chesterfield, forcing an early retirement from League football.

Sid Reid, capped for Ireland while in Derby Reserves.

Tony Rhodes.

George Richards

REID
Sidney Edward   *Left-back*

Born: Belfast.
Career: Cliftonville Strollers. Belfast Distillery. Derby County December 1929. Reading June 1936.
Division One runners-up 1935-6.

Such was Derby County's talent in the 1930s that Sid Reid played only 16 games, as reserve to George Collin, in more than six years at the Baseball Ground even though he was an Irish international. Reid played three times for Ireland while he was with the Rams, who paid Distillery £1,150 for him.

REVELL
Charles H.   *Defender*

Born: Belvedere, 5 June 1919.
Career: Callenders Athletic. Tottenham Hotspur January 1937. Northfleet. Charlton Athletic May 1939. Derby County March 1951. Player-manager, Eynesbury Rovers, June 1952. Manager, Edgware Town, 1955 to 1957. Player-coach, Canterbury City Reserves August 1957. Manager,
Erith and Belvedere, June 1958. Coach, Crystal Palace.

Charlie Revell was a stop-gap signing by Stuart McMillan after Tim Ward had joined Barnsley. His impact at the Baseball Ground was limited and he returned south after 15 months.

RHODES
John Anthony   *Centre-half*

Born: Dover, 17 September 1946.
Career: Juniors, Derby County: professional October 1963. Halifax Town November 1970. Southport August 1976.

Tony Rhodes was a steady Central League player for Derby County, making only seven senior appearances in seven years as a professional before joining Halifax Town for £4,000.

RICHARDS
Frederick.   *Inside-forward*

Career: Burton Wanderers. Derby County December 1898. Sheffield Wednesday February 1899. Burton Wanderers August 1899. Woodville
Excelsior. Trent Rovers January 1903.

Played two matches for Derby County immediately after being signed.

RICHARDS
George Henry   *Wing-half/Inside-forward*

Born: Bulwell, 10 May 1880. Died: Derby, 1 November 1959.
Career: Castle Donington Juniors. Whitwick White Cross. Derby County April 1902. Retired 1914.
FA Cup Finalists 1902-03. Division Two champions 1911-12.

George Richards, a basketmaker by trade, spent most of his life in Castle Donington. His early Derby days saw him playing inside-left to George Davis, a partnership as close off the field as it was successful on it. Jimmy Methven once said: "They were partners in the noble game of nap, in which they had phenomenal luck. They are said to have set up a library with their winnings." Richards became even better when he moved to left-half and played for England against Austria in Vienna in June 1909. It was a reward for some brilliant performances by the noted ball-juggler, known as the 'Corkscrew'. He was reserve for England against Scotland in 1910 and later that year toured South Africa with an FA side. Injured for much of the following season, Richards fought back. During World War One he guested for Queen's Park Rangers and Chelsea.

RICHARDS
John Peter *Centre-forward*

Born: Warrington, 9 November 1950.
Career: Apprentice, Wolverhampton Wanderers: professional July 1969. Derby County, loan, November 1982. Maritimo Funchal (Portugal) August 1983.

John Richards had a tremendous career with Wolverhampton Wanderers, scoring 144 League goals for them in 387 appearances, 22 of which were as substitute. He was involved in two League Cup winning teams, the UEFA Cup Final in 1972 and a Second Division championship, earning an England cap against Northern Ireland in May 1973. Richards was in Wolves' Reserves when he heard that Peter Taylor was desperate for players and joined Derby on loan, doing an excellent job in a successful fight against relegation from the Second Division.

RICHARDS
Wayne *Left-back*

Born: Scunthorpe, 10 May 1961.
Career: Normanby Park Works, Scunthorpe. Apprentice, Derby County: professional May 1979. Matlock Town August 1982. Heanor Town November 1982.

A determined performer at Central League level, Wayne Richards provided cover for Steve Buckley.

RICHARDSON
John *Right-back*

Born: Worksop, 20 April 1945.
Career: Apprentice, Derby County: professional April 1962. Notts County July 1971. King's Lynn July 1973.
Division Two champions 1968-9.

John Richardson was Derby County's first apprentice professional when the scheme was introduced. He showed promise in Tim Ward's time as manager, forming a youthful partnership with Peter Daniel at full-back. The introduction of John Robson and the shift of Ron Webster to right-back limited Richardson's

John Richards.

Wayne Richards.

Paul Richardson.

John Richardson.

opportunities under Brian Clough and he broke a leg after moving to Notts County.

RICHARDSON
Paul Andrew *Midfield*

Born: Hucknall, 7 November 1962.
Career: Rolls-Royce, Hucknall. Eastwood Town February 1981. Nuneaton Borough August 1983. Derby County August 1984. Retired from League football on medical advice. Kettering Town August 1986. Eastwood Town, loan, October 1988. Boston United, loan, September 1990. Barnet October 1990. Boston United

August 1991. Redbridge Forest November 1991.

Paul Richardson was signed before Arthur Cox's first season as manager and was starting to make an impact at League level until he suffered from tiredness. Hospital checks showed that blood was entering his lungs and he was advised to retire. He later returned successfully with Kettering Town and would have joined Scarborough but for complications over the insurance.

RICHMOND
John Frederick *Wing-half*

Born: Derby, 17 September 1938.
Career: Derby Boys. Derby Corinthians.

John Richmond.

Derby County January 1956. Chelmsford City June 1963.

A sound Central League player who had only limited opportunities in Derby County's Second Division side.

RIDDELL
Frederick William   *Inside-right*

Born: c.1888.
Career: Newhall Swifts. Derby County September 1907. Bristol Rovers cs 1909.

Fred Riddell played six senior games in two seasons with Derby County.

RIOCH
Bruce David   *Midfield*

Born: Aldershot, 6 September 1947.
Career: Apprentice, Luton Town: professional September 1964. Aston Villa July 1969. Derby County February 1974. Everton December 1976. Derby County November 1977. Birmingham City, loan, December 1978. Sheffield United, loan, March

Bruce Rioch, 54 goals, mostly from midfield, for Derby.

1979. Seattle Sounders March 1980. Player-coach, Torquay United, October 1980 (alternating with Seattle). Manager, Torquay United, July 1982 to January 1984. Coach, Seattle Sounders, July 1985 to January 1986. Assistant manager, Middlesbrough, January 1986: manager, February 1986 to March 1990. Manager, Millwall, April 1990 to March 1992. Manager, Bolton Wanderers, May 1992.

Division One champions 1974-5.

Dave Mackay bought Bruce Rioch from Aston Villa for £200,000 because he wanted more scoring power in midfield. The choice paid off in 1974-5 when Rioch, leading scorer with 15 League goals, was vital to Derby's second Championship success. In March of

that season he scored one of his most memorable goals with a surging run from near the half-way line against Newcastle United at St James' Park. The following season he hit a thunderous free-kick in the FA Cup sixth-round tie against Newcastle at the Baseball Ground. As an attacking player he had pace, power and a magnificent shot, qualities which took Rioch — with his Scottish parentage — into the Scotland side. He won 18 of his 24 caps while with Derby and captained his country in the 1978 World Cup in Argentina. In October 1976, Rioch scored four goals against Spurs at Derby, but two months later Colin Murphy sold him to Everton for £180,000. Within a year Tommy Docherty had bought him back to form a midfield trio with Gerry Daly and Don Masson. "Come and see my three Van Goghs," said Docherty, but the promised artistry did not materialise. Rioch's second spell was unhappy. He was sent off twice in 1977-8 and had rows with Docherty and his successor, Colin Addison. Rioch won medals with Luton Town, Fourth Division champions in 1967-8, and Aston Villa, Third Division winners in 1971-2. He also found success as a manager, taking Middlesbrough from liquidation to promotion from the Third Division in 1986-7 and to the First Division in 1988.

RITCHIE
Archibald   *Left-back*

Born: Stenhousemuir.
Career: Stenhousemuir. Dumbarton July 1914. Glasgow Rangers 1919. Derby County June 1920. Player-manager, Guildford City July 1927.
Division Two promotion 1925-6.

Archie Ritchie served with the Royal Engineers in World War One and was awarded the Distinguished Conduct Medal for bravery at Nieuport in 1917. He returned to win a Scottish League championship medal with Glasgow Rangers and joined Derby to partner veteran Jack Atkin. He looked even more settled in 1921-2 with Bert Chandler on the other flank but his days as a first-team regular were ended by a nasty knee injury against West Ham United in December 1921. Cecil Potter bought Tom Crilly before the start of the following season and although Ritchie played his part in promotion from Division Two, he was never again as effective.

RITCHIE
Duncan   *Outside-left*

Career: Dumbarton. Raith Rovers cs 1911. Sheffield United November 1911. Derby County July 1913.

Duncan Ritchie played only twice for Derby, in the 1913-14 relegation season.

RITCHIE
William   *Inside-right*

Born: Carlisle, 1897.
Career: Amateur, Derby County, August 1919: professional November 1919. Millwall May 1923. Ashington July 1924. Barrow June 1925.

William Ritchie joined Derby County after serving in World War One and scored on his debut in September 1919, the only goal of the game against Aston Villa. He made only three more appearances and emigrated to Canada after finishing his League career with Barrow.

ROBERTS
Edward   *Inside-forward*

Born: Chesterfield, 2 November 1916.
Career: Glapwell Colliery. Derby

Archie Ritchie DCM, decorated for bravery in World War One.

County April 1934. Coventry City March 1937. King's Lynn August 1952. Banbury Spencer September 1952. Bedworth Town January 1954. Coach, Coventry City, to December 1961.
Division One runners-up 1935-6.

Ted Roberts stood in for Peter Ramage for four matches in March 1936, when Derby County were on their way to second position in the League. He gave many years of excellent service to Coventry City, although World War Two took a chunk out of his career. His heading ability and reputation as a team-man made him very popular at Highfield Road. He scored 87 goals 223 League and Cup appearances for Coventry, later returning on the coaching staff. His son Dudley played for Coventry, Mansfield Town,

Doncaster Rovers and Scunthorpe United.

ROBERTS
William   *Right-back*

Died: Nottingham, c1937.

William Roberts was a drummer with the Sherwood Foresters at Normanton Barracks when he played for the Rams in 1890-91. His performances were impressive enough for Derby County to want to sign him permanently but he declined to be bought out of the Army.

ROBERTSON
John Neilson   *Outside-left*

Born: Uddingston, 20 January 1953.
Career: Drumchapel Amateurs.

John Robertson.

Apprentice, Nottingham Forest: professional May 1970. Derby County June 1983. Nottingham Forest August 1985. Corby Town August 1986. Stamford March 1987. Assistant manager, Grantham, August 1987. Assistant manager, Shepshed Charterhouse, June to September 1989. Manager, Grantham, February 1990 to March 1992.

John Robertson touched greatness in Nottingham Forest's most successful period. Out on the left, Robertson was the main outlet for defenders and Forest's most creative player as, in the space of four seasons, they were promoted from the Second Division, won the League Championship, the League Cup twice and the European Cup twice. With good players around him, Robertson was a major force and Peter Taylor was desperate to sign him for Derby County. A tribunal set a fee of £135,000 but Robertson was not the man to turn a struggling team. He underwent a cartilage operation in his first season at Derby, which ended his

Scotland career. He had won the last two of his 28 caps after moving to the Baseball Ground. Arthur Cox allowed him to return to the City Ground on a free transfer.

ROBINSON
A.   *Outside-left*
Career: Alfreton Town. Tibshelf Colliery. Derby County May 1909.

Robinson played once in December 1909, standing in for Jack Davis. His son was on Derby's books in the 1930s.

ROBINSON
John William   *Goalkeeper*
Born: Derby, 22 April 1870. Died: Derby, 28 October 1931.
Career: Derby Midland. Lincoln City January 1889. Derby County June 1891. New Brighton Tower August 1897. Southampton May 1898. Plymouth Argyle April 1903. Millwall November 1905. Exeter City December 1905. Green Waves (Plymouth) cs 1907. Exeter City November 1908. Stoke City May 1909. Rochester (New York) October 1912.

Division One runners-up 1895-6.

Jack Robinson, an agile and daring goalkeeper, had spent six excellent seasons with Derby County and broken into the England team when, in August 1897, he rocked the club by joining New Brighton Tower. An FA commission, held in Manchester on 11 August, ruled that the registration was invalid as the club was not affiliated. Only after New Brighton joined the FA via the Cheshire FA did the transfer go

Jack Robinson.

through and a tart contemporary report gave the opinion: 'If Robinson thinks he can enhance his reputation by joining a mushroom organisation like the New Brighton club, whose purse may not always be so heavy as at present, he has done well to leave Derby.' It did not do Robinson any harm, for he retained his England place and, a year later, joined Southampton. At The Dell he took his total of England caps to 11, played in two FA Cup Final defeats, by Bury in 1900 and Sheffield United in 1902, and was involved in three Southern League championships — in 1898-9, 1900-01 and 1902-03. Robinson, who was reported to the FA for allegedly trying to poach Steve Bloomer for Southampton, may have been a wayward character. For four years, however, he was indisputably the best goalkeeper in England.

ROBINSON
Thomas Charles   *Wing-half*
Born: Burton upon Trent.
Career: Derby County December 1926. Bury April 1930. Torquay United February 1933.

Division One runners-up 1929-30.

Tom Robinson joined Derby County from local football in Burton and provided useful cover for the wing-half positions for more than three years.

ROBINSON
William   *Forward*
Career: Lincoln City. Derby County May 1909.

Played three times in 1909-10.

ROBSON
James W.   *Centre-half*
Born: Cambois, 16 August 1900.
Career: Seaton Delaval. Derby County January 1922. Durham City September 1924.

Played three times as replacement for Harry Wightman after joining Derby County from non-League football.

ROBSON
John Cecil   *Outside-left*
Born: Birtley, 24 March 1906. Died: Ashbourne, 20 October 1966.
Career: Birtley. Hull City March 1923. Reading August 1925. Derby County June 1928. Southend United June 1932. Chester August 1933. Rochdale November 1933. Oldham Athletic June 1934. Retired 1936.

Division One runners-up 1929-30.

A powerfully-built winger who cost Derby County £1,500, Jack Robson spent most of his time at the Baseball Ground as reserve to George Mee. When the Rams were runners-up in the First Division in 1929-30, Robson scored five goals in his five

Jack Robson.

appearances. He missed only one match when Reading won the Third Division South in 1925-6. Robson was later a licensee in Hull, Derby and Belper.

ROBSON
John Dixon *Left-back*

Born: Consett, 15 July 1950.
Career: Birtley YC. Derby County October 1967. Aston Villa December 1972.

Division Two champions 1968-9. Division One champions 1971-2.

It was said that Peter Taylor earned his salary for that year simply by signing John Robson from North-East junior football in October 1967. Taylor had spotted the 17-year-old playing for Birtley Youth Club and knew at once that he must have him at Derby. The following season Robson was an ever-present member of the side which stormed away with the Second Division championship and he missed only one game as the Rams won the First Division title for the first time, three years later. Robson was not a physically commanding full-back, but he rarely gave an inch to opposing forwards and was far from out of place in a defence which included Roy McFarland and Colin Todd. But Brian Clough wanted Leicester City's classy David Nish and as soon as the player was eligible for the later stages of the 1972-3 European Cup, Clough allowed Robson to join

John Robson, joined Villa after 211 games for the Rams.

Aston Villa for £90,000 — then a record incoming fee for Derby. It was a happy move for the England Under-23 defender and he played in the Villa team which won promotion in 1975 and took the League Cup in 1975 and 1977. Sadly, Robson's career was ended in 1978 by multiple sclerosis.

ROBSON
Norman *Inside-forward*

Born: Ryton-on-Tyne, 1908.
Career: West Stanley. Preston North End June 1926. Derby County May

1930. Bradford City March 1933. Wigan Athletic September 1934.

An £850 signing from Preston, Norman Robson acted as cover for Bobby Barclay and Peter Ramage. He began 1932-3 as first-choice at inside-right but it was a position which was to cause problems for two years.

ROBSON
William *Left-back*

Born: Castletown. Died: Oxford, 11 August 1960.
Career: Hylton Colliery. Derby County

January 1927. West Ham United May 1933. Reading June 1934. Coach, Newbury Town, 1946.

Division One runners-up 1929-30.

A sound reserve whose opportunities were limited by the consistency of George Collin. Robson had five seasons with Reading before World War Two shortened his career.

ROBY
Donald   *Outside-right*

*Born: Billinge, 15 November 1933.
Career: Juniors. Notts County: professional February 1951. Derby County August 1961. Burton Albion June 1965. Loughborough United July 1970.*

Don Roby.

Don Roby was a traditional winger with considerable skill. He spent ten years with Notts County before Harry Storer bought him for £10,000. He was first choice for almost two seasons until a cartilage operation ruled him out. Roby faded into the background when Tim Ward signed Gordon Hughes.

ROSE
Charles H.   *Inside-forward*

Career: Derby Midland. Derby County June 1891.

One of the players who joined Derby County when Derby Midland folded.

ROSE
Walter   *Wing-half*

Born: Borrowash. Died: Draycott February 1953.

Walter Roulstone.

Career: Derby Midland. Derby County June 1891. Loughborough Town 1893. Ilkeston Town June 1897.

Known as Golly Rose. Like his brother, joined the Rams from Derby Midland. Each played five senior games for Derby County.

ROULSTONE
Frank   *Left-back*

Career: Sawley Rangers. Derby County.

Played once in the first League season, 1888-9.

ROULSTONE
Walter   *Left-half*

*Died: Castle Donington, 20 February 1953.
Career: Sawley Rangers. Derby County 1887. Heanor Town September 1895. Castle Donington Town October 1897. Heanor Town. Castle Donington Town December 1898.*

One of Derby County's foremost early players. He played in the opening League game in September 1888, held his place for the rest of the winter and was still good enough when the Rams began to import more experienced professionals. He was the first Derby County player to complete 100 senior appearances.

ROUND
Stephen John   *Full-back*

*Born: Derby, 9 November 1970.
Career: Trainee, Derby County: professional July 1989.*

Steve Round was the last of five players

Steve Round.

from a successful Derby Youth team to make a senior debut. He followed Robbie Briscoe, Jonathan Davidson, Craig Ramage and Paul Williams when, in March 1992, he stood in for the suspended Michael Forsyth at left-back for two games. He more often played at right-back in the Reserves.

ROWE
George William   *Left-back*

*Born: Saltburn, 1899. Died: Derby, 8 November 1966.
Career: Loftus (Cleveland League). Hartlepools United December 1921. Derby County June 1923. Norwich City May 1927. Chesterfield September 1928. Chester January 1930.*

Division Two promotion 1925-6.

Played once in the Second Division promotion season, figuring in a 2-0 defeat by Swansea Town in February 1926.

ROWE
Valentine Norman   *Right-back*

*Born: Shouldham, 14 February 1926.
Career: King's Lynn. Derby County December 1949. Walsall August 1952.*

Norman Rowe appeared in two First Division games for Derby County in May 1952.

RUDDY
Thomas   *Centre-forward*

*Born: Stockton-on-Tees, 1 March 1902.
Died: Cleveland, 11 November 1979.
Career: Stockton Shamrock. Amateur, Darlington, November 1921: profes-*

sional, February 1922. Derby County May 1928. Chesterfield December 1931. Southampton September 1932. Spennymoor United cs 1934.

Division One runners-up 1929-30.

George Jobey paid £500 for Tom Ruddy as a centre-forward prospect but his chances were limited, first by Harry Bedford and then by Jack Bowers. Ruddy, who scored five goals for Darlington against South Shields in 1927, also filled in at inside-left.

RUSSELL
John   *Inside-forward*

Career: Derby County December 1898.

Russell played twice in place of Steve Bloomer in 1898-9.

RUTHERFORD
James B.   *Inside-forward*

Career: St Mirren. Derby County August 1898. Darwen January 1899.

Rutherford scored in his only match, a 3-3 draw against Nottingham Forest in December 1898.

RYAN
Gerard Joseph   *Outside-left*

Born: Dublin, 4 October 1955.
Career: Bohemians. Derby County September 1977. Brighton & Hove Albion September 1978.

Gerry Ryan.

Gerry Ryan showed flair and an ability to lift crowds after Tommy Docherty had bought him from Bohemians at the same time as Fran O'Brien, who failed his medical. Ryan won the first of his 16 Republic of Ireland caps in his year at Derby. He was in Brighton's Second Division promotion team in 1978-9 and came on as substitute in their drawn 1983 FA Cup Final against Manchester United. A broken leg in a match against Crystal Palace in April 1985, brought a premature end to his career.

Reg Ryan, the Rams' most influential skipper since Raich Carter?

RYAN
Reginald Alphonsus

Wing-half/inside-forward

Born: Dublin, 30 October 1925.
Career: Nuneaton Borough. Coventry City, amateur, March 1943. West Bromwich Albion April 1945. Derby County July 1955. Coventry City September 1958. Retired November 1960. Coventry City, pools organiser, November 1960. West Bromwich Albion, pools organiser, December 1961: chief scout, September 1962 to October 1976.

Division Three North champions 1956-7 (captain).

When Harry Storer took over the Rams in 1955 his priority was to sign West Brom's international inside-forward Reg Ryan for £3,000. Ryan had starred in Albion's 1954 FA Cup Final victory over Preston North End and was the very man to carry Storer's work on to the field. Ryan, who played Gaelic football for his school, appeared 16 times for the Republic of Ireland — once while with Derby — and once for Northern Ireland before southern players were barred from the Home International Championship. Ryan's first job was to instil some spirit back into a Derby side which had sunk to rock bottom. Soon he welded a happy family and he was the link between Storer and the players. In three seasons he missed only three matches — two because of injury and one through international duty — and his part in the Rams' promotion drive of 1956-7 cannot be overestimated. On the Rams' return to Division Two, Ryan was leading scorer and looked equally at home at wing-half. In 1955, he played for the Third Division North team against the Third South.

Dean Saunders, 57 goals in 131 senior games before a record move to Liverpool.

SAGE
Melvyn   *Right-back*

Born: Gillingham, 24 March 1964.
Career: Apprentice, Gillingham: professional March 1982. Derby County August 1986.

Division Two champions 1986-7.

Derby County were well aware of Mel Sage's potential in 1985-6, their Third

Mel Sage.

Division promotion season, because they met Gillingham five times, in the League, FA Cup and Freight/Rover Trophy. What they could not forecast was how consistently unlucky Sage would be with injuries after an independent tribunal fixed the fee at £60,000. He quickly adapted to the Second Division and was one of Derby's most consistent players until, in February 1987, he broke a collarbone against Sunderland at Roker Park. The following season, he had a niggling groin injury and, most seriously, underwent a knee ligaments operation in December 1991. As quiet on the field as he is off it, Sage has a neat touch on the ball but the succession of injuries prevented him from realising expectations at the Baseball Ground.

SAUNDERS
Dean Nicholas   *Striker*

Born: Swansea, 21 June 1964.
Career: Apprentice, Swansea City: professional June 1982. Cardiff City, loan, March 1985. Brighton and Hove Albion August 1985. Oxford United March 1987. Derby County October 1988. Liverpool July 1991.

Little more than three years after being given a free transfer by Swansea manager John Bond, Dean Saunders became Derby's first £1-million signing. The transfer, between two clubs owned by the Maxwell family, cost Oxford manager Mark Lawrenson his job, because he made his objections public, but was immensely popular at Derby. Saunders, who made his debut for Wales when he was at Brighton, not only scored goals regularly, but also excited Derby supporters by his speed, flair and sheer love of playing. When he joined Paul Goddard in attack, Derby surged to fifth place in the First Division in 1988-9 but, because of Robert Maxwell's policies, were unable to develop the team. Saunders was leading scorer in each of his three seasons before joining Liverpool for a then British domestic record of £2.9 million. The main benefit from the transfer of Saunders and Mark Wright was that Derby were able to buy out Maxwell's shares. Saunders was in Liverpool's 1992 FA Cup winning team but, despite that and his goals, he did not look as happy at Anfield as he had at Derby. His father Roy played for Liverpool and Swansea.

SAUNDERS
Samuel   *Left-half*

Career: Alfreton Town. Derby County April 1904. Sutton Town December 1909.

Saunders played in the last seven games of 1904-5 and the first one of the following season. After a lengthy period out with injury he joined Sutton Town, where he earned a benefit.

SAVIN
Keith Anthony   *Left-back*

Born: Oxford, 5 June 1929.
Career: Oxford City. Derby County May 1950. Mansfield Town May 1957. Nuneaton Borough July 1959. Bourne Town March 1960.

Keith Savin.

A neat left-back who seemed to lack the confidence to carry his Central League form into the senior team. He had several good runs, especially in Derby's first season in the Third Division North, but Harry Storer signed Roy Martin for his promotion side.

SAWYER
Thomas   *Inside-forward*

Career: Derby County August 1894. Macclesfield 1895. Stockport County April 1896.

Sawyer played twice as partner to Steve Bloomer but his contract was cancelled after only five months with Derby County.

SAXTON
Robert   *Centre-half*

Born: Bagby, 6 September 1943.
Career: Derby County February 1962. Plymouth Argyle February 1968. Exeter City September 1975: player-manager, January 1977. Manager, Plymouth Argyle, January 1979. Manager, Blackburn Rovers, May 1981 to December 1986. Adviser, Preston North End, January 1987. Manager, York City, June 1987. Assistant manager, Blackpool, September 1988. Assistant manager, Newcastle United, December 1988 (caretaker manager March 1991) to April 1991. Chief scout, Manchester City, October 1991.

Bobby Saxton developed into a sound centre-half under Tim Ward and later became a respected manager. Because

Bobby Saxton, played in a League Cup semi-final for the Rams

Ernald Scattergood.

Roy McFarland was ineligible, Saxton played through the 1967-8 run to the League Cup semi-finals before joining Plymouth Argyle for £12,000. He earned promotion from the Fourth Division as player-manager of Exeter City in 1976-7, continuing John Newman's good work, and came close to more honours as Blackburn manager.

SCARBOROUGH
Brian   *Outside-left*

Born: Ironville, 11 December 1941.
Career: Juniors, Derby County: professional January 1959. Burton Albion July 1961. Heanor Town June 1962. Bourne Town August 1963.

Scarborough played four League games under Harry Storer before he was released in 1961.

SCATTERGOOD
Ernald Oak   *Goalkeeper*

Born: Riddings, 29 May 1887. Died: Worksop, 2 July 1932.

Career: Riddings. Ripley Athletic February 1906. Derby County August 1907. Bradford October 1914. Alfreton Town cs 1925.

Division Two champions 1911-12, 1914-15.

Yet another in the long line of Derbyshire-produced goalkeepers, Ernald Scattergood took over from Harry Maskrey — who was also signed from Ripley Athletic. Scattergood was different from the two previous goalkeepers — Maskrey and Fryer — in that he stood only 5ft 8in tall. But he punched well and played for England against Wales at Ashton Gate in March 1913. In 1911-12 he was the only ever-present in the Rams team which won the Second Division title and the following season he became the club's regular penalty taker. Scattergood scored three out of three, more by virtue of a powerful shot than astute placing. He joined Bradford in their first season in Division One, survived being gassed in World War One and went on to play 288 games for them, scoring six goals. He took

their penalties in 1921-2 until, on Easter Saturday, South Shields goalkeeper Willis Walker saved one. Scattergood was involved in a frantic and successful race to return to his own line.

SCATTERGOOD
Kenneth   *Goalkeeper*

Born: Riddings.
Career: Wolverhampton Wanderers November 1931. Bristol City August 1933. Stoke City May 1934. Derby County July 1935.

Ken Scattergood was the son of Ernald Scattergood. He had a fearsome debut for the Rams on Christmas Day 1936, when Everton put seven goals past him at Goodison Park, but was on the winning side against them three days later. Scattergood's chances at the Baseball Ground were limited by injuries and he was released in 1938.

SCOTT
Archibald Teasdale   *Half-back*

Born: Airdrie, 27 July 1905. Died: Gosport, 2 May 1990.
Career: Bellshill Athletic. Gartsherrie. Airdrieonians August 1925. Derby County April 1927. Brentford July 1934. Trainer, Reading.
Division One runners-up 1929-30.

Archie Scott was one of the candidates to take over from Johnny McIntyre at right-half and also covered for the centre-half position. When McIntyre left, Jack Nicholas stepped in and after playing 32 games in seven seasons, Scott joined Brentford. He played a couple of games in their 1934-5 Second Division championship team.

SCOTT
Kenneth
Outside-right

Born: Maltby, 13 August 1931.
Career: Denaby United. Derby County August 1950. Denaby United March 1952. Mansfield Town July 1952.

Ken Scott was given a chance in 1950, playing twice when Reg Harrison was out, but found the step up to the First Division too much for him.

SEAL
Chris E.
Left-back

Career: Hyson Green. Derby County May 1905.

Seal played once for Derby County, standing in for Charlie Morris in November 1905.

SELVEY
Scotch
Wing-half

Born: Derby, 1 November 1863. Died: Derby, 19 March 1947.
Career: Derby St Luke's. Derby Midland. Derby County 1888.

Made one senior appearance, in October 1888.

SELVEY
Walter
Inside-forward

Born: Derby.
Career: Derby Midland. Derby County 1888. Derby Junction.

Like his brother, played once in the first League season.

SHANKS
Thomas
Inside-left

Born: New Ross, County Wexford, 1880.
Career: Wexford. Derby West End. Derby County April 1898. Brentford October 1901. Woolwich Arsenal January 1903. Brentford May 1904. Leicester Fosse October 1906. Leyton cs 1909. Clapton Orient 1911. York City 1912.

Tom Shanks never quite established himself as first choice with Derby County but later played three times for Ireland, twice while with Woolwich Arsenal, and once in his second spell with Brentford. He scored 24 goals when Arsenal were promoted from Division Two in 1903-04 and was one of five players with Derby connections in the Leicester Fosse team which won promotion from the Second Division in 1907-08.

SHARMAN
Donald William
Goalkeeper

Born: Rothwell, 2 February 1932.
Career: Juniors, Derby County: professional February 1949. Ilkeston Town September 1951. Gresley Rovers June 1955. Bradford City June 1956. Burton Albion July 1958. Long Eaton United August 1959. Wilmorton and Alvaston.

Frank Sheridan, scored twice on his Rams debut.

'Joe' Sharman played two First Division games as a teenager in April 1951.

SHARPE
Ivan Gordon
Outside-left

Born: St Albans, 15 June 1889. Died: Southport, 9 February 1968.
Career: St Albans Abbey. Watford October 1907. Glossop August 1908. Derby County October 1911. Leeds City June 1913. One match for Leeds United in 1920.
Division Two champions 1911-12.

Ivan Sharpe, journalist and amateur international, won a gold medal with the Great Britain football team at the 1912 Olympic Games in Stockholm. He had close connections with two of Derby County's immortals. John Goodall signed him for Southern League Watford and Sharpe played in the same team as Steve Bloomer. He entered League football when he joined the *Glossop Chronicle* and left the Rams to take up an appointment on the *Yorkshire Post*. When he succeeded Jimmy Catton as editor of *Athletic News* in 1924, he discovered in a desk drawer a letter of application he had written to the newspaper in 1909. Sharpe, whose journalistic career

continued well after World War Two, always played as an amateur and made occasional appearances for English Wanderers, Brighton & Hove Albion, in the FA Cup, Nottingham Forest Reserves and Luton Town Reserves.

SHEPHERD
George
Forward

Career: Rocester. Derby County September 1919.

Shepherd played only two senior games, one at inside-left and the second on the wing.

SHERIDAN
Frank Michael
Midfield/central defender

Born: London, 9 December 1961.
Career: Apprentice, Derby County: professional July 1978. Torquay United June 1982. Teignmouth 1984.

Frank Sheridan had a remarkable debut in October, 1980, when he scored twice against Queen's Park Rangers from midfield and later lay on the treatment table, emotionally exhausted. He had a good run at centre-half in 1981-2 after Alan Ramage was injured but was released at the end of the season. He was unlucky with Torquay, suffering a ruptured spleen.

Peter Shilton, broke the League appearances record with the Rams

SHILTON
Peter Leslie   *Goalkeeper*
Born: Leicester, 18 September 1949.
Career: Apprentice, Leicester City:
professional September 1966. Stoke
City November 1974. Nottingham
Forest September 1977. Southampton
August 1982. Derby County July 1987.
Player-manager, Plymouth Argyle,
March 1992.

Peter Shilton was already a legend when he became Derby County's first major signing in Robert Maxwell's time as chairman. When Mark Wright followed from Southampton it was assumed that Arthur Cox was to be given the money to build a top-class team quickly but it did not turn out like that. Shilton had been an England player for almost 17 years when he joined Derby. He made his debut for Leicester at the age of 16 and was so good as a teenager that one of England's greatest goalkeepers, Gordon Banks, was allowed to move to Stoke City. Shilton succeeded Banks again at Stoke but his greatest days in club football were with Nottingham Forest. Brian Clough and Peter Taylor had wanted him at Derby in the early 1970s. With Shilton in goal, Forest won their first League title, a League Cup and two European Cups. Mark Wallington, who had taken over from Shilton at Leicester, gave way to him at Derby 13 years later and, in November 1987, Shilton marked his 800th League appearance with a fantastic display against Newcastle United at St James' Park. Eight days later he played in his 1,000th competitive club match and broke Terry Paine's record of 824 League appearances in April 1988, at Watford. Amazingly, he had equalled it against Southampton, not only the club from which he joined Derby but also the one for which Paine had played most of his career. Shilton won a world record 125 caps before bowing out of international football after the 1990 World Cup. Unfortunately, Maxwell's promise to build a great team in front of Shilton was not fulfilled and he suffered relegation before stepping into management with Plymouth Argyle.

SHINER
Albert J.   *Centre-forward*
Career: Seaview FC (Isle of Wight).
Derby County September 1920.

Shiner played in one match, soon after signing.

SHIRTCLIFFE
Edward   *Outside-right*
Career: Derby County October 1901.
Ripley Town September 1902.

Shirtcliffe played four times in place of Richard Wombwell towards the end of 1901-02.

Paul Simpson, soon regarded as a bargain buy at £500,000.

SIMPSON
Paul David   *Winger*
Born: Carlisle, 26 July 1966.
Career: Apprentice, Manchester City:
professional August 1983. Oxford
United October 1988. Derby County
February 1992.

An England Youth international, Paul Simpson made his debut for Manchester City as a 16-year-old and earned five Under-21 caps. Oxford United were able to sign him with some of the cash received when Dean Saunders joined Derby. His scoring record from the left wing, 50 goals in 167 games for Oxford, attracted Arthur Cox, who made his move when Oxford were struggling for cash after the collapse of the Maxwell empire. There was an immediate return for the Rams, four goals in his first five games. Simpson also hit dangerous corners and free-kicks, soon coming to be regarded as a bargain at £500,000.

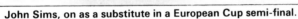

John Sims, on as a substitute in a European Cup semi-final.

Glenn Skivington, eventually returned to Barrow and played for England at non-League level.

SIMS
John
Forward

Born: Belper, 14 August 1952.
Career: Apprentice, Derby County: professional December 1972. Luton Town, loan, November 1973. Oxford United, loan, September 1974. Colchester United, loan, January 1975. Notts County December 1975. Exeter City December 1978. Plymouth Argyle October 1979. Torquay United August 1983. Exeter City February 1984. Player-coach, Torquay United, November 1984: manager, August to September 1985. Saltash United 1985. Player-manager, Waldon Athletic.

John Sims, a member of Derby County's Central League championship team in 1971-2, played in only three League games for Derby but came on as substitute in the European Cup semi-final against Juventus. Sims later played for all three West Country teams and was Torquay manager for 33 days before becoming a licensee in the resort.

SKIVINGTON
Glenn
Midfield

Born: Barrow, 19 January 1962.
Career: Barrow. Derby County July 1980. Halifax Town, loan, March 1983. Southend United August 1983. Barrow 1984.

Skivington was playing Alliance Premier League football while still at Barrow Sixth Form College and looked a fine prospect when he made his debut for the Rams against Grimsby Town at Blundell Park in September 1980. He always showed flashes of skill but did not seem to have the appetite for full-time football. In 1989-90, Skivington became an England non-League international and helped Barrow win the FA Trophy, while studying for a law degree.

SMITH
Frederick
Left-back

Born: Buxton.
Career: Buxton 1904. Stockport County September 1906. Derby County September 1909. Macclesfield 1910. Southampton May 1913.

His five games for Derby were at left-back but he played on the other flank in his Southern League season with Southampton. After one year at The Dell, he returned to the Macclesfield area, where he worked as a motor mechanic.

SMITH
Frederick Edward
Centre-forward

Born: Draycott, 7 May 1926.
Career: Draycott. Derby County June 1947. Sheffield United March 1948.

Manchester City May 1952. Grimsby Town September 1952. Bradford City July 1954. Frickley Colliery December 1954.

Fred Smith's muscular qualities as leader of the attack brought him only one senior game for Derby County, against Burnley in September 1947, but attracted several other clubs. Manchester City paid £6,000 for him and Grimsby £4,000.

SMITH
Herbert
Left-back

Born: Witney, 22 November 1879. Died: Oxford, 6 January 1951.
Career: Reading 1900 to 1909 as amateur. Also played for Oxford City, Witney, Richmond, Stoke, Derby County, Oxfordshire.

A distinguished amateur who won a gold medal with the Great Britain football team in the 1908 Olympic Games in London. An amateur international 17 times and an Amateur Cup Finalist with Oxford City in 1903, he also won four full caps. Smith played once for Derby County, in April 1907, and was later president of the Oxfordshire FA.

SMITH
J.
Centre-half

Made a dozen appearances in Derby County's first two League seasons.

SMITH
John William   *Goalkeeper*

Born: Beeston.
Career: Long Eaton St Helen's. Derby County November 1903. Newark Town March 1908. Nottingham Forest May 1909. Ilkeston United July 1911.

Reserve to Harry Maskrey for more than four seasons before Ernald Scattergood came on the scene.

SMITH
Joseph   *Right-back*

Born: Sutton upon Trent.
Career: Worksop North End. Sheffield United April 1907. South Shields cs 1913. Derby County August 1914.
Division Two champions 1914-15.

Smith began Derby County's Second Division championship season but gave way to Jack Atkin after six months.

SMITH
Michael John   *Centre-half*

Born: Quarndon, 22 September 1935.
Career: Juniors, Derby County: professional October 1952. Bradford City June 1961. Crewton Sports August 1967. Lockheed Leamington September 1967.

An England schoolboy international in

Mike Smith.

1950-51, Mike Smith was a centre-half but played several of his senior games for Derby County at full-back. Bradford City signed him for £1,000 and he gave them good service for five seasons, during which he made 142 senior appearances. He retired in 1967 following an attack of jaundice.

SMITH
Sydney Joseph   *Centre-forward*

Born: Aston, Birmingham, 11 July 1895.
Career: Aston Manor. War service. Aston Park Rangers. Stourbridge. Cradley Heath St Luke's 1920. Derby County August 1921. Norwich City June 1923. Gillingham July 1924.

Played once, against Barnsley in September 1922.

SMITH
Valentine   *Outside-right*

Born: Sandiacre.
Career: Newark Town. Derby County October 1925.
Division Two promotion 1925-6.

Signed from Newark Town for £450 and deputised for George Thornewell on four occasions.

SOAR
Thomas Albert   *Outside-right*

Born: Heanor, 20 May 1881.
Career: Nottingham Forest. Alfreton Town 1898. Derby County January 1903. Fulham May 1903. Watford May 1906.

Albert Soar played only twice in his short stay with Derby County but was a popular player with Fulham and was involved in their Southern League championship in 1905-6.

SPILSBURY
Benjamin Ward   *Inside-forward*

Born: Findern, 1 August 1864. Died: Vancouver, 15 August 1938.
Career: Cambridge University 1884 to 1887. Corinthians 1885 to 1888. Derby County 1884 to 1889.

Benjamin Spilsbury had the honour of scoring the first goal recorded by Derby County. It came in the Rams' second match, against Blackburn Olympic at the County Ground on 27 September 1884, and although Derby lost 4-3 Spilsbury had a fine game. Less than six months later he was in the England team, the first of three caps he won. Spilsbury was educated at Repton School where he played soccer and cricket for the First Eleven and won the long jump four years in succession, breaking the school record in 1882. Spilsbury went to Jesus College, Cambridge, in October 1983, won his soccer Blue (1884-7), captained the team in his last season and also gained an athletics Blue. He was a talented goalscorer — he netted five for England, including four against Ireland in 1886 — and was known as a most dangerous opponent. Spilsbury is not credited with being a Derby player on his international appearances, but although his club is given as Cambridge University, he turned out for Derby until 1889. When the Rams met Small Heath in the 1885-6 FA Cup third round, one reporter noted that 'practically half the home team made the point of waiting upon Spilsbury, feeling convinced that, if only they could hamper his movements, they would have a great chance of keeping their goal intact'. Spilsbury was hampered and failed to score in Derby's 4-2 defeat, but it says much for his reputation that the Birmingham side should mark him so closely. Spilsbury gained a degree and moved to Canada as a land agent.

Steve Spooner.

SPOONER
Stephen Alan   *Midfield*

Born: Sutton, 25 January 1961.
Career: Apprentice, Derby County: professional December 1978. Halifax Town, loan, December 1981. Halifax Town February 1982. Chesterfield July 1983. Hereford United August 1986. York City July 1988. Rotherham United July 1990. Mansfield Town March 1991.

Steve Spooner made his debut as a

teenager in Tommy Docherty's time. He made a good career in the lower divisions and played an important part in Chesterfield's 1984-5 Fourth Division championship. He had another promotion with Mansfield Town in 1991-2.

SPRINGTHORPE
James A.   *Outside-right*

Career: Derby County October 1907. Draycott.

Made two League appearances in October 1907.

STALEY
Jonathon   *Left-back*

Born: Newhall.
Career: Derby Midland. Derby County June 1891. Ripley Athletic October 1901.

Division One runners-up 1895-6. FA Cup Finalists 1898-9.

'Jonty' Staley

When Derby Midland folded in 1891, Derby County were quick to sign their best players. Jonty Staley gave the Rams sound and loyal service for a decade. He went into the side as Jimmy Methven's partner but was injured in October 1892. Tom McLean came in for a couple of matches before Joe Leiper took over for six seasons, keeping Staley as a patient reserve. His reward came in 1898-9, when Leiper suffered an early injury. Staley played for the rest of the season, including the FA Cup Final defeat by Sheffield United. "He's one of those all-in players," said Methven. "You know the

style — it's either you or me for it, but something must happen."

STALLARD
Mark   *Striker*

Born: Derby, 24 October 1974.
Career: Trainee Derby County: professional October 1991.

Derby County were keen to sign Mark Stallard after his scoring feats for Derby Boys. He was still 16 when he made

Mark Stallard.

his League debut as a substitute at Oxford in September 1991 and scored in a Full Members' Cup tie at Middlesbrough the following month. He was leading scorer for the Reserves in his first season as a professional.

STAMPS
John David   *Centre-forward*

Born: Thrybergh, 2 December 1918.
Died: Winshill, Burton upon Trent, 19 November 1991.
Career: Mansfield Town October 1937. New Brighton August 1938. Derby County January 1939. Shrewsbury Town December 1953. Burton Albion August 1954: player-coach, June 1955: general assistant (coaching and scouting), June 1956: re-signed as a player, October 1956: assistant manager, May 1957: temporary manager, November 1957: manager, February 1958 to October 1959.

FA Cup winners 1945-6.

'A rare battler' was how the 1946 FA Cup Final programme summed up Derby County centre-forward Jack Stamps. It was an astute judgement for Stamps was one of the bravest players to wear the Rams colours, but it undersold his considerable skill. Stamps was given a free transfer by Mansfield and snapped-up by New Brighton, then a Third Division North club. His goalscoring exploits soon had the scouts hurrying to Cheshire and George Jobey won the race to sign him for £1,500. Like so many players of his time, Stamps lost his best years to the war — he was one of the last members of the BEF to be evacuated from Dunkirk in 1940 — but in 1946 he scored two goals at Wembley as the

Jack Stamps watches Harry Medhurst collect the ball at Chelsea in January 1947.

Jack Stamps, scored exactly 100 League goals for Derby in a career which marked him as one of the bravest of players.

Rams lifted the FA Cup. Stamps was originally an inside-forward and no less an expert than Raich Carter is quick to extol his virtues as a fine footballing forward. But it is as a big, burly centre-forward that most fans choose to remember him and it was from that position that he scored the majority of his 100 League goals for Derby, playing between Doherty and Carter, and later between Morris and Steel. One memory is of him heading a goal against Birmingham and then spitting out his teeth after the goalkeeper accidentally punched him in the mouth. Those who played alongside, and against him, will testify to his courage. Stamps, who became totally blind, was invited to become an honorary vice-president of Derby County in January 1983.

Frank Stapleton - a relegation battle was a new experience.

Eric Steele, two more promotions.

STAPLETON
Francis Anthony   *Striker*

Born: Dublin, 10 July 1956.
Career: St Martin's. Bolton Athletic (Dublin). Apprentice, Arsenal: professional September 1973. Manchester United August 1981. Ajax Amsterdam July 1987. Derby County, loan, March 1988. Le Havre October 1988. Blackburn Rovers August 1989. Aldershot September 1991. Player-coach, Huddersfield Town, October 1991. Player-manager, Bradford City, December 1991.

Frank Stapleton was the Republic of Ireland captain when Derby County took him on loan from Ajax Amsterdam. His unhappy eight months with the Dutch giants had included a back operation for the removal of a disc. Arthur Cox, desperate for experience in attack, gambled on Stapleton, who played in his 61st international immediately after the loan deal. With Arsenal and, after his £900,000 transfer, Manchester United, Stapleton played in five FA Cup Finals, three times as a winner. He also appeared in the 1980 European Cup-winners' Cup Final for Arsenal, when they lost on penalties to Valencia. At his best, he was one of the finest strikers in Britain, creative as well as sharp. After a brilliant debut for Derby at Coventry, he struggled to find his scoring touch and a relegation battle was a new experience for him. It did, however, help him back to match fitness for the 1988 European Championship Finals.

STEEL
William   *Inside-left*

Born: Denny, 1 May 1923. Died: Los Angeles, 13 May 1982.
Career: Dunipace Thistle. Bo'ness Cadora. Leicester City groundstaff January 1939. St Mirren, amateur, cs 1939. Morton cs 1941. Derby County June 1947. Dundee September 1950. Los Angeles Danes (officially transferred) January 1956. Hollywood.

Derby paid a British record fee of £15,500 for blond-haired Billy Steel in June 1947 after he had made overnight headlines with an electrifying display for Great Britain against the Rest of Europe the previous month. Although he had played only a handful of League games for Morton, and one international for Scotland, Steel fitted in well with the other forwards, Stanley Matthews, Wilf Mannion, Tommy Lawton and Billy Liddell, and scored the most spectacular of Britain's six goals. Although he had many fine games for Derby with his terrific left-foot shot and brilliant ball control, Steel was difficult to play with and was a law unto himself. His team mates felt that he reserved his best for Scotland or games in London. They resented his status and the fact that he had other 'jobs' which increased his earnings in the days of the maximum wage. His pleasant smile also masked an intolerant side to his character. Eventually Dundee paid a Scottish record of £23,000 for the player whom many former Rams players of his era still blame for the decline of the 1950s, after several unsettled stars left the club. Steel helped Dundee to two League Cup Final victories and a Scottish Cup Final before emigrating to America in August 1954, taking up a position in advertising.

STEEL
William Gilbert   *Left-back*

Born: Blantyre, 6 February 1908.
Career: Bridgton Waverley. St Johnstone September 1926. Liverpool August 1931. Birmingham March 1935. Derby County February 1939. Trainer, Airdrieonians, April 1950: manager April 1954. Manager, Third Lanark, January 1963 to June 1964.

Billy Steel did not miss a match for St Johnstone for three seasons before moving south. He made his Liverpool debut against Derby County and later joined the Rams for £1,275. His career was curtailed by the outbreak of World War Two.

STEELE
Eric Graham   *Goalkeeper*

Born: Wallsend, 14 May 1954.
Career: Amateur, Newcastle United: professional, July 1972. Peterborough United, loan, December 1973. Peterborough United July 1974.

Billy Steel, helped repay the record fee Derby paid for him with 35 goals in 124 League and Cup games.

Bob Stephenson.

George Stephenson – 56 goals in 120 games – won England honours with Derby.

Brighton & Hove Albion February 1977. Watford October 1979. Cardiff City, loan, March 1983. Derby County August 1984. Southend United August 1987. Mansfield Town, loan, March 1988. Notts County October 1988. Wolverhampton Wanderers March 1989.

Division Three promotion 1985-6. Division Two champions 1986-7.

Eric Steele was an amateur with Newcastle United while completing his GCE 'A' levels and playing for England Schools Under-18. He made his League debut with Peterborough and began a sequence of promotions with them. His rises continued with Brighton and Watford and even in a loan spell with Cardiff. Steele added two more promotions at the Baseball Ground, twice coming in at important stages when Mark Wallington was injured.

At most of his clubs, he did a great deal of unpublicised charity work and ran successful goalkeeping schools. In July 1992, he returned to the Baseball Ground as a specialised goalkeeping coach.

STEPHENSON
George Robert   *Outside-right*

Born: Derby, 19 November 1942.
Career: Derwent Sports. Juniors, Derby County: professional September 1960. Shrewsbury Town June 1964. Rochdale July 1965. Lockheed Leamington July 1967. Worcester City October 1967. Buxton August 1968.

Bob Stephenson, the son of pre-war international George, won greater fame as a county cricketer. He played 14 senior games for Derby County and made his Derbyshire debut in 1967

when Bob Taylor was injured. The presence of Taylor made the future bleak for Stephenson, a wicketkeeper, and he joined Hampshire, playing for them from 1969 to 1980. He was Hampshire captain in 1979 and shared in 661 dismissals in his career.

STEPHENSON
George Ternent   *Inside-forward*

Born: New Delaval, 3 September 1900.
Died: Derby, 18 August 1971.
Career: New Delaval Villa. Leeds City August 1919. Aston Villa October 1919. Stourbridge, loan, August 1920 to May 1921. Derby County November 1927. Sheffield Wednesday February 1931. Preston North End July 1933. Charlton Athletic May 1934: chief scout 1939. Manager, Huddersfield Town, August 1947 to March 1952.

Division One runners-up 1929-30.

When Leeds City were expelled from the League in 1919, their players were put up for auction at the Metropole Hotel, Leeds, in October. Among them were two later to be with Derby County. Thomas Lamph went to Manchester City and George Stephenson was sold to Aston Villa, where he joined his brother Clem, for £250 and was promptly loaned to Stourbridge. Stephenson had matured into a clever inside-forward by the time George Jobey signed him and his impact was immediate. After making his debut in a 3-0 defeat by Everton, he scored 13 goals in the next 11 League and Cup games. He played for England against France and Belgium the same season, scored four in a 5-4 defeat of Grimsby Town in December 1929 and was an integral member of the team until he and Tommy Davison were suddenly, and suprisingly, transferred to Sheffield Wednesday. Stephenson was involved in three successive promotions, from the Second Division with Preston North End in 1933-4 and from the Third Division South to the First with Charlton. Like his brother Clem, also an England international, he became manager of Huddersfield Town and coached Derby's 'A' team in the early 1960s. His son, Bob, also played for the Rams.

STEVENSON
James
Inside-left

Born: Paisley, Scotland, 1876. Killed in World War One.

Jimmy Stevenson.

Career: Clyde. Derby County January 1895. Newcastle United October 1898. Grimsby Town September 1901. Leicester Fosse January 1902. Clyde October 1902.

Division One runners-up 1895-6. FA Cup Finalists 1897-8.

Jimmy Stevenson's dribbling ability caught the eye of commentators but he was also reckoned to be unselfish and his scoring rate with Derby, 32 goals in 84 senior games, shows his effectiveness. Unlucky with injuries after his £225 move to Newcastle United. At Leicester he was suspended within two months of signing on, as an internal disciplinary action.

STEWART
Arthur
Midfield

Born: Ballymena, 13 January 1942.
Career: Ballymena 1957. Glentoran August 1961. Derby County December 1967. Ballymena August 1970: player-manager August 1971. Manager, Glentoran, 1977. Coaching in New Jersey 1979. Manager, Ballyclare Comrades, 1981.

Division Two champions 1968-9.

Brian Clough and Peter Taylor signed Arthur Stewart to stiffen their defence and midfield in their first season at the Baseball Ground. He won four of his seven caps for Northern Ireland while at Derby but, after beginning the Second Division championship season as first choice, he lost his place when Willie Carlin was signed.

Arthur Stewart.

STEWART
F.Harry
Outside-left

Career: Dundee. Derby County March 1900. Blackburn Rovers September 1900.

Harry Stewart scored on his debut against Everton in April 1900, one of only two games he played in his six months with Derby.

STOCKILL
Reginald Robert
Inside-right

Born: York, 23 November 1913.
Career: York City August 1929. Scarborough February 1931. Arsenal May 1931. Derby County September 1934. Luton Town August 1939.

Division One runners-up 1935-6.

Reg Stockill.

Reg Stockill, an England schoolboy international, made his debut in York City's first Third Division North match, against Wigan Borough in August 1929, aged 15 years and 281 days. George Jobey signed him for £2,000 from Arsenal, after nipping in ahead of Liverpool, Huddersfield and Newcastle. Stockill made a tremendous start with Derby and supporters were hailing a new star until, on Boxing Day 1934, he was carried off with a badly damaged right knee. Out until March 1936, he was never the same player again.

STOKOE
James   *Inside-forward*

Born: Jarrow.
Career: Jarrow. Swindon Town June 1920. Derby County August 1922. Durham City June 1923.

Stokoe played eight times in 1922-3 but was allowed to leave at the end of his only season with Derby.

STORER
Harry   *Wing-half/inside-forward*

Born: Liverpool, 2 February 1898. Died: Derby, 1 September 1967.
Career: Ripley Town. Eastwood. Amateur, Notts County, 1918. Amateur, Grimsby Town, February 1919: professional, April 1919. Derby County March 1921. Burnley February 1929. Manager, Coventry City, June 1931. Manager, Birmingham City, June 1945. Manager, Coventry City, November 1948 to November 1953. Manager, Derby County, July 1955 to May 1962.
Division Two promotion 1925-6.

Although he was born in Liverpool and came to the Rams from Grimsby Town for £4,500, Harry Storer had fine Derbyshire connections. His father, Harry, was born in Ripley and played in goal for Derby Midland, Woolwich Arsenal and Liverpool, as well as cricket for Derbyshire. Uncle William was a Rams forward and a Derbyshire and England cricketer. Harry junior also played for Derbyshire from 1920 to 1936, scoring 13,513 runs (average 27.63) with 18 centuries and taking over 200 wickets. He was one of Derbyshire's finest opening batsmen and a member of the 1936 Championship team. His career with the Rams was just as distinguished. Although he played most of his games in the half-back line, he had one outstanding season at inside-forward when he scored 24 League goals in 1923-4, including four when the Rams won 8-0 at Bristol City. At the end of that season he won the first of his two caps, at inside-left against France in Paris. Storer was a hard player and a tough manager. He was firm with his players and successful: the Division Three South title with Coventry in 1935-6, the Second Division championship with Birmingham in 1947-8 and the Third North success with the Rams in 1956-7.

STORER
William   *Forward*

Born: Butterley, 25 January 1867. Died: Derby, 28 February 1912.
Career: Derby Midland. Derby County June 1891. Loughborough Town August 1893. Glossop North End May 1895.

William Storer was brother to Liverpool and Woolwich Arsenal goalkeeper Harry and uncle of Harry junior, a Rams and England player. William was better known as a Derbyshire and England wicketkeeper. He played for Derbyshire from 1887 to 1905, appeared in six Tests against Australia and, in all first-class cricket, scored 12,966 runs (average 28.87). Apart from being international class behind the stumps, he also captured 214 wickets for the county as a bowler. The first professional to score two hundreds in a match, against Yorkshire at Derby in 1896. In 27 games for the Rams, he appeared in all five forward positions.

STRAW
Raymond   *Centre-forward*

Born: Ilkeston, 22 May 1933.
Career: Ilkeston MW. Ilkeston Town August 1951. Derby County October 1951. Coventry City November 1957. Mansfield Town August 1961. Lockheed Leamington July 1963.
Division Three North champions 1956-7

There have been few less complicated characters to play for Derby County than Ray Straw, the former Ilkeston

Harry Storer.

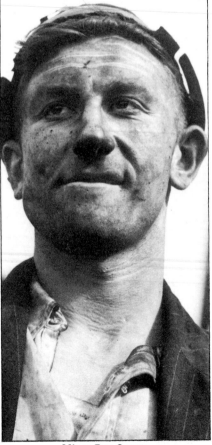
Miner Ray Straw.

William Storer.

miner who equalled Jack Bowers' record of 37 League goals in a season. Straw's tally came in the Third Division North promotion season and a large proportion of them were headed in from Tommy Powell's centres. His training in the days of Harry Storer's management consisted mainly of heading in centres from Powell and Woodhead, the two wingers. It paid Straw twice over. Before the 1956-7 season began, his brother had offered him half-a-crown a goal and ten shilling for every hat-trick (he scored three). Straw joined the Rams when

they were still in Division One. He played in the top flight, making his debut in a 1-1 home draw with Chelsea in the last game of 1951-2, but did not establish himself until Derby had been relegated twice, when he became the key man in attack. He injured his ankle during the 1957 close season tour of Holland and by the time he had regained full fitness and form, Storer had sold him to Coventry. Straw, known in his playing days as 'Toffee' because of his passion for sweets, enjoyed two more promotions, from the Fourth Division with Coventry in

1958-9, thereby appearing in all six divisions of the Football League, and Mansfield Town in 1962-3. The goals still flowed, 85 in 151 games for Coventry and 14 in 49 for Mansfield.

STREETE
Floyd Anthony   *Defender*

Born: Lionell Town, Clarendon, Jamaica, 5 May 1959.
Career: Rivet Sports. Cambridge United July 1976. FC Utrecht cs 1983. SC Cambuur 1983-4. Derby County September 1984. Wolverhampton Wanderers October 1985. Reading July 1990

Division Three promotion 1985-6.

Floyd Streete.

Straw in more familar pose. His 60 Rams goals included a seasonal record.

Floyd Streete was a powerfully-built and versatile player. He made his debut in Cambridge United's Fourth Division championship season and had a larger part in their next promotion. After a year in Dutch football, Streete joined Derby, initially on a non-contract basis, to cover while Rob Hindmarch was injured. He proved a useful short-term signing and helped Wolverhampton Wanderers to win Division Four and the Sherpa Van Trophy in 1987-8 followed by the Division Three title in 1988-9.

STURRIDGE
Dean Constantine   *Forward*

Born: Birmingham, 27 July 1973.
Career: Trainee, Derby County:
professional July 1991.

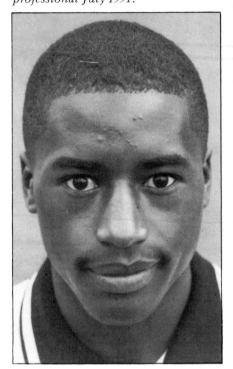

Dean Sturridge.

A winger or central striker with
considerable speed, Dean Sturridge was
still learning his trade in the Reserves
when he made his senior debut at
Southend in January 1992. His brother
Simon is a Birmingham City player.

SUGG
Frank Howe   *Centre-forward*

Born: Ilkeston, 11 January 1862. Died:
Liverpool, 29 May 1933.
Career: Derby County 1884. Everton
1888. Burnley 1889.

Frank Sugg appeared in Derby
County's first FA Cup tie in 1884. He
played cricket for Derbyshire between
1884 and 1886. He had previously
appeared for Yorkshire and played for
Lancashire from 1887 to 1899. His two
Tests against Australia came in 1888.

SUMMERS
John Lawrence   *Outside-right*

Born: Chorlton, 8 February 1915. Died:
Southampton, 12 April 1991.
Career: Manchester North End 1931.
Burnley February 1932. Fleetwood,
loan, 1932. Preston North End 1933.
Tunbridge Wells Rangers 1933.
Leicester City April 1934. Derby
County May 1935. Southampton
October 1936. Retired 1938.
Division One runners-up 1935-6.

A member of Derby's Central League
championship team in 1935-6,
Summers also deputised for Sammy
Crooks in two First Division matches.

Steve Sutton, finally joined the club he had supported as a boy.

SUTTON
Stephen John   *Goalkeeper*

Born: Hartington, 16 April 1961.
Career: Apprentice, Nottingham
Forest: professional September 1979.
Mansfield Town, loan, March 1981.
Derby County, loan, January 1985.
Coventry City, loan, February 1991.
Luton Town, loan, November 1991.
Derby County March 1992.

Steve Sutton, who slipped through
Derby's fingers as a schoolboy, was one
of two Nottingham Forest goalkeepers
taken on loan in 1984-5. Ronnie
Sinclair did not make a senior appearance but Sutton, kept out of the Forest
team by Hans Segers, played extremely

well while Eric Steele was injured.
Arthur Cox would have signed Sutton
had the money been available. Sutton
was in the Forest team which won the
Littlewoods Cup and the Simod Cup
in 1988-9 but fell out of favour at the
City Ground after rejecting a new
contract. He finally joined Derby, the
team he supported as a boy, for £300,000
as Peter Shilton's successor.

SWALLOW
Raymond   *Forward*

Born: Southwark, 15 June 1935.
Career: Tooting and Mitcham.
Amateur, Arsenal, March 1952;

groundstaff September 1952; professional December 1952. Derby County September 1958. Poole Town August 1964.

Harry Storer paid Arsenal £3,600 for Ray Swallow, who played over 100 League games for Derby. He was more effective than his plodding gait suggested and he also played cricket for Derbyshire from 1959 to 1963, having made his first-class debut for MCC against Scotland in 1957. His one century for Derbyshire was against Oxford University in 1962.

SWINDLEHURST
David — *Striker/midfield*

Born: Edgeware, 6 January 1956.
Career: Apprentice, Crystal Palace: professional January 1973. Derby County, loan, February 1980. Derby County April 1980. West Ham United March 1983. Sunderland August 1985. Anorthosis (Cyprus) July 1987. Wimbledon March 1988. Colchester United June 1988. Peterborough United, loan, December 1988. Manager, Bromley, June 1989 to January 1990, remaining as a director.

David Swindlehurst became Derby's first £400,000 player and set a transfer record which lasted until Mark Wright was signed for £760,000 more than seven years later. He had spent two months on loan with the Rams before Colin Addison clinched a £410,000 deal with Crystal Palace. The signing was completed on the pitch before Derby played Manchester City but, despite a Rams victory, they lost their First Division status that afternoon. Swindlehurst's partnership with Alan Biley was designed to lead Derby to an immediate return, but the team was not good enough. Biley joined Everton in July 1981 and Swindlehurst spent the rest of his time helping Derby avoid a further drop into the Third Division. He was a strong runner and performed with equal effect in midfield. Frustration at the Rams' inability to make progress was a partial explanation for his being sent off three times in Derby's colours and, with his contract nearing an end, he joined West Ham for £160,000 as Derby sought to ease their crippling financial problem.

SYLVESTER
Tom — *Right-back*

Career: Derby County October 1907.

Sylvester stood in for Nicholas twice in 1908-9.

TAFT
Douglas — *Centre-forward*

Born: Leicester, 9 March 1926. Died: Derby, 29 September 1987.
Career: Army football. Derby County November 1947. Wolverhampton Wanderers July 1949. Chelmsford City

David Swindlehurst, 32 goals in 125 games for the Rams.

Ray Swallow.

Doug Taft.

August 1950. Bedford Town May 1952. Peterborough United June 1953. Kettering Town June 1955. Rugby Town July 1956. Player-manager, Hinckley Athletic, June 1957. Long Eaton United February 1959.

Doug Taft scored on his debut against Stoke City in December 1948, his only goal in the nine games in which he stood in for Jack Stamps. He was for many years a publican in Derby, keeping the Spotted Horse and later the Osmaston Park Hotel.

TATE
Geoffrey Michael   *Outside-right*

Born: Leicester, 16 December 1937.
Career: Juniors, Derby County. Juniors, Leicester City. Professional, Derby County, August 1955. Rugby Town July 1958. Burton Albion June 1961. Loughborough United November 1961.

An England schoolboy international, Geoff Tate scored in his only match for Derby County, against Oldham Athletic in September 1955.

TAYLOR
Kevin   *Midfield*

Born: Wakefield, 22 January 1961.
Career: Apprentice, Sheffield Wednesday: professional October 1978. Derby County July 1984. Crystal Palace March 1985. Scunthorpe United October 1987. Farsley Celtic 1991.

Kevin Taylor.

Kevin Taylor was the first player for whom Arthur Cox paid a transfer fee, around £10,000. He did a steady job for Derby County without making a lasting impression.

TAYLOR
Martin James   *Goalkeeper*

Born: Tamworth, 9 December 1966.
Career: Mile Oak Rovers. Derby County July 1986. Carlisle United, loan, September 1987. Scunthorpe United, loan, December 1987.

Martin Taylor.

Martin Taylor had the first chance to succeed Peter Shilton in March 1992 but, with promotion the aim, his bad error against Tranmere Rovers at Prenton Park cast doubts and Steve Sutton soon took over. After early loan spells to gain experience, Taylor became a very competent Reserves goalkeeper. His handling was excellent but he could not carry the same composure into his limited senior opportunities.

TAYLOR
Robert Craig   *Outside-left*

Born: 4 December 1897.
Career: Seaton Delaval. Derby County January 1922.

Played two games immediately before the arrival of Lionel Murphy ended any problems with the outside-left position for the next five years.

THOMAS
Andrew Mark   *Forward*

Born: Oxford, 16 December 1962.
Career: Apprentice, Oxford United:

professional December 1980. Fulham, loan, December 1982. Derby County, loan, March 1983. Newcastle United September 1986. Bradford City June 1988. Plymouth Argyle July 1989.

Andy Thomas was a talented striker unlucky with injuries. Peter Taylor signed him on loan but gave him only one substitute appearance. Persistent back injuries forced him to retire in February 1991.

THOMAS
Edward   *Forward*

Born: Newton-le-Willows, 23 October 1933.
Career: Juniors, Everton: professional October 1951. Blackburn Rovers February 1960. Swansea Town July 1962. Derby County August 1964. Orient September 1967. Nuneaton Borough, loan, February 1968. Heanor Town August 1968.

Eddie Thomas was one of the best bargains Tim Ward ever picked up, so good that the deal ultimately worked against Ward as directors expected him to find gems for under £10,000. Thomas cost around £6,000 and, for two years, formed a deadly inside-forward partnership with Alan Durban. They were on target with a remarkably high percentage of their shots but the Rams did not derive full value because they conceded so many goals. Brian Clough sold Thomas to Orient for £5,000.

THOMAS
Michael Reginald   *Midfield*

Born: Mochdre, 7 July 1954.
Career: Amateur, Wrexham: apprentice: professional April 1972. Manchester United November 1978. Everton August 1981. Brighton & Hove Albion November 1981. Stoke City August 1982. Chelsea January 1984. West Bromwich Albion September 1985. Derby County, loan, March 1986. Wichita Wings August 1986. Shrewsbury Town August 1988. Leeds United June 1989. Stoke City, loan, March 1990. Stoke City August 1990. Wrexham August 1991.

Division Three promotion 1985-6.

Mickey Thomas enjoyed a glittering, if slightly erratic, career after developing under John Neal at Wrexham. He played 51 times for Wales, helped Wrexham to win the Third Division and, after a £300,000 move, was in Manchester United's 1978-9 FA Cup Final team beaten by Arsenal. Chelsea won the Second Division in 1983-4 with Thomas in the side and his all-action style, coupled with his experience, persuaded Arthur Cox to take him on loan. Thomas played nine times as Derby neared promotion from the Third Division but did not make the expected impact. At the age of 37, however, he was still able to make a dramatic contribution to Wrexham's FA Cup victory over Arsenal in 1992.

THOMAS
Roderick John   *Right-back*

Born: Glyncorrwg, 11 January 1947. Career: Gloucester City. Swindon Town July 1964. Derby County November 1973. Cardiff City October 1977. Newport County March 1982. Bath City 1982-3.

Division One champions 1974-5.

Dave Mackay went back to Swindon Town, where he had started his managerial career, for his first signing after taking over at Derby. Rod Thomas, already established in the Wales team, cost Derby £80,000. The first to react was Ron Webster who, presented with a threat to his position, asked Mackay where he stood. Mackay assured him that he would remain in the team while his form justified selection. Thomas had to wait until an injury to Webster let him in and in the second half of the 1974-5 Championship-winning season he was at last able to show his quality. He was deceptively quick and a long leg would often stretch around an opponent who thought he had escaped. He played in

Andy Thomas.

Mickey Thomas.

Rod Thomas, 118 appearances after Ron Webster's injury let him in.

Eddie Thomas.

the Swindon team which beat Arsenal in the 1969 League Cup Final and won 50 Welsh caps, 19 of them with Derby. Thomas and Francis Lee were joint owners of a racehorse.

THOMPSON
Cyril Alfred   *Centre-forward*

Born: Southend, 18 December 1918. Career: Southend United, amateur, July 1945. Derby County July 1948.

Brighton & Hove Albion March 1950.
Watford March 1951.

Cyril Thompson found the transition from the Third Division South to the First Division difficult and struggled at the Baseball Ground.

THOMPSON
George Alexander *Outside-right*

Born: South Shields, 23 March 1883.
Career: South Shields Bertram 1904-05.
South Shields Adelaide 1905. North
Shields. Sheffield United October 1906.
Derby County September 1908.
Newcastle United. Manager, Luton
Town, February to October 1925.

For two seasons, George Thompson was the most consistent of several players competing for the outside-right position. A boiler-maker by trade, he was briefly manager of Luton.

THOMPSON
George H.   *Inside-forward*

Career: Ticknall. Derby County
December 1920.

One of 32 players used in 1920-21, when Derby County were relegated from the First Division.

THOMPSON
James   *Wing-half*

Career: Derby County February 1898.

Played one match, against Aston Villa in March 1898.

THOMPSON
Peter   *Centre-forward*

Born: Blackhall, 16 February 1936.
Career: Blackhall CW. Amateur,
Wrexham, November 1955.
Professional, Hartlepools United, July
1957. Derby County November 1958.
Bournemouth & Boscombe Athletic
January 1962. Hartlepools United
September 1963. Boston United August
1966.

Peter Thompson was an England amateur international before turning professional. He was Derby's leading scorer in 1959-60 but was never sure of a regular place at the Baseball Ground and moved after Bill Curry had established himself.

THOMS
Harry   *Centre-half*

Born: Greatham, 19 November 1896.
Died: Newcastle upon Tyne, December
1970.
Career: Greatham. Service in World
War One. Amateur, Hartlepools
United, December 1919: professional
January 1920. Derby County August
1922. Crystal Palace May 1928.
Division Two promotion 1925-6
(captain).

In his youth Harry Thoms played relatively little football and trained as

Harry Thoms, 90 minutes from Wembley in his first season with the Rams.

an electrical engineer. Then his potential was noted and he signed for his local club, Hartlepools United. After three seasons with United, Thoms followed manager Cecil Potter and fellow defender Tommy Crilly to Derby. He became the Rams' regular centre-half and captained the side which won promotion in 1925-6. The £500 fee which Derby had to pay turned out to be a bargain and Thoms produced many sterling displays, powerful shoulder-charging being a feature of his play. In his first season at the Baseball Ground Thoms went with Derby to the FA Cup semi-final against West Ham and was only 90 minutes away from appearing in the first Wembley Final. He had twice been wounded in France but survived to form, with McIntyre and Plackett, one of Derby's soundest half-back lines. Thoms and Crilly left together, moving to Crystal Palace with Jimmy Gill.

THORNEWELL
George   *Outside-right*

Born: Romiley, April 1898. Died:
Derby, 6 March 1986.
Career: Rolls-Royce. Derby County
May 1919. Blackburn Rovers December

George Thornewell, 295 League and Cup appearances for Derby after World War One.

North title in 1930-31, played with Newark Town and for many years kept a pub at Duffield, at the same time playing an active role on the committee of the Derby County Supporters' Association.

TINKLER
Alfred   *Inside-forward*

Died: Croydon, 1950.
Career: Derby County January 1909. Heanor United. Ilkeston United May 1911. Birmingham December 1911. Burton United 1915.

Tinkler played twice in 1909-10 but returned more successfully to League football with Birmingham. A teacher by profession, he walked out of Derby County but the reputation as a trouble-maker did not resurface.

TODD
Colin   *Central defender/midfield*

Born: Chester-le-Street, 12 December 1948.
Career: Apprentice, Sunderland: professional December 1966. Derby County February 1971. Everton September September 1978. Birmingham City September 1979. Nottingham Forest August 1982. Oxford United February 1984. Vancouver Whitecaps May 1984. Luton Town October 1984. Youth coach, Middlesbrough, May 1986: assistant-manager September 1986: manager March 1990 to June 1991. Assistant-manager, Bradford City, January 1992. Assistant manager, Bolton Wanderers, June 1992.
Division One champions 1971-2, 1974-5.

"We're not signing Colin Todd. We can't afford him," said Brian Clough in answer to reporters' persistent questions one day in February 1971. Clough promptly got into his car and, 24 hours later, produced Todd to those same reporters. Derby paid Sunderland £170,000 for one of the most promising young players in the country and Clough, once Sunderland's youth coach, knew he had a cast-iron certainty. Todd, paired with Roy McFarland, was a central defender with the capacity to both excite and produce ripples of appreciative applause. He was devastatingly fast and strong in the tackle. He made the game look so easy, because all he did was to catch opponents, take the ball off them and give it to one of his own players. He played 40 games in the 1971-2 Championship side, but 1974-5 was his greatest season. Peter Daniel stood in admirably for the injured McFarland and Todd made scarcely an error. Deservedly he was elected as the Professional Footballers' Association Player of the Year. He could easily have won more than 27 England caps and there was great resentment when Tommy Docherty sold him to Everton for £300,000 in

1927. Chesterfield August 1929. Newark Town August 1932.
Division Two promotion 1925-6.

Nippy little George Thornewell was a regular fixture in the Rams' team in the years following World War One. The youngest of eight children, Thornewell moved to Derby after his father died. He became an apprentice at Rolls-Royce and during World War One was training as a pilot. When peace was restored, he went back to Royces and played with the Rams in the 1919 Midland Victory League. Later that year the former schoolboy

star was making his First Division debut against Manchester United at the Baseball Ground. Thereafter Thornewell was the Rams' regular outside-right, making 295 appearances, until the appearance of Sammy Crooks, and played for England four times, twice each against Sweden and France. Thornewell, a cheeky little winger who liked to hug the touchline, helped Derby to promotion in 1925-6. He moved to Blackburn and a few months later, in the 1928 FA Cup Final victory over Huddersfield Town, was involved in a first-minute goal. Later he helped Chesterfield to the Third Division

Colin Todd, made 371 first-team appearances for the Rams and gained two Championship medals and 27 England caps.

September 1978. Todd helped Birmingham City to promotion from the Second Division in 1980 and gave Oxford United a vital thrust towards the Third Division title in 1984. He became Bruce Rioch's assistant at Middlesbrough before being manager for 15 months and they were together again with Bolton Wanderers.

TODD
Thomas Bell   *Centre-forward*

Born: Stonehouse, 1 June 1926.

Career: Burnbank Athletic. Motherwell 1944. Airdrieonians. Stonehouse Violet. Hamilton Academical January 1951. Crewe Alexandra August 1955. Derby County November 1955. Rochdale May 1956.

Tommy Todd, a £750 buy from Crewe Alexandra, scored on his debut against Chester in November 1955 and hit three goals in his four League games for Derby. He lost his place to Ray Straw, a move which proved crucial when Derby won the Third Division North the following season.

TOOTLE
James   *Full-back*

Born: Skelmersdale, April 1899. Died: Westhead, 18 November 1947.

Career: Skelmersdale. Southport May 1922. Derby County December 1924.

Division Two promotion 1925-6.

Tootle was signed on Christmas Day 1924, and provided cover for the full-back positions. He played in the first three games of the 1925-6 promotion season before Harry Wightman returned to the team.

TOWIE
Thomas
Wing-forward

Career: Dumbarton Union. Preston North End August 1891. Glasgow Celtic cs 1892. Renton. Derby County August 1893. Rossendale January 1896.

Towie played on both wings but made only occasional appearances for Derby County.

TOWNSEND
William
Goalkeeper

Born: Bedworth, 27 December 1922. Died: Thornton Cleveleys, 21 December 1988.
Career: Nuneaton Borough. Derby County May 1939. Burton Albion July 1953. Banbury Spencer June 1957. Burton Albion September 1959: player-manager, October 1959: secretary-manager, May to October 1962.

More than half-a-dozen goalkeepers were preferred to Billy Townsend after he had made his peacetime debut in the 1946 FA Cup quarter-finals against Aston Villa. Townsend had built up considerable experience during World War Two but contemporary players felt he was liable to freeze in Cup ties. So the Rams seemed to be constantly searching for other goalkeepers but Townsend out-lasted most of them. He had a spell managing Burton Albion and was later their pools promoter and

chairman of the supporters' club. In 1966, he became groundsman to Fylde RFC and in 1969 was appointed sales manager in Everton's development office.

TRAVIS
Henry
Centre-forward

Born: Manchester, 26 December 1911.
Career: Manchester City October 1931. Oldham Athletic June 1932. Accrington Stanley July 1933. Leeds United June 1934. Bradford City June 1935. Derby County February 1937. Tranmere Rovers November 1938. Kidderminster Harriers July 1939.

Travis had to make several moves before he found any success at League level, with Bradford City. George Jobey signed him for £825 but he did not fully adapt to First Division demands.

TREMELLING
Solomon
Centre-forward

Born: Newhall, 1885.
Career: Newhall Swifts. Derby County November 1905. Burton United 1909. Ilkeston United November 1909. Gresley Rovers 1911. Bradford City March 1913. Mansfield Town 1915. Gresley Rovers.

Tremelling was signed as a centre-forward but the second of his two League appearances was at centre-half.

TRUEMAN
Ronald
Outside-right

Career: Macclesfield Town. Derby County May 1908. Sutton Town May 1910. Macclesfield 1911. Sutton Town July 1912.

In two successive seasons, Trueman began as first-choice without being able to consolidate his position.

TURNER
Arthur D.
Outside-right

Born: Farnborough, June 1877. Died: Hartley Witney, 4 April 1925.
Career: Aldershot North End 1892. South Farnborough. Camberley St Michael's. Southampton May 1899. Derby County May 1902. Newcastle United January 1903. Tottenham Hotspur February 1904. Southampton cs 1904.

Arthur Turner had a rapid rise to fame, playing for England against Ireland in his first Southern League season. He won a second cap, was a member of Southampton's Southern League championship team in 1900-01 and played in their 1900 and 1902 FA Cup Final teams. He spent only eight months with Derby but was a regular choice until Newcastle United signed him. He returned to Southampton in 1904 but spent only a further year in the professional game.

Billy Townsend watches anxiously with Bert Mozley close at hand.

Jimmy Turner.

TURNER
James Albert
Left-half

Born: Black Bull, Staffordshire 1866. Died: Stoke, 9 April 1904.
Career: Black Lane. Radcliffe. Bolton

Wanderers July 1888. Stoke September 1894. Derby County June 1896. Stoke August 1898. Retired 1899.

FA Cup Finalists 1897-8.

Jimmy Turner developed with Bolton Wanderers, winning the first of his three England caps while with them. He became an increasingly important member of the Bolton team before moving to Stoke, where he gained his second call-up for England. After a dispute with Stoke, Turner joined Derby County and played his third game for England, against Ireland in March 1898. In the same year, he played in Derby's second Cup Final, the 4-1 defeat by Sheffield United. He patched up his differences with Stoke and returned for a second spell.

UDALL
Edward William   *Right-back*

Born: Atherstone, 1912.
Career: Atherstone Town. Leicester City November 1931. Derby County May 1934. Retired because of injury. Manager, Atherstone Town, July 1945.

Division One runners-up 1935-6.

Ted Udall became Derby County's regular right-back when England international Tommy Cooper joined Liverpool. His injury problems began on Easter Monday 1935, when he

dislocated a shoulder against Everton. He was only out for one game and was encouragingly consistent the following season until he aggravated the injury in the sixth-round FA Cup tie against Fulham. From then on, Udall was always liable to shoulder trouble and the injury was so persistent that he needed 12 operations after leaving the Baseball Ground. In the early post-war years, Udall was manager of Atherstone Town.

UPTON
Frank   *Wing-half/full-back*

Born: Ainsley Hill, 18 October 1934.
Career: Nuneaton Borough. Northampton Town March 1953. Derby County June 1954. Chelsea August 1961. Derby County September 1965. Notts County September 1966. Worcester City July 1967. Player-manager, Workington, January to July 1968. Coach, Northampton Town, October 1969. Coach, Aston Villa, January 1970. Coach, Chelsea, August 1977: temporary manager, December 1978. Coach, Randers Freja, February 1979 to February 1980. Coach, Dundee, August 1980. Coach, Al Arabi, 1981. Coach, Wolverhampton Wanderers, October 1982. Coach, Bedworth United, October 1984. Coach, assistant-manager, Coventry City, December

Frank Upton.

1984 to April 1986. Coach, IBK Keflavik, May 1987. State coach, Borneo, May 1989. Caretaker-manager, Burton Albion, January to February 1990. Youth development officer, Northwich Victoria, April 1990. YTS officer, Cheltenham Town to November 1990.

Division 3 North Champions 1956-57.

Bone-crunching tackles and rocket-powered shots were the trade mark of Frank 'The Tank' Upton. After 17 League appearances for Northampton Town, Upton's first Derby career lasted six years. He was just the sort of player to capture Harry Storer's eye, although he played only a handful of games when the Rams won promotion in 1956-7. Later he regained a regular place until Storer sold him to Chelsea. Upton was a success at Stamford Bridge, playing some of his 74 League matches at centre-forward, helping them to promotion from the Second Division in 1962-3 and picking up a League Cup winners' prize in 1964-5. Tim Ward re-signed him for Derby and a year later he was off again, making the short trip to Meadow Lane. As a coach, he earned a good reputation for working with young players but had ups and downs, winning an industrial tribunal for wrongful dismissal by Wolves and becoming a globe-trotter in search of football.

Ted Udall, took over from Tommy Cooper.

VANN
Bernard W. *Centre-forward*

Career: Northampton Town. Burton United February 1907. Derby County March 1907. Leicester Fosse June 1907.

Vann stayed only three months at the Baseball Ground, playing three League games as Derby County were heading towards relegation for the first time in their history. A master at Ashby Grammar School.

VARNEY
Herbert *Outside-right*

Born: Belper, 1880. Died: c1951.
Career: Belper Town. Derby County April 1902. Belper Town cs 1903. West Bromwich Albion October 1905. Belper Town May 1907.

Varney appeared in two League matches for the Rams.

WALKER
Colin *Wing-half*

Born: Long Eaton, 7 July 1929.
Career: Juniors, Derby County: professional October 1946. Gresley Rovers February 1955.

Colin Walker worked in the Derby County offices before gaining a professional contract. He always looked a polished player, but did not have the confidence to assert himself.

WALKER
John A. *Half-back*

Career: Derby Junction. Derby County 1889. Notts County October 1891.

Played 13 senior games after joining Derby County from one of the early rivals. Walker was a member of the Junction team that reached the FA Cup semi-final in 1887-8 by beating mighty Blackburn Rovers 2-1 on Arboretum Field.

WALKER
James Harry *Wing-half*

Born: Wirksworth. Died: 1934.
Career: Clay Cross. Derby County May 1910. Notts County June 1920. Fulham March 1921. Aberdare Athletic May 1923. Bournemouth & Boscombe Athletic March 1924. Chesterfield June 1924.

Division Two champions 1911-12, 1914-15.

Harry Walker played a small part in the 1911-12 Second Division championship, but established himself as a steady wing-half in the 1914-15 success. He was still at the club in the difficult first season after World War One, then made several moves in quick succession.

WALKER
James McIntyre *Midfield*

Born: Northwich, 10 June 1947.
Career: Northwich Victoria. Derby County February 1968. Hartlepool, loan, March 1970. Brighton & Hove Albion September 1974. Peterborough United, loan, October 1975. Peterborough United February 1976. Chester November 1976. Coach, Al-Arabi 1983. Physiotherapist, Blackburn Rovers 1985. Physiotherapist, Aston Villa July 1987.

Division Two champions 1968-9. Division One champions 1971-2.

Jim Walker was one of the players who helped to point Derby County back to the First Division under Brian Clough and Peter Taylor. He was a regular in the 1968-9 Second Division championship team until the turn of the year, when John McGovern took over. From then on Walker, with his ability to hold the ball, was a valuable cover player. His major contribution to the

Colin Walker.

Jim Walker, played in First and Second Division championship teams.

Mark Wallington, played his part in two promotions.

Phil Waller, over 100 games for Derby

first League Championship was the only goal of the game against Crystal Palace at Selhurst Park. He had a good spell with Chester, where he first moved towards the physiotherapy side of the game.

WALLACE
John Martin   *Goalkeeper*

Born: Deantown, 13 April 1911. Died: 1978.
Career: Wallyford Bluebell. Raith Rovers December 1930. Blackpool February 1934. Derby County February 1948. Leith Athletic August 1948.

Jock Wallace, father of the Rangers, Leicester City and Seville manager, was in the veteran stage when Derby County signed him to take over from Billy Townsend. The main attraction was that Wallace, who had been in Blackpool's Second Division promotion team in 1936-7, was eligible for the FA Cup. He played in the quarter-finals against Queen's Park Rangers and the semi-final defeat by Manchester United at Hillsborough.

WALLER
Philip   *Wing-half*

Born: Leeds, 12 April 1943.
Career: Juniors, Derby County: professional April 1960. Mansfield Town March 1968. Player-manager, Ilkeston Town, June 1972. Boston United January 1973. Matlock Town August 1974. Burton Albion October 1974. Player-coach, Belper Town, July

1975. *Kimberley Town November 1976. Manager, Burton Albion, March 1977 to November 1978.*

Phil Waller was one of the young players developed by Tim Ward and did a steady job in the Second Division. He was in the team which reached the League Cup semi-finals in 1967-8 and then moved to Mansfield Town for £6,000. Waller was in two Northern Premier League championship teams with Boston United and in the side which achieved an FA Cup third round draw at the Baseball Ground in 1974, raising echoes of the 6-1 defeat by Boston in 1955.

WALLINGTON
Francis Mark   *Goalkeeper*

Born: Sleaford, 17 September 1952.
Career: Walsall October 1971. Leicester City March 1972. Derby County July 1985. Lincoln City August 1988: player-coach July 1990.

Division Three promotion 1985-6.
Division Two champions 1986-7.

In 1974, the developing talent of Mark Wallington enabled Leicester City to cash in on a major asset by selling Peter Shilton to Stoke City. By a strange quirk, Shilton took over from Wallington at the Baseball Ground almost 13 years later. In between, Wallington had a long and distinguished career at Leicester, playing twice for England Under-23 and, between January 1975 and March 1982, appearing in 332 consecutive club games. Arthur Cox went through his first season at Derby

with only one senior goalkeeper, Eric Steele, and spent £25,000 to sign Wallington. It was money very well spent, for Wallington brought quality, experience and a wholly beneficial influence in the dressing-room. He played a major part in two promotions, with Steele as admirable cover when injury struck on both occasions. After Shilton's arrival. Wallington passed on some of his model professionalism to the Central League team.

WALSH
Wilfred   *Outside-right*

Born: Pentelottyn, 29 July 1917. Died: 1977.
Career: Margate (Arsenal nursery). Arsenal May 1936. Derby County June 1939. Walsall March 1947. Hednesford Town 1948. Player-manager, Redditch Town, 1949. Player-manager, Hednesford Town, 1952

George Jobey paid £2,000 for Wilf Walsh, who played in the three matches before the outbreak of World War Two halted the 1939-40 season, and saw him as a successor to Sammy Crooks. He played in the first League game after the war.

WALTON
Gordon   *Right-back*

Career: Sevenoaks. Derby County April 1906.

Walton played only once, in the 7-0 defeat by Wolverhampton Wanderers at Molineux in April 1906.

WALTON
John
Left-half

Career: West Stanley. Derby County
November 1920. Walsall August 1922.

One of several players Jimmy Methven
signed from the North-East as he tried
to put together a team after World War
One.

WARD
Timothy Victor
Wing-half

Born: Cheltenham, 17 October 1917.
Career: Cheltenham Town. Derby
County April 1937. Barnsley March
1951. Manager, Exeter City, March 1953
(for eight days while still registered
with Barnsley). Manager, Barnsley,
March 1953. Manager, Grimsby Town,
February 1960. Manager, Derby
County, June 1962 to May 1967.
Manager, Carlisle United, June 1967
to September 1968.

A part-timer with his local club,
Cheltenham Town, Tim Ward was
spotted by Jackie Whitehouse and in
his first trial match for Derby County
'A', scored with his first kick. George
Jobey paid Cheltenham £100 and Ward
became a full-time professional. In
January 1938 he took over at left-half
in the League side, displacing England
international Errington Keen. Ward
was the regular number six until the
outbreak of war. Although he played
in the first game of the 1945-6 FA Cup
run, at Luton, Ward was in Germany
with the BAOR side for most of the
season. As a result he had no chance
of displacing Bullions and Musson, but
looked back philosophically. "So many
of my friends were killed in the war,"
he said, "and I regarded myself lucky
to emerge from it, rather than unlucky
to miss Wembley." Later that year
Arsenal offered £10,000 for him but
Derby found him a place at right-half
and in that position he went on to win
two England caps and skipper the
Rams. In the late 1940s, Ward had no
superior as a stylish wing-half and in
1950 he went on the FA tour of Canada.
His sudden sale to Barnsley shook not
only supporters but Ward himself
although he later returned to Derby as
manager.

WARREN
Arnold R.
Outside-right

Born: Codnor, 2 April 1875. Died:
Codnor, 3 September 1951.
Career: Heanor Town May 1895.
Ripley Athletic. Glossop November
1899. Ripley Town December 1899.
Derby County November 1901. Brent-
ford July 1902. Ripley Town April
1903.

Arnold Warren had one season with
Derby County, but gained more lasting
fame as a Derbyshire fast bowler. He
took 939 wickets in first-class cricket
between 1897 and 1920 and shared in

Tim Ward, made 260 appearances and later managed Derby.

Arnold Warren.

a world record ninth-wicket partnership of 283 with Jack Chapman for
Derbyshire against Warwickshire at
Blackwell in 1910. Warren played once
for England, against Australia at Leeds
in 1905. He took five for 57 in the first
innings, including distinguished vic-
tims in Victor Trumper, Monty Noble,
Warwick Armstrong and Joe Darling,
but was never picked again. Derbyshire
people have always believed that Test
selectors regarded the county as unfa-

shionable. While on Brentford's staff
he was involved in a pub brawl,
convicted of assault and served a prison
sentence.

WARREN
Benjamin
Wing-half/inside-forward

Born: Newhall, 1879. Died: Newhall,
15 January 1917.
Career: Newhall Town. Newhall
Swifts. Derby County May 1899. Chel-
sea August 1908. Retired February 1912.
FA Cup Finalists 1902-03.

For five years Ben Warren was probably
the finest wing-half in the League. As
late as 1972 his 13 caps held fourth place
in the list of Derby County's England
internationals. Warren rose to national
fame, yet his death at the age of 38 was
tragic. He was essentially a right-half,
a position in which he played 19
consecutive games for England with his
two clubs, but he was also an effective
inside-forward. In 1902, he scored eight
FA Cup goals, including a hat-trick
against Lincoln. Warren was a cour-
ageous player who allied a fierce tackle
to perfect ball control and abundant
hard work. After Derby were relegated
in 1907 he stayed another season and
then resumed his First Division career
with Chelsea, although he found it a
wrench to leave the Baseball Ground
and every Saturday night caught the
first available train back to his South
Derbyshire home. After his enforced
retirement, Chelsea played a testimon-

Ben Warren.

Darren Wassall, signed from Nottingham Forest for £600,000.

ial for him. Warren was certified insane and spent a period in Derbyshire Lunatic Asylum. It was a terrible end for a great player.

WARRINGTON
Joseph   *Forward*

Born: Macclesfield.
Career: Derby Wanderers. Derby County April 1901. Brentford May 1904. Portsmouth May 1905. New Brompton December 1906.
FA Cup Finalists 1902-03.

Joe Warrington was essentially an outside-right but played in four different forward positions for Derby County. He was one of those overwhelmed in the 1903 FA Cup Final.

WASSALL
Darren Paul James *Centre-half*

Born: Edgbaston, 27 June 1968.
Career: Apprentice, Nottingham

Forest: professional September 1986. Hereford United, loan, October 1987. Bury, loan, March 1989. Derby County June 1992.

After a long battle to establish himself with Nottingham Forest, Darren Wassall appeared to have broken through in 1991-2, especially when he played heroically against Manchester United — and Mark Hughes — in the League Cup Final despite a broken jaw. When Des Walker joined Sampdoria, Wassall appeared to be the natural successor, not least because of his speed. Instead, he joined Derby for £600,000.

WATERHOUSE
Frank   *Right-half*

Born: Langley Green, c1889. Died: 1940s.
Career: Langley St Michael's. Langley St Michael's Guild. Langley Green.

Wednesbury Old Athletic. West Bromwich Albion February 1908. Derby County March 1920.

An ever-present in West Bromwich Albion's 1910-11 Second Division championship team, Waterhouse joined Derby to assist in a late fight against relegation in 1919-20, along with another wing-half, Thomas Lamph. The drop was postponed for only 12 months.

WATSON
Alexander Francis *Centre-half*

Born: Liverpool, 5 April 1968.
Career: Apprentice Liverpool: professional May 1985. Derby County, loan, August 1990. AFC Bournemouth January 1991.

Derby County were forced to rely on loan signings to bolster their squad in 1991-2, when chairman Robert Max-

Alex Watson.

Dave Watson.

Robert Waugh.

well turned his back on the club. Alex Watson played five games early in the season and was sold to Bournemouth after returning to Anfield. His brother Dave also began with Liverpool, going on to play for Norwich City, Everton and England.

WATSON
David Vernon   *Centre-half*

Born: Stapleford, 5 October 1946.
Career: Stapleford Old Boys. Notts County January 1967. Rotherham United January 1968. Sunderland December 1970. Manchester City June 1975. Werder Bremen June 1979. Southampton October 1979. Stoke City January 1982. Vancouver Whitecaps April 1983. Derby County September 1983. Fort Lauderdale Sun May 1984. Player-coach, Notts County, September 1984. Kettering Town August 1985.

Dave Watson was in the veteran stage when Peter Taylor signed him for Derby County in the hope that his experience would preserve a Second Division place. There were too many problems, on and off the field, and Derby went down. Watson played for England 65 times and was capped with five clubs, a record unique among England internationals until Peter Shilton was picked for the first time as a Derby County player. Watson, superb in the air, was in Sunderland's 1973 FA Cup winning team and Manchester City's League Cup winners in 1976.

WAUGH
Robert   *Left-back*

Born: Newcastle upon Tyne.
Career: Newcastle Bentonians. Newcastle United January 1908. Derby County August 1912. Jarrow 1919.

David Webb, a great favourite in his brief time at Derby.

Division Two champions 1914-15.

Waugh was originally signed as cover for Charlie Betts and was then reserve to Tommy Barbour.

WEBB
David James   *Central defender*

Born: East Ham, 9 April 1946.
Career: Amateur, West Ham United.

Ron Webster, who made 535 senior appearances after joining Derby when Harry Storer was manager and going on to share in the enormous successes under Brian Clough.

Professional, Leyton Orient, May 1963. Southampton March 1966. Chelsea February 1968. Queen's Park Rangers July 1974. Leicester City September 1977. Derby County December 1978. Player-coach, AFC Bournemouth, May 1980: manager, December 1980 to December 1982. Manager, Torquay United, February 1984 to August 1985: managing-director to June 1986. Manager, Southend United, June 1986 to March 1987: General Manager, Southend United, December 1988 to May 1992.

David Webb was a short-term signing by Tommy Docherty, but his terrific enthusiasm made him a favourite at the Baseball Ground. After being involved in Southampton's promotion from the Second Division in 1965-6, Webb had his best days with Chelsea, scoring the winning goal in the 1970 FA Cup Final replay, being successful again in the European Cup-winners' Cup Final a year later and appearing in the 1972 League Cup Final. He played twice for Torquay in 1984-5 when he was the club's managing director.

WEBB
George H. *Half-back*

Born: Birmingham, c1900.
Career: Aston Villa 1918. Nuneaton Borough (remaining registered with Villa). Derby County June 1921. Bristol Rovers September 1922.

George Webb made two senior appearances in 1921-2.

WEBB
John Armstrong *Full-back*

Born: Sunderland, 19 May 1908. Died: Derby, 12 January 1984.
Career: Southwick. Derby County May 1927. Newport County June 1937. Ilkeston Town September 1947. Trainer, Wilmorton and Alvaston, August 1958.
Division One runners-up 1929-30, 1935-6.

Jack Webb spent ten years at the Baseball Ground as a reserve full-back, being briefly involved in two teams to finish runners-up. He became Derbyshire County Cricket Club's masseur in 1937, but continued to play, helping Newport County to win the Third Division South in 1938-9. He returned to Derby during the World War Two and, along with Jack Nicholas, played a major part in re-forming the club.

WEBSTER
Ronald *Right-back/wing-half*

Born: Belper, 21 June 1943.
Career: Juniors, Derby County: professional, June 1960. Minnesota Kicks, loan, April 1976. Minnesota Kicks April 1978. Youth coach, Derby County, August 1978 to November 1982.

Terry Webster, finally established himself in the Third Division North.

Division Two champions 1968-9. Division One champions 1971-2, 1974-5.

Ron Webster was the one local man in Derby County's League Championship teams. First as a player then as youth coach, he served under eight managers at the Baseball Ground. Harry Storer was in the manager's office when the young Webster went to ask why he was not in the first team and his promise brightened considerably in what was then, under Tim Ward, an average Second Division team. Bigger clubs saw Webster's potential but he stayed at Derby and, under Brian Clough and Peter Taylor, became the regular right-back in the surge towards the top. He was not a flamboyant player and tended to shun publicity. Because he had been around for a long time, managers as well as Press observers often underestimated him but his hallmarks were utter reliability and dedicated professionalism. He was a top-class defender and his rare goals in the 1970s — one in

each of the Championship seasons — assumed a prophetic significance. Dave Mackay bought Rod Thomas to play right-back but Webster, characteristically, made the Welsh international wait. Only when Webster was injured did he lose his place. When he turned to coaching he had made more senior appearances than any other player in the Rams' history. Kevin Hector subsequently took the record off him but Webster was a popular and effective youth coach until he became a victim of Peter Taylor's reorganisation.

WEBSTER
Terence Charles *Goalkeeper*

Born: Doncaster, 9 July 1930.
Career: Intake YC, Sheffield. Doncaster Rovers June 1948. Derby County October 1948. Skegness Town July 1958 to July 1961.
Division Three North champions 1956-7.

Terry Webster had not played a senior game for Doncaster Rovers before he moved to Derby County as part of a deal taking George Antonio in the opposite direction. Before the end of that season he found himself opposite such great goalkeepers as Ted Sagar (Everton), Frank Swift (Manchester City) and Gil Merrick (Birmingham City). Webster was small for a goalkeeper, standing barely 5ft 8in, but he performed competently after replacing Bill Townsend. He lost his place after the first 13 games of 1949-50 and found himself on the fringes of selection, not appearing in the senior team for two seasons after Ray Middleton had been signed. Webster finally established his place during the Rams' first season in Division Three North, missing only four games through injury. He was absent only once when the Rams won the Northern Section title the following season, Harry Storer giving Terry Adlington a run-out against bottom club Crewe. In Division Two, Derby had defensive problems and late in 1957 Webster let in seven goals in two games, including four at home to Huddersfield when teenaged Denis Law scored a penalty. He was replaced by Ken Oxford and signed for Skegness Town, but Derby still had much the better of the Antonio deal.

WHEATCROFT
Frederick George   Centre-forward

Born: Alfreton, 1882. Died: Bourlon Wood, France, 26 November 1917.
Career: Alfreton Town. Derby County May 1903. Swindon Town January 1905. Fulham March 1906. Derby County (one game in April 1906). Derby County, professional, February 1907. Reading May 1908. Swindon Town May 1909.

A schoolmaster who played much of his career as an amateur and, therefore, was able to shift around several clubs. He was as England amateur international, but Jimmy Methven persuaded him to turn professional in 1907. Wheatcroft was involved in four Southern League championships, with Fulham in 1905-6 and 1906-7, then with Swindon Town in 1910-11 and 1913-14. During World War One, he was a lieutenant in the 5th East Surrey Regiment and was killed in France.

WHEATLEY
Steven Peter   Outside-right

Born: Hinckley, 26 December 1929.
Career: Hinckley United. Derby County January 1950. Boston United July 1954. Chesterfield July 1955. Boston United September 1955.

Steve Wheatley played four League games for Derby County.

WHEELER
William   Outside-left

Career: Chesham. Watford 1910. Derby County April 1911.

Wheeler was signed from the Southern League and given a trial in Derby's final match of the 1910-11 season.

WHITE
Alfred   Centre-forward

Born: Spennymoor, 1910.
Career: Spennymoor United. Derby County November 1927. Bournemouth & Boscombe Athletic October 1931. Wrexham October 1935.

Alfie White managed only four senior games in four years with Derby, but found greater success when he moved to Bournemouth.

WHITE
William   Goalkeeper

Born: Clackmannan, 25 September 1932.
Career: Alva Albion. Rangers. Motherwell July 1952. Accrington Stanley August 1953. Mansfield Town May 1954. Derby County August 1955. Mansfield Town September 1955. Bacup Borough cs 1956.

An injury to Terry Webster in August 1955 caused Harry Storer to look around for a goalkeeper. Bill White came on a temporary transfer from Mansfield, long before the concept of loan deals had been introduced, and played three times before returning to Field Mill.

WHITEHOUSE
John Charles   Inside-forward

Born: Smethwick, 4 April 1897. Died: Halesowen, 3 January 1948.
Career: Smethwick Hall. Blackheath Town. Redditch. Birmingham August 1916. Derby County May 1923. Sheffield Wednesday February 1929. Bournemouth & Boscombe Athletic August 1930. Folkestone Town May 1933. Player-manager, Worcester City, 1935.
Division Two promotion 1925-6.

Jackie Whitehouse, who had guested for Derby County and Chelsea during World War One, was a vital signing from Birmingham. The following season he helped Derby to become Division Two's leading scorers — one more goal and they would have been promoted — and with Storer and Galloway formed a prolific inside trio. Had injury not prevented him from playing in the final two League games, thus robbing him of an ever-present record, the Rams might have found the goal they needed for promotion, because he scored 86 in his 200 senior appearances for the Rams. Whitehouse could scheme as well as score and was equally at home at centre or inside-forward. When Derby did win promo-

Jackie Whitehouse.

tion he proved himself a First Division player and scored four when the Rams beat Sheffield Wednesday 8-0 in March 1927. Perhaps Wednesday remembered that when they signed him a little under two years later. In the late 1930s, he was a Derby County scout.

WHITTAKER
Walter   Goalkeeper

Born: Manchester, 20 September 1878. Died: 1927.
Career: Molyneaux (Manchester League). Buxton. Newton Heath February 1896. Fairfield cs 1896. Grimsby Town May 1897. Reading May 1898. Blackburn Rovers February 1900. Grimsby Town December 1901. Derby County April 1903. Brentford May 1904. Reading May 1906. Clapton Orient August 1907. Exeter City July 1910. Player-manager, Swansea Town, July 1912 to April 1914. Manager, Llanelli, June to November 1914.

A much-travelled goalkeeper who had first chance to succeed Jack Fryer in 1903. After 12 games, he gave way to Harry Maskrey.

WHYMARK
Trevor John   Forward

Born: Burston, 4 May 1950.
Career. Diss Town. Ipswich Town May 1969. Vancouver Whitecaps November 1978. Sparta Rotterdam, loan, September 1979. Derby County, loan,

December 1979. Grimsby Town December 1980. Southend United January 1984. Peterborough United August 1985. Colchester United November 1985.

Trevor Whymark was a top striker with Ipswich Town, winning one England cap as substitute against Luxembourg in October 1977. Following a North American Soccer League Super Bowl success with Vancouver Whitecaps, Whymark joined Derby via Holland but, after failing to complete his second game, was laid low with glandular fever.

Trevor Whymark.

WICKS
Stephen John *Centre-half*

Born: Reading, 3 October 1956.
Career: Apprentice, Chelsea: profess-ional June 1974. Derby County January 1979. Queen's Park Rangers September 1979. Crystal Palace June 1981. Queen's Park Rangers March 1982. Chelsea July 1986. Coach, Tampa Bay Rowdies, August 1988. Assistant manager, Ports-mouth, January to July 1989. Wycombe Wanderers August 1989. Manager, Crawley Town, May 1992.

Tommy Docherty signed the imposing Steve Wicks, but he stayed only eight months at Derby. He rejoined Docherty and shifted around the London clubs. He was hampered by injuries and probably never reached full potential. Back trouble forced Wicks to retire in August 1988, when he was close to signing for Tottenham Hotspur.

Steve Wicks, an imposing defender who spent only eight months at Derby.

WIGHTMAN
Harold *Centre-half/full-back*

Born: Sutton-in-Ashfield, 19 June 1894.
Died: Nottingham, 5 April 1945.
Career: Sutton Town. Eastwood Rangers January 1913. Chesterfield May 1913. Nottingham Forest (wartime football) September 1915. Derby County May 1919. Assistant manager, Derby County, 1928. Chesterfield May 1929. Team manager/coach, Notts County, May 1930. Manager, Luton Town, June 1931 to October 1935. Chief scout, Derby County, November
1935. Manager, Mansfield Town, January 1936. Manager, Nottingham Forest, May 1936 to March 1939.
Division Two promotion 1925-6.

Harry Wightman played for Not-tingham Forest during World War One and in 1919 was one of several useful signings made by Jimmy Methven. In the first post-war League season Wight-man was one of three ever-presents, along with Jack Atkin and George Thornewell. Wightman was a steady centre-half for most of his Derby career but, when Harry Thoms was signed, he also proved himself at right-back.

Harold Wightman.

Under George Jobey, he played a significant part in the Second Division promotion at right-back, partnering both Tommy Crilly and Archie Ritchie, but the Rams bought a future England star in Tommy Cooper. Wightman closed his Derby career as Jobey's assistant and was later involved with all three League clubs in Nottinghamshire. He was the first team manager to be appointed by Forest, his predecessors having combined the role with that of secretary.

WIGNALL
Frank　　　　　　　　　*Forward*

Born: Blackrod, 21 August 1939.
Career: Horwich RMI. Amateur, Everton, May 1958: professional May 1960. Nottingham Forest June 1963. Wolverhampton Wanderers March 1968. Derby County February 1969. Mansfield Town November 1971. Player-manager, King's Lynn, July 1973. Burton Albion August 1974. National coach, Qatar, October 1974. Manager, Shepshed Charterhouse, July 1981 to March 1983.

Division Two champions 1968-9.
Division One champions 1971-2.

Brian Clough and Peter Taylor bought Wignall as cover and insurance for the final run-in towards the Second Division title and he did a steady job for more than two years. Wignall was a

Frank Wignall, 17 goals in 57 games for Derby, 18 of which were as a substitute.

powerfully-built striker whose best days were with Nottingham Forest. He won two England caps in 1964-5, against Wales and Holland, and was in the Forest team which finished First Division runners-up and reached the FA Cup semi-finals in 1966-7.

WILCOX
George E.　　　　　*Right-back*

Born: Treeton, 23 August 1917.
Career: Denaby United. Derby County October 1936. Rotherham United July 1948.

George Wilcox's chance of a regular place disappeared when Jack Nicholas moved to right-back in 1938. World War Two took away his best years.

WILEMAN
Sydney　　　　　*Inside-forward*

Born: Coalville.
Career: Gresley Rovers, Derby County April 1931. Port Vale June 1938.

A patient reserve who made 11 senior appearances in seven years before joining Port Vale for £500. Later secretary of the Coalville & District Referees' Society.

WILKES
Harry Theodore   *Goalkeeper*

Born: Sedgeley, 24 June 1907. Died: Derby, 5 April 1984.
Career: Sedgeley Congregationals. Wellington Town. Derby County February 1927. Sheffield United March 1934. Rhyl October 1935. Heanor Town August 1936.

Division One runners-up 1929-30.

Goalkeeper Harry Wilkes was having a trial for Wellington Town (now Telford United) when he was spotted by the old Aston Villa star Harry Hampton. Hampton, two-goal hero of the 1905 FA Cup Final, sent him to Villa Park but they said he was too small for a goalkeeper. George Jobey brought Wilkes into League soccer and he made his Rams debut against Arsenal in 1927, taking over from Ben Olney. Derby won 4-0 and, just before his death in 1984, Wilkes recalled, "I was a real little hero that night." In March 1930 a football journalist wrote, 'Wilkes gets about his goal like a cat but that is not to confuse him with the dancing dervish type of player. His movements come of purpose backed by anticipation. There is no fuss.' Wilkes was remarkably agile and knew just when to leave his line. He went to Sheffield United, then to Rhyl, where Tommy Davison was manager, and finally to Heanor Town for £1 per week 'when they remembered to pay us'.

WILKINS
Raymond John Hamilton
                          Centre-forward
Born: Crossley, 16 August 1928.
Career: Loughborough College. Moira
United. Derby County January 1950. Boston United July 1954. Wrexham May 1957: later third-team coach. Oswestry Town June 1960. Macclesfield Town February 1962. Gresley Rovers September 1962. Wilmorton & Alvaston February 1963. Manager, Crewton, October 1964 to July 1966.*

A spirited centre-forward who met with some success in his 30 League games and returned to the Baseball Ground with Boston United when they were shock 6-1 winners in the FA Cup. Ray Wilkins trained as a teacher and became a headmaster in Derby.

WILLIAMS
David Geraint   *Midfield*
Born: Cwn-parc, 5 January 1962.
Career: Apprentice, Bristol Rovers: professional January 1980. Derby

Harry Wilkes.

Geraint Williams, 332 games before a £650,000 move to Ipswich.

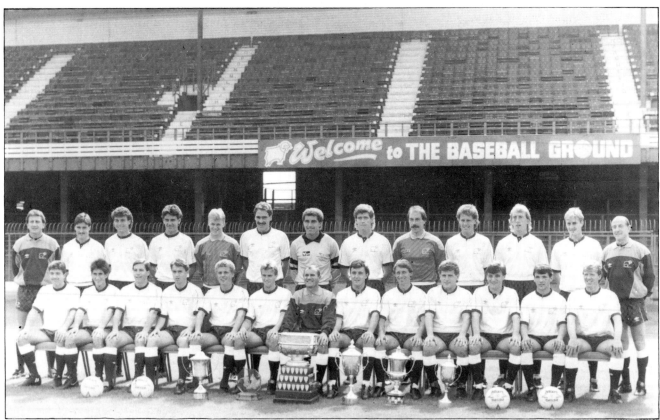

Rams squad on the eve of the club's return to Division One in 1987. Back row (left to right): Roy McFarland (assistant manager), Ross MacLaren, Michael Forsyth, John Gregory, Martin Taylor, Dick Pratley, Peter Shilton, Rob Hindmarch, Mark Wallington, Andy Garner, Mark Lillis, Paul Blades, Gordon Guthrie (physiotherapist). Front row: Brian McCord, Nigel Callaghan, Geraint Williams, Mel Sage, Steve Cross, Phil Gee, Arthur Cox (manager), Bobby Davison, Gary Micklewhite, Mickey Lewis, David Penney, Robbie Briscoe, Steve McClaren.

County March 1985. Ipswich Town July 1992.

Division Three promotion 1985-6. Division Two champions 1986-7.

Arthur Cox pursued Geraint Williams for five months before Bristol Rovers agreed to sell him for £43,500 on the eve of the 1985 transfer deadline. He had won two Welsh Under-21 caps at Eastville and proved an excellent signing for the Rams. Through two promotions, Williams took each division in his stride and his midfield industry was essential to Derby. Although his goals were rare, he had a sharp eye for danger, often popping up as a back man, and his most fruitful partnership was with John Gregory. The blend was right and Williams won 11 caps for Wales. When the Rams were relegated in 1990-91, Williams had an almost impossible burden, trying to keep the midfield afloat virtually on his own. Supporters voted him Player of the Year after the Second Division championship and he bounced back in style as captain in 1991-2. Ipswich Town signed Williams for £650,000 on a four-year contract, John Lyall seeing him as a man who could help cement their Premier League status.

WILLIAMS
Paul Darren   *Midfield*
Born: Burton upon Trent, 26 March 1971.
Career: Trainee, Derby County: profes-

sional July 1989. Lincoln City, loan, November 1989.

After developing at left-back in the Youth team, Paul Williams settled into a senior slot in midfield. He provided one of the few bright spots of the 1990-91 relegation season with a hat-trick in the 6-2 victory over Southampton. Williams' strength developed quickly and he won the first of six England Under-21 caps in the same season. When the Rams returned to the Second Division, Williams was leading scorer with 16 goals from midfield, seven of them from fiercely struck penalties. In 1991-2 he played for the Second Division team against the Italian Serie 'B' but a back injury kept him out of a second Toulon Under-21 tournament.

WILLIAMS
Peter John   *Outside-left*
Born: Nottingham, 21 October 1931.
Career: South Normanton. Derby County August 1952. Boston United July 1954. Chesterfield July 1955. Boston United February 1956. King's Lynn December 1956. Arnold St Mary's 1959.

Peter Williams played twice in 1952-3, an unsettled season which ended with Derby losing their First Division place.

WILLIAMSON
Albert   *Right-half*
Career: Sawley Rangers. Derby County

Albert Williamson.

1884. Notts County 1891.

Williamson joined Derby County in their first season and was one of the regular players when the Football League was formed in 1888.

Paul Williams, scored some spectacular goals from midfield as well as becoming the Rams' penalty-taker.

WILLIAMSON
Michael   *Outside-left*

Born: *Ashbourne, 30 May 1942.*
Career: *Ashbourne Town. Derby County August 1961. Gillingham July 1964. Ramsgate Athletic July 1966: later player-manager.*

Williamson spent three years at the Baseball Ground, mainly in the Central League.

WILSON
Angus   *Outside-right*

Career: *Derby County May 1898. Darwen January 1899*

Wilson played once for Derby County, in November 1898.

WILSON
Albert   *Outside-left*

Born: *Rotherham, 28 January 1915.*
Career: *Rotherham YMCA. Rawmarsh Welfare. Stafford Rangers. Derby County May 1936. Mansfield Town July 1938. Crystal Palace January 1939. Rotherham United June 1946. Grimsby Town July 1947. Boston United June 1948.*

Signed from Stafford Rangers for £125, Wilson played once for Derby County but his career spanned World War Two. He was later Rotherham United's groundsman.

WILSON
Cyril K.   *Inside-forward*

Career: *West Bromwich Albion, amateur. Derby County, amateur, March 1923.*

An amateur from the Sheffield area who had one match for Derby County, in March 1923.

WILSON
Ian William   *Inside-forward*

Born: *Aberdeen, 27 March 1958.*
Career: *Juniors, Aberdeen: Juniors, Dundee. Elgin City. Leicester City April 1979. Everton September 1987. Besiktas, Turkey, cs 1989. Derby County, loan, February 1991. Bury August 1991.*

In a last bid to stay in the First Division, Derby County took Ian Wilson on loan from Turkish champions Besiktas in February 1991 but he was unable to deflect the inevitable relegation. Wilson cost Leicester City £30,000 when he was signed from the Highland League and was involved in two Second Division promotions, under Jock Wallace in 1979-80 and Gordon Milne in 1982-3. He won two of his five Scotland caps before joining Everton for £300,000. He was substitute in the 1989 FA Cup Final defeat by Liverpool before Milne signed him for Besiktas.

Ian Wilson.

WILSON
James   *Inside-forward*

Born: *Seaham Harbour, c.1916*
Career: *Seaham Colliery. Lincoln City July 1937. Derby County June 1939. Linfield.*

Wilson played in the first match of the 1939-40 season, which came to an abrupt end because of the outbreak of World War Two. He joined Linfield during the war and was still living in Northern Ireland in 1991. Wilson and Redfern, who played only in the abandoned wartime season, have been Derby's forgotten men.

WILSON
Kevin James   *Centre-forward*

Born: *Banbury, 18 April 1961.*
Career: *Ruscote Sports. Banbury United 1978. Derby County December 1979. Ipswich Town January 1985. Chelsea June 1987. Notts County March 1992.*

A sprightly striker, signed from non-League football by Colin Addison. Kevin Wilson had trials with Sheffield United and Stoke City before Derby gave him his chance. Although he was leading scorer in 1981-2, his most

Kevin Wilson, hit 41 goals in 141 games before moving to Portman Road.

prolific period was at the start of Arthur Cox's first season. He scored four goals against Hartlepool United in the Milk Cup and a hat-trick against Bolton Wanderers before breaking an arm against Plymouth Argyle. When he recovered, he joined Ipswich Town for £150,000, money used to fund the incoming transfers of Trevor Christie and Gary Micklewhite. With Ipswich, Wilson became a Northern Ireland international and they more than doubled their money when he joined Chelsea. His goals helped Chelsea win the Division Two title in 1988-9 but he could not help Notts County stay in Division One.

WOMACK
Albert Roy   *Outside-left*

Born: Denaby, 20 September 1934.
Career: Denaby United. Derby County October 1957. Southampton May 1959. Workington July 1960. Denaby United cs 1961. Sutton Town March 1962. Goole Town July 1962. Bourne Town June 1964.

Roy Womack played two League games after being signed for £750. Southampton paid £500 for him, but he stayed at The Dell for only one season.

WOMBWELL
Richard   *Forward*

Born: Nottingham.
Career: Bulwell. Ilkeston Town December 1898. Derby County May 1899. Bristol City July 1902. Manchester United March 1905. Heart of Midlothian January 1907. Brighton & Hove Albion June 1907. Blackburn Rovers February 1908. Ilkeston United August 1910.

Wombwell was a versatile forward who played in all five front positions during his three years at the Baseball Ground and was a steady scorer. He joined Bristol City for their second season in the Football League and played for Hearts in the 1906-7 Scottish Cup Final defeat by Celtic.

WOOD
Alfred E.   *Centre-half/wing-half*

Born: Smallthorne, near Burslem.
Career: Smallthorne Albion. Burslem Port Vale. Stoke October 1895. Aston Villa March 1901. Derby County May 1905. Bradford May 1907.

Alf Wood had plenty of experience when he joined Derby County for two seasons. He began at centre-half, but moved to allow Ben Hall to establish himself. Wood joined Bradford when they were playing in the Southern League, before being elected to the Second Division.

Dennis Woodhead, helped the Rams out of the Third Division North.

WOOD
John   *Inside-forward*

Career: Southern United. Derby County March 1906. Manchester City June 1907. Plymouth Argyle July 1909.

John Wood was a regular choice in his 15 months at the Baseball Ground, but Derby County began to decline when Steve Bloomer was sold to Middlesbrough. After the Rams had been relegated for the first time, Wood moved on.

WOODHEAD
Dennis   *Outside-left*

Born: Huddersfield, 2 September 1924.
Career: Hillsborough Boys' Club. Amateur, Sheffield Wednesday, June 1942: professional, April 1945. Chesterfield September 1955. Derby County January 1956. Southport February 1959. Derby County March 1959. Frickley Colliery July 1959. Worksop Town July 1960. Manager, Retford Town, April 1964 to March 1967.
Division Three North champions 1956-7.

Dennis Woodhead was a flight engineer in the RAF during World War Two and flew on around 30 operational bombing missions. He spent ten years with Sheffield Wednesday and was involved in two Second Division promotions, in 1949-50 and, as champions, 1951-2. Harry Storer spent £1,500 to bring him from Chesterfield for his experience, good distribution and explosive shooting. All those qualities were vitally important when the Rams won the Third Division North. Woodhead went to Southport for £750 but, on League orders, was transferred back the following month because of knee trouble. After working on Chesterfield's office staff, he was Sheffield Wednesday's commercial manager from 1971 to 1987.

Vic Woodley and his defenders under attack at Wembley in 1946, when the Rams won the FA Cup by beating Charlton 4-1.

Vic Woodley, came out of semi-retirement to win a Cup medal.

WOODLEY
Victor Robert   *Goalkeeper*

Born: Cippenham, 26 February 1910. Died: Bradford-on-Avon, 23 October 1978.

Career: Windsor & Eton. Chelsea May 1931. Bath City December 1945. Derby County March 1946. Bath City May 1947: player-manager, to December 1949.

FA Cup winners 1945-6.

Vic Woodley was a fixture in Chelsea's goal through most of the 1930s and was England's number one from April 1937, when he made his debut against Scotland at Hampden Park, until the outbreak of World War Two. During that time, he made 19 consecutive international appearances, the best sequence recorded until Ron Springett passed it in the early 1960s. Derby County gave Woodley an unexpected chance to crown his distinguished career. Following an injury to Frank Boulton, they needed an experienced goalkeeper for their FA Cup campaign, so Stuart McMillan negotiated with Chelsea, who held Woodley's registration, and Bath City, his club at the time. He played in the semi-finals, where players reckon a superb save from Harold Bodle in the replay against Birmingham City at Maine Road kept them in the Cup, and the Wembley victory.

WOOLLEY
Albert   *Outside-left*

Died: Manchester 1896.
*Career: Park Mills. Aston Villa August
1892. Derby County January 1895.*

Albert Woolley played 14 games in
Aston Villa's 1893-4 League Championship team, but managed only six
appearances after joining Derby
County. Woolley succumbed to tuber-
culosis, an illness which brought about
his early death.

WRIGHT
Henry Edward   *Goalkeeper*

*Born: Tottenham, June 1912.
Career: Harwich & Parkeston. Amateur, Charlton Athletic, June 1932:
professional, December 1932. Aldershot
May 1936. Derby County September
1937. Colchester United July 1946.
Guildford City. Coach in Norway.
Manager-coach, St Albans City, May
1951. Trainer, Walsall, December 1952.
Trainer, Luton Town, January 1954.
Trainer, Everton, October 1956. Coach
in Lebanon. Coach, National Institute
of Sport, Patiala, 1961 to 1965.*

George Jobey paid £2,500 for Harry
Wright, who immediately took over
from Ken Scattergood in Derby's goal.
Wright was first choice in 1937-8, but
then gave way to Frank Boulton.

WRIGHT
Horace   *Outside-right*

*Career: Bulwell White Star. Ilkeston
United August 1910. Derby County
September 1910. Portsmouth August
1912. Coventry City cs 1913. Aberavon.*

*Abertillary May 1921. Sutton Town
December 1921.
Division Two champions 1911-12.*

Horace Wright shared the right-wing
duties with Billy Grimes in 1910-11,
but managed only three games when
Derby County won the Second Division
the following season. He joined Southern League Portsmouth for £35.

WRIGHT
Levi George   *Half-back*

*Born: Oxford, 15 January 1862. Died:
Derby, 11 January 1953.
Career: Derby Midland. Derby County.
Derby Junction.*

L.G.Wright was more notable as
Derbyshire's leading batsman, but he
played four times for Derby County in
the first League season. He was with
Derbyshire from 1883 to 1909, during
which time he scored 14,800 runs for
the county, with 20 centuries, and
15,166 (average 26.10) in all first-class
cricket. Wright also won fame as a
remarkable point, always fielding close
to the bat.

WRIGHT
Mark   *Centre-half*

*Born: Dorchester-on-Thames, 1 August
1963.
Career: Apprentice, Oxford United:
professional August 1980. Southampton March 1983. Derby County August
1987. Liverpool July 1991.*

The early days of Robert Maxwell's
chairmanship were full of optimism.
Peter Shilton was signed from Southampton and when Arthur Cox

Levi Wright.

returned to The Dell for England
centre-half Mark Wright, it was felt that
a formidable team was taking shape.
Wright cost £760,000, shattering the
club record of £410,000 which had stood
for more than seven years since the
signing of David Swindlehurst. The
Rams would probably not have survived their first season back in Division
One without Wright and Shilton. The
centre-half continued to grow in stature

Rams manager Arthur Cox and Mark Wright after the England centre-half signed for the Rams.

A bloodied Mark Wright in action against Arsenal.

and, although he fell out with England manager Bobby Robson after the 1988 European Championship finals, returned splendidly for the 1990 World Cup in Italy. Wright was twice voted Derby's Player of the Year but was also sent off three times while he was with the club. A move became inevitable in 1991, when the Rams were desperate to get rid of Maxwell, and it was no great surprise when Wright moved to Liverpool for £2.3 million. As captain, Wright led Liverpool to victory in the 1992 FA Cup Final but missed the European Championships in Sweden because of a tendon injury.

WRIGHT
Patrick Daniel Joseph *Full-back*

Born: Oldbury, 17 November 1940.
Career: Springfield BC. Birmingham City November 1959. Shrewsbury Town September 1962. Derby County September 1967. Southend United,

Pat Wright.

loan, March 1970. Player-coach, Rotherham United, September 1970. Coach, Portsmouth, July 1971 to April 1976: player-manager of nursery club Waterlooville, 1971. National coach, Zambia, 1976. National coach, Saudi Arabia, 1978: youth team manager 1979. Coach, United Arab Emirates, 1979. Coach, Al Nasr, Dubai, 1980 to 1984.

One of the least successful buys made by Brian Clough and Peter Taylor. Pat Wright began in the first team, but Derby County moved towards their most successful blend when Ron Webster switched to right-back.

WYER
Peter William   *Inside-right*

Born: Coventry, 10 February 1937.
Career: Coventry City October 1955. Derby County June 1956. Coventry City July 1958. Rugby Town July 1959. Nuneaton Borough.
Division Three North champions 1956-7.

Peter Wyer scored on his debut, in a 6-1 win over Bradford, but made only one more senior appearance.

YORK
Charles H.   *Forward*

Born: Edinburgh, 1882.

Ray Young, a skilful centre-half who made 269 appearances for the Rams.

Career: Reading April 1901. Derby County April 1902. Sunderland January 1904. Heart of Midlothian May 1904. Southampton December 1904.
FA Cup Finalists 1902-03.

Charlie York began at centre-forward when he joined Derby, but moved to inside-right, replacing the injured Steve Bloomer in the later stages of Derby's run to their third FA Cup Final. That was where York played in the 6-0 defeat by Bury, but he did not have a lasting effect at the Baseball Ground.

YOUNG
George Raymond   *Centre-half*

Born: Derby, 14 March 1934.
Career: Juniors, Derby County: professional March 1951. Heanor Town September 1966. Burton Albion May 1967.
Division Three North champions 1956-7.

When Ray Young joined Derby in 1949, after a successful schoolboy career in which he played for England Boys, there were high hopes that this skilful and intelligent centre-half would develop into another Leon Leuty. Young was nursed through Colts and Reserves before making his League debut at Doncaster in 1954. It was felt that he would make the number-five spot his own, yet he did not until his career was almost over. When he was playing well, Young looked international class. He seemed to have time on his hands and strolled around the back with consummate ease. But then he would become too casual and his lack of pace could be exposed. There were those who felt that he was too 'philosophical' in his approach to the game. He lost many appearances to the cold steel of Martin McDonnell and later Les Moore. Nevertheless, Young gave a touch of style to Derby County, flourishing more under Tim Ward than Storer.

The Who's Who of Rams Managers

As Derby County entered their centenary year in 1984, Arthur Cox became the 18th Rams manager to be appointed by the club since the first, Harry Newbould, assumed office 84 years earlier, and counting Roy McFarland who held the post temporarily for nine games at the end of 1983-4.

Harry Newbould

FA Cup Finalists 1902-03.

HARRY Newbould, Derby County's first manager, joined the club in 1896 as assistant secretary. He was a qualified accountant and gained sporting fame in the Midlands as a fine sprinter. He also played on the right wing for Derby St Luke's, then a leading local club.

Newbould was promoted to secretary and continued his administrative duties when he was appointed manager in 1900, a common combination in the football of the times. During his time, fine players such as Charlie Morris, Ben Warren, George Richards, Harry Maskrey and Ben Hall were brought in but he also sold Steve Bloomer to Middlesbrough. The instruction would have come from the board and it hastened relegation, although Newbould did not stay to see it.

Harry Newbould

The Derby directors were 'surprised and disappointed' when he was appointed secretary-manager of Manchester City in July 1906. He arrived at Hyde Road in the wake of a bribery and illegal payments scandal, which led to wholesale suspensions. Newbould took City to third place and, after a relegation, steered them to the Second Division title in 1910.

He left City in 1912 and, a year later, became secretary of the Players' Union, a position in which he served diligently until his death in 1929.

Jimmy Methven

Division Two champions 1911-12, 1914-15.

WHEN Jimmy Methven was appointed Rams manager on 7 August 1906 he continued an association with the club he joined as a player in the close season of 1891.

Jimmy Methven

Methven's appointment was the first of its kind in Derby's history since the previous manager was also secretary. Methven was uncluttered by such administrative chores, yet just how much control he had over Derby's playing affairs is open to question. Throughout his period as Derby manager, from 1906 to 1922, with a break during World War One when he worked at Rolls-Royce, there were continual references to the 'selection committee'. Similarly, players were bought 'by the Derby directors', though presumably on Methven's recommendations. His son Alfred clearly remembered his father coming home in

the small hours of the morning after long scouting trips.

Methven was unable to prevent Derby, without Bloomer, from being relegated in his first season as manager and the following years were fraught with financial problems with little money to buy new blood. He was successful in bringing Bloomer back to Derby in 1910, a move which led directly to the first of two Second Division titles, and had notable captures in inexperienced strikers Alf Bentley and Horace Barnes. Immediately after World War One his efforts were described as 'unsparing in difficult days of financial crisis'.

In 1922 Methven, suffering from glaucoma, was admitted to hospital for what turned out to be an unsuccessful eye operation. As manager he just faded from the scene and in June of that year, his job was advertised.

Cecil Potter

WHEN 33-year-old Cecil Potter was offered the Derby manager's job in July 1922, the Rams had just finished 12th in Division Two. Although Potter never achieved promotion for Derby, he did build the basis of a side good enough to win back a place in Division One the season after he left.

Potter was born in West Hoathly, Sussex, in November 1888, the son of a Congregational minister. He signed for Norwich City and was their joint top Southern League scorer in 1911-12 and 1914-15. After military service — and a few wartime games for Spurs — Potter went to Hull in 1919 and then to Hartlepools United as secretary, player and manager in 1920, steering them into League football.

When Methven retired at Derby, rumours swept the town that the famous Newcastle United and England player Colin Veitch was to become the Rams manager. In fact Veitch never applied for the job and on 4 July 1922, Derby announced that, after interviewing four candidates, Potter was their man.

Potter brought with him from Hartlepools two players, full-back Tommy Crilly and centre-half Harry Thoms, and although his first season saw the Rams finish an all-time low 14th in Division Two, Potter soon developed a side which narrowly missed promotion in 1924 and 1925 and which went within 90 minutes

Cecil Potter

of the first Wembley FA Cup Final in 1923. In 1923-4 he made the important signing of Birmingham goalscorer Jackie Whitehouse.

Potter took Derby close to promotion before leaving in 1925. He had originally intended to take a dairy business in Sussex, but a week after leaving the Baseball Ground he was approached by Huddersfield and went on to complete their hat-trick of League Championships started by Herbert Chapman. He resigned after 13 months, despite this triumph, giving health and family as the reasons. He was tempted back by Norwich and managed them until January 1929 before failing to survive the humiliation of being knocked out of the FA Cup, 5-0 by the amateur Corinthians. He died in October 1975.

George Jobey

Division Two promotion 1925-6. Division One runners-up 1929-30, 1935-6. Central League champions 1935-6.

AFTER Brian Clough and Dave Mackay, George Jobey must rank as the most successful manager in Derby County's history. His 16-year reign at the Baseball Ground, from August 1925 into World War Two, was the Rams' most consistently successful period in Division One, not withstanding the two Championships of the 1970s.

Jobey was born on Tyneside and played as a half-back with Newcastle, Arsenal (where he scored the first goal to be netted at Highbury) and Leicester. He also had short spells with Bradford

George Jobey

and Hamilton and in 1922 became manager-coach at Wolves. After they had won the Third Division North in 1923-4, Jobey went into the hotel business and it was the Rams' good fortune that they brought him back into football.

He reinforced Potter's side, notably with Harry Bedford, and won promotion in his first season. Thereafter, his shrewdness in the transfer market served Derby well and although he was not afraid to back judgement with cash, three of his greatest signings, Jack Barker, Jack Bowers and Sammy Crooks, cost the Rams next to nothing. He signed some of the finest players in Derby's history, although it must be said that he brought a large number to the Baseball Ground and not all were as successful.

He had the imagination to go for Hughie Gallacher when Bowers was injured, and proved also that he had the character to tame a player like the difficult Scotsman. Rams players would tremble before him and those who played for him still wince at the thought of his waspish tongue. George Collin, his left-back for almost nine years, recalled a favourite saying of Jobey: "The strong will live and the weak will die."

Tim Ward remembers how Jobey would rarely attend training, but when he did he was quite likely to order two or three players straight off for a haircut. Ward once received a tongue-lashing for asking for first-team money — then found

out next pay-day that he had been awarded his rise. Though, with the exception of the irrepressible Sammy Crooks, they feared him, they were all Jobey's men to the end, Crooks included.

George Jobey presented the Derby public with an impressive array of talent, particularly centre-forwards from Bedford to Dave McCulloch, throughout the 1930s and people sometimes wondered how he managed it. In 1941 they had their question partly answered. A joint FA-League Commission, sitting at the Midland Hotel, Derby, found that between 1925 and 1938 the Rams had paid out illegal bonuses and inducements, balancing their books with some inventive entries.

Jobey was suspended permanently from all football, five directors received *sine die* suspensions, and the club was fined £500. Although Jobey's suspension was lifted in 1945, it was not until 1952 that he made a managerial comeback with Mansfield, only to be sacked for 'lack of interest'. Jobey died at his home in Bangor Street, Chaddesden, in May 1962, aged 76. With him went a significant part of Derby County's history.

Ted Magner

Football League North champions, Midland Cup winners 1944-5.

TED Magner managed the Rams for a brief but significant period during World War Two. When he took over in March 1944 the vagaries of wartime soccer were still dominant. When he left 22 months later he had persuaded both Raich Carter and Peter Doherty to sign officially, and the Rams were on the way towards winning the FA Cup for the first time.

A native of Newcastle, Magner signed for Gainsborough Trinity, then a Second Division club, at the age of 17, and his second League appearance was against Derby County. Magner also played for Everton against the Rams in an FA Cup match at the Baseball Ground in 1911, when Bloomer scored twice in Derby's 5-0 win. From Goodison Park Magner moved to St Mirren and scored five goals against Queen's Park to set a Scottish League Division One record.

During World War One Magner served in the Northumberland Fusiliers, during which time he contracted malaria, and when peace was restored he worked as a coach in Amsterdam and elsewhere on the Continent before returning to become a tutor on FA coaching refresher courses at Leeds and Loughborough.

In 1938 he was appointed assistant manager of Huddersfield and when Clem Stephenson left in June 1942, Magner stepped up. He left Leeds Road in September 1943 and six months later he was at Derby.

From an ever-shifting parade of players Magner fashioned a team which did the double of Football League North championship and Midland Cup in 1944-5. The following year the FA Cup proper resumed and Magner got both Carter and Doherty to commit themselves to Derby County.

Says Doherty, "Ted Magner was an

Ted Magner

Stuart McMillan

Jack Barker

outstanding manager and if he had not left Derby, then I would have stayed. His man-management was superb and he had an immense knowledge of the game. He would take us out on to the pitch and hit the crossbar from the 18-yard line, six times out of six, just to show us that he could play''.

Magner saw the Rams to the fourth round before going back to work abroad in January 1946. Had he stayed, and lived, he might have become a great Derby manager and the decline of the 1950s might not have happened.

In 1948 illness prevented him from taking up a Continental appointment. In July of that year he died at his home in Sunny Hill Avenue and was buried in Nottingham Road Cemetery. Perhaps his career is best summed up by his first club. it was called Expansion FC.

Stuart McMillan

FA Cup winners 1945-6.

STUART McMillan stands unique among Derby managers in that he was in charge when the Rams won the FA Cup.

The son of Johnny McMillan, a star in Bloomer's day, Stuart McMillan was a fine all-round sportsman, although he played only one League game, at outside-right, for Derby.

After World War One, he was briefly with Chelsea, then played for Gillingham, when his father was manager, Wolves under Jobey, Bradford City, Nottingham Forest and Clapton Orient. He also played four first-class cricket matches for Derbyshire, as well as golf for Derbyshire and billiards for Derby Institutes.

McMillan took over the Nag's Head, Mickleover, scouted for the Rams and often drove officials to matches. In 1942

he was appointed advisor to the club and when Magner left, McMillan inherited his Wembley-bound team.

Though he twice broke the British transfer record for Derby, buying first Billy Steel and then Johnny Morris, he never enjoyed the same success in the transfer market as Jobey had experienced and to which he had contributed as a scout. The signing of Steel actually worked against him when several senior players became unsettled and left.

Ageing stars were not replaced by men of the same calibre and McMillan did not survive the Rams sailing perilously close to Division Three. In November 1953 he was replaced by Jack Barker and went to the Station Hotel, Ashbourne, where he died in September 1963. Raich Carter was one of the mourners at the funeral of this quiet and essentially modest man.

Jack Barker

JACK Barker was a giant at centre-half in George Jobey's entertaining team of the 1930s and Derby County hoped that he would bring the same strength to management when they appointed him in November 1953. His previous experience was scanty, eight months as manager of Bradford City in the first full season after World War Two, 1946-7, a brief spell in Ireland with Dundalk and two months as Oldham Athletic's coach.

Derby were on the slide when they summoned Barker to succeed Stuart McMillan but, with the players already at the Baseball Ground, he managed to avoid relegation in 1953-4. He spent around £40,000 the following year, on goalkeeper George Hunter, winger Stewart Imlach, former England centre-

forward Jesse Pye and, as a last gamble, Hull forwards Ken Harrison and Alf Ackerman. They could not avoid the drop to the Third Division North for the first time in the club's history and a depressing period for supporters also left Barker bitter as he resigned in April 1955 and found employment as a fitter's mate at the Carriage and Wagon railway works.

"It was a rotten experience," he said later. "I wouldn't be a manager again for £10,000 a week. The trouble is that the people you are working for know nothing about the game."

Harry Storer

Division Three North champions 1956-7.

FORMER Derby County and England player Harry Storer faced a daunting task when he took over from Jack Barker in July 1955. Derby had dropped into the Third Division North, their lowest ever in 67 years of the League, and the club was bereft of the spirit and skill which had produced such a fine Division One side in the 1930s and 1940s.

Storer was a hard wing-half for Derby in the 1920s, an unselfish and intelligent player who gave his absolute all for the team.

As a manager he was equally hard and dedicated. He took Coventry to the

Harry Storer in his office at the Baseball Ground with his dog, Billy.

Tim Ward

WHEN Tim Ward succeeded Harry Storer as manager in June 1962, he was still remembered as a classy wing-half, good enough to play twice for England, in the immediate post-war years. His sudden move to Barnsley in March 1951 surprised supporters as much as it did Ward.

He played only 33 League games for Barnsley and, in March 1953, was named as Exeter City's new manager. It was an extraordinary episode. Ward travelled with Exeter for a Third Division South match against Ipswich Town at Portman Road on 7 March but Barnsley had never released him. He was recalled to Oakwell on 12 March and appointed manager of Barnsley on 30 March. They were relegated in his first season but Ward brought them back as Third Division North champions in 1954-5. Barnsley slipped back to the Third Division in 1959 but Ward was comfortably established at Oakwell until Grimsby Town appointed him in January 1960.

Everything was completed rapidly as Ward was preferred to Raich Carter, his former colleague at Derby, and ex-Newcastle captain Joe Harvey. He enjoyed another promotion at Blundell Park, from the Third Division in 1961-2, before Derby came in for him. They were always close to Ward's heart and remained so in later years, when he ran the ex-Rams football side and was instrumental in the formation of the Former Players' Association in 1991, becoming the first chairman.

Tim Ward

Second Division in 1936 and Birmingham to the First in 1948. Two years earlier he had won the Football League South title for the Blues and pushed the Rams hard in the FA Cup semi-final. While manager of Coventry he helped Derbyshire become cricket's champion county in 1936.

Storer's first signing as Derby manager was Reg Ryan. The former West Brom schemer says, "I chose the manager as well as the club. I'd always admired Harry Storer. He had a sharp tongue, a heart of gold, and a fantastic knowledge of the game. If Storer was alive today he'd be one of the great managers of our time."

Storer took the Rams to promotion in his second season and by the time he retired in 1962 he had reduced the club's overdraft from £60,000 to around £23,000. His biggest signing was Bill Curry who came for £12,000. The former Brighton and Newcastle centre-forward typified what Storer liked best in a player — skill, guts and character. He had much time for the likes of Frank Upton, Glyn Davies and Martin McDonnell, all ferocious defenders; and much time also for the delightful skills of Tommy Powell who, during the Third Division days, would be told by Storer, "Go out and play where you like."

There are plenty of Harry Storer tales, like the time Joe Mercer asked him if he would discipline the five players who, Mercer claimed, had been clogging during a match with Sheffield United, then managed by Mercer. Storer's reply was typical: "No, but I'm going to give the others a good rollicking!".

In May 1962, Storer retired, saying that it was about time to make way for a younger man. He died in Derby in May 1967, unfortunately not living long enough to see the success enjoyed by his disciples Brian Clough and Peter Taylor.

Ward's five years as manager of Derby were not happy because he was so hampered by lack of cash and a parochial attitude in the boardroom. He made some important signings, Alan Durban from

Cardiff City and, to the surprise of supporters, Kevin Hector from Bradford for £40,000. Ward had to work for months before he persuaded the directors to make a record investment and Hector was so successful that some of the board promptly tried to claim the credit. Colin Boulton and Peter Daniel, who were to play important parts in League Championship teams, came in as youngsters, but one of his most successful captures, Eddie Thomas from Swansea Town, worked against him.

When told his contract would not be renewed, Ward said: "The job has been the toughest I have ever had and the shortage of money has been frustrating. The trouble with this club is that you can't put a threepenny stamp on a letter without consulting the board personally. I was told that money was available but I could never get an answer when I asked how much.

"Perhaps the worst thing I ever did was to sign Eddie Thomas for £3,500, because he proved a marvellous bargain and after that I was expected to sign other players as cheaply." Ward was even more upset by the dismissal of two other former Derby players, chief scout Sammy Crooks and trainer Ralph Hann. Ward spent 15 months with Carlisle United, his last post in management.

Brian Clough & Peter Taylor

Division Two champions 1968-9. Division One Champions 1971-2. Texaco Cup winners 1971-2. Central League champions 1971-2.

BRIAN Clough and Peter Taylor transformed Derby County. When they arrived from Hartlepools United in July 1967 on the strong recommendation of Len Shackleton, Derby were pottering along aimlessly in the Second Division. Their first season brought no improvement in results but the buying attracted a public starved of success.

The first three in were John O'Hare, Roy McFarland and Alan Hinton at a combined cost of less than £75,000 and when Dave Mackay and Willie Carlin arrived for 1968-9, Derby County took off. They won the Second Division in a canter, the team was ready for the First Division and the signings became more ambitious and exciting. Terry Hennessey was Derby's first £100,000 player, Archie Gemmill and Colin Todd arrived and David Nish was a British record signing at £225,000. When Nish was signed, Derby were reigning Champions, having won the League in 1971-2 for the first time in thier history. In 1972-3, they reached the semi-finals of the European Cup.

There was a great hunger for success in Clough, perhaps because his career was cut short by a knee injury. He was born in Middlesbrough on 21 March 1935 and, after working as a clerk at ICI, became a professional at Ayresome Park in May 1952. It was more than three years before he made his debut but he began to score so regularly from centre-forward that it became impossible to leave him out. He hit 204 goals in 222 senior games for 'Boro, winning two England caps. While he was there, he formed a close friendship with Taylor but Clough moved to Sunderland for £45,000 in July 1961. He added another 63 goals in 74 games but severely damaged knee ligaments in a collision with Bury goalkeeper Chris Harker on Boxing Day 1962. After a spell as Sunderland's Youth coach, Clough

Brian Clough

became manager of Hartlepool United in October 1965 and persuaded Taylor to become his assistant.

Clough and Taylor formed a partnership in every sense of the word, their talents and their moods complementing each other. They did not buy many players after their initial clear-out but

Brian Clough and Peter Taylor with chairman Sam Longson on the day the pair joined the Rams.

they bought brilliantly and the new prosperity at the Baseball Ground was given tangible form by the building of the Ley Stand after promotion had been earned. Seats were sold out for two seasons even before it had been completed.

Clough, controversial but always interesting, became a target for newspapers and television, and because he was not afraid to stir a few things, worried League and FA officials as well as his chairman, Sam Longson. There were constant suggestions that Clough and Taylor would move to another club and the party they threw after the final match of 1971-2 had originally been intended as a farewell before they left to take over Coventry City. Disputes between board and management became more bitter until, in October 1973, Clough and Taylor resigned.

They had come to a confrontation with Longson and another director, Jack Kirkland, and decided they must go. The players were as upset as the vast majority of the supporters but not even the formation of a protest movement could change events.

Clough and Taylor went to Brighton then, while Taylor stayed, Clough had a brief and unhappy spell with Leeds United. They rejoined forces at Nottingham Forest and were even more spectacularly successful than at Derby; a first Championship for Forest, two League Cup victories, a third Final and two European Cup triumphs.

On his own, Clough continued to produce teams that illustrated the best aspects of the game. He was rewarded with League Cup Final victories in 1989 and 1990, followed by an FA Cup Final appearance in 1991.

The Executive Stand at the City Ground mirrored their talent as surely as the Ley Stand. As a partnership they were magnificent and it was infinitely sad that the parting in 1982 was so acrimonious. Derby and Forest have never known anybody like them.

Dave Mackay

Division One Champions 1974-5.

DAVE Mackay walked into a situation unique in football when, in October 1973, he left Nottingham Forest with his assistant Des Anderson to manage Derby County. It was the best of jobs, because there was a talented team awaiting him, and the worst of jobs because the Baseball Ground was in turmoil following the departure of Brian Clough and Peter Taylor. Mackay, a hero as a player at Derby, had to fight for acceptance because the players wanted Clough and Taylor back but gradually won his way through.

After six weeks without a victory under Mackay, Derby revived to finish third and qualify for the UEFA Cup.

Mackay bought Rod Thomas and Bruce Rioch and, before the start of the following season, the 30-year-old Francis Lee from Manchester City.

Derby were Champions again in 1974-5, a magnificent achievement by

Dave Mackay and his assistant Des Anderson lead out Derby County, the Football League Champions, against Carlisle United for the final game of 1974-5.

Mackay and Anderson, and a year later, with Charlie George in the side and Leighton James becoming their first £300,000 player, finished fourth and reached the semi-finals of the FA Cup. Derby were beaten at Hillsborough by Tommy Docherty's young Manchester United side and, disappointing though that performance was, few realised that the great days had come to a full stop in one afternoon. The following season began badly and there was increasing criticism from the boardroom of Mackay's free-wheeling style.

In November 1976 Mackay sought a vote of confidence and when the directors felt they could not give this, he and Anderson were sacked. It was an astonishing decision because they were at least entitled to be given time. Mackay had a brief spell with Walsall, then went to work in Kuwait. After a year in Dubai, Mackay returned to English football with Doncaster Rovers in December 1987. He joined Birmingham City before again finding success abroad, this time with the Egyptian club, Zamalek.

It seemed that the worst thing a manager could do at the Baseball Ground was to win the Championship and nothing that has happened since has in any way diminished Mackay's stature and achievements. Third, first and fourth in his three seasons: those credentials should have impressed even Derby's board.

Colin Murphy

COLIN Murphy, who had been Reserve-team coach under Dave Mackay with Nottingham Forest and Derby County, became Derby's manager in November 1976, at first on a temporary basis. A Londoner, he never played League football, although he was with Crystal Palace as well as Cork Hibernian, Wimbledon and Hastings United.

He brought in Dario Gradi as his assistant but the early season struggles continued and only five of the first 23 League matches had been won when, in February, chairman George Hardy and the board invited Brian Clough and Peter Taylor to leave Nottingham Forest and return to Derby. Murphy had, it seemed, merely been keeping the seat warm but when Clough and Taylor shattered Derby's plans by deciding to stay with Forest, Murphy was asked to continue in office.

Murphy had invested more than £300,000 in Derek Hales and, in March 1977, bought Gerry Daly from Manchester United for £175,000. Daly watched Derby go to the foot of the First Division when they lost to West Bromwich Albion at The Hawthorns and Sam Longson, by then president, called publicly for Dave Mackay to return. It was humiliating for Murphy but he stuck to it to steer clear of the relegation zone. The 1977-8 season

Colin Murphy

Tommy Docherty

Colin Addison

with York City, Nottingham Forest, Arsenal and Sheffield United before joining Hereford United as player-manager. He saw them into the Football League and, after working with Durban City, had a good year with Newport County.

He came to Derby from West Bromwich Albion, where he worked under Ron Atkinson, and appointed John Newman as his assistant.

was only six matches old when Murphy had to watch a draw against Leeds United knowing that Tommy Docherty was on the way to the Baseball Ground to succeed him. It had been an extraordinary ten months for Murphy and the shameful final day in office reflected no credit on Derby County. After a spell with Jimmy Sirrel at Notts County, Murphy became manager of Lincoln City. He returned to Sincil Bank after two spells with Stockport County and year in Saudi Arabia to guide Lincoln out of the GM Vauxhall Conference. He worked with David Pleat as Youth coach at Leicester and assistant manager at Luton, before succeeding David Webb as manager of Southend United in May 1992.

Tommy Docherty

CHANGES were needed to a Derby County squad which had lost its impetus but Tommy Docherty's 20 months of buying and selling seriously diminished the quality of the players at the Baseball Ground.

Docherty, born in Glasgow on 24 April 1928, was a rugged wing-half with Celtic, Preston North End and Arsenal, winning 25 caps for Scotland. With him in the side, Preston won the Second Division in 1950-51, were twice First Division runners-up and reached the 1954 FA Cup Final. One of his team mates at Deepdale was former Derby forward Angus Morrison.

Docherty joined Chelsea as player-caoch, became manager in January 1962 and created a fine young team. He was equally liable to break up teams and managed Rotherham United, Queen's Park Rangers, Aston Villa and Oporto. He was briefly assistant manager at Hull, then Scotland's team manager from September 1971 to December 1972.

After a hectic career, Docherty appeared

to have found the right niche with Manchester United but, after winning the FA Cup with an exciting team in 1977, he lost his job as the result of an affair with the physiotherapist's wife. Docherty and his assistant, Frank Blunstone, were still very much tuned in to United in their first season. In the second, Docherty was in and out of court, suffering a major setback with the collapse of his libel action against Willie Morgan and Granada Television. Docherty kept Derby in the First Division but the departure of players such as Colin Boulton, Colin Todd, Archie Gemmill, Kevin Hector, Charlie George and Leighton James worried supporters. Of all Docherty's purchases, only Steve Buckley proved a long-term investment and the midfield trio of Gerry Daly, already there when Colin Murphy left, Don Masson and Bruce Rioch flopped despite the manager's description of them as three Van Goghs.

In May 1979 Docherty resigned to become manager of Queen's Park Rangers for a second time, leaving Derby still paying for players who were of limited use to them. He also managed Sydney Olympic, twice, Preston North End, Wolverhampton Wanderers and Altrincham before concentrating on radio work and after-dinner speaking.

Colin Addison

GEORGE Hardy was chairman when Colin Addison was appointed as manager. By the time Derby lined up for the pre-season photograph, Richard Moore had taken the chair. It was an unsettling start for Addison, especially when coupled with a police investigation, began during the summer of 1979 into the affairs at the Baseball Ground.

Addison, born in Taunton on 18 May 1940, was a goalscoring inside-forward

The Derby job was hard, for the club had been in decline for three years, and despite paying more than £1 million for Barry Powell, Alan Biley and David Swindlehurst, Derby's first £400,000 player, Addison's first season ended in relegation. Derby were also beginning to lose control of their finances. They were never good enough to challenge for promotion in 1980-81 and, with the downward trend continuing, Addison was sacked in January 1982, rejoining Newport. In 1986-7 he took Celta Vigo to promotion from the Spanish Second Division, then rejoined Atkinson at West Bromwich. They went together to Atletico Madrid, where Addison succeeded Atkinson in January 1989. He also managed Cadiz, had another spell with Hereford and coached Al Arabi in Kuwait.

John Newman

AFTER proving himself in the lower divisions with Exeter City and Grimsby Town, John Newman joined Derby County as Colin Addison's assistant and succeeded him in January 1982, although only on a temporary, untitled basis until March. During that time, the directors talked about appointing a managing director, rather hoping that Brian Clough would be interested. It was typical of the atmosphere in which Newman had to work and, at a time when Derby changed chairmen as often as managers, he had little chance of success.

John Newman

Newman was born in Hereford on 13 December 1933 and began his career with Birmingham City, where he was in the Second Division Championship team of 1954-5 and played in the 1956 FA Cup Final as deputy for Roy Warhurst. He joined Leicester City in search of more regular first-team football and spent almost eight years with Plymouth Argyle before joining Exeter City where, in April 1969, he was appointed player-manager, succeeding Frank Broome. He left a promotion-bound team to take over at Grimsby in January 1977 and moved to Derby after a Fourth Division promotion at Blundell Park.

His immediate task after taking over from Addison was to keep Derby in the Second Division. He brought back Charlie George, signed Brian Attley and John McAlle and achieved his objective. When Mike Watterson took over the club, it was obvious that Newman's days were numbered. He was dismissed in November 1982 and, typically for that time, the sacking was handled without dignity or compassion.

Newman managed Hereford United from March 1983 to October 1987, briefly assisted Bobby Saxton at York, was assistant to John Barnwell at Notts County and worked with George Foster as chief scout at Mansfield. His nine months in charge at the Baseball Ground must have seemed like a lifetime.

Peter Taylor

PETER Taylor had been in retirement for six months when new chairman Mike Watterson brought him back to the Baseball Ground. Taylor engaged Roy McFarland and Mick Jones from Bradford City and thereby involved the club in a costly controversy. The Rams were fined £10,000 by the Football League for

Peter Taylor and Roy McFarland urging on the Rams.

illegally inducing McFarland to break his contract at Valley Parade and were then ordered to pay £55,000 in compensation.

Taylor, facing a desperate fight against relegation, brought Archie Gemmill back to Derby and paid substantial fees for Bobby Davison, Paul Futcher and Paul Hooks. A run of 15 League games without defeat was a fine achievement and victory over Fulham in the final game ensured safety. Even then, with thousands of spectators around the touchline in the closing minutes, there was more controversy.

The summer signings of John Robertson and Bobby Campbell seemed to point Derby towards better days but they never recovered from a dreadful start and the financial crisis came to a head with the Inland Revenue issuing a winding-up petition. When Derby cleared themselves in the High Court, they parted company with Taylor in April 1984. Taylor's second season was disastrous and Derby were as good as down when he left, despite an FA Cup run to the sixth round.

His greatest days were with Clough, first with Derby, then with Nottingham Forest. Taylor was born in Nottingham on 2 July 1928 and was on Forest's books

as an amateur goalkeeper before joining Coventry City in May 1946. He was deeply influenced by Harry Storer's methods and personality before, in August 1955, he joined Middlesbrough, there becoming a close friend of Brian Clough. He was briefly with Port Vale before entering management with Burton Albion and steering them to the Southern League Cup in 1963-4 with a team including Richie Barker.

Taylor, a private man happiest with his family, died in Majorca in October 1990. His funeral in the Nottinghamshire village of Widmerpool was packed with the kind of class players he loved.

Roy McFarland

AFTER Peter Taylor's departure, Roy McFarland had nine games in which to save Derby County from relegation and convince the board that he was the right man for the job. By playing a settled side, he brought an improvement in results but could not make up an alarming deficit in a short time. McFarland was put on the short list of four for the manager's job but Arthur Cox was appointed. McFarland stayed as Cox's assistant.

Christie, Gary Micklewhite and Geraint Williams to add to three outstandingly successful free transfers, Charlie Palmer, Rob Hindmarch and Eric Steele.

After a gruelling battle, Derby were promoted from the Third Division in 1985-6, Cox's second season, and won the Second Division 12 months later. When Derby regained their First Division place, Robert Maxwell became chairman, made lavish promises and initially backed the purchases of Peter Shilton and Mark Wright. The first year was a struggle but Cox was able to improve the squad in 1989, when Dean Saunders became Derby's first £1-million player, and they finished fifth. They could have gone on from there but Maxwell refused to invest or, as revelations after his death suggested, was unable to. Without a turnover of players, and with an alarming list of long-term injuries, Derby deteriorated from the start of 1990 until their inevitable relegation 15 months later.

It was an awful period but Cox maintained his dignity in failure as he had in success and Maxwell was ultimately bought out at a cost of £3-million. That money came from the sale of Wright and Saunders to Liverpool but not until Lionel Pickering took over in November 1991 did Cox, by then a director, have money at his disposal. Instead of fighting a losing battle with a chairman who should never have been in football, Cox had the freedom to invest and, after a near miss for promotion in 1991-2, hopes to recreate his earlier success.

Arthur Cox, now the Rams' longest-serving manager since George Jobey.

Arthur Cox

Division Three promotion 1985-6. Division Two champions 1986-7. Central League champions 1985-6.

ARTHUR Cox had just clinched promotion to the First Division with Newcastle United when he was appointed manager of Derby County in May 1984. The Rams were about to mark their centenary and Cox was their ninth manager in less than 11 years, a statistic which goes some way towards explaining why they were celebrating as a Third Division club. Towards the end of the 1991-2 season, he had become Derby's longest-serving manager since George Jobey.

Cox was born in Southam on 14 December 1939 and joined Coventry City as a junior. His playing career ended when he was 18, the result of a badly broken leg, and he turned to coaching. He was Coventry's Youth coach as a teenager and subsequently worked at Walsall, Aston Villa with Tommy

Docherty, Halifax Town and Preston North End. He was Bob Stokoe's assistant when Sunderland won the FA Cup in 1973 and, after a brief spell in Turkey as Galatasaray's coach, entered League management at Chesterfield in October 1976. He took them agonisingly close to promotion from the Third Division before Newcastle appointed him in September 1980. Cox rebuilt an ailing team before leaving on a matter of principle about the duration of a contract.

He faced an even bigger challenge at the Baseball Ground, although he took over only nine years after the Rams had won their second League Championship. At first, Cox believed he was starting from scratch but, in August 1984, the Maxwell family moved in and Ian was appointed chairman while his father stayed with Oxford United. There was a measure of financial stability but it was necessary to sell Kevin Wilson to Ipswich Town before Cox could invest in Trevor

Gordon Guthrie, the Rams' physiotherapist who has served 11 different managers at the Baseball Ground. Guthrie played for Derby County Reserves as a part-time professional before injury ended his career and he joined the training staff.

Rams Internationals

In June 1988, Peter Shilton became the first player associated with Derby County to play in 100 internationals. Appearances given here refer to caps won when with the Rams. The Republic of Ireland first played as a separate nation in 1924 but Eire-born players appeared for Northern Ireland until after World War Two.

England

Bagshaw J.J. 1919-20 v Ireland (1).

Barker J.W. 1934-5 v Wales, Italy, Northern Ireland, Scotland, Holland; 1935-6 v Northern Ireland, Germany, Wales, Scotland, Austria; 1936-7 v Wales (11).

Bloomer S. 1894-5 v Ireland, Scotland; 1895-6 v Ireland, Wales; 1896-7 v Ireland, Wales, Scotland; 1897-8 v Scotland; 1898-9 v Ireland, Wales, Scotland; 1899-1900 v Scotland; 1900-01 v Wales, Scotland; 1901-02 v Wales, Ireland, Scotland; 1903-04 v Scotland; 1904-05 v Ireland, Wales, Scotland (21).

Bowers J.W.A. 1933-4 v Northern Ireland, Wales, Scotland (3).

Buckley F.C. 1913-14 v Ireland (1).

Carter H.S. 1946-7 v Northern Ireland, Republic of Ireland, Wales, Holland, Scotland, France, Switzerland (7).

Cooper T. 1927-8 v Northern Ireland; 1928-9 v Northern Ireland, Wales, Scotland, France, Belgium, Spain; 1930-31 v France; 1931-2 v Wales, Spain; 1932-3 v Scotland; 1933-4 v Scotland, Hungary, Czechoslovakia; 1934-5 v Wales (15).

Cox J.D. 1891-2 v Ireland (1).

Crooks S.D. 1929-30 v Scotland, Germany, Austria; 1930-31 v Northern Ireland, Wales, Scotland, France, Belgium; 1931-2 v Northern Ireland, Wales, Spain, Scotland; 1932-3 v Northern Ireland, Wales, Austria; 1933-4 v Northern Ireland, Wales, France, Scotland, Hungary, Czechoslovakia; 1934-5 v Northern Ireland; 1935-6 v Wales, Scotland; 1936-7 v Wales, Hungary (26).

Davis G.H. 1903-04 v Wales, Ireland (2).

Dix R.W. 1938-9 v Norway (1).

George C.F. 1976-7 v Republic of Ireland (1).

Goodall J. 1890-91 v Wales, Scotland; 1891-2 v Scotland; 1892-3 v Wales. 1893-4 v Scotland; 1894-5 v Ireland, Scotland; 1895-6 v Wales, Scotland. 1897-8 v Wales (10).

Hector K.J. 1973-4 v Poland (sub), Italy (sub) (2).

Howe J.R. 1947-8 v Italy; 1948-9 v Northern Ireland, Scotland (3).

Keen E.R.L. 1932-3 v Austria; 1936-7 v Wales, Northern Ireland, Hungary (4).

Kinsey G. 1895-6 v Ireland, Wales (2).

Lee J. 1950-51 v Northern Ireland (1).

McFarland R.L. 1970-71 v Malta, Greece, Malta, Northern Ireland, Scotland; 1971-2 v Switzerland, Greece, West Germany, Wales, Scotland; 1972-3 v Wales, Wales, Northern Ireland, Wales, Scotland, Czechoslovakia, Poland, USSR, Italy; 1973-4 v Austria, Poland, Italy, Wales, Northern Ireland; 1975-6 v Czechoslovakia, Scotland; 1976-7 v Republic of Ireland, Italy (28).

Maskrey H.M. 1907-08 v Ireland (1).

Moore J. 1922-3 v Sweden (1).

Morris J. 1948-9 v Norway, France; 1949-50 v Republic of Ireland (3).

Mozley B. 1949-50 v Republic of Ireland, Wales, Northern Ireland (3).

Nish D.J. 1972-3 v Northern Ireland; 1973-4 v Portugal, Wales, Northern Ireland, Scotland (5).

Quantrill A.E. 1919-20 v Wales, Scotland; 1920-21 v Ireland, Wales (4).

Richards G.H. 1908-09 v Austria (1).

Robinson J.W. 1896-7 v Ireland, Scotland (2).

Scattergood E.O. 1912-13 v Wales (1).

Shilton P.L. 1987-8 v West Germany, Turkey, Yugoslavia, Holland, Scotland, Colombia, Switzerland, Republic of Ireland, Holland; 1988-9 v Denmark, Sweden, Greece, Albania, Albania, Chile, Scotland, Poland, Denmark; 1989-90 v Sweden, Poland, Italy, Yugoslavia, Brazil, Czechoslovakia, Denmark, Uruguay, Tunisia, Republic of Ireland, Holland, Egypt, Belgium, Cameroon, West Germany, Italy (34).

Stephenson G.T. 1927-8 v France, Belgium (2).

Storer H. 1923-4 v France; 1927-8 v Northern Ireland (2).

Thornewell G. 1922-3 v Sweden, Sweden; 1923-4 v France; 1924-5 v France (4).

Todd C. 1971-2 v Northern Ireland; 1973-4 v Portugal, Wales, Northern Ireland, Scotland, Argentina, East Germany, Bulgaria, Yugoslavia; 1974-5 v Portugal (sub), West Germany, Cyprus, Cyprus, Northern Ireland, Wales, Scotland; 1975-6 v Switzerland, Czechoslovakia, Portugal, Northern Ireland, Scotland, Brazil, Finland; 1976-7 v Republic of Ireland, Finland, Holland (sub), Northern Ireland (27).

Turner J.A. 1897-8 v Ireland (1).

Ward T.V. 1947-8 v Belgium; 1948-9 v Wales (2).

Warren B. 1905-06 v Ireland, Wales, Scotland; 1906-07 v Ireland, Wales, Scotland; 1907-08 v Ireland, Wales, Scotland, Austria, Austria, Hungary, Bohemia (13).

Wright M. 1987-8 v Israel, Holland (sub), Colombia, Switzerland, Republic of Ireland, Holland; 1989-90 v Czechoslavakia (sub), Tunisia (sub), Holland, Egypt, Belgium, Cameroon, West Germany, Italy; 1990-91 v

Peter Shilton (left) and Mark Wright (right) both enjoyed good World Cups in Italy in 1990. The competition marked the end of Shilton's long international career but Wright could look forward to more caps, although he fell foul of new England manager Graham Taylor after choosing to remain in Liverpool and celebrate winning the FA Cup rather than fly immediately to Sweden for the 1992 European Championships. Injury eventually ruled him out of the European Finals.

Hungary, Poland, Republic of Ireland, Cameroon, Republic of Ireland, USSR, Argentina, Australia, New Zealand, Malaysia (24).

Scotland

Duncan D. 1932-3 v Wales, England; 1933-4 v Wales, Austria; 1934-5 v Wales, England; 1935-6 v Wales, Northern Ireland, England; 1936-7 v Germany, Northern Ireland, Wales, England; 1937-8 v Wales (14).
Gallacher H.K. 1934-5 v England (1).
Gemmill A. 1970-71 v Belgium; 1971-2 v Portugal, Holland, Peru, Northern Ireland, Wales, England; 1975-6 v Denmark, Romania, Wales, Northern Ireland, England; 1976-7 v Finland, Czechoslovakia, Wales, Wales, Northern Ireland (sub), England (sub), Chile (sub), Argentina, Brazil; 1977-8 v East Germany (sub) (22).
McCulloch D. 1938-9 v Wales, Hungary (2).
Masson D.S. 1977-8 v Northern Ireland, England, Peru (3).
Napier C.E. 1936-7 v Northern Ireland, Austria (2).
O'Hare J. 1969-70 v Northern Ireland, Wales, England; 1970-71 v Denmark, Belgium, Wales, Northern Ireland; 1971-2 v Portugal, Belgium, Holland (sub), Peru, Northern Ireland, Wales (13).
Rioch B.D. 1974-5 v Portugal, Wales, Northern Ireland, England, Romania; 1975-6 v Denmark, Denmark,

Geraint Williams, seen here organising his defence, won 11 full caps for Wales as a Derby County player.

Romania, Wales, Northern Ireland, England; 1976-7 v Finland, Czechoslovakia, Wales; 1977-8 v Northern Ireland, England, Peru, Holland (18).
Robertson J.N. 1983-4 v Uruguay, Belgium (2).
Steel W. 1947-8 v Northern Ireland, Wales, England, France; 1948-9 v Wales, Northern Ireland, England, France; 1949-50 v Northern Ireland, Wales, England, Switzerland, Portugal, France (14).

Wales

Astley D.J. 1938-9 v England, Scotland (2).
Durban W.A. 1965-6 v Brazil (sub); 1966-7 v Northern Ireland; 1967-8 v England, Scotland, Northern Ireland, West Germany; 1968-9 v West Germany, East Germany, Scotland, England, Northern Ireland; 1969-70 v East Germany, Italy, England, Scotland, Northern Ireland; 1970-71 v Romania, Czechoslovakia, Scotland, England, Northern Ireland, Finland; 1971-2 v Finland, Czechoslovakia, England, Scotland, Northern Ireland (27).
Hennessey W.T. 1969-70 v England, Scotland, Northern Ireland; 1971-2 v Finland, Czechoslovakia, England, Scotland; 1972-3 v England (8).
James L. 1975-6 v Yugoslavia, Scotland, England, Northern Ireland, Yugoslavia; 1976-7 v West Germany, Scotland, Czechoslovakia, Scotland, England, Northern Ireland; 1977-8 v Kuwait, Kuwait (13).
Morris C.R. 1900-01 v Scotland, England, Ireland; 1901-02 v England; 1902-03 v England, Scotland, Ireland; 1903-04 v Ireland; 1904-05 v Scotland, England, Ireland; 1905-06 v Scotland; 1906-07 v Scotland; 1907-08 v Scotland, England; 1908-09 v Scotland, England, Ireland; 1909-10 v Scotland, England, Ireland (21).
Pembridge M.A. 1991-2 v Holland, Japan (sub) (2).
Saunders D.N. 1988-9 v Israel, Sweden, West Germany; 1989-90 v Finland, Holland, West Germany, Sweden, Costa Rica; 1990-91 v Denmark, Belgium, Luxembourg, Republic of Ireland, Belgium, Iceland, Poland, Germany (16).
Thomas R.J. 1973-4 v England, Scotland, Northern Ireland; 1974-5 v Hungary, Luxembourg, Hungary, Luxembourg, Scotland, England, Northern Ireland; 1975-6 v Austria, Yugoslavia, England; 1976-7 v Czechoslovakia, Scotland, England, Northern Ireland; 1977-8 v Kuwait, Scotland (19).
Williams D.G. 1987-8 v Czechoslovakia, Yugoslavia, Sweden, Malta, Italy; 1988-9 v Holland, Israel, Sweden, West Germany; 1989-90 v Finland, Holland (11).

Northern Ireland (and Ireland before 1924)

Caskey W.T. 1978-9 v Bulgaria, England, Bulgaria, England, Denmark (sub); 1979-80 v England (sub) (6).
Doherty P.D. 1946-7 v England (1).
Goodall A.L. 1898-9 v Wales, Scotland; 1899-1900 v Wales, England; 1900-01 v England; 1901-02 v Scotland; 1902-03 v England, Wales (8).
Halligan W. 1910-11 v Wales (1).
Mercer J.T. 1903-04 v England, Wales; 1904-05 v Scotland (3).
Moreland V. 1978-9 v Bulgaria (sub), Bulgaria (sub), England, Scotland; 1979-80 v England, Republic of Ireland (6).
O'Brien M.T. 1926-7 v Wales (1).
Reid S.E. 1933-4 v England, Wales; 1935-6 v England (3).
Stewart A. 1967-8 v Wales; 1968-9 v Israel, Turkey (sub), Turkey (4).

Republic of Ireland

Daly G.A. 1976-7 v France, Bulgaria; 1977-8 v Bulgaria, Turkey, Denmark; 1978-9 v Northern Ireland, England, Denmark, Bulgaria; 1979-80 v Northern Ireland, England, Cyprus, Switzerland, Argentina (14).
Fagan F. 1959-60 v Chile, West Germany, Sweden; 1960-61 v Wales, Norway, Scotland (6).
Langan D.F. 1977-8 v Turkey, Norway; 1979-80 v Switzerland, Argentina (4).
Macken A. 1976-7 v Spain (1).
O'Brien M.T. 1926-7 v Italy (1).
Ryan G.J. 1977-8 v Turkey (1).
Ryan R.A. 1955-6 v Spain (1).
Stapleton F.A. 1987-8 v Romania, Yugoslavia, Norway, England, USSR, Holland (6).

England 'B'

Forsyth M.E. 1989-90 v Yugoslavia (1).
Hill G.A. 1977-8 v Malaysia, New Zealand (three times), Singapore (5).
Leuty L.H. 1948-9 v Finland, Holland; 1949-50 v Holland (3).
Morris J. 1948-9 v Finland (1).

Wartime and Victory Internationals

England
Bagshaw J.J. 1919-20 v Wales (1).
Carter H.S. 1945-6 v Switzerland, France (2).

Scotland
McCulloch D. 1939-40 v England (1).

Wales
Redfern W.J. 1939-40 v England (1).

Northern Ireland
Doherty P.D. 1945-6 v Wales (1).

Under-23 Internationals

England
Davies R. 1973-4 v Scotland (sub) (1).
McFarland R.L. 1968-9 v Holland, Holland, Belgium, Portugal; 1969-70 v Scotland (5).
Powell S. 1974-5 v Scotland (1).
Robson J.D. 1970-71 v West Germany, Sweden, Scotland; 1971-2 v Wales, Scotland, East Germany (6).
Todd C. 1970-71 v Scotland; 1971-2 v Wales; 1974-5 v Wales (3).

Scotland
McGovern J.P. 1971-2 v Wales; 1972-3 v Wales (2).
O'Hare J. 1969-70 v France, England, Wales (3).

Wales
Durban W.A. 1963-4 v England, Scotland, Northern Ireland (3).

David Langan (left) made four appearances for the Republic of Ireland and won 25 full caps altogether after moving to Birmingham City and then Oxford United. Michael Forsyth (right) has been capped at 'B' and Under-21 levels for England.

Under-21 Internationals

England
Forsyth M.E. 1987-8 v Switzerland (1).
Johnson T. 1991-2 v Mexico, Czechoslovakia (sub) (2).
Kitson P. 1991-2 v Mexico, Czechoslovakia, France (3).
Ramage C.D. 1990-91 v Wales; 1991-2 v France (sub) (2).
Williams P.D. 1990-91 v Senegal, Mexico, USSR; 1991-2 v Germany, Turkey, Poland (6).

Wales
Clark J. 1978-9 v England (1).

Football League Representatives

Barker J.W. 1934-5 v Scottish League; 1935-6 v Irish League; 1936-7 v Irish League (3).
Bedford H. 1925-6 v Scottish League (1).
Bloomer S. 1896-7 v Irish League, Scottish League; 1897-8 v Irish League; 1898-9 v Irish League, Scottish League; 1899-1900 v Irish League, Scottish League; 1900-01 v Irish League; 1901-02 v Irish League, Scottish

After Arsenal's Eddie Hapgood, Sammy Crooks (left) was England's most capped player between the wars with 26 appearances. He also made five appearances for the Football League. John Goodall (right) was already an England player when he joined Derby from Preston in 1889 but he won ten of his 14 caps with the Rams.

League; 1902-03 v Irish League; 1903-04 v Irish League, Scottish League; 1904-05 v Scottish League; 1910-11 v Scottish League (15).

Bowers J.W.A. 1933-4 v Irish League, Scottish League (2).

Carter H.S. 1946-7 v Scottish League (1).

Cooper T. 1926-7 v Irish League; 1928-9 v Irish League; 1932-3 v Irish League; 1934-5 v Irish League, Scottish League (5).

Crooks S.D. 1930-31 v Irish League, Scottish League; 1931-2 v Scottish League; 1933-4 v Irish League; 1936-7 v Scottish League (5).

Dix R.W. 1938-9 v Scottish League (1).

Goodall J. 1890-91 v Football Alliance; 1891-2 v Scottish League; 1893-4 v Scottish League; 1895-6 v Scottish League (4).

Hector K.J. 1970-71 v Irish League; 1971-2 v League of Ireland; 1973-4 v Scottish League (sub) (3).

Keen E.R.L. 1936-7 v Scottish League (1).

Leuty L.H. 1947-8 v Scottish League; 1948-9 v League of Ireland (2).

Maskrey H.M. 1905-06 v Irish League (1).

McFarland R.L. 1969-70 v Scottish League; 1970-71 v Scottish League; 1971-2 v League of Ireland; 1972-3 v Scottish League; 1973-4 v Scottish League; 1975-6 v Scottish League (6).

Morris J. 1949-50 v Irish League; 1950-51 v Irish League, Scottish League (3).

Mozley B. 1947-8 v Scottish League (1).

Musson W.U. 1949-50 v Irish League (1).

Nish D.J. 1972-3 v Scottish League; 1973-4 v Scottish League (2).

Robson J.D. 1970-71 v Irish League (1).

Saunders D.N. 1990-91 v Italian League (sub) (1).

Shilton P.L. 1987-8 v Rest of the World (1).

Todd C. 1971-2 v League of Ireland (sub); 1973-4 v Scottish League (2).

Warren B. 1905-06 v Scottish League; 1906-07 v Irish League, Scottish League; 1907-08 v Scottish League (4).

Wright M. 1990-91 v Italian League (1).

Rams full-back Bert Mozley won two England caps, making his debut in England's first home defeat by 'foreign' opposition, against the Republic of Ireland at Goodison Park in 1949. Mozley was a classy defender, occasionally used in attack. Here he is playing at centre-forward against Arsenal at Highbury in September 1951. The Arsenal defenders are goalkeeper George Swindin, Joe Mercer (6) and Ray Daniel (5).

In September 1894, John and Archie Goodall played for the Rest of the Football League against champions Aston Villa in a testimonial match for William McGregor, the founder of the League.

Jimmy Moore played for the Football League against a Nottingham XI at Meadow Lane in December 1913. It was a testimonial for Tom Harris, a member of the Management Committee and director of Notts County.

In May 1935, Jack Barker and Sammy Crooks represented the Football League against West Bromwich Albion at The Hawthorns in a match celebrating the Jubilee of King George V. The League used the game to test a system of two referees.

In March 1992, Simon Coleman and Paul Williams played for the Football League Second Division against the Italian Serie 'B' in Caserta.

Other Appearances by Competitions

Test Match (1894-95)

S.Bloomer 1, J.Cox 1, P.Francis 1, A.Goodall 1, J.Goodall 1, J.Leiper 1, J.McMillan 1, J.Methven 1, J.Paul 1, J.Robinson 1, J.Staley 1.
Goalscorers: Bloomer 1, McMillan 1.

Texaco Cup (1971-72)

C.Boulton 8, T.Hennessey 8, A.Hinton 8, K.Hector 6, J.McGovern 6, J.Robson 6, C.Todd 6, P.Daniel 5, J.O'Hare 5, R.Webster 5, A.Durban 4, J.Walker 2/2, B.Butlin 3, A.Gemmill 3, F.Wignall 3, A.Bailey 2/1, R.McFarland 2, S.Powell 2, J.Bourne 1, R.Davies 1, A.Lewis 1, A.Parry 1.
Goalscorers: O'Hare 4, Hinton 3, Hector 2, Walker 2, Butlin 1, Davies 1, Durban 1, Durban 1, McGovern 1, Robson 1, Todd 1, Wignall 1.

European Cup (1972-73 and 1975-76)

C.Boulton 12, C.Todd 12, A.Gemmill 11, K.Hector 11, R.McFarland 11, J.McGovern 8, D.Nish 8, J.O'Hare 8, A.Hinton 6/1, S.Powell 6, R.Davies 4/1, P.Daniel 4, C.George 4, T.Hennessey 4, H.Newton 4, R.Thomas 4, R.Webster 4, J.Bourne 0/4, F.Lee 3, B.Rioch 3, J.Robson 3, A.Durban 2/1, J.Sims 0/1.
Goalscorers: George 4, Hector 4, Lee 2, McFarland 2, Bourne 1, Gemmill 1, Hinton 1, McGovern 1, Nish 1, O'Hare 1.

Goalkeeper Colin Boulton played in all 12 of the Rams' European Cup games but gave way to Graham Moseley in their second season in the UEFA Cup.

UEFA Cup (1974-75 and 1976-77)

A.Gemmill 10, B.Rioch 10, K.Hector 9, C.Todd 9, H.Newton 8, D.Nish 8, R.Webster 6/1, C.Boulton 6, P.Daniel 6, F.Lee 6, J.Bourne 4/2, R.Thomas 5, C.George 4, L.James 4, R.McFarland 4, G.Moseley 4, A.Macken 2/2, A.Hinton 0/4, S.Powell 3, R.Davies 2/1, J.King 0/2.
Goalscorers: Hector 12, George 6, Rioch 4, James 3, Bourne 2, Lee 2, Daniel 1, Hinton 1, Nish 1.

FA Charity Shield (1975-76)

C.Boulton 1, A.Gemmill 1, C.George 1, K.Hector 1, F.Lee 1, R.McFarland 1, H.Newton 1, D.Nish 1, B.Rioch 1, R.Thomas 1, C.Todd 1.
Goalscorers: Hector 1, McFarland 1.

Freight/Rover Trophy (1984-85 and 1985-86)

P.Blades 3/1, S.Buckley 3, A.Garner 3, M.Lewis 3, R.Pratley 3, E.Steele 3, G.Ablett 2, T.Christie 2, R.Davison 2, C.Palmer 2, J.Robertson 2, S.Biggins 1/1, J.Chandler 1/1, P.Gee 1/1, J.Gregory 1/1, G.Harbey 1/1, P.Hooks 1/1, R.Hindmarch 1, S.McClaren 1, R.MacLaren 1, G.Micklewhite 1, D.Penney 1, S.Powell 1, F.Streete 1, K.Taylor 1, M.Wallington 1, G.Williams 1.
Goalscorers: Davison 2, Christie 1, Taylor 1.

Full Members' Cup (1986-87 to 1991-92)

M.Forsyth 12, G.Williams 10, M.Sage 8, P.Shilton 8, S.Cross 3/5, T.Hebberd 7, D.Saunders 7, M.Wright 7, P.Gee 6, G.Micklewhite 6, P.Blades 5/1, N.Callaghan 5, P.Goddard 5, R.Hindmarch 5, K.McMinn 4, J.Gregory 3, R.MacLaren 3, N.Pickering 3, M.Patterson 2/1, D.Penney 0/3, R.Davison 2, A.Garner 2, M.Harford 2, J.Kavanagh 2, M.Taylor 2, M.Wallington 2, P.Williams 2, C.Ramage 0/2, J.Chandler 1, S.Coleman 1, A.Comyn 1, G.Harbey 1, S.Hayward 1, M.Lewis 1, S.McClaren 1, R.Pratley 1, M.Stallard 1, M.Chalk 0/1, J.Davidson 0/1, K.Francis 0/1, B.McCord 0/1.
Goalscorers: Micklewhite 6, Saunders 5, Cross 2, Callaghan 1, Garner 1, Goddard 1, McCord 1, Penney 1, Stallard 1, Opponent own-goal: Trewick (Birmingham City) 1.

Second Division Play-offs (1991-92)

S.Coleman 2, A.Comyn 2, M.Forsyth 2, M.Gabbiadini 2, T.Johnson 2, J.Kavanagh 2, P.Kitson 2, K.McMinn 2, P.Simpson 2, S.Sutton 2, P.Williams 2, G.Micklewhite 0/1, C.Ramage 0/1.
Goalscorers: Comyn 1, Gabbiadini 1, Johnson 1, McMinn 1.

Roy McFarland (left) missed only one European Cup game, being suspended after he was dubiously booked in the Rams' 1973 semi-final first-leg game against Juventus in Italy. When he signed as a professional for Derby under Harry Storer in June 1960, Ron Webster (right) could hardly have imagined that he would one day play for the Rams in the European Cup.

100 Consecutive Appearances

League

151	Archie Goodall	Oct 1892 to Sep 1897
122	Steve Buckley	Nov 1983 to May 1986
117	Steve Buckley	Jan 1978 to Nov 1980
112	Gary Micklewhite	Feb 1985 to Sep 1987
108	Peter Shilton	Aug 1987 to Mar 1990
107	Les Green	Aug 1968 to Dec 1970
106	Dean Saunders	Oct 1988 to May 1991
105	Bobby Davison	Sep 1983 to Dec 1985
105	Kevin Hector	Mar 1970 to Oct 1972
104	Jack Nicholas	Jan 1937 to Sep 1946

All Matches

167	Archie Goodall	Oct 1892 to Sep 1897
131	Colin Boulton	Jan 1971 to Apr 1973
130	Dean Saunders	Nov 1988 to May 1991
130	Colin Todd	Nov 1974 to Mar 1977
129	Les Green	Aug 1968 to Dec 1970
127	Steve Buckley	Jan 1978 to Nov 1980
126	Bobby Davison	Sep 1983 to Dec 1985
124	Michael Forsyth	Apr 1988 to Jan 1991
124	Peter Shilton	Aug 1987 to Jan 1990
120	Jack Nicholas	Jan 1937 to Sep 1946
119	Steve Buckley	Nov 1983 to Jan 1986
115	Colin Boulton	Apr 1973 to Sep 1975
113	Kevin Hector	Nov 1972 to Dec 1974
109	Jack Nicholas	Jan 1933 to Apr 1935
100	Geraint Williams	Nov 1988 to Nov 1990

Bobby Davison (left) made 105 consecutive League appearances for the Rams and also scored 106 goals for the club. Colin Todd (right), pictured with the PFA Player of the Year award he won in 1975, ran up 130 consecutive appearances in all matches.

Ever-Present in a Football League Season

Season	Games	
1888-89	22	L.Plackett.
1889-90	22	W.Roulstone.
1890-91	22	A.Goodall, J.McLachlan, W.Roulstone.
1891-92	26	J.Methven.
1892-93	30	J.Robinson.
1893-94	30	J.Allan, A.Goodall, J.McMillan, J.Methven.
1894-95	30	A.Goodall, J.Methven.
1895-96	30	A.Goodall, G.Kinsey, J.Miller, J.Robinson.
1896-97	30	A.Goodall, H.McQueen, J.Robinson.
1897-98	30	H.McQueen.
1898-99	34	—
1899-1900	34	J.May, J.Methven.
1900-01	34	R.Wombwell.
1901-02	34	—
1902-03	34	J.Methven.
1903-04	34	—
1904-05	34	B.Warren.
1905-06	38	—
1906-07	38	—
1907-08	38	—
1908-09	38	—
1909-10	38	J.Bauchop, A.Bentley.
1910-11	38	—
1911-12	38	E.Scattergood.
1912-13	38	J.Atkin.
1913-14	38	—
1914-15	38	T.Benfield, J.Moore.
1919-20	42	J.Atkin, G.Thornewell, H.Wightman.
1920-21	42	—
1921-22	42	A.Chandler.
1922-23	42	T.Crilly.
1923-24	42	—
1924-25	42	J.McIntyre, L.Murphy, B.Olney.
1925-26	42	S.Plackett.
1926-27	42	H.Thoms.
1927-28	42	—
1928-29	42	—
1929-30	42	H.Bedford.
1930-31	42	T.Cooper.
1931-32	42	—
1932-33	42	G.Collin.
1933-34	42	J.Nicholas.
1934-35	42	P.Ramage.
1935-36	42	J.Kirby, J.Nicholas.
1936-37	42	—
1937-38	42	D.Astley, J.Nicholas.
1938-39	42	R.Dix, D.Duncan, R.Hann, J.Nicholas.
1946-47	42	—
1947-48	42	—
1948-49	42	F.Broome.
1949-50	42	—
1950-51	42	—
1951-52	42	R.Harrison, R.Middleton.
1952-53	42	—
1953-54	42	—

Season	Games	
1954-55	42	—
1955-56	46	—
1956-57	46	—
1957-58	42	—
1958-59	42	G.Barrowcliffe.
1959-60	42	—
1960-61	42	A.Conwell.
1961-62	42	—
1962-63	42	J.Parry.
1963-64	42	G.Barrowcliffe, R.Matthews.
1964-65	42	A.Durban, J.Parry, R.Webster.
1965-66	42	G.Hughes, R.Matthews.
1966-67	42	—
1967-68	42	J.O'Hare.
1968-69	42	L.Green, R.McFarland, J.Robson.
1969-70	42	L.Green, A.Hinton.
1970-71	42	K.Hector, D.Mackay, J.O'Hare.
1971-72	42	C.Boulton, K.Hector.
1972-73	42	—
1973-74	42	C.Boulton, K.Hector.
1974-75	42	C.Boulton, B.Rioch.
1975-76	42	A.Gemmill, C.Todd.
1976-77	42	—
1977-78	42	D.Langan.
1978-79	42	S.Buckley.
1979-80	42	S.Buckley.
1980-81	42	R.Jones.
1981-82	42	—
1982-83	42	M.Brolly (41 plus 1 sub).
1983-84	42	—
1984-85	46	S.Buckley, R.Davison.
1985-86	46	S.Buckley, R.MacLaren, G.Micklewhite.
1986-87	42	J.Gregory, R.MacLaren, G.Micklewhite.
1987-88	40	N.Callaghan, P.Shilton, G.Williams.
1988-89	38	P.Blades, M.Forsyth, P.Shilton.
1989-90	38	M.Forsyth, D.Saunders, G.Williams.
1990-91	38	D.Saunders.
1991-92	46	A.Comyn.

Most Ever-Present Seasons
5   A.Goodall, J.Methven.
4   S.Buckley, J.Nicholas.
3   C.Boulton, K.Hector, J.Robinson.

Progressive Goalscoring Records

Sandy Higgins set the first target in Derby County's opening League season scoring 11 League goals and adding another in the FA Cup. This chart shows how individual scoring records have been equalled and beaten since then.

	League		All Matches			League		All Matches	
1888-89	Sandy Higgins	11	Sandy Higgins	12	1900-01	Steve Bloomer	24		
1889-90	Sandy Higgins	14	Sandy Higgins	14	1907-08	Alf Bentley	27		
1890-91			John Goodall	14	1908-09			Alf Bentley	32
1891-92	John Goodall	15	John Goodall	15	1909-10	Alf Bentley	30		
1893-94	Steve Bloomer	19	John McMillan	21	1929-30	Harry Bedford	30		
1895-96	Steve Bloomer	22	Steve Bloomer	27	1930-31	Jack Bowers	37	Jack Bowers	39
1896-97	Steve Bloomer	24	Steve Bloomer	31	1932-33			Jack Bowers	43
1898-99	Steve Bloomer	24			1956-57	Ray Straw	37		

Steve Bloomer broke the Rams' scoring record three times. His 28 England goals were a record until 1956.

Individual Scoring Feats

Six goals in a game

S.Bloomer v Sheffield Wednesday (h), Division One ....21 Jan 1899

Five goals in a game

A.Higgins v Aston Villa (h), Football League ....28 Dec 1889
J.McMillan v Wolves (h), Football League.............10 Jan 1891
J.Moore v Crystal Palace (h), Division Two ....25 Dec 1922
H.Gallacher v Blackburn Rovers (a), Division One .....15 Dec 1934
R.Davies v Luton Town (h), Division One ....29 Mar 1975
K.Hector v Finn Harps (h), UEFA Cup ....15 Sep 1976

Four goals in a game

A.Higgins v Aston Villa (h), Football League ....9 Mar 1889
S.Bloomer v Wolves (h), Division One ....19 Sep 1896
J.Stevenson v Blackburn Rovers (h), Division One .....21 Nov 1896
A.Bentley v Barnsley (a), Division Two ....14 Sep 1907
A.Bentley v Leeds City (h), Division Two...............19 Oct 1907
A.Bentley v Leeds City (a), Division Two ....19 Sep 1908
H.Leonard v Fulham (h), Division Two ....4 Nov 1911
J.Lyons v Rotherham County (h), Division Two ....29 Apr 1922
H.Storer v Bristol City (a), Division Two ....29 Sep 1923
H.Storer v Nelson (h), Division Two ....26 Dec 1923
A.Fairclough v Fulham (h), Division Two.............13 Sep 1924
H.Bedford v Bradford City (a), FA Cup ....8 Jan 1927
J.Whitehouse v Sheffield Wednesday (h), Division One 19 Mar 1927
H.Bedford v Cardiff City (h), Division One............31 Mar 1928
H.Bedford v West Ham United (h), Division One ....8 Dec 1928
G.Stephenson v Grimsby Town (h), Division One ......14 Dec 1929
J.Bowers v Chelsea (h), Division One ....6 Dec 1930
J.Bowers v Portsmouth (h), Division One..............7 Feb 1931

J.Bowers v Manchester United (h), Division One ....18 Apr 1931
J.Bowers v Tottenham Hotspur (h), Division One ....7 Apr 1934
J.Bowers v Manchester United (h), Division One........5 Sep 1936
J.Stamps v Luton Town (a), FA Cup ....5 Jan 1946
H.Carter v Sunderland (h), Division One ....14 Feb 1948
J.Stamps v Blackpool (h) Division One ....30 Sep 1950
J.Lee v Sunderland (h), Division One ....16 Dec 1950
A.Ackerman v Accrington S (h), Division Three North   7 Apr 1956
A.Hinton v Stockport County (h), FL Cup..............4 Sep 1968
B.Rioch v Tottenham Hotspur (h), Division One ....16 Oct 1976
K.Wilson v Hartlepool United (h), FL Cup ....29 Aug 1984

Three goals in a game

18 times S.Bloomer.
11   J.Bowers
10   H.Bedford.
 6   K.Hector.
 5   J.Bauchop, A.Bentley, J.Goodall
 4   A.Durban, J.Stamps.
 3   D.Astley, W.Curry, R.Davison, C.George, J.Lee,
      D.Saunders, R.Straw.
 2   K.Havenhand, J.McMillan, J.Morris, J.Parry, B.Spilsbury.
 1   T.Arkesden, R.Barclay, H.Barnes, A.Biley, J.Boag,
      H.Carter, J.Chandler, S.Crooks, R.Davies, A.Fairclough,
      N.Fordham, H.Gallacher, A.Garner, E.Garry, A.Gemmill,
      J.Gill, M.Harford, R.Harrison, W.Hodgkinson,
      W.Hodgson, L.James, H.Leonard, J.Miller, J.Moore,
      A.Morrison, J.O'Hare, W.Paterson, J.Pye, G.Stephenson,
      R.Stockill, H.Storer, B.Warren, P.Williams, K.Wilson.

Dean Saunders, seen here wheeling away after scoring for the Rams, achieved three hat-tricks for the club before his record move.

Leading Goalscorers
1888-89 to 1991-92

	League		All Matches			League		All Matches	
1888-89	A.Higgins	11	A.Higgins	12	1948-49	F.Broome	14	W.Steel	15
1889-90	A.Higgins	14	A.Higgins	14		W.Steel	14		
1890-91	J.Goodall	13	J.Goodall	14	1949-50	J.Stamps	22	J.Stamps	29
1891-92	J.Goodall	15	J.Goodall	15	1950-51	J.Lee	28	J.Lee	29
1892-93	J.Goodall	13	J.Goodall	14	1951-52	J.Parry	11	J.Morris	11
1893-94	S.Bloomer	19	J.McMillan	21				J.Parry	11
1894-95	S.Bloomer	10	S.Bloomer	11	1952-53	J.Lee	16	J.Lee	17
1895-96	S.Bloomer	22	S.Bloomer	27	1953-54	H.McLaren	11	H.McLaren	11
1896-97	S.Bloomer	24	S.Bloomer	31	1954-55	J.Dunn	8	J.Dunn	8
1897-98	S.Bloomer	15	S.Bloomer	20		T.Powell	8	T.Powell	8
1898-99	S.Bloomer	24	S.Bloomer	30				J.Pye	8
1899-1900	S.Bloomer	19	S.Bloomer	19	1955-56	J.Parry	24	J.Parry	27
1900-01	S.Bloomer	24	S.Bloomer	24	1956-57	R.Straw	37	R.Straw	37
1901-02	S.Bloomer	15	S.Bloomer	18	1957-58	R.Ryan	14	R.Ryan	14
1902-03	S.Bloomer	12	S.Bloomer	13	1958-59	J.Parry	15	J.Parry	16
1903-04	S.Bloomer	20	S.Bloomer	25	1959-60	P.Thompson	11	P.Thompson	12
1904-05	S.Bloomer	13	S.Bloomer	13	1960-61	W.Curry	19	W.Curry	20
1905-06	S.Bloomer	12	S.Bloomer	12	1961-62	W.Curry	18	W.Curry	25
1906-07	G.Davis	8	J.Long	9	1962-63	W.Curry	21	W.Curry	22
	J.Long	8						B.Hutchinson	22
1907-08	A.Bentley	27	A.Bentley	28	1963-64	A.Durban	9	A.Durban	11
1908-09	A.Bentley	24	A.Bentley	32	1964-65	A.Durban	22	A.Durban	24
1909-10	A.Bentley	30	A.Bentley	31		E.Thomas	22	E.Thomas	24
1910-11	S.Bloomer	20	S.Bloomer	24	1965-66	A.Durban	17	A.Durban	17
1911-12	S.Bloomer	18	S.Bloomer	19				E.Thomas	17
1912-13	H.Leonard	15	H.Leonard	15	1966-67	K.Hector	16	K.Hector	16
1913-14	H.Barnes	24	H.Barnes	25	1967-68	K.Hector	21	K.Hector	24
1914-15	J.Moore	22	J.Moore	22	1968-69	K.Hector	16	K.Hector	20
1919-20	N.Burton	12	N.Burton	13	1969-70	J.O'Hare	13	K.Hector	16
	H.Leonard	12						J.O'Hare	16
1920-21	W.Paterson	8	W.Paterson	8	1970-71	J.O'Hare	13	J.O'Hare	15
1921-22	J.Moore	16	J.Moore	17	1971-72	A.Hinton	15	A.Hinton	20
1922-23	J.Lyons	11	J.Moore	16	1972-73	K.Hector	14	K.Hector	23
	J.Moore	11			1973-74	K.Hector	19	K.Hector	19
1923-24	H.Storer	24	H.Storer	27	1974-75	B.Rioch	15	K.Hector	21
1924-25	A.Fairclough	22	A.Fairclough	22	1975-76	C.George	16	C.George	24
1925-26	H.Bedford	27	H.Bedford	28	1976-77	L.James	9	C.George	17
1926-27	H.Bedford	22	H.Bedford	26	1977-78	C.George	11	G.Daly	12
	J.Gill	22			1978-79	G.Daly	13	G.Daly	13
1927-28	H.Bedford	27	H.Bedford	28	1979-80	A.Biley	9	A.Biley	9
1928-29	H.Bedford	27	H.Bedford	30	1980-81	D.Swindlehurst	11	D.Swindlehurst	11
1929-30	H.Bedford	30	H.Bedford	31	1981-82	K.Wilson	9	K.Wilson	9
1930-31	J.Bowers	37	J.Bowers	39	1982-83	R.Davison	8	D.Swindlehurst	11
1931-32	J.Bowers	25	J.Bowers	26		D.Swindlehurst	8		
1932-33	J.Bowers	35	J.Bowers	43	1983-84	R.Davison	14	R.Davison	18
1933-34	J.Bowers	34	J.Bowers	37	1984-85	R.Davison	24	R.Davison	26
1934-35	H.Gallacher	23	H.Gallacher	24	1985-86	R.Davison	17	R.Davison	23
1935-36	H.Gallacher	15	H.Gallacher	16	1986-87	R.Davison	19	R.Davison	22
1936-37	D.Astley	25	D.Astley	29	1987-88	P.Gee	6	P.Gee	6
1937-38	D.Astley	17	D.Astley	17		J.Gregory	6	J.Gregory	6
1938-39	R.Dix	16	R.Dix	16	1988-89	D.Saunders	14	D.Saunders	15
	D.McCulloch	16	D.McCulloch	16	1989-90	D.Saunders	11	D.Saunders	21
1946-47	H.Carter	19	H.Carter	21	1990-91	D.Saunders	17	D.Saunders	21
1947-48	H.Carter	15	R.Harrison	18	1991-92	P.Williams	13	P.Williams	16
	R.Harrison	15							

Raich Carter, leading scorer in the first two post-war seasons, the second time jointly with Reg Harrison.

John Gregory (arm raised) and Phil Gee (9) were joint top scorers in 1987-8 with six goals each, the lowest individual totals of any leading marksmen in the club's history.

Jack Bowers' 43 League and Cup goals in 1932-3 is a Rams record for one season.

Kevin Hector is the Rams' appearances record holder in both League and all matches and stands second in the list of leading scorers in all games.

Top 20 Goalscorers

	All Matches			*League Matches*	
1.	Steve Bloomer	332	1.	Steve Bloomer	293
2.	Kevin Hector	201	2.	Jack Bowers	167
3.	Jack Bowers	183	3.	Kevin Hector	155
4.	Harry Bedford	152	4.	Harry Bedford	142
5.	Jack Stamps	126	5.	Jack Parry	105
=6.	Alf Bentley	112	6.	Sammy Crooks	101
=6.	Alan Durban	112	7.	Jack Stamps	100
8.	Sammy Crooks	111	8.	Alf Bentley	99
9.	Jack Parry	110	9.	Alan Durban	93
10.	Bobby Davison	106	10.	Bobby Davison	91
11.	Jackie Whitehouse	86	11.	Jackie Whitehouse	82
12.	John Goodall	85	12.	John Goodall	76
13.	Alan Hinton	83	13.	Jimmy Moore	75
14.	Jimmy Moore	82	14.	Horace Barnes	74
15.	John O'Hare	81	15.	Harry Leonard	72
16.	Horace Barnes	78	16.	Jimmy Bauchop	68
17.	Bill Curry	76	17.	Bill Curry	67
18.	Harry Leonard	73	18.	John O'Hare	65
19.	Jimmy Bauchop	72	19.	Alan Hinton	64
20.	Douglas Duncan	69	20.	Douglas Duncan	63

Totals include League, FA Cup, League Cup, League Test Match, League Play-offs, FA Charity Shield, European Cup, UEFA Cup, Texaco Cup, Freight/Rover Trophy and Full Members' Cup. The Watney Cup is not included as it was played out of season and, in some years, with experimental laws.

Top 20 Appearances

	All Matches			*League Matches*	
1.	Kevin Hector	581/8	1.	Kevin Hector	478/8
2.	Ron Webster	530/5	2.	Jack Parry	482/1
3.	Roy McFarland	525/5	3.	Geoff Barrowcliffe	475
4.	Steve Bloomer	525	4.	Steve Bloomer	474
5.	Jack Parry	516/1	5.	Jimmy Methven	458
6.	Jimmy Methven	511	6.	Ron Webster	451/4
7.	Geoff Barrowcliffe	503	7.	Roy McFarland	437/5
8.	Sammy Crooks	445	8.	Sammy Crooks	408
9.	Archie Goodall	423	=9.	Archie Goodall	380
10.	Steve Powell	409/11	=9.	Tommy Powell	380
11.	Tommy Powell	406	11.	Steve Powell	342/10
12.	Archie Gemmill	404	12.	Johnny McIntyre	349
13.	Alan Durban	388/15	13.	Jack Nicholas	347
14.	Jack Nicholas	383	14.	Alan Durban	336/10
15.	Colin Todd	371	15.	Jack Barker	326
16.	Johnny McIntyre	369	16.	Archie Gemmill	324
17.	Steve Buckley	366	17.	Steve Buckley	323
18.	Jack Barker	353	18.	George Collin	309
19.	Colin Boulton	344	19.	Jack Atkin	308
20.	George Collin	334	20.	Bert Mozley	297

Totals include League, FA Cup, League Cup, League Test Match, League Play-offs, FA Charity Shield, European Cup, UEFA Cup, Texaco Cup, Freight/Rover Trophy and Full Members' Cup. The Watney Cup is not included as it was played out of season and, in some years, with experimental laws.

Three main officers of the Derby County Former Players' Association, pictured in earlier times as Ian Hall (now the Association's secretary) signs for Mansfield Town watched by Rams manager Tim Ward (chairman of the Association) and Mansfield boss Raich Carter (Association president).

Rams Career Records 1884-1992

Below are the career records (League, FA Cup, and League Cup) of every Rams first-team player since the club's first FA Cup match in 1884. The years given are the first years of seasons. Thus, 1946 means 1946-7. In the 'Others' list are all the competitions not accounted for in the rest of the table. This list contains figures for the 1894-5 Test Match, 1975 FA Charity Shield, Texaco Cup, European Cup, UEFA Cup, Freight/Rover Trophy, Full Members' Cup and 1991-2 League Play-offs. It should be noted that in 1889-90 the Rams fielded only ten men at Preston. Substitute appearances are given to the right of full appearances (eg 26/2).

Player	Played	League App	League Gls	FA Cup App	FA Cup Gls	Lg Cup App	Lg Cup Gls	Others App	Others Gls	TOTAL App	TOTAL Gls
ABBOTT S.W.	1911	1	0	0	0	0	0	0	0	1	0
ABBOTT W.L.	1893	4	1	0	0	0	0	0	0	4	1
ABDALLAH T.	1920-21	15	1	0	0	0	0	0	0	15	1
ABLETT G.I.	1984	3/3	0	0	0	0	0	2	0	5/3	0
ACKERMAN A.A.E.	1954-56	36	21	0	0	0	0	0	0	36	21
ADLINGTON T.	1956-61	36	0	1	0	4	0	0	0	41	0
AINSWORTH C.	1908	8	0	0	0	0	0	0	0	8	0
AINSWORTH F.	1919	1	0	0	0	0	0	0	0	1	0
ALDERMAN A.E.	1928-33	21	0	3	0	0	0	0	0	24	0
ALLAN J.	1893-94	36	5	4	1	0	0	0	0	40	6
ALLEN H.	1898-99	15	3	5	2	0	0	0	0	20	5
ALTON T.W.	1937	3	0	0	0	0	0	0	0	3	0
ANTONIO G.R.	1946-47	18	2	0	0	0	0	0	0	18	2
ARKESDEN T.A.	1898-1900	50	14	1	0	0	0	0	0	51	14
ARMSTRONG A.	1906-07	4	1	0	0	0	0	0	0	4	1
ASTLEY D.J.	1936-38	93	45	5	4	0	0	0	0	98	49
ATKIN J.T.	1907-21	308	3	17	0	0	0	0	0	325	3
ATTLEY B.R.	1981-83	54/1	1	2	0	4	0	0	0	60/1	1
BACON A.	1925-27	8	3	1	0	0	0	0	0	9	3
BAGSHAW J.J.	1906-19	226	6	14	0	0	0	0	0	240	6
BAILEY A.D.	1971	1	0	0	0	0	0	2/1	0	3/1	0
BAILEY H.P.	1909	3	0	0	0	0	0	0	0	3	0
BAILEY L.A.	1937-38	26	0	2	0	0	0	0	0	28	0
BAKER J.	1890	8	0	2	0	0	0	0	0	10	0
BAKER W.E.	1914-20	44	7	0	0	0	0	0	0	44	7
BAKEWELL G.	1884-90	49	9	15	3	0	0	0	0	64	12
BALKWILL A.	1901	11	1	0	0	0	0	0	0	11	1
BANOVIC V.	1981-83	35	0	0	0	3	0	0	0	38	0
BARBOUR T.	1908-20	273	3	21	0	0	0	0	0	294	3
BARCLAY R.	1928-30	61	23	3	3	0	0	0	0	64	26
BARKER F.C.	1903-04	4	2	0	0	0	0	0	0	4	2
BARKER J.W.	1928-38	326	2	27	0	0	0	0	0	353	2
BARKER R.	1967-68	30/8	12	0	0	7	2	0	0	37/8	14
BARNES H.	1908-13	153	74	14	4	0	0	0	0	167	78

Player	Played	League App	League Gls	FA Cup App	FA Cup Gls	Lg Cup App	Lg Cup Gls	Others App	Others Gls	TOTAL App	TOTAL Gls
BARNES J.	1921	4	0	0	0	0	0	0	0	4	0
BARROWCLIFFE G.	1951-65	475	37	22	1	6	1	0	0	503	39
BARTLETT P.	1977-79	7/6	0	0	0	0	0	0	0	7/6	0
BARTON J.S.	1981-83	68/1	1	8	0	5	0	0	0	81/1	1
BAUCHOP J.R.	1909-12	126	68	9	4	0	0	0	0	135	72
BAYLISS H.H.R.	1920	1	0	0	0	0	0	0	0	1	0
BEDFORD H.	1925-30	203	142	15	10	0	0	0	0	218	152
BELL C.	1950-54	77	2	2	0	0	0	0	0	79	2
BELL D.	1934-38	52	0	3	0	0	0	0	0	55	0
BELLHOUSE E.W.	1888	2	0	0	0	0	0	0	0	2	0
BENFIELD T.C.	1914	38	15	1	0	0	0	0	0	39	15
BENTLEY A.	1906-10	151	99	17	13	0	0	0	0	168	112
BESTWICK T.H.	1886-88	1	0	6	0	0	0	0	0	7	0
BETTS A.C.	1911-13	71	0	3	0	0	0	0	0	74	0
BEVAN F.W.	1907-09	51	17	1	1	0	0	0	0	52	18
BIGGINS S.J.	1984-85	8/2	1	1	0	0	0	1/1	0	10/3	1
BILEY A.P.	1979-80	47	19	2	0	2	0	0	0	51	19
BIRD D.W.C.	1934-35	5	2	0	0	0	0	0	0	5	2
BIRDSALL G.	1921	8	0	0	0	0	0	0	0	8	0
BLACKETT J.	1900	17	1	0	0	0	0	0	0	17	1
BLADES P.A.	1982-89	157/9	1	12	0	9/3	0	8/2	0	186/14	1
BLESSINGTON J.	1899	2	0	0	0	0	0	0	0	2	0
BLOCKLEY J.P.	1977	0	0	1	0	0	0	0	0	1	0
BLOOMER P.	1895	1	0	0	0	0	0	0	0	1	0
BLOOMER S.	1892-1905 1910-13	474	293	50	38	0	0	1	1	525	332
BLOORE V.F.	1933-34	15	0	0	0	0	0	0	0	15	0
BOAG J.	1896-1903	117	27	23	10	0	0	0	0	140	37
BOSWORTH S.	1898	2	1	0	0	0	0	0	0	2	1
BOULTON C.D.	1964-77	272	0	29	0	16	0	27	0	344	0
BOULTON F.P.	1938-45	39	0	7	0	0	0	0	0	46	0
BOURNE J.	1970-76	35/14	9	7/3	2	2/1	0	5/6	3	48/24	14
BOWDEN O.	1932-33	10	1	0	0	0	0	0	0	10	1
BOWER T.A.	1886	0	0	1	0	0	0	0	0	1	0
BOWERS J.A.	1959-65	65	19	0	0	3	1	0	0	68	20

Player	Played	League App	League Gls	FA Cup App	FA Cup Gls	Lg Cup App	Lg Cup Gls	Others App	Others Gls	TOTAL App	TOTAL Gls
CHERRY S.R.	1979-83	77	0	8	0	5	0	0	0	90	0
CHESTERS C.W.	1977-78	6/3	1	0	0	0/1	0	0	0	6/4	1
CHIEDOZIE J.O.	1988	2	0	0	0	0	0	0	0	2	0
CHOLERTON W.	1966	1	0	0	0	0	0	0	0	1	0
CHRISTIE T.	1984-85	65	22	7	3	5	0	2	1	79	26
CLAMP E.	1948	1	0	0	0	0	0	0	0	1	0
CLARK B.	1954-57	16	0	1	0	0	0	0	0	17	0
CLARK J.	1978-80	48/5	3	4	0	4	0	0	0	56/5	3
CLAYTON J.	1978-81	21/3	4	1	0	1/1	0	0	0	23/4	4
CLEAVER F.I.	1905-06	11	3	1	0	0	0	0	0	12	3
CLEEVELY N.R.	1964-66	15/1	3	1	0	1	0	0	0	17/1	3
CLIFTON G.	1886-88	1	0	2	0	0	0	0	0	3	0
COLEMAN S.	1991	43	2	3	0	3	0	3	0	52	2
COLLIN G.	1927-35	309	0	25	0	0	0	0	0	334	0
COMYN A.J.	1991	46	1	3	1	3	0	3	1	55	3
CONWELL A.	1959-61	98	1	2	0	7	0	0	0	107	1
COOKE J.A.	1898-99	11	2	0	0	0	0	0	0	11	2
COOP M.A.	1981	17/1	0	1	0	2	0	0	0	20/1	0
COOPER G.F.	1885	0	0	3	0	0	0	0	0	3	0
COOPER L.	1885-91	50	23	8	4	0	0	0	0	58	27
COOPER T.	1925-34	248	1	18	0	0	0	0	0	266	1
CORISH R.	1977	0/1	0	0	0	0	0	0	0	0/1	0
COWELL W.	1926	1	0	0	0	0	0	0	0	1	0
COX J.D.	1890-99	212	7	25	0	0	0	1	0	238	7
CRAWFORD A.	1977-79	16/5	4	0/2	0	1/1	1	0	0	17/8	5
CRAWFORD J.	1900-01	42	1	1	0	0	0	0	0	43	1
CRESSWELL P.F.	1954-56	12	2	2	0	0	0	0	0	14	2
CRILLY T.	1922-27	197	0	14	0	0	0	0	0	211	0
CROOKS S.D.	1927-46	408	101	37	10	0	0	0	0	445	111
CROPPER W.	1886	0	0	1	0	0	0	0	0	1	0
CROSS S.C.	1986-91	42/31	3	3/2	0	4/4	0	3/5	2	52/42	5
CROWSHAW A.A.	1956-57	18	6	0	0	0	0	0	0	18	6
CRUMP F.	1899	6	1	0	0	0	0	0	0	6	1
CULLEN M.J.	1962-64	24	5	1	0	1	0	0	0	26	5
CURRAN E.	1977	26	2	3	0	0	0	0	0	29	2
CURRY W.M.	1960-64	148	67	8	4	8	5	0	0	164	76
CUSHLOW R.	1948-49	2	0	0	0	0	0	0	0	2	0
DAFT T.	1890	3	0	0	0	0	0	0	0	3	0
DALY G.A.	1976-79	111/1	31	5	2	5	1	0	0	121/1	34
DALZIEL I.	1981-82	22	4	1/1	0	3/1	0	0	0	26/2	4
DANIEL P.A.	1965-78	188/7	7	18/1	0	16/1	1	15	0	237/9	8
DARWIN G.H.	1957-60	94	32	3	1	0	0	0	0	97	33
DAVIDSON J.S.	1989-91	7/5	0	0/2	0	1	0	0/1	0	8/8	0
DAVIES F.	1902	1	0	0	0	0	0	0	0	1	0
DAVIES G.	1953-61	200	5	9	0	4	0	0	0	213	5
DAVIES R.	1971-75	120/16	34	12/4	8	5	1	7/2	1	144/22	44

Player	Played	League App	League Gls	FA Cup App	FA Cup Gls	Lg Cup App	Lg Cup Gls	Others App	Others Gls	TOTAL App	TOTAL Gls
BOWERS J.W.A.	1928-36	203	167	17	16	0	0	0	0	220	183
BOWLER G.H.	1912	1	0	0	0	0	0	0	0	1	0
BOXLEY H.	1919	7	0	0	0	0	0	0	0	7	0
BOYD J.M.	1935-36	9	1	0	0	0	0	0	0	9	1
BRADBURY J.J.L.	1899	7	1	0	0	0	0	0	0	7	1
BRAND R.	1890	3	0	0	0	0	0	0	0	3	0
BRINTON J.V.	1937	8	2	0	0	0	0	0	0	8	2
BRISCOE R.D.	1989-90	10/3	1	0	0	4/1	0	0	0	14/4	1
BROLLY M.J.	1982	41/1	4	3	0	5	1	0	0	49/1	5
BROMAGE E.	1888-89	17	0	1	0	0	0	0	0	18	0
BROMAGE E.	1923-26	4	2	2	1	0	0	0	0	6	3
BROMAGE H.	1899-1901	5	0	0	0	0	0	0	0	5	0
BROOKS G.	1914	33	0	1	0	0	0	0	0	34	0
BROOKS J.T.	1894	3	0	0	0	0	0	0	0	3	0
BROOME F.H.	1946-49	112	45	7	0	0	0	0	0	119	45
BROWN G.	1956-59	53	20	1	0	0	0	0	0	54	20
BROWN H.T.	1949-50	37	0	3	0	0	0	0	0	40	0
BUCHANAN J.	1954-56	32	12	0	0	0	0	0	0	32	12
BUCKLEY F.C.	1911-13	92	3	5	0	0	0	0	0	97	3
BUCKLEY S.	1977-85	323	21	19	1	21	3	3	0	366	25
BULLIONS J.L.	1945-47	17	0	12	0	0	0	0	0	29	0
BUNYAN C.	1889-91	9	0	2	0	0	0	0	0	11	0
BURNS K.	1982										
BURRIDGE J.	1983-84	36/2	2	3	0	4	0	0	0	43/2	2
BURTON J.H.	1984	6	0	0	0	2	0	0	0	8	0
BURTON N.	1897-98	10	3	0	0	0	0	0	0	10	3
BUTLIN B.D.	1919-20	56	16	5	2	0	0	0	0	61	18
BUTTERWORTH C.E.	1891	1	0	5	0	0	0	3	1	9	1
BUXTON I.R.	1959-67	144/1	41	2	0	11	2	0	0	157/1	43
CALLAGHAN N.I.	1986-88	88	11	4	1	3	0	5	1	100	13
CALLAN W.	1990	1	0	0	0	0	0	0	0	1	0
CALLENDER R.H.	1921	5	0	0	0	0	0	0	0	5	0
CAMPBELL R.M.	1983	11	4	0	0	1	0	0	0	12	4
CARGILL D.A.	1958-60	56	8	3	3	0	0	0	0	59	11
CARLIN W.	1968-70	89	14	5	0	14	2	0	0	108	16
CARR W.P.	1925-32	102	0	7	0	0	0	0	0	109	0
CARRUTHERS E.	1976	0/1	0	0	0	0	0	0	0	0/1	0
CARTER H.S.	1945-47	63	34	20	16	0	0	0	0	83	50
CARTER S.C.	1978-79	32/1	1	1	0	1	0	0	0	34/1	1
CASKEY W.T.	1978-79	26/2	3	0	0	1	0	1	0	28/2	3
CHALK M.P.G.	1991	4/3	1	3	1	0	0	0/1	0	7/4	2
CHALMERS B.	1902	20	1	2	0	0	0	0	0	22	1
CHANDLER A.	1919-24	169	0	14	0	0	0	0	0	183	0
CHANDLER J.G.	1985-86	45/1	9	7	4	7	3	2/1	0	61/2	16
CHATTERTON W.	1884-88	5	1	1	0	0	0	0	0	6	1

Derby County with the FA Cup in 1946. Back row (left to right): Jimmy Bullions, Jack Nicholas, Vic Woodley, Leon Leuty, Jack Howe, Chick Musson. Front row: Stuart McMillan (manager), Reg Harrison, Raich Carter, Jack Stamps, Peter Doherty, Dally Duncan, Dave Willis (trainer).

Player	Played	League App	League Gls	FA Cup App	FA Cup Gls	Lg Cup App	Lg Cup Gls	Others App	Others Gls	TOTAL App	TOTAL Gls
FLETCHER T.	1904-06	33	8	2	1	0	0	0	0	35	9
FLOWERS J.	1885	0	0	2	0	0	0	0	0	2	0
FORD D.	1898	6	0	0	0	0	0	0	0	6	0
FORDHAM N.M.	1913-14	13	5	1	1	0	0	0	0	14	6
FORMAN F.	1894	8	0	0	0	0	0	0	0	8	0
FORMAN F.R.	1892	4	3	0	0	0	0	0	0	4	3
FORSYTH M.E.	1986-91	234	5	10	0	26	1	14	0	284	6
FOSTER G.W.	1982	30	0	3	0	5	0	0	0	38	0
FOX W.	1925	1	0	0	0	0	0	0	0	1	0
FRAIL J.	1897	10	0	0	0	0	0	0	0	10	0
FRANCIS K.D.M.	1989-90	0/10	0	1/2	1	1/2	0	0/1	0	2/15	1
FRANCIS P.O.	1893-95	16	6	3	1	0	0	1	0	20	7
FRITH R.W.	1910	1	0	0	0	0	0	0	0	1	0
FRYER J.S.	1897-1902	173	0	26	0	0	0	0	0	199	0
FULTON W.	1901	13	1	0	0	0	0	0	0	13	1
FUTCHER P.	1982-83	35	0	4	0	1	0	0	0	40	0
GABBIADINI M.	1991	20	6	0	0	0	0	2	1	22	7
GALLACHER H.K.	1934-35	51	38	4	2	0	0	0	0	55	40
GALLOWAY S.R.	1922-24	66	25	10	5	0	0	0	0	76	30
GAMBLE F.	1981-82	5/1	2	1	0	1	0	0	0	7/1	2
GARDEN H.W.	1892	1	0	0	0	0	0	0	0	1	0
GARDNER W.	1920	5	1	0	0	0	0	0	0	5	1
GARNER A.	1983-87	48/23	17	4/3	2	1/4	0	5	1	58/30	20
GARRY E.	1907-12	120	18	9	1	0	0	0	0	129	19
GEE P.J.	1985-91	107/17	26	6/1	2	11/2	3	7/1	0	131/21	31
GEMMILL A.	1970-77, 1982-83	324	25	35	6	20	1	25	1	404	33
GEORGE C.F.	1975-78	117	36	11	6	10	4	9	10	147	56
GIBSON A.M.	1980-81	0/2	0	0	0	0/1	0	0	0	0/3	0
GILCHRIST L.	1904	11	0	0	0	0	0	0	0	11	0
GILL J.	1925-27	65	35	1	0	0	0	0	0	66	35
GILLETT L.F.	1884	0	0	0	0	0	0	1	1	1	1
GODDARD P.	1988-89	49	15	1/1	0	7	2	5	1	62/1	18
GOLBY J.A.	1922	1	0	0	0	0	0	0	0	1	0
GOODALL A.L.	1889-1902	380	48	42	4	0	0	1	0	423	52
GOODALL J.	1889-98	211	76	26	9	0	0	1	0	238	85
GOODCHILD G.	1896	2	0	0	0	0	0	0	0	2	0
GORHAM C.	1884	0	0	1	0	0	0	0	0	1	0
GRANT A.F.	1946-47	12	0	3	0	0	0	0	0	15	0
GREEN J.	1894	7	0	0	0	0	0	0	0	7	0
GREEN L.	1968-70	107	0	5	0	17	0	0	0	129	0
GREEN R.E.	1931	1	0	0	0	0	0	0	0	1	0
GREENWOOD R.T.	1978-79	26/5	1	1	0	1	0	0	0	28/5	1
GREGORY J.C.	1985-87	103	22	9	1	8	0	4/1	0	124/1	23
GRIMES W.J.	1909-14	161	11	8	0	0	0	0	0	169	11
GROVES A.	1933-35	64	17	5	1	0	0	0	0	69	18

Player	Played	League App	League Gls	FA Cup App	FA Cup Gls	Lg Cup App	Lg Cup Gls	Others App	Others Gls	TOTAL App	TOTAL Gls
DAVIS G.H.	1900-07	134	27	21	2	0	0	0	0	155	29
DAVIS J.W.	1904-09	138	9	15	4	0	0	0	0	153	13
DAVISON R.	1982-87, 1991	213/3	91	11	7	18	6	4	2	246/3	106
DAYKIN R.B.	1925-30	83	5	2	0	0	0	0	0	85	5
DEACY E.S.	1959-61	4	1	0	0	0	0	0	0	4	1
DEVINE S.B.	1983-84	10/1	0	0	0	0	0	0	0	10/1	0
DEVONSHIRE W.J.	1914	7	1	0	0	0	0	0	0	7	1
DILLY T.	1907	10	2	0	0	0	0	0	0	10	2
DIX R.W.	1936-38	94	35	2	0	0	0	0	0	96	35
DOBBS A.	1933	3	1	0	0	0	0	0	0	3	1
DOCHERTY J.	1893-94	35	0	3	0	0	0	0	0	38	0
DOCKERY G.	1893	5	0	0	0	0	0	0	0	5	0
DOHERTY P.D.	1945-46	15	7	10	10	0	0	0	0	25	17
DONAGHY E.	1926	6	0	0	0	0	0	0	0	6	0
DONALD D.M.	1909-11	45	2	0	0	0	0	0	0	45	2
DRAPER D.	1966	8	1	1	0	0	0	0	0	9	1
DUNCAN D.	1931-46	261	63	28	6	0	0	0	0	289	69
DUNCAN J.P.	1978-80	35/1	12	0/1	0	2	0	0	0	37/2	12
DUNN G.	1890	1	0	0	0	0	0	0	0	1	0
DUNN J.	1952-54	57	21	1	0	0	0	0	0	58	21
DURBAN W.A.	1963-72	336/10	93	16/3	10	30/1	8	6/1	1	388/15	112
EADIE W.P.	1914	31	0	0	0	0	0	0	0	31	0
EDWARDS J.W.	1908	2	1	0	0	0	0	0	0	2	1
EGGLESTON T.	1945	1	1	0	0	0	0	0	0	1	1
EKINS F.G.	1891-92	18	3	0	0	0	0	0	0	18	3
EMERY S.R.	1979-81	73/2	4	3	0	2	0	0	0	78/2	4
EMSON P.D.	1978-82	112/15	13	1/3	0	4/3	0	0	0	117/21	13
EVANS G.	1884-86	0	0	5	6	0	0	0	0	5	6
EVANS W.	1907	1	0	0	0	0	0	0	0	1	0
EXHAM P.G.	1884	0	0	1	0	0	0	0	0	1	0
FABIAN A.H.	1931-32	12	1	4	2	0	0	0	0	16	3
FAGAN F.	1959-60	24	6	1	0	0	0	0	0	25	6
FAIRCLOUGH A.	1924-26	37	26	0	0	0	0	0	0	37	26
FAZACKERLEY S.N.	1925	3	2	0	0	0	0	0	0	3	2
FELLOWS P.J.	1913	2	1	0	0	0	0	0	0	2	1
FEREDAY D.T.	1928-29	16	2	1	0	0	0	0	0	17	2
FERGUSON A.	1888-90	49	0	2	0	0	0	0	0	51	0
FERGUSON R.B.	1962-65	121	0	8	0	0	0	0	0	129	0
FIFE	1889	2	0	0	0	0	0	0	0	2	0
FINDLAY J.W.	1983	1	0	0	0	0	0	0	0	1	0
FINDLAY T.	1922-23	4	0	0	0	0	0	0	0	4	0
FISHER W.	1896	11	5	4	3	0	0	0	0	15	8
FLANDERS F.	1910	13	0	3	0	0	0	0	0	16	0
FLETCHER F.	1894	3	0	0	0	0	0	0	0	3	0

Les Green (left), Dave Mackay (centre) and Alan Durban in training at the Baseball Ground in 1969.

Hughie Gallacher (left), Alan Hughes (centre) and Jack Nicholas at St Pancras station in December 1934, on their way to a match at Chelsea.

Player	Played	League App	Gls	FA Cup App	Gls	Lg Cup App	Gls	Others App	Gls	TOTAL App	Gls
HINTON A.T.	1967-75	240/13	64	18/2	3	23/1	11	14/5	5	295/21	83
HODGKINSON W.H.	1903	16	9	0	0	0	0	0	0	16	9
HODGSON W.	1965-67	78	17	2	0	6	3	0	0	86	20
HOFFMAN E.H.	1922	1	0	0	0	0	0	0	0	1	0
HOLMES S.	1889-90	21	8	1	0	0	0	0	0	22	8
HOLYOAKE J.E.	1901	1	0	0	0	0	0	0	0	1	0
HOOKS P.	1982-84	46/2	4	3	0	6	0	1/1	0	56/3	4
HOPE J.	1926-29	9	2	0	0	0	0	0	0	9	2
HOPEWELL W.	1888	5	0	0	0	0	0	0	0	5	0
HOPKINS W.	1890	8	0	0	0	0	0	0	0	8	0
HOPKINSON M.E.	1960-67	112/3	4	6	1	10	1	0	0	128/3	6
HOUNSFIELD R.E.	1904-05	23	4	3	0	0	0	0	0	26	4
HOWARD E.	1899	1	0	0	0	0	0	0	0	1	0
HOWARD F.J.	1919	5	0	0	0	0	0	0	0	5	0
HOWE J.R.	1935-49	223	2	21	0	0	0	0	0	244	2
HUGHES A.	1934	2	1	0	0	0	0	0	0	2	1
HUGHES G.	1963-67	184	22	4	0	13	2	0	0	201	24
HUGHES W.	1977	17/2	8	0	0	1	0	0	0	18/2	8
HUNT A.	1904-05	15	1	0	0	0	0	0	0	15	1
HUNT D.	1977	5	0	0	0	0	0	0	0	5	0
HUNT J.	1901-03	5	0	0	0	0	0	0	0	5	0
HUNT R.A.R.	1958	24	10	0	0	0	0	0	0	24	10
HUNTER G.I.	1954	19	0	0	0	0	0	0	0	19	0
HURST W.	1922	3	0	0	0	0	0	0	0	3	0
HUTCHINSON F.	1886	0	0	1	0	0	0	0	0	1	0
HUTCHINSON J.B.	1960-63	107	51	3	2	6	4	0	0	116	57
HUTCHISON D.	1931-33	29	4	1	0	0	0	0	0	30	4
IMLACH J.J.S.	1954	36	2	1	0	0	0	0	0	37	2
JACKSON J.H.	1921	13	4	1	0	0	0	0	0	14	4
JAMES L.	1975-77	67/1	15	11	2	7	1	4	3	89/1	21
JARDINE R.J.	1889	1	1	0	0	0	0	0	0	1	1
JEFFRIES A.	1936-38	15	1	0	0	0	0	0	0	15	1
JESSOP F.S.	1930-37	84	7	9	0	0	0	0	0	93	7
JOHNSON T.	1991	12	2	0	0	0	0	2	1	14	3
JOHNSTON J.M.	1923	1	0	0	0	0	0	0	0	1	0
JONES N.E.	1922	3	0	0	0	0	0	0	0	3	0
JONES R.	1980-81	59	0	3	0	3	0	0	0	65	0
JONES V.	1937	2	0	0	0	0	0	0	0	2	0
KAVANAGH J.C.	1990-91	27/9	0	3	0	0	0	4	0	34/9	0
KEAY W.	1893-94	24	7	5	0	0	0	0	0	29	7
KEEN E.R.L.	1930-37	219	4	18	1	0	0	0	0	237	5
KEETLEY F.	1921-25	76	8	6	0	0	0	0	0	82	8
KELHAM H.	1908	1	0	0	0	0	0	0	0	1	0
KELLY D.	1926-27	5	0	0	0	0	0	0	0	5	0

Player	Played	League App	Gls	FA Cup App	Gls	Lg Cup App	Gls	Others App	Gls	TOTAL App	Gls
GWYNNE Revd L.H.	1887	0	0	1	0	0	0	0	0	1	0
HADDOW D.	1890	16	0	0	0	0	0	0	0	16	0
HAGAN J.	1935-38	30	7	1	0	0	0	0	0	31	7
HAIG J.	1898	3	0	0	0	0	0	0	0	3	0
HALES D.D.	1976-77	22/1	4	6	2	1	1	0	0	29/1	7
HALEY W.T.	1924-26	9	1	2	0	0	0	0	0	11	1
HALFORD D.	1935	6	3	3	1	0	0	0	0	9	4
HALL B.	1903-10	245	11	24	3	0	0	0	0	269	14
HALL I.W.	1959-61	44	13	1	0	6	3	0	0	51	16
HALLIGAN W.	1909-10	22	8	0	0	0	0	0	0	22	8
HAMILTON J.	1894	12	2	0	0	0	0	0	0	12	2
HAMPTON J.W.	1927-29	12	0	0	0	0	0	0	0	12	0
HANDLEY G.	1897-98	15	2	0	0	0	0	0	0	15	2
HANN R.	1932-38	115	0	5	0	0	0	0	0	120	0
HANNAY J.	1920	1	0	0	0	0	0	0	0	1	0
HANNIGAN J.L.	1958-60	72	19	3	0	0	0	0	0	75	19
HARBEY G.K.	1983-86	35/5	1	1/2	0	5	1	2/1	0	43/8	2
HARBOARD	1888	1	0	0	0	0	0	0	0	1	0
HARDCASTLE D.S.	1905	5	1	1	0	0	0	0	0	6	1
HARDMAN J.A.	1913-14	14	0	1	0	0	0	0	0	15	0
HARDY A.	1891-92	3	1	0	0	0	0	0	0	3	1
HARDY J.J.	1924	3	0	0	0	0	0	0	0	3	0
HARFORD M.G.	1989-91	58	15	1	0	7	3	2	0	68	18
HARRISON K.	1954-55	15	3	1	0	0	0	0	0	16	3
HARRISON R.F.	1945-54	254	52	27	7	0	0	0	0	281	59
HARRISON T.W.	1901	1	0	0	0	0	0	0	0	1	0
HART J.L.	1925-26	4	3	0	0	0	0	0	0	4	3
HARVEY J.A.H.	1894	5	0	0	0	0	0	0	0	5	0
HASLAM H.B.	1900-01	8	0	0	0	0	0	0	0	8	0
HAVENHAND K.	1961	26	14	3	0	0	0	0	0	29	14
HAWDEN K.	1953	2	0	0	0	0	0	0	0	2	0
HAYWARD S.L.	1989-91	4/7	0	0	0	0/2	0	1	0	5/9	0
HAYWOOD F.	1906	1	0	0	0	0	0	0	0	1	0
HAZLEDINE D.	1952-53	26	6	2	0	0	0	0	0	28	6
HAZLEDINE G.	1953	1	0	0	0	0	0	0	0	1	0
HEBBERD T.N.	1988-90	70/11	10	5	2	13	2	7	0	95/11	14
HECTOR K.J.	1966-77	478/8	155	34	12	42	15	27	19	581/8	201
HENNESSEY W.T.	1969-72	62/1	4	3/2	0	2	1	12	0	79/3	5
HICKINBOTTOM E.	1888-93	50	0	3	0	0	0	0	0	53	0
HICKLING W.	1903	9	0	0	0	0	0	0	0	9	0
HIGGINS A.F.	1888-89	42	25	3	1	0	0	0	0	45	26
HILL A.R.	1981-83	19/3	2	3	1	3	1	0	0	25/3	4
HILL G.A.	1930-37	22/2	5	1	0	2	1	0	0	25/2	6
HINCHLIFFE T.	1938	6	1	0	0	0	0	0	0	6	1
HIND F.	1889	1	0	0	0	0	0	0	0	1	0
HINDMARCH R.	1884-89	164	9	13	1	13	0	6	0	196	10

Player	Played	League App	League Gls	FA Cup App	FA Cup Gls	Lg Cup App	Lg Cup Gls	Others App	Others Gls	TOTAL App	TOTAL Gls
McALLISTER A.	1904	24	0	0	0	0	0	0	0	24	0
McANDREW R.	1963	1	0	0	0	0	0	0	0	1	0
McCAFFERY A.	1978-79	31/6	4	0	0	4	0	0	0	35/6	4
McCANN J.	1962-63	55	2	3	0	0	0	0	0	58	2
McCLAREN S.	1985-87	23/2	1	0	0	5	1	2	0	30/2	1
McCONNACHIE A.	1897	23	9	3	0	0	0	0	0	26	9
McCORD B.J.	1987-89	3/2	0	3	0	1	0	0/1	1	7/3	1
McCORMICK H.	1946-47	7	0	0	0	0	0	0	0	7	0
McCULLOCH D.	1938	31	16	1	0	0	0	0	0	32	16
MacDONALD W.J.	1898-99	23	4	6	3	0	0	0	0	29	7
McDONNELL L.M.	1955-57	93	0	6	0	0	0	0	0	99	0
MacDOUGALL A.L.	1928	2	0	0	0	0	0	0	0	2	0
McFARLAND R.L.	1967-80	437/5	44	33	0	37	1	18	3	525/5	48
McGILL J.	1946-47	8	0	0	0	0	0	0	0	8	0
McGOVERN J.P.	1968-73	186/4	16	18	0	15	2	14	2	233/4	20
McINTYRE J.M.	1921-31	349	9	20	0	0	0	0	0	369	9
MACKAY D.C.	1968-70	122	5	7	0	16	2	0	0	145	7
McKELLAR D.	1978-79	41	0	2	0	0	0	0	0	43	0
MACKEN A.	1975-77	20/3	1	4/1	0	3/2	0	2/2	0	29/8	1
McLACHLAN J.	1890-94	63	17	3	0	0	0	0	0	66	17
McLACHLAN S.	1938-52	58	1	5	1	0	0	0	0	63	2
McLAREN H.	1949-53	119	53	12	3	0	0	0	0	131	56
MacLAREN R.	1985-87	113/9	4	9	0	13	1	4	0	139/9	5
McLAVERTY B.	1920-27	115	1	2	0	0	0	0	0	117	1
McLEAN T.	1892	2	0	0	0	0	0	0	0	2	0
McMILLAN J.S.	1890-95	116	45	9	4	0	0	1	1	126	50
McMILLAN S.T.	1914	1	0	0	0	0	0	0	0	1	0
McMINN K.C.	1987-91	102/2	7	6	1	10	3	6	1	124/2	12
McQUEEN H.	1895-1900	150	18	18	4	0	0	0	0	168	22
McQUILLAN D.	1952-55	18	1	0	0	0	0	0	0	18	1
MALLOCH G.C.	1927-31	93	0	4	0	0	0	0	0	97	0
MANN H.H.	1928	4	0	2	0	0	0	0	0	6	0
MARSHALL J.	1888	16	0	0	0	0	0	0	0	16	0
MARTIN B.	1919	6	0	0	0	0	0	0	0	6	0
MARTIN R.	1955-59	81	0	4	0	0	0	0	0	85	0
MASKREY H.M.	1902-09	202	0	20	0	0	0	0	0	222	0
MASSON D.S.	1977	23	1	3	2	0	0	0	0	26	3
MATTHEWS R.D.	1961-67	225	0	7	0	14	0	0	0	246	0
MATTHEWS W.	1912	1	0	0	0	0	0	0	0	1	0
MAY H.	1902	6	0	0	0	0	0	0	0	6	0
MAY J.	1898-1903	179	17	21	0	0	0	0	0	200	17
MAYCROFT D.	1884	0	0	1	0	0	0	0	0	1	0
MAYS A.E.	1949-59	272	21	9	0	0	0	0	0	281	21
MEE G.W.	1925-31	148	15	7	0	0	0	0	0	155	15
MERCER J.T.	1903-04	26	1	6	0	0	0	0	0	32	1
METCALFE R.	1966	1	0	0	0	0	0	0	0	1	0

Player	Played	League App	League Gls	FA Cup App	FA Cup Gls	Lg Cup App	Lg Cup Gls	Others App	Others Gls	TOTAL App	TOTAL Gls
KIDD J.	1919-21	20	0	1	0	0	0	0	0	21	0
KIFFORD J.	1898-99	6	0	0	0	0	0	0	0	6	0
KING F.O.	1937	3	0	0	0	0	0	0	0	3	0
KING J.	1975-77	12/2	0	1/1	0	1/2	0	0/2	0	14/7	0
KING W.G.	1905	1	0	0	0	0	0	0	0	1	0
KINSEY G.	1895-96	36	0	5	0	0	0	0	0	41	0
KIRBY J.	1929-37	173	0	18	0	0	0	0	0	191	0
KITSON P.	1991	12	4	0	0	0	0	2	0	14	4
KNOWLES F.E.	1921	3	1	0	0	0	0	0	0	3	1
KNOX J.J.	1886	0	0	2	1	0	0	0	0	2	1
LAMB S.	1905-06	30	1	3	0	0	0	0	0	33	1
LAMPH T.	1919-20	16	0	1	0	0	0	0	0	17	0
LANE M.A.E.	1924	0	0	1	0	0	0	0	0	1	0
LANE S.B.	1983	1	0	0	0	0	0	0	0	1	0
LANGAN D.F.	1976-79	143	1	6	0	6	0	0	0	155	1
LANGLAND A.	1889	2	0	0	0	0	0	0	0	2	0
LATHAM A.	1886-90	48	1	8	0	0	0	0	0	56	1
LAW C.R.	1952-53	33	2	0	0	0	0	0	0	33	2
LAWRENCE G.H.	1910-23	137	0	8	0	0	0	0	0	145	0
LAWRENCE S.E.	1887	0	0	4	0	0	0	0	0	4	0
LEACH S.	1897	1	0	0	0	0	0	0	0	1	0
LECKIE C.T.	1898-1904	126	1	13	0	0	0	0	0	139	1
LEE F.H.	1974-75	62	24	5/2	1	4	1	10	4	81/2	30
LEE J.	1950-53	93	54	6	2	0	0	0	0	99	56
LEES J.	1888-89	10	2	0	0	0	0	0	0	10	2
LEIGH A.S.	1919	2	0	0	0	0	0	0	0	2	0
LEIPER J.	1892-99	157	0	20	0	0	0	1	0	178	0
LEONARD H.D.	1911-19	144	72	6	1	0	0	0	0	150	73
LEONARD J.	1897	1	1	2	1	0	0	0	0	3	2
LEUTY L.H.	1945-49	131	1	27	0	0	0	0	0	158	1
LEWIS A.T.	1971-72	2	0	0	0	0	0	1	0	3	0
LEWIS M.	1984-87	37/6	1	0/1	0	2	0	4	0	43/7	1
LEWIS W.L.	1931	8	3	0	0	0	0	0	0	8	3
LIEVESLEY W.	1920	1	0	0	0	0	0	0	0	1	0
LILLIS M.A.	1986-87	6/9	1	0/1	0	2/1	0	0	0	8/11	1
LINACRE J.H.	1898	2	0	0	0	0	0	0	0	2	0
LITTLE T.	1892-93	16	1	1	1	0	0	0	0	17	2
LLOYD A.	1903	1	0	0	0	0	0	0	0	1	0
LLOYD G.H.	1901-02	10	1	2	0	0	0	0	0	12	1
LONG J.	1906-07	61	18	4	1	0	0	0	0	65	19
LOVATT J.	1981	2/2	0	0	0	0	0	0	0	2/2	0
LOWELL E.J.	1953	0	1	1	0	0	0	0	0	1	1
LUNTLEY W.	1885	0	0	3	0	0	0	0	0	3	0
LYLE R.C.	1910	7	0	0	0	0	0	0	0	7	0
LYONS J.	1919-22	80	31	6	2	0	0	0	0	86	33
McALLE J.E.	1981-83	51/7	1	3/1	1	4	0	0	0	58/8	2

Rams skipper Dave Mackay holds aloft the Second Division championship trophy in April 1969, after Derby's 5-0 win over Bristol City.

Player	Played	League App	League Gls	FA Cup App	FA Cup Gls	Lg Cup App	Lg Cup Gls	Others App	Others Gls	TOTAL App	TOTAL Gls
NICHOLLS H.	1885	0	0	1	0	0	0	0	0	1	0
NIELSON N.F.	1951-53	57	8	3	1	0	0	0	0	60	9
NISH D.J.	1972-78	184/4	10	16	1	16	1	17	2	233/4	14
OAKDEN H.	1898	9	5	3	0	0	0	0	0	12	5
O'BRIEN M.T.	1926-27	3	0	2	0	0	0	0	0	5	0
O'BRIEN R.C.	1983	4	0	0	0	0	0	0	0	4	0
O'HARE J.	1967-73	247/1	65	17	3	28/2	8	13	5	305/3	81
OLIVER J.A.	1947-49	16	2	1	0	0	0	0	0	17	2
OLIVER J.H.K.	1949-57	184	1	9	0	0	0	0	0	193	1
OLNEY B.A.	1920-27	223	0	17	0	0	0	0	0	240	0
O'RIORDAN D.J.	1976-77	2/4	1	0	0	0/1	0	0	0	2/5	1
ORMONDROYD I.	1991	25	8	3	1	3	0	0	0	31	9
O'ROURKE J.	1900	5	0	0	0	0	0	0	0	5	0
OSGOOD K.	1979-81	61/8	10	2	0	3	0	0	0	66/8	10
OSMAN R.C.H.	1953-54	2	0	0	0	0	0	0	0	2	0
OXFORD K.	1957-62	151	0	6	0	5	0	0	0	162	0
PALMER C.A.	1984-85	51	2	1	0	7	0	2	0	61	2
PALMER D.F.	1961	18	6	2	0	1	0	0	0	21	6
PARKIN A.G.	1949	9	0	0	0	0	0	0	0	9	0
PARKIN R.	1936	1	0	0	0	0	0	0	0	1	0
PARNELL G.F.	1903-04	9	0	0	0	0	0	0	0	9	0
PARR J.	1945-52	112	0	22	0	0	0	0	0	134	0
PARRY A.J.	1971-72	4/2	0	0	0	0	0	1	0	5/2	0
PARRY J.	1948-65	482/1	105	20	5	14	0	0	0	516/1	110
PATTERSON R.	1897-99	19	0	2	0	0	0	0	0	21	0
PATTERSON W.	1920-23	66	24	2	0	0	0	0	0	68	24
PATON T.H.	1904-05	35	4	3	0	0	0	0	0	38	4
PATRICK R.	1952-55	49	0	1	0	0	0	0	0	50	0
PATTERSON M.	1988-91	24/9	3	1	0	5/2	0	2/1	0	32/12	3
PATTISON J.W.	1921	15	2	0	0	0	0	0	0	15	2
PAUL D.D.	1953-55	2	0	0	0	0	0	0	0	2	0
PAUL J.	1894-97	28	9	1	0	0	0	1	0	30	9
PAYNE F.E.	1947	0	0	1	0	0	0	0	0	1	0
PEART J.G.	1919	9	1	0	0	0	0	0	0	9	1
PEART R.	1946	1	0	0	0	0	0	0	0	1	0
PENNEY D.M.	1985-88	6/13	0	1	0	2/3	0	1/3	1	10/19	3
PHILBIN J.	1934	1	0	0	0	0	0	0	0	1	0
PHILLIPS J.L.	1990	3	1	0	0	0	0	0	0	3	1
PICKERING N.	1988-91	35/10	3	3	0	7/1	0	3	0	48/11	3
PITMAN R.	1888-89	5	0	2	0	0	0	0	0	7	0
PLACE C.A.	1955	2	0	0	0	0	0	0	0	2	0
PLACKETT H.	1888	16	2	0	0	0	0	0	0	16	2
PLACKETT L.	1886-88	22	7	8	1	0	0	0	0	30	8
PLACKETT S.	1921-26	140	3	16	0	0	0	0	0	156	3
PLUMMER C.A.	1983	23/4	3	3/1	1	2	0	0	0	28/5	4
POPPITT J.	1946-49	16	0	0	0	0	0	0	0	16	0

Player	Played	League App	League Gls	FA Cup App	FA Cup Gls	Lg Cup App	Lg Cup Gls	Others App	Others Gls	TOTAL App	TOTAL Gls
METHVEN J.	1891-1906	458	0	52	0	0	0	1	0	511	0
METHVEN J.Jnr	1913	1	0	0	0	0	0	0	0	1	0
MICKLEWHITE G.	1984-91	219/15	31	8/2	4	23/2	2	7/1	6	257/20	43
MIDDLETON F.	1901-05	65	3	3	0	0	0	0	0	68	3
MIDDLETON J.	1977-79	73	0	3	0	4	0	0	0	80	0
MIDDLETON R.	1951-53	116	0	4	0	0	0	0	0	120	0
MILARVIE R.	1889	14	4	1	0	0	0	0	0	15	4
MILLER D.	1947	1	0	0	0	0	0	0	0	1	0
MILLER J.	1895-97	62	20	9	5	0	0	0	0	71	25
MILLIN A.	1955	1	0	0	0	0	0	0	0	1	0
MILLS G.R.	1982	18	2	3	0	2	0	0	0	23	2
MILLS S.	1891-92	45	7	2	0	0	0	0	0	47	7
MINNEY G.	1920	2	0	0	0	0	0	0	0	2	0
MITCHELL H.	1905	1	0	0	0	0	0	0	0	1	0
MITCHELL J.D	1958-59	6	0	0	0	0	0	0	0	6	0
MONEY R.	1981	5	0	1	0	0	0	0	0	6	0
MONKS I.	1887-88	3	0	3	2	0	0	0	0	6	2
MOORE J.	1904-05	5	0	0	0	0	0	0	0	5	0
MOORE J.	1913-25	203	75	15	7	0	0	0	0	218	82
MOORE J.L.	1957-63	144	3	7	0	5	0	0	0	156	3
MOORE R.	1919	1	0	0	0	0	0	0	0	1	0
MOORE W.C.	1906-08	11	0	0	0	0	0	0	0	11	0
MORAN J.	1954	2	0	0	0	0	0	0	0	2	0
MORELAND V.	1978-79	38/4	1	1	0	1/1	0	4	0	40/5	1
MORLEY H.A.	1884-88	4	0	6	0	0	0	0	0	10	0
MORRIS C.R.	1900-09	276	1	35	1	0	0	0	0	311	2
MORRIS J.	1948-52	130	44	10	3	0	0	0	0	140	47
MORRISON A.C.	1945-47	52	21	16	1	0	0	0	0	68	22
MORTON W.H.	1920-21	24	1	1	0	0	0	0	0	25	1
MOSELEY G.	1972-76	32	0	4	0	4	0	4	0	44	0
MOZLEY B.	1946-54	297	2	24	0	0	0	0	0	321	2
MURPHY L.	1921-27	221	46	14	3	0	0	0	0	235	49
MURRAY W.	1920	31	3	3	1	0	0	0	0	34	4
MUSSON W.U.	1945-53	246	0	34	0	0	0	0	0	280	0
MYNARD L.D.	1949-50	14	2	0	0	0	0	0	0	14	2
NAPIER C.E.	1935-37	80	24	8	2	0	0	0	0	88	26
NASH R.W.	1885-87	0	0	3	1	0	0	0	0	3	1
NEAL R.M.	1931	10	1	2	2	0	0	0	0	12	3
NEEDHAM G.W.	1919	5	0	0	0	0	0	0	0	5	0
NEEDHAM T.	1887-89	15	3	5	3	0	0	0	0	20	6
NELSON E.	1926	2	0	0	0	0	0	0	0	2	0
NELSON J.	1890	4	2	0	0	0	0	0	0	4	2
NEVE E.	1912-13	47	1	2	0	0	0	0	0	49	1
NEWBERY P.J.	1958-60	5	2	0	0	0	0	0	0	5	2
NEWTON H.A.	1973-76	111/6	5	15	1	10/1	0	13	0	149/7	6
NICHOLAS J.T.	1928-46	347	14	36	2	0	0	0	0	383	16
NICHOLAS W.J.	1905-10	130	0	13	0	0	0	0	0	143	0

Player	Played	League App	League Gls	FA Cup App	FA Cup Gls	Lg Cup App	Lg Cup Gls	Others App	Others Gls	TOTAL App	TOTAL Gls
POWELL B.I.	1979-81	86	7	2	1	4	0	0	0	92	8
POWELL K.	1946	13	0	0	0	0	0	0	0	13	0
POWELL S.	1971-84	342/10	20	31/1	0	24	1	12	0	409/11	21
POWELL T.	1948-61	380	57	24	7	2	0	0	0	406	64
PRATLEY R.G.	1983-86	29/2	1	0/1	0	4	0	4	0	37/3	1
PUMFORD G.L.	1924	2	0	0	0	0	0	0	0	2	0
PYE J.	1954-56	61	24	4	3	0	0	0	0	65	27
PYNEGAR A.	1904	1	0	0	0	0	0	0	0	1	0
QUANTRILL A.E.	1914-20	72	5	4	0	0	0	0	0	76	5
RAISBECK W.	1901	3	0	3	0	0	0	0	0	6	0
RAMAGE A.	1980-81	32/1	2	2	0	3	0	0	0	37/1	2
RAMAGE C.D.	1989-91	30/6	4	3	1	6/1	2	0/3	0	39/10	7
RAMAGE P.	1928-36	233	55	22	5	0	0	0	0	255	60
RAMSELL E.A.	1905	5	0	0	0	0	0	0	0	5	0
RANCE C.S.	1920-21	23	0	0	0	0	0	0	0	23	0
RANDALL J.	1930-34	52	4	0	0	0	0	0	0	52	4
RANSFORD J.	1906	15	3	2	1	0	0	0	0	17	4
RATCLIFFE E.	1902-05	16	0	0	0	0	0	0	0	16	0
RAYBOULD S.	1894	5	2	0	0	0	0	0	0	5	2
READER A.R.	1913	4	0	0	0	0	0	0	0	4	0
REID A.J.	1980-82	27/3	1	1/1	0	2	0	0	0	30/4	1
REID S.E.	1931-35	16	0	0	0	0	0	0	0	16	0
REVELL C.H.	1950-51	22	2	0	0	0	0	0	0	22	2
RHODES J.A.	1964-70	5	0	0	0	1/1	0	0	0	6/1	0
RICHARDS F.	1898	2	0	0	0	0	0	0	0	2	0
RICHARDS G.H.	1901-13	284	33	25	4	0	0	0	0	309	37
RICHARDS J.P.	1982	10	2	0	0	0	0	0	0	10	2
RICHARDS W.	1979-81	16/3	0	3	0	0/1	0	0	0	19/4	0
RICHARDSON J.	1962-70	118	4	3	1	12	0	0	0	133	5
RICHARDSON P.A.	1984	7/7	0	1	0	0/2	0	0	0	8/9	0
RICHMOND J.F.	1957-62	6	0	0	0	0	0	0	0	6	0
RIDDELL F.W.	1907-08	6	1	0	0	0	0	0	0	6	1
RIOCH B.D.	1973-76	146/1	38	12	7	11	5	14	4	183/1	54
RITCHIE A.	1920-26	87	1	6	0	0	0	0	0	93	1
RITCHIE D.	1913	2	0	0	0	0	0	0	0	2	0
RITCHIE W.	1919	4	1	0	0	0	0	0	0	4	1
ROBERTS E.	1935	4	0	0	0	0	0	0	0	4	0
ROBERTS W.	1890	5	0	0	0	0	0	0	0	5	0
ROBERTSON J.N.	1983-84	72	3	5	0	6	1	2	0	85	4
ROBINSON A.	1909	1	0	0	0	0	0	0	0	1	0
ROBINSON J.W.	1891-96	163	0	16	0	0	0	1	0	180	0
ROBINSON T.C.	1927-29	9	0	2	0	0	0	0	0	11	0
ROBINSON W.	1909	3	0	0	0	0	0	0	0	3	0
ROBSON J.C.	1928-31	38	10	2	0	0	0	0	0	40	10
ROBSON J.D.	1967-72	170/1	3	12	1	19	0	9	1	210/1	5

Player	Played	League App	League Gls	FA Cup App	FA Cup Gls	Lg Cup App	Lg Cup Gls	Others App	Others Gls	TOTAL App	TOTAL Gls
ROBSON J.W.	1921	3	0	0	0	0	0	0	0	3	0
ROBSON N.	1930-32	35	6	0	0	0	0	0	0	35	6
ROBSON W.	1927-31	13	0	3	0	0	0	0	0	16	0
ROBY D.	1961-64	70	6	5	0	6	1	0	0	81	7
ROSE C.H.	1891-92	5	0	0	0	0	0	0	0	5	0
ROSE W.	1891-92	5	0	0	0	0	0	0	0	5	0
ROULSTONE F.	1888	1	0	0	0	0	0	0	0	1	0
ROULSTONE W.	1887-94	118	4	11	0	0	0	0	0	129	4
ROUND S.J.	1991	2/1	0	0	0	0	0	0	0	2/1	0
ROWE G.W.	1925	1	0	0	0	0	0	0	0	1	0
ROWE V.N.	1951	2	0	0	0	0	0	0	0	2	0
RUDDY T.	1928-31	22	9	0	0	0	0	0	0	22	9
RUSSELL J.	1898	2	0	0	0	0	0	0	0	2	0
RUTHERFORD J.B.	1898	1	1	0	0	0	0	0	0	1	1
RYAN G.J.	1977-78	30	4	2	1	2	0	0	0	34	5
RYAN R.A.	1955-58	133	30	6	1	0	0	0	0	139	31
SAGE M.	1986-91	137/3	4	4	0	22/1	0	8	0	171/4	4
SAUNDERS D.N.	1988-90	106	42	6	0	12	10	7	5	131	57
SAUNDERS S.	1904-05	8	0	0	0	0	0	0	0	8	0
SAVIN K.A.	1950-55	65	0	1	0	0	0	0	0	66	0
SAWYER T.E.	1894	2	0	0	0	0	0	0	0	2	0
SAXTON R.	1964-67	94/2	1	3	0	9	0	0	0	106/2	1
SCARBOROUGH B.	1958-60	4	0	0	0	0	0	0	0	4	0
SCATTERGOOD E.O.	1907-14	182	3	10	0	0	0	0	0	192	3
SCATTERGOOD K.	1936-37	22	0	3	0	0	0	0	0	25	0
SCOTT A.T.	1927-33	27	0	5	0	0	0	0	0	32	0
SCOTT K.	1950	2	0	0	0	0	0	0	0	2	0
SEAL C.E.	1905	1	0	0	0	0	0	0	0	1	0
SELVEY S.	1888	1	0	0	0	0	0	0	0	1	0
SELVEY W.	1888	1	0	0	0	0	0	0	0	1	0
SHANKS T.	1898-1900	27	9	1	0	0	0	0	0	28	9
SHARMAN D.W.	1950	2	0	0	0	0	0	0	0	2	0
SHARPE I.G.	1911-12	54	12	3	0	0	0	0	0	57	12
SHEPHERD G.	1919-20	2	0	0	0	0	0	0	0	2	0
SHERIDAN F.M.	1980-81	41/2	5	0	0	1	0	0/1	0	42/2	5
SHILTON P.L.	1987-91	175	0	10	0	18	0	8	0	211	0
SHINER A.J.	1920	1	0	0	0	0	0	0	0	1	0
SHIRTCLIFFE E.	1901	4	0	0	0	0	0	0	0	4	0
SIMPSON P.D.	1991	16	7	0	0	0	0	2	0	18	7
SIMS J.	1972	2/1	0	0	0	0	0	0/1	0	2/2	0
SKIVINGTON G.	1980-82	39/7	2	4	0	4	1	0	0	43/7	3
SMITH A.	1884-85	0	0	4	2	0	0	0	0	4	2
SMITH F.	1909	5	0	0	0	0	0	0	0	5	0
SMITH F.E.	1947	1	0	0	0	0	0	0	0	1	0
SMITH H.	1906	1	0	0	0	0	0	0	0	1	0
SMITH J.	1888-89	12	0	0	0	0	0	0	0	12	0
SMITH J.	1914	6	0	0	0	0	0	0	0	6	0

Player	Played	League App	League Gls	FA Cup App	FA Cup Gls	Lg Cup App	Lg Cup Gls	Others App	Others Gls	TOTAL App	TOTAL Gls
SMITH J.W.	1903-06	9	0	1	0	0	0	0	0	10	0
SMITH M.J.	1957-60	22	0	0	0	1	0	0	0	23	0
SMITH S.J.	1922	1	0	0	0	0	0	0	0	1	0
SMITH V.	1925-26	4	0	0	0	0	0	0	0	4	0
SOAR T.A.	1902	2	0	0	0	0	0	0	0	2	0
SPILSBURY B.W.	1885-88	1	1	8	7	0	0	0	0	9	8
SPRINGTHORPE J.A.	1907	2	0	0	0	0	0	0	0	2	0
SPOONER S.A.	1978-81	7/1	0	0	0	0	0	0	0	7/1	0
STALEY J.	1891-1900	128	0	12	0	0	0	1	0	141	0
STALLARD M.	1991	2/1	0	1/1	0	0	0	1	1	4/2	1
STAMPS J.D.	1938-53	233	100	29	26	0	0	0	0	262	126
STAPLETON F.A.	1987	10	1	0	0	0	0	0	0	10	1
STEEL W.	1938	11	0	0	0	0	0	0	0	11	0
STEEL W.	1947-49	109	27	15	8	0	0	0	0	124	35
STEELE E.G.	1984-86	47	0	1	0	2	0	3	0	53	0
STEPHENSON G.R.	1961-62	11	0	1	0	2	0	0	0	14	1
STEPHENSON G.T.	1927-30	111	53	9	3	0	0	0	0	120	56
STEVENSON J.	1894-98	73	31	11	1	0	0	0	0	84	32
STEWART A.	1967-69	29/1	1	1	0	4	1	0	0	34/1	2
STEWART F.H.	1899	2	1	0	0	0	0	0	0	2	1
STOCKILL R.R.	1934-38	66	29	3	1	0	0	0	0	69	30
STOKOE J.	1922	8	1	0	0	0	0	0	0	8	1
STORER H.	1920-28	257	60	17	3	0	0	0	0	274	63
STORER W.	1891-92	25	10	2	1	0	0	0	0	27	11
STRAW R.	1951-57	94	57	4	3	0	0	0	0	98	60
STREETE F.A.	1984-85	35	0	1	0	4	0	1	0	41	0
STURRIDGE D.C.	1991	1	0	0	0	0	0	0	0	1	0
SUGG F.H.	1884	0	0	1	0	0	0	0	0	1	0
SUMMERS J.L.	1935	2	0	0	0	0	0	0	0	2	0
SUTTON S.J.	1984	24	0					2	0	26	0
SWALLOW R.	1958-63	118	21	4	1	6	0	0	0	128	22
SWINDLEHURST D.	1979-82	110	29	6	0	9	3	0	0	125	32
SYLVESTER T.	1908	2	0	0	0	0	0	0	0	2	0
TAFT D.	1948	6	1	3	1	0	0	0	0	9	2
TATE G.M.	1955	1	1	0	0	0	0	0	0	1	1
TAYLOR K.	1984	22	2	0	0	4	0	1	1	27	3
TAYLOR M.J.	1989-91	15	0	0	0	2	0	2	0	19	0
TAYLOR R.C.	1921	2	0	0	0	0	0	0	0	2	0
THOMAS A.M.	1982	0/1	0	0	0	0	0	0	0	0/1	0
THOMAS E.	1964-67	102/3	43	2	0	6	6	0	0	110/3	49
THOMAS M.R.	1985	9	0	0	0	0	0	0	0	9	0
THOMAS R.J.	1973-77	89	2	10	0	9	0	10	0	118	2
THOMPSON C.A.	1948-49	16	3	0	0	0	0	0	0	16	3
THOMPSON G.A.	1908-10	46	5	9	1	0	0	0	0	55	6
THOMPSON G.H.	1920	4	0	0	0	0	0	0	0	4	0
THOMPSON J.	1897	1	0	0	0	0	0	0	0	1	0
THOMPSON P.	1958-61	52	19	2	2	1	1	0	0	55	22
THOMS H.	1922-27	179	4	16	0	0	0	0	0	195	4
THORNEWELL G.	1919-27	275	23	20	3	0	0	0	0	295	26
TINKLER A.	1909	2	0	0	0	0	0	0	0	2	0
TODD C.	1970-78	293	6	30	2	20	1	28	1	371	10
TODD T.B.	1955	4	3	1	0	0	0	0	0	5	3
TOOTLE J.	1924-25	7	0	0	0	0	0	0	0	7	0
TOWIE T.	1893	8	1	0	0	0	0	0	0	8	1
TOWNSEND W.	1945-52	79	0	14	0	0	0	0	0	93	0
TRAVIS H.	1936-38	12	4	0	0	0	0	0	0	12	4
TREMELLING S.	1905-07	2	0	0	0	0	0	0	0	2	0
TRUEMAN R.	1908-09	16	0	3	1	0	0	0	0	19	1
TURNER A.D.	1902	21	1	0	0	0	0	0	0	21	1
TURNER J.A.	1896-97	51	2	10	0	0	0	0	0	61	2
UDALL E.W.	1934-36	81	0	7	0	0	0	0	0	88	0
UPTON F.	1954-60	259	17	8	1	5	0	0	0	272	18
VANN B.W.	1906	3	0	0	0	0	0	0	0	3	0
VARNEY H.	1901-02	2	0	0	0	0	0	0	0	2	0
WALKER C.	1948-54	25	0	0	0	0	0	0	0	25	0
WALKER J.A.	1889-90	11	0	2	0	0	0	0	0	13	0
WALKER J.H.	1911-19	84	4	4	0	0	0	0	0	88	4
WALKER J.M.	1967-73	35/7	3	0/1	0	8	0	2/2	2	45/10	5
WALLACE J.M.	1947	16	0	3	0	0	0	0	0	19	0
WALLER P.	1961-67	102/2	5	3	0	8	0	0	0	113/2	5
WALLINGTON F.M.	1985-86	67	0	8	0	11	0	3	0	89	0
WALSH W.	1946	1	0	0	0	0	0	0	0	1	0
WALTON G.	1905	1	0	0	0	0	0	0	0	1	0
WALTON J.	1921	7	0	1	0	0	0	0	0	8	0
WARD C.	1884	0	0	1	0	0	0	0	0	1	0
WARD T.V.	1937-50	238	4	22	1	0	0	0	0	260	5
WARMBY H.	1885-87	0	0	9	0	0	0	0	0	9	0
WARREN A.R.	1901	8	2	0	0	0	0	0	0	8	2
WARREN B.	1899-1907	242	19	27	14	0	0	0	0	269	33
WARRINGTON J.	1901-03	29	7	9	4	0	0	0	0	38	11
WATERHOUSE F.	1919-20	26	0	2	0	0	0	0	0	28	0
WATSON A.F.	1990	5	0	0	0	0	0	0	0	5	0
WATSON D.V.	1983	34	1	3/2	0	2	0	0	0	39/2	1
WAUGH R.	1912-14	28	0	1	0	0	0	0	0	29	1
WEBB D.J.	1978-79	25/1	1	1	0	2	0	0	0	28/1	1
WEBB G.H.	1921	2	0	0	0	0	0	0	0	2	0
WEBB J.A.	1929-36	25	0	0	0	0	0	0	0	25	0
WEBSTER R.	1961-77	451/4	7	30	0	34	0	15/1	0	530/5	7
WEBSTER T.C.	1948-57	172	0	6	0	0	0	0	0	178	0

Ray Young, a former schoolboy star who had a long career with the Rams.

Player	Played	League App	League Gls	FA Cup App	FA Cup Gls	Lg Cup App	Lg Cup Gls	Others App	Others Gls	TOTAL App	TOTAL Gls
WHEATCROFT F.G.	1903-04 1905 1906-07	25	8	0	0	0	0	0	0	25	8
WHEATLEY S.P.	1951-52	4	0	0	0	0	0	0	0	4	0
WHEELER W.	1910	1	0	0	0	0	0	0	0	1	0
WHITE A.	1927-31	4	0	0	0	0	0	0	0	4	0
WHITE W.	1955	3	0	0	0	0	0	0	0	3	0
WHITEHOUSE J.	1923-28	186	82	14	4	0	0	0	0	200	86
WHITTAKER W.	1903	12	0	0	0	0	0	0	0	12	0
WHYMARK T.J.	1979	2	0	0	0	0	0	0	0	2	0
WICKS S.J.	1978-79	24	0	0	0	0	0	0	0	24	0
WIGHTMAN H.	1919-27	180	9	9	0	0	0	0	0	189	9
WIGNALL F.	1968-71	29/16	15	3	1	4/2	0	3	1	39/18	17
WILCOX G.E.	1937-46	12	0	0	0	0	0	0	0	12	0
WILEMAN S.	1933-36	9	1	2	0	0	0	0	0	11	1
WILKES H.T.	1927-32	208	0	12	0	0	0	0	0	220	0
WILKINS R.J.H.	1949-53	30	11	0	0	0	0	0	0	30	11
WILLIAMS D.G.	1984-91	276/1	9	17	0	26/1	1	11	0	330/2	10
WILLIAMS P.D.	1989-91	67/3	18	3	2	4	1	4	0	78/3	21
WILLIAMS P.J.	1952	2	0	0	0	0	0	0	0	2	0
WILLIAMSON A.	1885-90	41	0	12	1	0	0	0	0	53	1
WILLIAMSON M.	1961-63	12	0	1	0	1	0	0	0	14	0
WILSON A.	1898	1	0	0	0	0	0	0	0	1	0
WILSON A.	1936	1	0	0	0	0	0	0	0	1	0
WILSON C.K.	1922	1	0	0	0	0	0	0	0	1	0
WILSON I.W.	1990	11	0	0	0	0	0	0	0	11	0
WILSON K.J.	1979-84	106/16	30	8	3	8/3	8	0	0	122/19	41
WOMACK A.R.	1957	2	0	0	0	0	0	0	0	2	0
WOMBWELL R.	1899-1901	85	17	10	1	0	0	0	0	95	18
WOOD A.E.	1905-06	60	2	6	1	0	0	0	0	66	3
WOOD J.	1905-06	37	7	3	0	0	0	0	0	40	7
WOODHEAD D.	1955-58	94	24	3	1	0	0	0	0	97	25
WOODLEY V.R.	1945-46	30	0	4	0	0	0	0	0	34	0
WOOLLEY A.	1894	6	3	0	0	0	0	0	0	6	3
WRIGHT H.	1910-11	15	2	1	0	0	0	0	0	16	2
WRIGHT H.E.	1937-38	25	0	1	0	0	0	0	0	26	0
WRIGHT L.G.	1888	4	1	0	0	0	0	0	0	4	1
WRIGHT M.	1987-90	144	10	5	0	15	0	7	0	171	10
WRIGHT P.D.J.	1967	12/1	0	0	0	0	0	0	0	12/1	0
WYER P.W.	1956	2	1	0	0	0	0	0	0	2	1
YORK C.H.	1902-03	24	6	3	0	0	0	0	0	27	6
YOUNG G.R.	1953-65	253/1	5	6	0	9	0	0	0	268/1	5

Tim Ward leads out an All Stars XI at the Baseball Ground for a match against the Rams, staged in aid of the family of Chick Musson, who died in April 1955. Following Ward are former Derby colleagues Bill Townsend, Frank Broome and Reg Harrison..

SUBSCRIBERS

PRESENTATION COPIES

1 Derby County Football Club • 2 Lionel Pickering
3 Arthur Cox • 4 Roy McFarland
5 Michael Dunford • 6 Gerald Mortimer

7 Mrs D E Twells
8 J A Harris
9 Chris Kendall
10 Chris Kendall, Football Programmes
11 Roy K Shoesmith
12 Harry Lewis
13 David Keats
14 David R Earnshaw
15 Fred Lee
16 Gary Wynne
17 Simon Baker
18 Andrew J Ellis
19 J S Pyke
20 Brian Flint
21 Raymond Shaw
22 Derek Hyde
23 Michael Holder
24 Phil Hollow
25 David J Godfrey
26 Douglas Lamming
27 Derek Wheatcroft
28 Garth Dykes
29 Brian H Hobbs
30 W D Phillips
31 Nigel Craigie
32 Christer Svensson
33 Trond Isaksen
34 David Sullivan
35 Maurice Curtin
36 Jonny Stokkeland
37 Colin Cameron
38 Filippo Rossi
39 J Gardiner
40 Mike Purkiss
41 Jonathan Hall
42 Nigel Turner
43 Michael McConkey
44 Stanley A Robinson
45 Gareth M Davies
46 B Lambert
47 Steve McGhee
48 John Qvarnberg
49 Gerald Hill
50 David Harby
51 Mike Young
52 Norman Green
53 Alan Hindley
54 Dave Hillam
55 Richard Stocken
56 Mike Jackman
57 A F Pearson Jnr
58 J Musgrove
59 Ian Griffiths
60 Christopher Taylor
61 Michael E Wells

62 Lars-Olof Wendler
63 L A Zammit
64 S Simpson
65 B M Lawton
66 P H Lawton
67 John van den Elsen
68 J A Retter
69 John Osgerby
70 L Groom
71 Paul Rowley
72 Mr D R Millward
73 David Horobin
74 Mick Derby
75 Richard Hill
76 Clive Moorcroft
77 Michael Rickwood
78 James Andrew Warren
79 David John Sheppard
80 J W Bant (Paddy)
81 William James Doyle
82 Samuel J Brindley
83 Kevin Beech
84 Janet Ball
85 Janet Ball
86 Alun Owen
87 Peter Bradly
88 Brian Redfern
89 John Newton
90 Ken Hales
91 Kevin Large
92 L Campbell
93 H Preston
94 P R Trembirth
95 David Thomas
96 S Cooper
97 Z Fugiel
98 Gary Alan Clarkson
99 Phillip Bennett
100 Jon David Banks
101 Leonard Matthews
102 Andy Pickers
103 Chris Jones
104 Mr Phillip Adams
105 Tony Deeming
106 Luke Renshaw
107 Mr A C Westley
108 Anna & James Beeson
109 Mervyn Richard Waring
110 David Clowes
111 Eric J Plumb
112 Steven Newiss
113 Stan Bridges
114 Timothy N Haskey
115 Andrew David Mitchell
116 Martin R Smith
117 Paul R Lester

118 Maxwell Bladon & Stella Barkley
119 Graham M Bolam
120 Martin Du Sautoy
121 Danny Simpson
122 K J Orpe
123 Peter Stephens
124 Neil A Beresford
125 Alan Cooke
126 Paul Barlow
127 Kenneth D Shipstone
128 Mark Ferris
129 G R Morley
130 Arnold Grace
131 Jason Bates
132 J A Bowler
133 G N Draper
134 Neil Paul Rhodes
135 Andy Rogers
136 Shaun Smalley
137 K H Frogson
138 Judith Margaret Peel
139 Stephen, Carole & Joseph Skaper
140 Wallace Scott
141 John E Lake
142 Sean Durkan
143 David Phillips
144 Andrew Phillips
145 George Ivor Phillips
146 Gary Holman
147 Mark Southwell
148 Dennis Ruston
149 Mr Iain Griffin
150 Richard J Pope
151 Philip J Ryde
152 Michael Taylor
153 Richard Foster
154 Gary A Holt
155 John S Marshall
156 Brian Moss
157 A M Winfield
158 Liam Kelly
159 Shane Sanghera
160 Simon Douglas Vickers
161 Gavin Perry
162 David E H Frost
163 Inge Haagensen
164 T R Bendle Moore
165 E Morley
166 Paul Watson
167 Arthur Watson
168 John Kenneth Boiling
169 Frederick Motson
170 P Stevenson
171 P Stevenson

172 Peter Wallis
173 Andrew Jarrett
174 Jonathan N Prime
175 C-Stander — Derby County Fanzine
176 Alan Featherstone
177 Graham Dent
178 John Anthony Walker
179 Richard Edward Hancock
180 Lee Stanley Bexson
181 Alan Toplis
182 Mr R S Twells
183 Tom Lungley, 266 Victoria Avenue, Ockbrook
184 Alan Richards
185 Jason Madeley
186 Tim Dolman
187 Judy & Harold Draycott
188 Wilf Cooper
189 I E Statham
190 Edward Fearn
191 Chris Cohen
192 Michael Cohen
193 Anthony John Peach
194 Bryan Linden Peach
195 John Michael Brown
196 Mr A J Froggatt
197 Barry Walker
198 Barbara Osborne
199 Peter Brindley
200 K & R J Jackson
201 G S Fish
202 Thomas William Bower
203 R J Latham
204 Gary Bowen
205 Simon A Brown
206 Frederick Tipper
207 Christopher Stephen Pritchard
208 Richard Bull
209 Richard H Sprenger
210 Deryck Burns
211 Terence Tattershaw
212 Brendan Colohan
213 John Murden
214 Inge Haagensen
215 Michael Scales
216 Andrew Cudworth
217 Glyn Mellor
218 Danny Townsend
219 Finn Morten Steen
220 Rosaleen A Simms
221 Kevin J Sims
222 Helen J Sims
223 Victoria A S Sims
224 Keith J Sims
225 George Selwood

226 Mr Steven R Greenhough
227 Ronald Bradley
228 Gareth A Jones
229 John Smith
230 A Harby
231 Neil Smith
232 Howard Bettany
233 Stven H Burgess
234 Huw Wright
235 Nigel Judd
236 Ruth, Edward, James & Julian Hill
237 Mr D Randall
238 Jim Wright
239 Mick Nordemann
240 Nicholas John Wrenn
241 Stephen Hawley
242 Mr Christopher George Boss
243 James R Woolley
244 B Snaith
245 Andrew Annison
246 Michael G Robinson
247 Duncan M Chambers
248 Peter Whilde
249 David Pease
250 Pat Thomas
251 Carol & Dennis Hawes
252 Andrew Hickling
253 Michael Wilson
254 Michael Wilson
255 Antony Holloway
256 Charlie Bolstridge
257 Nigel Wright
258 Phillip Cottrill
259 Leonard Dormer
260 Mr H S Miller
261 B M Morrow
262 Andrew Waterall
263 J R Littler
264 Michael Briggs
265 Mr J R Hewitt
266 Gary Wild
267 Colin Grimley
268 Steve Cooke
269 Stuart Burnett
270 Kevin George Wedgwood Litting
271 Marcus Edward Wedgwood Litting
272 Trevor R Titterton
273 Geoffrey Webb
274 Michael Edwards
275 John Hudson
276 Peter Haslam
277 P T Gerrard
278 Andrew Spalding

279 Andy Garner
280 Kevin John Rose
281 P D Wright
282 Roger Mather
283 Stephen John Knight
284 Mark Thompson
285 Mr Chris Gregory
286 Mr Jack Statham
287 John P Dyson
288 Timothy J Dorrington
289 Graham Barnett
290 Mr G Dickinson
291 Phil Abbott
292 Sue Hyett
293 Glyn Hodgetts
294 Kirk Taylor
295 Martin Bagshaw
296 Jordan Street
297 Matthew Hutchinson
298 Andrew Brewin
299 Philip Brewin
300 Anthony David Harrison
301 S Wood
302 James Paterson
303 Christopher Wood
304 Christopher J W Moorley
305 John Shirley
306 Mrs Jean Tighe
307 Robert & Jillian L Wood
308 Dave Rigley
309 Jeremy Webb
310 G E Blount
311 Percy Birkinshaw
312 Daniel John Skidmore
313 Alf Frantz
314 Ian Dogbone-Smith
315 Fred D Fisher
316 Mr M Stevenson
317 Michael Sydney Clarke
318 Carl Gregory
319 Barbara Storey
320 David Cundy
321 Gerard Carpenter
322 Ken Smith
323 David Stones
324 K A Jackson
325 Nick Shaw
326 Skeggy Ram
327 J E Harrison